DREAMBOOKS IN BYZANTIUM

Dreambooks in Byzantium
Six *Oneirocritica* in Translation,
with Commentary and Introduction

STEVEN M. OBERHELMAN
Texas A&M University, College Station, USA

ASHGATE

Steven M. Oberhelman has asserted his moral right under the Copyright, Designs and Patents Act, 1988, to be identified as the author of this work.

Published by
Ashgate Publishing Limited
Gower House
Croft Road
Aldershot
Hampshire GU11 3HR
England

Ashgate Publishing Company
Suite 420
101 Cherry Street
Burlington, VT 05401-4405
USA

www.ashgate.com

British Library Cataloguing in Publication Data
Dreambooks in Byzantium: Six *Oneirocritica* in Translation, with Commentary and
    Introduction
    1. Dream interpretation – Early works to 1800. 2. Dreams – Early works to 1800
    I. Oberhelman, Steven M.
    135.3

Library of Congress Cataloging-in-Publication Data
Dreambooks in Byzantium: Six *Oneirocritica* in Translation, with Commentary and
    Introduction / Steven M. Oberhelman.
        p.   cm.
    Includes bibliographical references and index.
    1. Dreams – Early works to 1800. I. Oberhelman, Steven M.
    BF1080.D74 2008
    135'.309495–dc22

2007050602

ISBN 978-0-7546-6084-2

Mixed Sources
Product group from well-managed
forests and other controlled sources
www.fsc.org Cert no. SA-COC-1565
© 1996 Forest Stewardship Council
FSC

Printed and bound in Great Britain by
MPG Books Ltd, Bodmin, Cornwall.

Contents

Acknowledgements

It was thirty years ago that as a young masters student in classics at the University of Minnesota, I first encountered the dream literature of the Hellenistic and medieval Greek periods. My graduate advisor, Gerald Erickson, the department's eccentric genius who taught courses on such bizarre aspects of ancient Greece and Rome as madness and deviant behavior, magic and witchcraft, and sexuality and eroticism, directed me to Artemidorus's magnificent second-century CE dreambook, with the suggestion that I write a thesis on Books 4 and 5. Later, in search of a dissertation subject, and not wishing to be the author of yet another study on Porson's Bridge and Euripidean iambic trimeters or a deconstructive analysis of the *Aeneid*, I turned to the tenth-century dreambook attributed to Achmet ibn Sereim, a Byzantine Greek who Christianised some Arabic dream manuals. In the course of my work on Achmet, I ran across six shorter but no less fascinating Byzantine dreambooks that seemed contemporaneous with Achmet. Many a long night in 1978 and 1979 was spent at the Blegen and Gennadius Libraries in Athens, Greece, in the company of these dreambooks authored, so the manuscripts claimed, by renowned Byzantine patriarchs, seers, and emperors. Achmet, however, beckoned, and so I put aside these dreambooks, relegating them, ultimately, to a drawer in one of my filing cabinets. As I turned to still other research projects, the dust accumulated atop my notes.

In 2002, I was asked by the journal *Speculum* to review *A Byzantine Book on Dream Interpretation: The Oneirocriticon of Achmet and Its Arabic Sources*, by Maria Mavroudi, who was later awarded a MacArthur Foundation Grant (the so-called Genius Award) for her work in the field of Arabic culture and Byzantine intellectual development. Professor Mavroudi's groundbreaking and truly brilliant investigation of Achmet never ceased to amaze me, and I walked away with a sense of humility at my own earlier efforts at understanding Achmet. The book struck a chord in another way. When I saw Professor Mavroudi's reference to the dreambook attributed to (or written for, depending on how one translates the title) Manuel II Palaeologus, the emperor of Byzantium from 1391 to 1425, I exclaimed (silently, to avoid startling the professor in the adjoining office), "I know that text!" Excavating my cabinet drawers with the passionate and reckless abandon of Heinrich Schliemann ripping through the strata at Hisarlik, I found my copy of the Greek text; and there immediately below were my copies of the other Byzantine dreambooks. An old, forgotten friendship was renewed.

In the course of the three years of writing this book, I have incurred many debts of appreciation and gratitude. Closest to home, I wish to thank Texas A&M University for its institutional support. A grant from the Program to Enhance Scholarly and Creative Activities freed me for one summer to conduct research and to finish writing Chapters 1 and 2. My department heads (and good friends for several decades now), Craig Kallendorf and Richard J. Golsan, offered me research funds, a reduction in teaching responsibilities, and, most of all, words of encouragement. I am also most thankful to the people at Ashgate Publishing. I am grateful to Kirsten Weissenberg, senior editor, for her professionalism and efficiency in overseeing the final product, and especially to Felicity Teague for her splendid copyediting and masterful eye, which improved the text in many places. John Smedley has been the ideal editor. With patience and energy, he has nurtured this project from its beginnings to its conclusion. He has provided detailed criticism and numerous suggestions for improving the manuscript, and has helped clarify my arguments and thoughts. Perhaps his greatest asset was his choice of truly exceptional readers. The primary reader, as it turned out, was Maria Mavroudi. I had asked Mr Smedley to inquire whether the reader would be willing to be identified by name—I was so greatly indebted to this person that expression of thanks to the "anonymous referee" seemed woefully inadequate and unjust. Professor Mavroudi agreed to have her identity revealed, and let me take advantage of this opportunity to acknowledge my deepest gratitude to her. She gave constructive advice, painstakingly checked the translations, and pointed out with a kind and gentle spirit the many places where I was in error; she was also responsible for a substantial rewriting and reorganisation of the opening chapters. Her influence informs every page and is responsible for what good one may find here. If I have not followed her advice here and there or disagreed with an interpretation of a difficult passage, it was from a sense of stubbornness that should perhaps be counted as foolishness.

Some parts of this present work have appeared elsewhere. I am grateful to Texas Tech University Press for permission to reuse some material from my 1991 study of Achmet's dreambook in Chapters 2 and 3, and to quote from it translations of Achmet's text. Translations of Artemidorus's dreambook are drawn from Robert White, *The Interpretation of Dreams = Oneirocritica by Artemidorus* (Park Ridge, NJ: Noyes Press, 1975), a book no longer in print. All other translations are my own.

The Greek texts of the *oneirocritica* translated here can be found as PDF documents on my webpage: http://euro.tamu.edu/~s-oberhelman/. The purpose of this page was to make the six dreambooks accessible to the reader. Only two have received modern treatment—Astrampsychus (Brodersen 2006) and Nicephorus (Guidorizzi 1980)—, but Guidorizzi's monograph is hard to secure, and the other dreambooks are found in very old and not widely distributed periodicals. Placing the texts on a webpage seemed the best way of extending to the interested reader the means of reading and checking the Greek texts, while at the same time limiting the pagination of this book.

Chapter 1

Authors, Dates, and Texts

Humans have an innate desire to gain knowledge of what the future has in store for them. The Greeks of antiquity were no different, and so they placed great emphasis on oracles, omens, necromancy, augury, haruspicy, and visions. Private diviners and soothsayers exercised considerable influence in the social, religious, and political life of the ancient Greek (and Roman) world, and no stigma was attached to the profession of divination. Not everyone was a diviner, however, nor did everyone have access to one, and so the future remained an indecipherable mystery for many. There was, though, one way accessible to anyone of any social and economic class, background, or gender to know the unknown: dreams. Everyone dreams, everyone receives images during their sleep. Thus, since it was agreed in the ancient and medieval worlds that dreams could unlock the future, the decoding of the symbolic images of a dream could accomplish on a personal level what professional diviners or oracles did for kings, governments, and the wealthy. All that a dreamer needed was a dream key manual.

Dream key manuals, or dreambooks (in Greek, *oneirocritica*), go back several millennia before the Byzantine era (330–1453). We have fragments of an Assyrian dreambook and records of Mesopotamian dream rituals,[1] while the thirteenth-century BCE Papyrus Chester Beatty III from Egypt, now in the British Museum, offers a dream key for dreamers. As we will see in Chapters 2 and 3 below, the Greeks and Romans up through the end of the Hellenistic period produced dreambooks. The Byzantines also sought to interpret their dreams through dream key manuals. The Church and State may have tried to control divination, but even patriarchs and emperors had to admit that dreams had a solid scriptural basis, and tradition and cultural lore insisted that throughout history God has sent prophetic visions and dreams to people whom He favors. Hagiographical writers related how saints and martyrs receive significant dreams, and although there was imperial legislation against divination, emperors like Justinian slept at night in churches in order to receive dream cures.[2]

But where could one find a dream key manual in Constantinople? That would have been a problematic issue in itself. The dreambooks of antiquity and the Hellenistic period had not disappeared, but they were thoroughly pagan and contained extended discussions of gods, mythology, sexuality, and (to the Church) deviant morality. In short, they were hardly the sort of tool that a good Christian, wishing to seek God's counsel and guidance in his dreams, would want to consult. What a Christian needed was a dreambook penned by a famous Church leader or saint for the godly.

---

[1] See A. L. Oppenheim 1956; Butler 1998.
[2] On all these points, see Chapter 3 below.

To meet this need for Christianised dream key manuals, a number of *oneirocritica* were written during the early and later periods of Byzantium.[3] The most famous example dates to the tenth century, when a Christian living on the eastern borders of the empire immersed himself in early Arabic dream manuals. Calling himself Achmet, this writer, as I will discuss below, Christianised his Arabic materials and published one of the longest and most comprehensive works on dream interpretation in Greek history. Intended for the current emperor or his court, this dreambook has attracted much scholarly attention.[4] But there were other dreambooks available to the Byzantines. Boasting authorship by biblical personalities, famous patriarchs, and even emperors, they did not display the paganism of pre-Byzantine works and therefore were appropriate for use by a Byzantine Greek audience. Indeed, as I hope to make clear in this chapter, these dreambooks were sought out and consulted by people of all backgrounds, from members of the imperial court and educated savants to the "everyman" walking the streets of the Byzantine capital.

The Daniel dreambook is commonly accepted as the earliest Byzantine *oneirocriticon*; some scholars even consider it the basic source text for all medieval dreambooks in both the East and the West.[5] Ascribed to the Hebrew prophet Daniel, under whose name a book of visions and prophecies has come down in the Hebrew canon,[6] the original text of the Daniel dreambook is post-Hellenistic or proto-Byzantine.[7] The most advocated date for the dreambook's writing is the fourth century,[8] although

---

[3]   As we will see below, no dreambook seems to have been written between the fifth and early ninth centuries, as this was a time of resistance and hostility to dreams.

[4]   Recent excellent studies are Lamoreaux 2002, Mavroudi 2002 and 2007, and Sirriyeh 2006.

[5]   Förster (1921, 58) calls the Daniel dreambook "the ultimate source for all European dreambooks up to the present day" ("die Urquelle für alle europäischen Traumbücher bis zum heutigen Tage").

[6]   The reason for the attribution of the dreambook to Daniel was his reputation for interpreting dreams and signs; see, e.g., the interpretations of Nebuchadnezzar's visions in Chapters 2 and 4 of the Book of Daniel, the first six chapters of which are historical in nature and may date to the period immediately after the Jews' return from exile in Babylon in 527 BCE. The final chapters (7–12), apocalyptic in nature, have been used in conjunction with the Book of Revelation by some Christian theologians, especially Dispensationalists with premillennialist and futurist theories, to outline the end of the world and the return of Christ. Many scholars, however, date the second half of the Book of Daniel to the second century BCE, specifically to the time of the Maccabean revolt. For a good overview of this argument (the so-called Maccabean thesis), see Ferch 1983; also DiTommaso 2005.

[7]   The dreambook, in my opinion, certainly does not go back so far as Artemidorus (second century CE); Artemidorus customarily cited the writers of those dreambooks he consulted, and we have no citation of, or reference to, the Daniel text. Detorakis (1996), who calls the Daniel dreambook παλαιό, notes the strong similarities between the two dreambooks, although he offers no proof of direct borrowing; many parallels can be explained simply by both authors using the same oneirocritic tradition. Guidorizzi (1980, 29) states that the dreambook in its original recension dates to the later imperial period ("risale, nella redazione originaria, all'epoca del tardo Impero").

[8]   So Förster 1921, 58 ("etwa im 4. Jahrhundert n. Chr. entstanden sein mag"). See also Brackertz 1993, 213–14; Guidorizzi 1977, 139–50 and 1980, 14; Detorakis 1996, 67; see the

the sixth and seventh have also been suggested.[9] The *terminus ante quem*, according to some scholars, is the seventh century, when the Greek text was translated into Latin in southern France.[10] I would note, however, that there is no extant manuscript of the Latin translation (called the *Somniale Danielis*) until the ninth century,[11] and so the seventh century may not be a reliable means of dating the Greek Daniel dreambook.[12] Overall, there are over 70 surviving Latin versions of the Daniel dreambook, but three early versions are important for recovering the text of the original Latin translation. The early eleventh-century British Library, MS. Tiberius A.III (=**T**) contains the *Somniale* on folia 27^v–32^v; the codex contains altogether 22 works dealing with dream interpretation, prognostication through thunder, calendar divination, omens, and lunar phenomena as they relate to medicine, bloodletting, and prophecy. The *Somniale* contains 302 dreams and interpretations, each entry listed alphabetically. Max Förster published (Förster 1910) both this text and an Old English interlinear gloss that appeared with it in the codex. The second main witness is the Wien, Österreichische Nationalbibliothek, MS. 271 (tenth century, with 158 dreams), which was published by Förster in 1911. Both traditions contain dreams not found in the other, and at times will contradict the other in interpretations. Problems remain, however, even with these best representations of the two traditions. **T**, for example, is structured in a puzzling fashion. Its first 249 entries are given in the usual format, in that each dream symbol is listed alphabetically and then followed by an interpretation applicable to all dreamers. Another 21 entries, not alphabetised, follow. These are extracts from another version of the dreambook, as some of the interpretations differ slightly or even contradict the interpretations in the first part. A final set of 32 dreams are composed in a wholly different style: the symbol is written as a conditional *si somniaveris …* ("If you have seen in your sleep that …") protasis, and then the interpretation is stated as an apodosis.[13] A third early witness was claimed by Martin (1979) to be the ninth-century British Library, MS. Harley 3017. The text is fragmentary. We have one dream starting with the letter "d,", then a series of symbols with an initial "e" through the letter "m,", and then three symbols beginning with "n." Altogether, there are 76 dreams, written in two columns on the front and back of the first folium of the codex. A third of the lines are incomplete or unreadable. However, more recent scholars like Epe (1995) have argued that a superior witness to the third tradition is, in fact, Uppsala, Universitätbibliothek, MS. C (ninth century). The reasons are two.

---

comments below to Daniel 53 and 83 (dreams involving animal sacrifices).

[9]   Turville-Petre 1968, with bibliography; De Stoop (1909, 94, 100) argues for a late Byzantine date. I would point out, however, that De Stoop also speculated that the dreambooks of Astrampsychus and Nicephorus were the sources for the Daniel text, a situation that is just the opposite of what we now know (see below), and that the Daniel dreambook was the last, not the earliest, of the Byzantine *oneirocritica*.

[10]   Brackertz 1993, 214; Förster 1921, 59–60; DiTommaso 2003–2004, 6–7.

[11]   See Wittmer-Butsch 1990, 172–81 for further fragmentary manuscripts from the ninth through thirteenth centuries. The most recent discussion is Semeraro 2002, 16–20.

[12]   Another *terminus ante quem* is the dreambook of Nicephorus, which dates to anywhere between the seventh and the eleventh century, although the late ninth or early tenth is most likely; see below.

[13]   The Cotton and Wien manuscripts are referenced in the commentaries below as "Beiträge, IV" and "Beiträge, V," respectively.

First, the Uppsala version (=**C**) is the earliest of all witnesses to the *Somniale*, predating even the Harley codex. Second, all of the Harley is found in **C**, in terms of both order of arrangement and contents. The Latin *Somniale Danielis* became extremely popular in Western Europe and was subsequently translated into languages like Old English, Middle English, Italian, French, German, Old Icelandic, Welsh, and Irish.[14]

Two versions of the Greek Daniel dreambook, each dating to the sixteenth century, have survived. The first is found on folia 4ᵛ–10ᵛ of Codex Berolinensis Phillips 1479 and was edited by De Stoop (1909). The text is incomplete, stopping at the letter *rho*. Another, and more extensive, version is Codex Vaticanus Palatinus Graecus 319 (published in Drexl 1926).[15] The text, found on folia 31ʳ–48ʳ, contains many more verses than the Berlin codex. Even excluding the verses after the letter *rho*, the Vatican codex has 133 additional interpretations. This is the codex translated below in Chapter 4.[16]

Both versions are clearly a conflation of the original text with material drawn from different sources. In the Berlin codex, for example, the same dream symbol may be interpreted in two different ways. For example,

218.   Seeing wild animals and associating with them signifies a disturbance caused by enemies.

225.   Seeing wild animals and going around with them will cause friendship with enemies.

324.   Dreaming of being stoned to death signifies being occupied in many business matters.

334.   Dreaming of being stoned to death means an accusation from one's enemies.

Conflation is also apparent in differences of vocabulary and terminology:

348.   Having sex with a prostitute means not a little profit.

372.   Having sex with a prostitute indicates distress.

Here, not only are the interpretations different, but there is a variation in the word to describe sexual relations: κοιμᾶσθαι versus συνδοιάσαι. In the next pair of dreams, we read ἐγχέλους and an interpretation of evil in the first dream, but ἐχέλυα and an interpretation of benefit in the second:

148.   Seeing or eating or, in short, handling eels means a great disturbance.

178.   Seeing or eating eels signifies a great amount of profit.

Conflation of this type is common in Byzantine (and Latin) dream manuals as scribes added dreams from other sources to the particular version before them. It is clear that dream key manuals were viewed as a template that one could revise and adapt at will. For example, one could add dreams from other oneirocritic sources at hand; as the

---

[14]   The bibliography on these translations is vast. I refer the reader to Martin 1981; Fischer 1982; Kruger 1992, 10–11, with 171 n. 27; DiTommaso 2003–2004, 5–10.

[15]   For a discussion of this manuscript, see ibid., 15–16.

[16]   Brackertz (1993) also translates this manuscript in his book.

commentaries below will make clear, Achmet's dreambook, once it was published, was heavily quoted by dreambook writers. A pious writer or scribe could also be offended by dreams that dealt with pagan matter, and so he would have Christianised them (a dream of sacrificing in a pagan temple would be transformed into a dream of taking the Eucharist) or simply excised them. Or, one would have rewritten some dreams to reflect new cultural codes. Artemidorus's extensive discussions of various forms of sexuality, for example, would have been taboo to some, and so they would have been suppressed or changed so as to espouse Christian virtues of virginity and monogamy. A similar practice of free adaptation of textual material occurs with the Byzantine medical manuals called *iatrosophia*. In this instance, Byzantine physicians took longstanding texts containing medical prescriptions, remedies, and recipes, and would continuously change, edit, and revise them as they became aware of new botanical and pharmacological knowledge and as their practice of medicine evolved.

We cannot reconstruct the original text of the Daniel dreambook. There are simply too many layers of added interpretations lifted from late Byzantine *oneirocritica* and unknown sources.[17] Now, one would think that it would be profitable simply to compare the two extant Greek manuscripts with our three earliest extant Latin versions (see above). If an agreement in both dream and interpretation exists between the Greek and Latin versions, then the original reading has been preserved. If we do this, then about 120 entries are in common among the various witnesses (although I would stress that not all the coincidences are exact—in fact, sometimes the dreams are interpreted in vastly different ways). If the original Daniel dreambook was indeed about 120 or so entries, the fact that the Greek version as preserved comprises 486 entries, is evidence that scribes could augment and revise oneirocritic texts by freely incorporating extraneous material. A parallel is the dreambook of Nicephorus (see below). The original text contained just over 130 verses, but eventually over 200 more verses were added to it, as copyists included material from other Byzantine dreambooks like Achmet's *Oneirocriticon*. Even so, we must be cautious in applying straightforward comparison of the Latin and Greek versions of the Daniel dreambook. Since our two Greek versions date to the sixteenth century, we cannot exclude a reverse line of influence. That is, some of our Greek text could be extracts from the Latin *Somniale*, which had been widely circulated throughout all of Europe for the previous 500 years and which had been subjected to constant revision (see Martin 1981 for full details). It is impossible to say with full confidence that the entries in our version of the Greek Daniel dreambook are all original, let alone that they belong to the Greek tradition and not to some Western European tradition.[18]

---

[17] The Latin *Somniale Danielis* suffered a similar fate. By the ninth century—that is, about 200 years after the Greek text had been translated into Latin—two competing versions of the text, augmented with many extraneous verses, had already emerged. Ultimately, there were four traditions of the Latin text from which over 70 Latin versions have been preserved: Martin 1981. More recently, Andreas Epe (1995) has argued for two versions and six recensions. See DiTommaso 2003–2004, 8–9 for further discussion.

[18] Because of such cross-borrowing, the exact relationship between our extant Byzantine *oneirocritica* in terms of chronology and sources is well-nigh impossible to sort out. Brackertz

The Greek Daniel dreambook in its original form (whatever that was) was a primary source for an *oneirocriticon* ascribed to "Nicephorus, patriarch of Constantinople."[19] The most likely candidate is Nicephorus I, who was patriarch from 806 to 815.[20] Nicephorus was a layperson appointed to the patriarchate on 12 April 806 (to the anger of many clergymen), and quickly became embroiled in the iconoclastic controversy. Among the many reasons for the outbreak of Iconoclasm, which occurred in three phases between the early eighth and the mid-ninth centuries,[21] foremost was the Church's uneasiness over icons, due to the prohibitions in the Hebrew Scriptures against idolatry and to the persistent survival of paganism in Byzantium. An imperial council, convened in 730, issued an order that religious images be destroyed. The patriarch Germanus I, who refused to comply with the council's directives, was forced to resign.[22] Emperor Constantine V (741–75), who was convinced that veneration of icons was tantamount to pagan idolatry and that the Eucharist alone represented the true image of Christ, commenced a persecution. Later, the Second Council of Nicaea in 787 condemned Iconoclasm and restored

---

(1993, 214) too observes that the relationship between these texts is not easy to determine ("nicht leicht zu entscheiden").

[19]   The indispensable work on this text is Guidorizzi 1980. Drexl's 1922 study is now lacking. I am embarrassed to say that I was not aware of Guidorizzi's work in my 1986 article (my 1980 article obviously came out before Guidorizzi's book); cf. Detorakis 1996, 69: "Εἶναι μάλιστα περίεργο ὅτι κατ' ἐξοχὴν μελετητῆς τῆς βυζαντινῆς ὀνειροκριτικῆς φιλολογίας St. M. Oberhelman φαίνεται νὰ ἀγνοεῖ καὶ τὸ ἀλεξανδρινὸ χειρόγραφο καὶ τὴν ἔκδοση τοῦ G. Guidorizzi." I corrected this oversight in my 1991 book on Achmet.

[20]   A good introduction to this patriarch is Alexander's (1958) monograph; see also the bibliography in Kazhdan and Talbot 1991 (hereafter, "*ODB*"), 3:1477. Not a candidate for authorship of the *oneirocriticon* is Nicephorus II, patriarch during 1260–61, since he lived after the earliest manuscript of the dreambook.

Two manuscripts of the Nicephorus dreambook attribute authorship to other theologians. Codex Marcianus 608 (fifteenth century) gives the author as Athanasius, probably the fourth-century Alexandrian theologian who vigorously fought Arianism. Codex Ambrosianus 592 (also fifteenth century) ascribes the dreambook to a Gregoras, perhaps Nicephorus Gregoras, who wrote a commentary on Synesius's book on dreams. These false ascriptions explain the various (and erroneous) lists of Byzantine dreambooks in older standard sources on Byzantine literature, e.g., Beck 1971, 203–4 and Krumbacher 1897, 629–30. See also Detorakis 1996, 68–9.

[21]   The three phases were, roughly: from the reign of Leo III (717–41) to the Council of Hiereia in 754; 754–75 (that is, to the death of Constantine V); and 815–42, or the reigns of Leo V, Michael II, and Theophilus: see Bowersock, Brown, and Grabar 1999 (hereafter, "*LAnt*"), 507–9. Among the many works on this subject are: Bryer and Herrin 1977; Grabar 1984; Stein 1980; *ODB* 2:975–7; Gregory 2005, 185–213 (with bibliography on 201); Treadgold 1997, 350–54, 360–66, 387–93, 399–401, 419–21, 432–45, 448–9, 552–5, 558–61; Haldon 1998, 7–9 (with nn. 3–4); Brubaker 1998b; Speck 1998; Cormack 1998. Krueger (2005, 314 n. 44) offers bibliography on the rise and early stages of icon cult. It should be noted that even during the iconoclast controversy, religious imagery in Hagia Sophia remained: Brubaker 1998a, 66. Karlin-Hayter (2002) discusses how the restoration of icon veneration was political, not religious, in motive.

[22]   Cf. *ODB* 2:846.

the veneration of images. In 815, however, Leo V (the Armenian) reinstituted Iconoclasm, and the patriarch Nicephorus I was deposed when he refused to sign a decree authorising the destruction of icons. Nicephorus was exiled to a monastery on the Bosphorus (a building, ironically, that he had constructed after his retirement as imperial secretary). Nicephorus wrote many treatises against Iconoclasm and in support of the veneration of images, notably the *Apologeticus minor* and *Antirrhetics* 1–3.[23] Because it was believed that dreams were sent by God—that is, they were divine images—Nicephorus's strong support of the imagery of icons, besides his authority as a respected patriarch, doubtlessly led to the dreambook being attributed to him.[24]

For a 1980 monograph, Guilio Guidorizzi collated 16 manuscripts of the Nicephorus dreambook. The earliest is Codex Parisinus Supplementus Graecus 690 (eleventh century), followed by the eleventh/twelfth-century Codex Marcianus Graecus 299; the other 14 manuscripts date from the thirteenth through the sixteenth century.[25] The collation proved two families of manuscripts (*a* and *b*), each of which presents numerous problems because of contaminations, copyists' changes, and later interpolations; family *b*, in fact, may be subdivided into four branches. The archetype of the dreambook cannot be recovered, although Guidorizzi believes that when *a* and *b* both agree, we have a reading preserved from the archetype.

In his monograph, Guidorizzi divides the many dreams in the 16 manuscripts into three sections. First, he offers 132 verses that, in his opinion, comprise more or less the original dreambook. In some cases, however, *a* and *b* are at variance either in the interpretation that they assign to a dream, or in the phrasing of the dream symbol. Guidorizzi denotes these differences by printing both versions of *a* and *b* in the body of the text, rather than relying on an apparatus criticus. For example,

28a. Consider a sweet fragrance a foul odor.

28b. Consider a foul odor displeasure.[26]

94a. Being bound with shackles is extremely inauspicious.

94b. Carrying shackles in your hands: expect to come into danger.

---

[23] I owe these references to ibid., 3:1477. For a discussion of Nicephorus's works and beliefs, see Travis 1984.

[24] Guidorizzi (1980, 27) comments that the attribution to Nicephorus I is spurious and reflects the pattern of other dreambooks in claiming authorship of famous historical and ecclesiastical people ("L'autenticità dell'attribuzione, sostenuta dalla maggioranza dei manoscritti, deve però essere negate. ... L'attribuzione pseudepigrafa a grandi personalità della Chiesa e della cultura è caratteristica della letteratura oniromantica bizantina ..."). Cf. Mavroudi 2002, 242 n. 30, who points out that ascriptions of dreambooks to famous Church leaders not only gave such profane texts validity, but also served to overcome the suspicions that the Church held concerning such writings.

[25] To these, add the two manuscripts discussed in Detorakis 1996, 69, 71–3.

[26] The first dream is interpreted according to antinomy (opposition), the second by analogy. Methods of dream interpretation in the Byzantine *oneirocritica* will be discussed in Chapter 2.

Guidorizzi affixes two appendices to his reconstruction of the original text. Appendix I contains all verses that appear in one of the two families but not in both; these are "old interpolations, since they already are contained in the subarchetypes of *a* and *b*."[27] Appendix II lists those verses that appear in only one or two manuscripts of either family. These are even later interpolations that subsequent copyists inserted into their text from *oneirocritica* they were acquainted with. Some dreams are clearly borrowed from sources like Achmet, but others have an unknown provenance. I have translated the Nicephorus dreambook in exact accordance with Guidorizzi's edition.[28]

Guidorizzi's conclusions on the manuscript tradition of the Nicephorean dreambook overturned all previous scholarship on the interrelationship between the dreambooks of Astrampsychus, Germanus, and Nicephorus. It had been the *communis opinio* that Astrampsychus's dreambook went back as far as the fourth century and, being the first of the three verse dreambooks, served as the source of the other two.[29] But as Guidorizzi proved, the Nicephorean dreambook was, in fact, penned first, and Astrampsychus's text is nothing more than a compilation of verses drawn from one of the witnesses of the manuscript tradition of Nicephorus and then inserted into the margins of several manuscripts of the Suda lexicon.[30] Likewise, nearly two-thirds of the Germanus dreambook derives from Nicephorus's text. The verses ascribed to the Astrampsychus dreambook are related to the *b* family of Nicephorus, while the Germanus dreambook is an independent witness. What variations and differences we see in the dreambooks are attributable to their copyists.

The date of the original Nicephorus dreambook, like those of the other Byzantine *oneirocritica*, can only be approximated. The *terminus ante quem* is the eleventh century, which is the date of the earliest manuscript.[31] Guidorizzi (1980, 27–8) notes that since this manuscript is not the archetype, an earlier *terminus ante quem* is warranted. As for the *terminus post quem*, Guidorizzi advocates a late seventh-century date on the basis of verse 47, which alludes to an Arab invasion ("Questo

---

[27]   Guidorizzi 1980, 47: "[S]ono interpolazioni assai antiche, contenute già nei subarchetipi *a* e *b*."

[28]   Brackertz (1993) translates Drexl's 1926 text. Drexl, however, used an inferior manuscript, Codex Oxoniensis Clark. 16 (fols 107^v–20^r), which is thoroughly interpolated and must be used with extreme caution (see Guidorizzi 1980, 40). I rely on Guidorizzi's text throughout this book, although when I refer to Brackertz's translation, I use Brackertz's numbering (which again is Drexl's numbering).

[29]   So I also stated in 1980; see also Krumbacher 1897, 629; Del Corno 1962, 341; Drexl 1922, 94. The reason for Astrampsychus's dreambook being first in chronology is never stated by any scholar, but the likely explanation is that there was an actual Astrampsychus who lived in the pre-Hellenistic period (see below), as opposed to Nicephorus and Germanus, who lived much later, in the mid-Byzantine period.

[30]   So Guidorizzi 1980, 28 ("E opinione corrente che fonte primaria di ps.-Niceforo siano stati 101 trimetri giambici di Astrampsychos, la cui composizione viene collocata nel IV secolo; in realtà quest'opera … è soltanto una redazione secondaria del nostro testo, e precisamente la raccolta di *interpretamenta somniorum* che si trova in margine al Lessico di Suda"). See below for the Suda and the Astrampsychus verses.

[31]   For this manuscript, see Gigli 1978; Mavroudi 2002, Appendix I; and below.

[sogno] presuppone evidentemente una datazione posteriore all'invasione araba, e quindi alla metà del VII secolo"). Ultimately, Guidorizzi opts for a date somewhere between the late seventh century and the mid-ninth century.[32] I would argue, however, that a more likely date is the years after the end of Iconoclasm—that is, the second half of the ninth century or the early tenth. We do not have dreambooks from previous centuries—except for the Daniel dreambook, which may date all the way back to the very beginning of the Byzantine period, perhaps earlier—because of Church censorship and imperial edicts (see Chapter 3 below). The advent of Iconoclasm and the hostile environment to imagery it created would have made the publication of a dreambook like Nicephorus's dangerous, if not impossible; an *oneirocriticon*, with its emphasis on symbolism and imaginary representation, would have been attacked or suppressed by iconoclasts. However, with the re-establishment and acceptance of imagery in all its forms—iconistic, artistic, visionary—in the second half of the ninth century, it became safe once again to discuss dreams and dream imagery, and so the climate for a dreambook's publication now became possible.[33] And who better to serve as "author" than Nicephorus, a pro-icon figure and a theologian with unshakeable orthodox credentials?[34] Moreover, as we will see in Chapter 3, iconophiles exploited dreams and visions in their own literature to advance their program.

Further proof for a late ninth or early tenth-century date for the Nicephorus dreambook is the lack of any reference to the tenth-century dreambook of Achmet, except in the late interpolations of certain codices (Guidorizzi lists these in his Appendix II).[35] For his source, the author of the Nicephorus dreambook uses Daniel, Artemidorus, and his own material and/or unknown texts;[36] he uses nothing from Achmet. The fact that Achmet's text is not cited proves that it was not yet in circulation: the authors of the Germanus and Anonymous dreambooks borrowed heavily from Achmet, the most extensive and most famous of all Byzantine dreambooks, and it is reasonable to assume that the author of the Nicephorus dreambook would have done likewise if he had access to it.

---

[32]   Guidorizzi 1980, 28 ("Per la datazione uno spazio cronologico esteso tra la fine del VII e la metà del IX secolo, ma non oltre questa data"). Brackertz (1993, 207) dates the dreambook to the time of Achmet ("Vermutlich entstand es um dieselbe Zeit wie das Werk des Achmet")—that is, to the ninth century (a date he bases on the mention of the caliph Mamun in Achmet's text); however, as Mavroudi (2002, Chap. 2) has convincingly demonstrated, Achmet's book belongs more appropriately to the tenth century (see also Lamoreaux 2002, 152–4; Sirriyeh 2006, 215–16). Gigli (1978, 67 n. 7), as I do here, situates Nicephorus in the late ninth century.

[33]   A parallel is the tenth-century dreambook of Achmet, where Church icons are openly discussed: Mavroudi 2002, 2–3.

[34]   This will be discussed in more detail in Chapter 3.

[35]   So Guidorizzi 1980, 29 ("[I]l libro di Achmet è invece completamente ignorato: le interpretazioni che dipendono da quest'opera sono interpolazioni successive, trasmesse soltanto da alcuni codici").

[36]   See ibid., 29 for discussion.

This dreambook should not be viewed as "low" or inferior literature, simply because of the genre to which it belongs.[37] As Guidorizzi demonstrates in his commentary, the vocabulary is unusually formal, the style elevated in tone, and popular forms rarely used.[38] The earliest extant version of the dreambook is found in a codex (Parisinus Supplementus Graecus 690) that contains 94 works of a literary, scientific, or medical nature. Moreover, the author uses metrical iambic trimeters, rather than the accentual dodecasyllables then used because of the loss of syllabic quantity.[39] A poetic text written in quantitative meters implies a learned author who doubtlessly intended his work for an audience of similar background.[40]

In the metrical schemes of the dreambook, the caesura usually falls after the fifth or seventh syllable. The verses are so structured that first the dream symbol is given, and then its interpretation. Since a dream's significance typically requires more space than its description, the author strives as often as possible (70 per cent of the time according to Guidorizzi) to have the interpretation of the symbol commence after the fifth foot. Thus,

Λέοντας ἰδεῖν δυσμενῶν δηλοῖ στίφη.
Λύκος κεχηνὼς φληνάφους δηλοῖ τρόπους.
Μύκητας ἔσθειν φαρμάκων δηλοῖ δόσιν.
Οἶνον ῥυπώδης ἐκτρανοῖ πολλὰς λύπας.

At other times, the interpretation begins after the caesura of the seventh foot:

---

[37]   Cf. Kruger 1992, 14–15, who states that the western dreambooks of the early Middle Ages also imply a learned literary audience; for example, some manuscripts of the *Somniale Danielis* appear in collections of medical texts. Kruger stresses that some readers of the *Somniale Danielis* were aristocrats or clerics: manuscripts were elaborately and richly produced, and two versions may have been given to King Richard II of England.

Miller (1994, 12) likewise laments the views of scholars who prefer to think of dream manuals as inferior products of literature. Such scholars divide literature "into two opposing categories: 'high' literature and 'low' vulgar practice. This model consigns late-antique interest in dreams to the latter category as something that only disreputable figures like magicians and other 'commoners' meddled in. The fact that such privileged representatives of 'high' culture as Augustine, Gregory of Nyssa, and Jerome were vitally interested in dreams is dismissed by this model as unimportant. ... When the distinction between elite and vulgar is abandoned, a shift in perspective occurs which allows the interpreter to focus on the thoughts and practices that highlight the shared human concerns of theologians like Augustine and users of magical spells, concerns that cut across lines of social status and intellectual attainment. ... [A]ll of the people who tapped into the resources of the imaginal forms of dreams can be viewed as ordinary people going about the ordinary business of trying to understand themselves and their world."

[38]   For example, Guidorizzi's comment ad verse 64: "Στίφη è parola di tono elevato, in armonia con le tendenze stilistiche dell'autore." Cf. his 29: "La lingua di ps.-Niceforo è singolarmente elevata per un libro dei sogni; dal punto di vista lessicale, le forme popolari o seriori sono rare."

[39]   Cf. *ODB* 1:643. The standard work on this meter is Maas 1903.

[40]   I owe this observation to Prof. Mavroudi.

Δαμασκηνὰ βρωθέντα μηνύει νόσον.
Στρουθοὺς κρατῶν φεύγοντας ἐκδέχου λάβην.

Or occasionally after the fourth foot:

Ἄστρα βλέπειν κάλλιστον ἀνθρώποις πέλει.
Βίβλον λαβὼν νόμιζε τιμὴν λαμβάνειν.[41]

The Nicephorus dreambook served as the primary source of two other verse *oneirocritica*. One is ascribed to Astrampsychus,[42] a magus who lived in Persia before the conquest of Alexander the Great.[43] A number of treatises, all spuriously ascribed to Astrampsychus, have survived: a book on the healing of donkeys (Suda, s.v. "Ἀστράμψυχος"); a work on geomancy (Tannery 1898); a discussion of lapidary stones for use in astrology (Mély and Ruelle 1896–1902, 2: 192–3; Brodersen 2006, 21, 144–5); a collection of oracles (Stewart 2001; Brodersen 2006, 7–21, 25–141); and a volume of love charms (British Museum Papyrus 122; Brodersen 2006, 23, 162–5).

Although Astrampsychus is credited with a dreambook, there is, in fact, no manuscript of any such treatise;[44] rather, we have 108 assorted verses written into the margins of two thirteenth-century manuscripts of the Suda (Codex Parisinus 2622 and Codex Parisinus 2625) and subsequently published in critical editions.[45] The copyists of these marginalia specifically state that the verses were drawn from the dreambook of Nicephorus;[46] however, Joseph Justus Scaliger, who later edited all but seven of these verses, attributed the verses not to Nicephorus, but to Astrampsychus.[47] As Guidorizzi observes, the true situation is that the "Astrampsychus dreambook," instead of being a separate work and the first Byzantine verse dreambook, is simply a collection of verses lifted from a version of the Nicephorus dreambook.[48] The

---

[41]   Drexl (1922, 96) assigned the occurrence of caesurae after the fourth, sixth, or eighth syllable to the tendencies of "folkish" writers who ignore the fine rules of art ("Dieses volkstümliche Erzeugnis wird sich um die feineren Regeln der Kunst nicht allzu sehr gesorgt haben").

[42]   For works ascribed to Astrampsychus, Brodersen 2006 is now indispensable; see also Harrauer 1997, who supplants Reiss 1896.

[43]   So Diogenes Laertius 1.2.

[44]   There are some verses on fol. 277ᵛ of Codex Parisinus 22 (twelfth century), and on folia 123ᵛ–5ʳ of Codex Parisinus Supplementus Graecus 90.

[45]   Brodersen 2006, 22.

[46]   See, e.g., Suda 2: 681; 4: 623, 634.

[47]   Opsopaeus (1599) notes this in his edition: "Doctissimus Io. Scaliger Ὀνειροκριτικόν illud emendavit, digessit et suo auctori Astrampsycho vindicavit, perperam Nicephori Patriarchae Constantinopolitani nomine olim editum." I owe this reference to Guidorizzi 1980, 45. See now Brodersen 2006, 22.

[48]   So Guidorizzi 1980, 44 ("Si ritiene infatti che il prontuario attribuito a questo personaggio risalga alla tarda età imperiale, e sia stato in seguito utilizzato da ps.-Niceforo per la composizione del suo libro; in realtà i 101 dodecasillabi a lui attribuiti sono soltanto una redazione del prontuario di ps.-Niceforo, ed esattamente quella che si può ricavare raccogliendo—con alcune omissioni—le glosse oniromantiche del Lessico di Suda").

Astrampsychus dreambook, in other words, is part of Nicephorus's manuscript tradition. As will become apparent in Chapter 6, the Astrampsychus verses are, in the main, related to the *b* family of Nicephorus. Sometimes, however, there are variations in phrasing, and a few interpretations are at odds with what we see in the Nicephorean dreambook. Thus, the source from which Astrampsychus's verses were drawn makes a contribution to the history of Byzantine oneirocriticism, and is worthy of inclusion in this study.[49]

The date of the Astrampsychus verses can only be approximated.[50] Some scholars have noted that the verses are written not in metrical iambic trimeters, like Nicephorus's, but in accentual dodecasyllables,[51] and so they advocate a later date, say the ninth or tenth century, on the grounds that the source from which the Astrampsychus verses were drawn dates to the period when quantity was not comprehended. This is a weak argument, however, since any trained author could use quantity, even in an anachronistic fashion, if he so opted. Better, perhaps, to imagine that someone rewrote the Nicephorus verses in a rhythmical scheme that his intended target audience could appreciate. Nicephorus was a learned person who wrote quantitative verses for an audience with an educated background, and it is reasonable to picture the person who recast Nicephorus's metrical lines into accentual ones as someone who was equally learned, but had a more general readership in mind. In the end, however, the only reliable time reference we have is the thirteenth century, to which the manuscripts containing the marginal verses date, and so this serves as our *terminus ante quem*. All we can say for sure is that the Astrampsychus verses are an accentual version of the Nicephorus dreambook and were produced sometime between the archetype of the Nicephorus dreambook (mid-ninth century at the earliest) and the thirteenth century.[52]

---

[49]   My translation is based on Brodersen 2006, who offers in parallel columns the editions of Opsopaeus and Rigault (published in 1599 and 1603, respectively). Brackertz (1993) used Scaliger's edition, the numbering of which is different from Rigault's and Opsopaeus's. Opsopaeus has only 100 verses, while Rigault, who followed Hadrianus Junius's text, has 101 verses. Scaliger also has 101 verses, but again his numbering sequence is different.

[50]   Hopfner's (1937, 2240) date of the second century CE is impossible. Gigli (1978, 66–7 n. 7) followed the then prevailing scholarship and placed the dreambook in the fourth century. Krumbacher (1897, 648) and Maas (1903, 287 n. 1) dated the verses to the sixth or seventh century.

[51]   Brackertz (1993, 201–2) remarks that although the verses are not quantitative but accentual, the metrical scheme was retained to serve as "an aid for memory" ("Es besteht aus 101 alphabetisch geordneten Zwölfsilbern, die den antiken iambischen Trimetern nahestehen, aber nicht quantitierend, sondern akzentuierend sind. Die metrische Form des Büchleins hatte vermutlich die Funktion einer Gedächtnisstütze"). Cf. Detorakis 1996, 68.

[52]   Cf. Brackertz 1993, 202, who opts for an earlier (ninth century) date ("Die Entstehungszeit der Schrift ist unbekannt, vermutlich ist die im 9. Jahrhundert abgefaßt"). Detorakis (1996, 68) accepts the tenth- or eleventh-century date offered in Oberhelman 1980, 490–92. Brodersen (2006, 23) simply observes that it is contested whether the Astrampsychus compilation comes prior to or later than the Nicephorean dreambook ("Ob nun die Sammlung von hundert Astrampsychos-Versen alter ist … oder aber jünger … ist in der Forschung umstritten").

The Nicephorus dreambook also formed a significant portion of a dreambook attributed to "Germanus, the patriarch of Constantinople." Two candidates are possible, although the ascription is assuredly false: Germanus I, patriarch from 11 August 715 to January 730,[53] and Germanus II, patriarch from 4 June 1223 to June of 1240.[54] Although either identification is possible, Germanus I is very likely intended. Germanus I was better known and was a hero to the Orthodox Church because of his pro-icon positions. His credentials, in other words, made him an excellent choice as author.[55]

This dreambook appears only on folia 311^r–19^r of Codex Vindoboniensis Theologicus Graecus 336. Although the codex itself is undated, Drexl assigned it to around 1300 by comparing its hand to manuscripts that can be securely dated.[56] The 1300 manuscript date, therefore, serves as the dreambook's *terminus ante quem*. The *terminus post quem* is the earliest that we can date the latest of the dreambook's known sources, which are the dreambooks of Daniel, Nicephorus, and Achmet.[57] Of these three sources, the latest is Achmet's text, which dates to the tenth century.[58] Thus, the Germanus dreambook falls anywhere between around 900 and 1300, a span of time that is very wide but cannot be narrowed.[59]

The dreambook contains 259 interpretations; some lines are written in prose, others in verse. The prose sections consist of 50 interpretations from Achmet and 36 from Daniel, while the verses are drawn from Nicephorus. Guidorizzi argues that although the verses seem to come from the *b* family of the Nicephorean manuscript tradition, the Germanus text actually represents an independent witness.[60] As will be noted in the commentary to Chapter 7 below, Germanus sometimes interprets a symbol in ways diametrically opposed to how Nicephorus and even Astrampsychus interpret, and there are variations in language in descriptions of dreams. The prose

---

[53]   The major study of Germanus I is Lamza 1975. As noted above, Germanus I's firm opposition to Iconoclasm caused his removal from office.

[54]   Germanus II was very anti-Roman Catholic, as evidenced in many of his treatises and sermons. His feelings were perhaps due to the fact that he barely escaped with his life during the Latins' sacking of Constantinople in 1204. See *ODB* 2:847.

[55]   My thanks to Prof. Mavroudi for this point. Drexl (1923, 428 n. 1) also dismisses Germanus II as author, preferring the icon-espousing Germanus I ("Zweifellos ist nicht der XIII. Jahrh. angehörende Patriarch Germanos II., sondern der ob seiner bilderfreudlichen Gesinnung verehrte erste Träger dieses Namens gemeint").

[56]   Drexl (1923, 428–9) used Codex Vaticanus Graecus 840 (date of 1330), Codex Parisinus Graecus 1735 (date of 1289), and Codex Parisinus Graecus 1671 (date of 1296).

[57]   Drexl 1923, 430–31; Brackertz 1993, 213.

[58]   One could argue that the earliest date is 813, the year when Mamun, who is mentioned throughout the dreambook, assumed the caliphate, but this is not the same thing as the actual writing of the text, which Mavroudi (2002) has proved to be approximately a century after Mamun's reign. Moreover, the favorable mention of icons in Achmet's dreambook points to a later date—that is, after 843; see Mavroudi 2002, 2–3, and notes 32–3 above.

[59]   See Drexl 1923, 430–31. Cf. Brackertz 1993, 213, who likewise places the date to a period between Achmet and 1300 ("Daraus ergibt sich, daß das Oneirokritikon des Germanos erst nach der Zeit des Achmet entstanden sein kann. Einen *terminus* [*ante*] *quem* bietet nur die Zeit der Handschrift, etwa das Jahr 1300").

[60]   See the discussion in Guidorizzi 1980, 43.

sections taken from the dreambooks of Daniel and Achmet are summative (one sentence may summarise an entire chapter in Achmet) or are glosses; yet they also betray the author's independent streak, as interpretations may be changed or rewritten. The impression one gets is of an author freely adapting a number of oneirocritic sources and revising them in order to create his own work. Certainly his idiomatic use of first- and second-person pronouns and adjectives, a stylistic device unique to the Byzantine dreambooks (the exception is the prologues in Achmet), reflects an attempt to label this dreambook as his own.

An anonymous dreambook of 440 dreams and their interpretations appears on folia 27ʳ–36ᵛ of Codex Parisinus Graecus 2511, dated to 1400.[61] The fact that the dreambook is anonymous is surprising, given the false ascriptions we see affixed to the other dreambooks.[62] The text is drawn primarily from three dreambooks: Daniel, Nicephorus (although the metrical verses have been changed into prose sentences), and Achmet. One dream (227), for example, reads: "Seeing or handling small pearls signifies misfortune; [other dream-interpreters] interpret them as tears." The former interpretation comes from Daniel 365, the latter from Nicephorus 68 (= Astrampsychus 41 = Germanus 138). The writer also displays originality, since 47 dreams and their interpretations are unique to this dreambook and do not appear in any other Byzantine dreambook.[63] As in the case of the Germanus dreambook, the earliest date that we can assign to this treatise is the earliest date of its latest known source, which is Achmet. The *terminus ante quem* is the codex's date of 1400.[64]

The final dreambook of the Byzantine era is a prose treatise ascribed to Manuel II Palaeologus.[65] Manuel, emperor of Byzantium from 1391 to 1425, was a prolific writer and scholar.[66] An example of Manuel's erudite interests and output is Codex Parisinus Graecus 3041, the production of which Manuel supervised and even edited with his own revisions.[67] Contained in this codex are such works as Manuel's

---

[61] This codex also contains a lunar dreambook, the Nicephorus dreambook, and a large section of Achmet's dreambook. The lunar dreambook is published in Delatte 1927–34, 2:615–18.

In the margins of the manuscript are dream interpretations written in two different hands; these are written in such a way as to coincide with the alphabetical listing of dream symbols. See Gigli 1978, 183–4, who describes them as glosses from Achmet and Nicephorus.

[62] The remarkable anonymity is noted by both Drexl (1925b, 348: "Es ist anonym; das ist verwunderlich, wenn man bedenkt, dass andere von demselben oder gar geringerem Umfang einem bestimmten, wenn auch fingierten Autor zugeschrieben werden") and Brackertz (1993, 215: "Es ist merkwürdig, daß diese doch umfangreiche Sammlung ohne den Namen eines bestimmten, wenn auch fingierten Verfassers überliefert ist"). DiTommaso (2003–2004, 15 n. 51) considers the manuscript to be a version of the Daniel dreambook, but Daniel serves as only one of several sources for the dreambook. For the use of false ascriptions in Byzantine literature, see *ODB* 2:797 with bibliography.

[63] So Brackertz 1993, 216 ("Nach meiner Zählung sind es mindestens 47 Deutungen, für die kleine Parallelen zu finden sind").

[64] See also Drexl 1925b, 348.

[65] The basic study of Manuel is Barker 1969.

[66] See ibid., 426–39, with Manuel's writings listed in the Index (579–81).

[67] Ibid., 426–33 with bibliography.

extensive correspondence, treatises on religious and secular topics, rhetorical exercises, a dialogue on marriage, a long liturgical poem on the Virgin Mary, a liturgy on Holy Saturday, and a discussion, based on classical Greek and Roman texts, of oneirology (folia 86ʳ–8ʳ).[68]

The *oneirocriticon* attributed to Manuel is found on folia 315ᵛ–19ʳ of the fifteenth-century Codex Parisinus Graecus 2419. A few fragments of this treatise appear on the final folium of Codex Leidensis Voss. 49 (late fifteenth century), but there are only a few readings and these are extracts from the Parisian manuscript.[69] It may well be the case, as Mavroudi (2002, 142; 2007, 53 n. 17) has argued, that the surviving text of the dreambook is a version somewhat removed in time from the original; the text we have is certainly fragmentary, and so may in fact be an extract or compilation. But even if our text is a redacted version and not the complete dreambook, the time between its writing and the publication of the original is quite short, leading one to conclude reasonably that the dreambook immediately became a popular hit.

The dreambook is unique among the other Byzantine *oneirocritica* under consideration here in that dreams and their interpretations are arranged by chapters, with each chapter given a summative header; this schematic framework emulates that found in Artemidorus and Achmet. Like Artemidorus, too, the author explains the derivations of some of his dream interpretations, the typical method of interpretation being etymological wordplay, puns, and analogy (for which, see Chapter 2). This does not mean, however, that the author made extensive or slavish use of Artemidorus. As I will make clear in the commentary in Chapter 9, parallels between Manuel and Artemidorus, and between Manuel and Achmet, certainly exist, but they are not many.[70] Where agreement does exist, this may reflect not a direct dependence, but the authors drawing on the same traditional dream material or of Artemidorean symbolism working its way into general culture.[71]

Is this dreambook a genuine work of the emperor Manuel? The dates of the manuscripts are very close to his *floruit*, so close in fact that it would have been hard for

---

[68]   This work on dreams is addressed to Andreas Asanēs and has been edited in Boissonade 1962, 239–46 (supplanting Migne 1847–1904 [hereafter, "PG"], 156:87–92); Calofonos (1990) offers a full discussion.

[69]   Cf. Mavroudi 2002, 142 n. 54.

[70]   Perhaps Manuel's reluctance to quote Achmet, who Christianised to some degree medieval Arabic texts, may derive from his bitter experiences with the Turks. Manuel was embroiled in wars with them off and on from 1382 until his death, and during the first year of his reign, he was forced to serve as a vassal to the sultan Bayezid I. See *ODB* 2:1291; Gregory 2005, 320–24; and below, Chapter 9, notes 43, 75–6.

[71]   Cf. Calofonos 1990, 454: "Although [the Manuel dreambook] belongs to the same oneiromantic tradition, it is original in its content." Detorakis's (1996, 71) comment on Manuel's dependence on Achmet and Artemidorus is surprising ("[Τὸ ὀνειροκριτικὸν] στηρίζεται στὰ ὀνειροκριτικὰ τοῦ Ἀρτεμιδώρου καὶ τοῦ Ἀχμέτ"). Mavroudi (2007, 53–4) likewise argues for a direct reliance on Artemidorus where Manuel and Artemidorus agree (although she does not argue for a systematic, thorough reliance). I would note that many of the examples Mavroudi chooses, such as apples as symbolic of love with women and cisterns, and vessels and wells as indicative of women, were traditional (and straightforward) analogies.

a false attribution to escape detection of the reading public.[72] Moreover, as Calofonos (1990, 454 n. 53) has noted, "The dreambook describes specific dreams of Byzantine officials of the times to illustrate various dream-symbols." Some of these persons are not known, but others are. In Chap. 11, Manuel talks about the Grand Duke Alexius Apocaucus, who dreamt that his son-in-law would die by drowning; the historian Kantakouzenus describes the death as occurring in 1343.[73] We read of a member of the Phakrases family, possibly Manuel Phakrases, an official under Manuel, who according to the dreambook suffered injurious loss at the hands of his enemy after dreaming of hard-shelled fish (Chap. 2). The writer also possesses genuine, firsthand knowledge of the imperial court.[74] My commentary provides many examples of this, but here I may adduce the following for illustrative purposes. The author's terminology is thoroughly imperial: we read of the *megas doux* (the admiral of the Byzantine fleet), the court physician (*aktuarios*), the *megas diermnēneutēs* (the emperor's chief interpreter, who participated in embassies, served as translator for other officials, and attended to documents written in other languages), and the *prōtospatharios* (a civil official with duties at court, or a commander of the military forces of the territories in the empire). We encounter the various honorific names and titles of the emperor and his family, such as *basileus* (the emperor), *despotēs* (heir-apparent, as well as the ruler of tracts of lands like the Morea and Thessalonica), *autokratōr* (senior emperor or the heir-presumptive among the co-emperors), *sebastokratōr* (the Augustus), *Kaisar* (the emperor's sons), and *despoinē* (the empress, princess, or queen mother). We read of descriptions of Galata, the suburb of Constantinople; Hagia Sophia and its ornamentation; imperial warships (*karabis*); the granting of honors of public office by the emperor or his heir; and royal clothing like purple shoes and the *skiadion* (the Palaeologan hat worn by the emperor and his courtiers). The author even gives the exact legal Byzantine term, *phthora*, for the deflowering of a virgin. He also expresses a fear of being overthrown by usurpers, and has a very strong aversion to the peasantry and the common people, who are called, among other things, "good-for-nothings," "vulgar," and "contemptible." We cannot say for sure if Manuel is the author, but if he is not, we must admire the pains he took to reconstruct the Palaeologan court and its goings-on—the empress using the royal interpreter to sell the hill next to the citadel of Galata to the Franks (an act said to have resulted in mob violence), the mute Palaeologan brother-in-law drowning to death, deaths of royal officials and officers in combat—as well as the accurate portrayal

---

[72]   Mavroudi (ibid., 53 n. 17) nicely observes that the title can be translated as "A Dreambook for Manuel," not necessarily "A Dreambook by Manuel."

[73]   See ibid., 53 n. 17 for details.

[74]   Ibid., 53 n. 17: "[T]here can be no doubt that this dreambook, even if not written by Manuel, was produced and used in Byzantine courtly circles, especially as it mentions names and incidents in the lives of known Byzantine aristocrats." And 2007, 55: "[The] target audience [of Manuel's dreambook] seems to be members of the aristocracy resident in Constantinople: in other words, a much more limited social stratum than the other dreambooks." Calofonos too remarks that if the author is not Manuel, he is probably a member of Manuel's court or "his immediate circle." If Manuel's authorship is spurious, the reason for the ascription would be the authentic treatise on dreams that Manuel wrote to Andreas Asanēs. For doubts on Manuel's authorship of the *oneirocriticon*, see the bibliography in Calofonos 1990, 447 n. 3; cf. Del Corno 1962, 342 with n. 14.

of Manuel's favoring the Franks (on whose support he was casting his hopes in his war with the Turks). We must also acknowledge that the author was very well read and learned. His methods of interpretation are sophisticated—in particular, his use of etymology to interpret dream symbols (see Chapter 2)—and his language, style, and method of composition exceeds anything we see from a Byzantine dreambook writer beyond Achmet.

These are the dreambooks that I have translated and commented on. It is difficult, if not impossible, to recover the original texts of these dreambooks. Their authorships are not known in any situation (excepting, perhaps, the dreambook of Manuel), and their contents often were lifted from other dreambooks and to such a degree that lines of influence are confused. Even their dates can only be approximated. These dreambooks, however, are invaluable, in that they are unique sources of information on the everyday life of the people of Byzantium, on their culture and society, on their very psyches.[75]

Appendix

Scholars have discussed several other premodern Greek dreambooks; however, I have not dealt with them here, since in my opinion they do not date to the Byzantine era, but rather are post-Byzantine and would contribute little to the Byzantine oneirocritic tradition.

Detorakis (1996) has uncovered a fragmented but very lengthy verse dreambook in Codex 22 of the Archaeological Museum in Heracleion, Crete. The codex's *titulus* gives us two facts. First, the dreambook is the work of an unknown author, and second, the dreams and interpretations have been taken from the Suda and a treatise written by Tarasius. Tarasius was patriarch of Constantinople from 25 December 784 to 18 February 806, and was a major force in attacking Iconoclasm in 787—hence, no doubt, the attribution of a dreambook to him. The extant part of the dreambook commences with a dream whose first word begins with the letter *delta*; this verse is an exact replication of verse number 29 of Nicephorus's dreambook. We have, altogether, 454 dreams with their interpretations. Detorakis remarks that the dreambook is one of the longest of the Byzantine *oneirocritica*, and certainly the longest verse dreambook, even taking into account the fact that we do not have the lines beginning with words with an initial *alpha, beta, gamma,* or *delta*: "Μολονότι ἔχει χαθεῖ μέγα μέρος τῆς ἀρχῆς (στοχεῖα α–δ) ἔχουμε σαφῶς τὸ πλουσιότερο ἔμμετρο βυζαντινὸ ὀνειροκριτικό." The codex itself is written in two hands, one from the seventeenth century and one from the eighteenth. It is not clear whether the dreambook is a copy of a Byzantine text on dreams, but given the manuscript's late date, it seems unlikely. It is more probable that a post-Byzantine author wrote an *oneirocriticon* by drawing on dreambooks, like the Nicephorus, with which he was acquainted. It is just not clear whether the dreambook in Codex 22 is a copy of a pre-existing text or the copyist's own work. A careful study of the MS may answer such questions.

---

[75] See Oberhelman 1997 further on this point.

Delatte published two prose dreambooks in his *Anecdota Atheniensia* (Liège and Paris 1927–39). One dreambook, found on folia 86ʳ–103ᵛ of the Athens National Library Codex 1350, is attributed to a "Blasius the Athenian," who is otherwise unknown.[76] The treatise is structured along the lines of the dreambooks of Artemidorus, Achmet, and Manuel; that is, dream symbols are listed as chapter headings ("Lion," "Sweets," "Cats"), and then exemplary dreams and their interpretations follow in paragraph format. The author discusses neither dream theory nor his methods of interpreting dreams; instead, he simply offers in each chapter a number of dreams that illustrate the different ways in which a symbol may be interpreted. The codex dates to the nineteenth century, thus hardly making it Byzantine; moreover, the dreambook's grammar and vocabulary place it closer to the modern era than to the Byzantine. Delatte's other dreambook, found on folia 60ʳ–71ᵛ of the same codex, is a dream key manual. As with the Daniel dreambook and the Byzantine verse dreambooks, we have an alphabetical catalog of dream symbols that are interpreted in a universal manner ("If you [dream that you] have a loaf of bread and then eat the entire loaf, this points to an imminent loss in your household: for it shows that you will die or some other person in your household will die"). Its language and style are easily post-Byzantine.[77]

Gigli (1978) has published a detailed analysis of Codex Parisinus Supplementus Graecus 690, an eleventh-century parchment manuscript.[78] The codex contains 94 texts, among which is the earliest version of Achmet's *oneirocriticon*. Folia 123ᵛ–32ᵛ contain a number of short texts dealing with dream interpretation. On folia 123ᵛ–4ᵛ are 153 iambic trimeters that show very close affinity to the verses in the Nicephorus dreambook; only a few verses are taken from other sources (for example, four verses derive from Germanus).[79] After five folia containing an abridged version of Achmet's text,[80] there follows a dreambook on folia 129ʳ–32ᵛ. The title identifies it only as an alphabetical dreambook ('Ονειροκριτικὸν κατὰ στοιχεῖον). It is incomplete (ending with the letter *pi*), although it contains 305 dreams and interpretations. The text has close affinities with the Anonymous and Daniel dreambooks (in the case of Daniel, the version in Codex Vaticanus Palatinus Graecus 319), although Gigli notes variations in the number and ordering of the interpretations, as well as differences in syntax and in how some dreams are interpreted. Such variation among manuscripts of a similar tradition, Gigli observes, is not uncommon in oneirocritic writing, such

---

[76] See Delatte 1935 for an analysis of this dreambook.

[77] I am currently preparing translations of, and commentaries on, these two dreambooks. I will be publishing a study of the Blasius dreambook, as it relates to *iatrosophia* and medical praxis of the Ottoman Greek era, in the fall of 2008 in the journal *Medicina nei Secoli*.

[78] See Gigli 1978; Mavroudi 2002, 92–8, 431–44.

[79] Gigli (1978) published his work before Guidorizzi's monograph appeared, and so his tally of 92 verses from Astrampsychus, 44 from Nicephorus and Germanus, 13 only from Nicephorus, and four from Germanus reflects an imperfect knowledge of the interrelationships of these verse dreambooks. This explains why his conclusion (77) that this dreambook should be dated to a period between Astrampsychus and Nicephorus should be ignored.

[80] See Mavroudi's (2002) Appendix 1 for a full treatment of this codex and for a correction of Gigli's observations.

as we see in the case of the Latin *Somniale Danielis*.[81] Gigli's dreambook awaits an edition and commentary.[82]

[81]   So Gigli 1978, 173 ("Quindi non deve stupire la diversa consistenza delle versioni presenti nei codici suddetti: anche gli onirocritici latini attribuiti al profeta presentano la stessa varietà nella lunghezza e nella formulazione").

[82]   Guidorizzi (1977, 138) mentions a dreambook in Codex Marcianus Graecus 608, but this dreambook is merely a version of the Nicephorus; see above, note 20.

Chapter 2

The Art of Interpreting Dreams

We know very little about ancient and Byzantine Greek dream interpreters except that they enjoyed popularity among people of all social strata.[1] According to our sources, interpreters were educated, learned scholars. Artemidorus, the most famous interpreter of the Greek and Roman worlds, recommended to his son that he become acquainted, to the best of his ability, with all aspects of philosophy, medicine, natural science, politics, and religion.[2] Artemidorus himself was knowledgeable in these very areas. As the *testimonia* in Pack's (1963) Teubner edition makes clear, the dreambook contains numerous references to such areas as philosophy, medicine, zoology, astronomy, and pharmacology. Moreover, Artemidorus dedicated his dreambook to Cassius Maximus (Maximus of Tyre), a well-known orator of the day, and the many quotations from authors like Homer, Aristotle, Theognis, Menander, and Euripides certainly say something about Artemidorus and his audience.[3] Because Artemidorus is the immediate predecessor of our Byzantine dream interpreters and because his work on dreams is the only pre-Byzantine *oneirocriticon* that we have beyond fragmentary remains,[4] a short discussion of Artemidorus and his theories is appropriate.

Artemidorus of Daldis, the son of Phocas, was born at Ephesus and lived near the beginning of the reign of the emperor Antoninus Pius (138–61 CE).[5] He wrote his

---

[1]   People also consulted magicians and spell-givers. Numerous magical papyri containing spells and charms for producing revelatory and divinatory dreams have survived; see, e.g., Preisendanz *et al.* 1973–74, 2.1–64, 64–183; 3.187–262; 4.3172–208; 7.222–49, 250–54, 359–69, 407–10, 478–90, 664–85, 703–26, 740–55, 795–845; 8.64–100; 12.107–21, 121–43, 190–92; 12b.27–31, 32–5. For discussion, see Eitrem 1991.

[2]   See the proems to Books 1 and 4 of Artemidorus's *oneirocriticon*. The same recommendation to interpreters that they immerse themselves in all facets of learning appears in the earliest Muslim dreambooks: Lamoreaux 2002, 29. In fact, early Muslim dream interpretation was first advanced by "the muhaddiths or transmitters of prophetic traditions and then by the ulema or religious scholars" (Lamoreaux 16).

[3]   Mavroudi 2007, 148 n. 3.

[4]   For ancient works on oneiromancy beyond Artemidorus, see Del Corno 1962, 1969, 1975. We have the names of 25 to 30 dream interpreters from antiquity (not including mythological persons); however, many of these are known only from Artemidorus. Del Corno (1969) discusses this in great detail.

[5]   The bibliography on Artemidorus is immense. To name just a few sources: Behr 1968, 181–90; Blum 1936; Del Corno 1975, 1607–13; Guidorizzi 1980, 157–70; Holowchak 2001a, 93–105; MacAlister 1992 and 1996, 72–4; Miller 1994, 77–91; Price 1990, esp. 371–78; Walde 1999 and 2001; Weber 2000; Winkler 1990, 17–44; and most recently, Mavroudi 2007, 48 n. 2, citing the introduction to her 2002 translation of Artemidorus's dreambook.

oneirocriticon to prove to his critics that the interpretation of dreams, if placed in the hands of a qualified person, was an empirical science.

Artemidorus divides all dreams into the non-predictive *enypnion* and the predictive *oneiros*.[6] The *enypnion* arises from physiological and psychological forces imposing themselves on the dreamer's soul; for example, a lover will dream of his beloved, a thirsty man of quenching his thirst.[7] The *enypnion* vanishes on awakening and has no predictive value.[8] The *oneiros*, on the other hand, is significant since it reveals messages regarding the future. Artemidorus subdivides the *oneiros* into two categories: the *allēgorikos* (allegorical or symbolic) and the *theōrēmatikos* (theorematic or straightforward). In his discussion of how theorematic dreams occur, Artemidorus cites Plato's theory that such dreams may occur in a purified soul; he also acknowledges the role of the gods who, in their desire to foretell to humans imminent events, may send theorematic dreams. As a rule, such dreams come true the very next day and in exactly the same manner as the imagery in the dream. For example, a person who has a theorematic dream of being shipwrecked and then drowning will experience that very fate the following day. The allegorical dream, on the other hand, contains symbols that foretell the future, and is fulfilled any point of time—in days, weeks, months, or years. The purpose of Artemidorus's *oneirocriticon*—in fact of any dreambook that uses a key code—is to explain and set forth the symbols of allegorical dreams and how they are to be interpreted. To this end, Artemidorus concocts a system of dream classification that, if carried to its extremes, represents 80 possible permutations.[9]

The correct interpretation of a dream depends on the skills of the interpreter, who must rely on his powers of observation (*tērēsis*) and on his experiential knowledge (*peira*) of a sufficient number of dreams and their outcomes. The interpreter's first task is to analyse the dream through six *stoicheia* (elements of analysis): nature, convention, habit, occupation, name, and time; he then must determine whether the dream is *kata* (in accordance with), or *para* (in opposition to), each of those elements. The two principle *stoicheia*, however, are *phusis* (nature) and *nomos* (convention), with the latter category subdivided into unwritten social rules (*ethē*) and written laws (*nomoi*). Thus, a dream that is *kata phusin* (in accordance with nature) foretells something good, while a dream *para phusin* (contrary to nature) signifies something evil.[10]

---

6   See Miller 1994, 77–91.

7   Freud, who knew Artemidorus's dreambook very well, quotes these same dreams in his *Interpretation of Dreams* to prove that some dreams do not have interpretative significance. Freud was inconsistent regarding symbolism in dreams, however. On the one hand, he believed that dreams have an originary script, but on the other he adhered to the generality and fixity of specific codes for some dream symbols. See Oberhelman 1991, 74–6 with notes.

8   Artemidorus in his proem to Book 4 states that most people have this type of dream.

9   See Behr 1968, 171–95 for full discussion.

10   Although the phrase *para phusin* literally means "in opposition to nature," Artemidorus often uses the phrase to denote "in opposition to culture." For example, Artemidorus labels certain sexual actions as *para phusin*. One action so described is penetration of a woman by a woman. Such activity is contrary to *phusis* (nature *and* culture) because in such intercourse the penetrating woman usurps the role of the insertive male, which Artemidorus glorifies in

The interpreter must be especially careful in how he collects and evaluates information concerning the dreamer and dream. No dream that is not completely remembered should be interpreted, while the situation and time of the dream must also be analysed since they too are significant. Absolutely crucial to any interpretation, however, is the interpreter's knowledge of a consultant's life and habits, for the images in a dream must be compared to the dreamer's biographical data: gender, number of children, marital status, social position, economic means, and so forth.[11] Since the meaning of a dream depends on the circumstances of each dreamer, the interpreter must question the dreamer about his or her life and then decode the dream's significance based on those answers.[12]

No Byzantine dreambook writer studied here offers theoretical discussions on dreaming, dream causation, and methods of interpretation.[13] There is no reason to think, however, that the writers' thoughts on these subjects would have differed too much from Achmet's discussions, which were contemporaneous and in wide circulation in Byzantium, and so let us turn to what Achmet has to say on these matters.

Achmet's theory on dream causation is simple: God sends prophetic dreams to His people (1, 2, 301). While Artemidorus had attributed dreams to a variety of factors—the passions, digestion, the gods, the soul itself, to name a few—Achmet considers the sole cause of dreams to be God Himself, who in His mercy foreshadows

---

his discussion of sex in 1.77–8; this usurpation violates the sexual hierarchy and, by extension, the social hierarchy. *Phusis* in Artemidorus's dreambook assumes that men are the critical players in sexual activity, and so woman–woman intercourse is *para phusin*. See Winkler 1990, Chap. 1; Oberhelman 1997.

[11]   See the superb study of MacAlister 1992; also Price 1990, 372–7.

[12]   For the flaws in this method, see Oberhelman 1991, 40. Briefly, there is the basic problem of determining whether a dream is allegorical or theorematic; very often only by hindsight can the difference be known. Also, every dream symbol has countless meanings, for if a symbol's significance is idiosyncratic to each dreamer, and further depends on the dreamer's circumstances, then any symbol is limitless in its interpretation and applicability. Finally, an interpreter must decide which of the many images in a dream has symbolic importance, and this often is a matter of guesswork. See also Miller 1994, 90–91.

[13]   The exception is the set of three prologues to the Nicephorus dreambook in Guidorizzi's edition. These verses, however, are not part of the original dreambook, but are later interpolations. According to the prologues, dreams are divided into prophetic messages sent by God and false images caused by wine, digestion, anxiety, sexual impurity, and passions. The prologues are based on the opening chapters of Books 1 and 4 of Artemidorus's dreambook, and on the theories of many Church Fathers (see below, Chapter 3).

If Manuel II Palaeologus wrote the dreambook ascribed to him, then he does give us his theories on dreams in his letter to Andreas Asanēs (see Chapter 1, note 68). Asanēs had asked the emperor for his views on oneirology and whether he was in agreement that all dreams are prophetic. In response, Manuel sets forth a classification of dreams based on Artemidorus and other classical Greek and Roman authors: dreams arising from the dreamer's mental and physical condition (these are not prophetic or significant); dreams that come from the dreamer's own soul (this is based on Neoplatonic ideas); dreams in which the dreamer reaches a solution to his problems; and dreams that are prophetic and are sent by God. Prophetic dreams are seen by deeply religious and pious people. Calofonos (1990) offers a detailed analysis.

goodness or evil to humans (2, 301). For proof, Achmet alludes to prophetic dreams in the Qur'an and the Hebrew Bible; although he does not explicitly mention these texts, he refers to them in phrases like "Holy Scripture" (10). Achmet does specifically mention the Christian New Testament ("Holy Gospels," 2), since he is adapting his Arabic material for a Christian audience.[14] Thus, even though the Byzantine dreambook writers do not discuss dream theory, we can confidently surmise, given the thoroughly Christian nature of their texts, that they followed Achmet in not distinguishing between internal and external causes of dreams, and in considering dreams predictive of the future and as the vehicle of God's guidance and help.

Achmet does not state how one receives a dream from God—whether the soul, the mind, or some other organ like the liver is the recipient. However, the terminology Achmet uses betrays an emphasis on cognitive processes. Artemidorus had used ἔδοξε ὅτι (it seemed that), but Achmet uses the sensory verbs ὁράω and θέομαι, both of which mean "I see." The vocabulary reflects the language of his Arabic sources, where dreams are invariably introduced with the verb *ra'a* (to see),[15] and signifies a perception process similar to what occurs during the waking state. The vocabulary also recalls religious dreams and visions where the dreamer sees, hears, and talks with God or a heavenly messenger just as he would in everyday life.

The Byzantine dreambook writers do not follow a standardised vocabulary to distinguish types of dreams and how a dreamer receives them. In the Daniel dreambook alone, we have three different words for dream: ὅραμα (e.g., 84, 184), ὄνειρος (e.g., 273), and ὄναρ (e.g., 110). While Artemidorus had reserved ὄνειρος for the predictive dream and ὅραμα for the dream vision, the Daniel author does not make a distinction between these terms. But Artemidorus's terminology and dream classifications do not appear in other texts, both Byzantine and classical, and so, as some scholars have argued, Artemidorus's system may have been idiosyncratic.[16] Moreover, inconsistency in dream terminology is a common phenomenon, such as we see in religious writings. In the Greek Septuagint we find ἐνύπνιον, the usual word for dream, but also ὅρασις, ὅραμα, and ὕπνος, while in the Old Testament Apocrypha, ὄνειρος is used (e.g., 2 Maccabees 15:11; 4 Maccabees 6:5). In the Christian New Testament, Matthew uses the phrase κατ' ὄναρ, but Luke prefers ὅραμα and ὄναρ.[17] In Byzantine hagiography we have a similar blurring of terminology, especially when visions and prophetic dreams are described.[18] What all this means is that there existed no standardised vocabulary for specifying types

---

[14]   The Qur'anic references reflect Achmet's reliance on medieval Arabic texts, while the New Testament references show Achmet's manipulation and adaptation of them. It would have been easier for Achmet to use the monotheistic Arabic texts than the polytheistic dreambook of Artemidorus.

[15]   As Prof. Mavroudi has reminded me, this lack of variety in the verb is already evident in the Arabic translation of Artemidorus by Hunayn b. Ishaq (ninth century). For this translation, see Rosenthal 1965; Lamoreaux 2002, 8–9, 47–51; Mavroudi 2002, 135–42; Mavroudi 2007, 51 n. 11 (comprehensive bibliography). For the use of *ra'a* in Muslim dreambooks, Lamoreaux 2002, 84–5.

[16]   See Behr 1968, 182–95.

[17]   See Oepke 1954, 220–21.

[18]   See Kenny 1996 for a detailed study.

and subtypes of dreams; an author had at hand many verbs and nouns that were largely synonymous and hardly reflected a developed technical terminology. What terminology an author chose to use probably came down to individual word choice and preference. Rhythmical considerations also played a role, as verbs like ὁράω, βλέπω, and θεωρέω were interchanged freely to fit the metrical or accentual scheme. Thus, we have variations in Nicephorus's metrical dreambook such as Κλαίων καθ' ὕπνους παγχαρὴς πάντως ἔσῃ (52); Κριθὰς θεωρεῖν εἰς κριτήριον φέρει (61); Κριοὶ φανέντες εὐτρεπίζουσι τρίβους (62); and Μορφὰς ἀγνὰς ἰδών τις εὐμενὴς νόει (74). Nicephorus may even omit the verb for dreaming because of rhythmical demands; for example, δώρων μετασχὼν οὐ μακρὰν κέρδους ἔσῃ (29) and θλασθεῖσα ῥάβδος οὐ καλὸν πέρας φέρει (41).

Neither the Byzantine writers nor Achmet explicitly followed Artemidorus's division of divinatory dreams into the two broad categories of simple (theorematic) and complex (allegorical/symbolic); however, they did think of some dreams as being wholly void of symbolism. Achmet states that such dreams will be fulfilled on the very next day and in exact accordance with the dream's content (301); because the dream is straightforward and occurs immediately, there is no need to seek professional help in interpreting it. Other than this extremely brief statement, mentioned as it were in an offhand manner, Achmet does not devote any space to such dreams, probably because of his desire to treat only those dreams that require a (paid) interpreter's skill. The vast majority of prophetic dreams, he writes, contain symbols or riddles that indicate the future, and therefore can be interpreted only through an interpreter or by consulting an *oneirocriticon*. An allegorical dream is fulfilled at a point determined by the hour of the night and the season of the year when the dream occurs. By examining these two factors, an interpreter can determine whether a dream is truthful or false, and how quickly it will come to pass:

> Furthermore, we must make a distinction between summer and winter: for these seasons are judged in conjunction with the trees and plants [that appear in one's dream]. ... The interpretation of dreams that occur in the morning is more truthful; that of dreams in the afternoon, less so. As for the moon, a dream's speed or slowness [in turning out] will depend on the moon's phase. Now if someone consults you about a dream, ask him in return as to what hour it was when he saw the dream. For from the first to the third hour of the night, [we calculate that] the dream will turn out at some point up to 20 years; from the third to the sixth hour, up to 15 or ten or eight years; from the sixth to the ninth hour, up to five or four or three years; from the ninth hour to dawn, up to one year or six or three months or one month or even within ten days; the dream at daybreak will turn out on that day or [after] two or three days. [301][19]

Using this system, Achmet's father, who is called "Sereim, the dream interpreter of the caliph Mamun,"[20] deciphered the following dream:

---

[19]   This section is actually Arabic in origin; see Mavroudi 2002, 155–60 for details; also Lamoreaux 2002, 62. The Babylonian Talmud likewise states that the dream seen just before waking will be fulfilled quickly: Parry 2004, 149.

[20]   Sereim would be Ibn Sirin, considered the founder of Muslim dream interpretation. Born in 654, he did not write any dreambooks, but was reputed to have been a master of interpretation; see Lamoreaux 2002, 19–25. Many of the 13 dream interpretations made by

A newly wedded man came and consulted Sereim ... as follows: "I saw in a dream that my penis was completely severed from me." Sereim asked: "At what hour of the night did you dream this?" He replied: "The sixth hour." Sereim then said: "From the sixth hour calculate six months, and in the sixth month you will die childless." And so it turned out at the end of six months. [96][21]

The authors of the Byzantine *oneirocritica* do not offer theoretical discussions of the prophetic dream;[22] they merely believed that dreams are prophetic and will be fulfilled in a time and way in accordance with God's purposes. The certainty that dreams do come true is denoted through verbs like δηλόω (indicate), σημαίνω (signify), and ἐμφαίνω (display); future indicatives (e.g., ἐλευθερωθήσεται [he will be set free: Daniel 387]; ἐμπεσεῖται [he will fall into: Anonymous 42]); imperatives (e.g., παραφυλάττου [be on your guard: Daniel 437] and προσδόκα [expect: Daniel 454]); causative verbs like ποιέω (cause) and φέρω εἰς (bring about, result in); and the verb μέλλω (be about to; used with the infinitive, this is Manuel's most common verb for dream fulfillment). These verbs reveal the writers' confidence that whatever events are portrayed in a dream will in fact happen.

As for when a dream will come true, the Byzantine dreambook writers are on the whole silent; they seem to have accepted the eventual inevitability of a dream whenever God deems it appropriate. There are a few exceptions to this, however. For example, Manuel mentions a dream that will come true on the same day:

If [someone who dreams that he lost his hat has a master], he is about to be far removed from that man's success and aid or he will be insulted in some other way on the very same day [as when the dream occurs]. [35]

Several dreambook writers interpret dreams in various units of time or in accordance with the season of the year; for example,

If someone dreams of holding eggs in his hands, he is about to be thrown out of his house or country; and the number of eggs he was holding will be the number of days he will be gone from his friends, relatives, and other [dear ones]. But if he already is on a trip [when this dream occurs], his absence will be a matter of months, not days. [Manuel 45]

Large bread rolls are judged as a trek that will last one year and turn out to be profitable because of the fineness [of the flour]; coarse bread, as distress and a trip that will last one year; small bread rolls, as a journey lasting one month; the small καλήτζα roll as a trip lasting seven days, [that is to say,] for a week. Likewise, sesame bread points to a yearlong

---

Sereim and recorded in Achmet's dreambook are derived from Muslim dreambooks; see the discussions in Lamoreaux 2002, 150–51 and, in richer detail, Mavroudi 2002, Chap. 9.

[21]　　The interpretation is based on the equivalence of the loss of the penis and the loss of one's children; see Achmet 95.

[22]　　Of course, Byzantine literature is not without extended discussions. For example, the fourteenth-century scholar Nicephorus Gregoras wrote a commentary on Synesius's book on dreams; the eleventh–century writers Michael Psellus and John Italus discuss categories of dreams and their causes; Manuel II Palaeologus, as we have seen, engaged in a philosophical discussion of dreams; and the twelfth-century John Tzetzes distinguished between types of dreams and dream visitations.

period of banishment that will turn out to be profitable, pleasant, and altogether quite nice. [Manuel 26]

To dream of candles being kindled signifies [good] opportunities; to hold extinguished candles, the opposite; to hold candles again in the same condition, a protracted period of time. Thick candles [are interpreted] as years, while slender ones as months and days depending on their quality and quantity. [Anonymous 143]

Wearing a wreath made of roses means something good, provided that roses are in season [at the time of the dream]; if they are out of season, it indicates torment. [Anonymous 364]

Other dreams are significant if they are seen during the day or on a particular day of the week:

A dream that occurs during the day is very clear [in its significance]. [Nicephorus, Appendix II, 108]

A dream on Saturday results in temporal power. [Germanus 165]

[A dream on] the first day of the week is a true dream. [Germanus 225]

The fact that every symbolic dream has an idiosyncratic value was the leading principle of Artemidorus's dreambook. Achmet fully agrees with Artemidorus on this point when he states that the significance of a dream symbol varies in accordance with the individual circumstances of the dreamer; thus, an interpreter must pay special attention to the dreamer's status, gender, occupation, wealth, and state of health (2, 301). On the basis of this information, a dream symbol's significance can be decoded:

Dreams, as already stated, are judged in different ways for various people. For, given the same dream, there is one interpretation for a king, another for his subjects; one for a warrior, another for a farmer; one for a nobleman, another for a poor man; one for a man, another for a woman. [301]

The interpreter obtains during the consultation process the information required to decipher the dream. After the consultant relates his dream, the interpreter, drawing on his experience, selects from the dream's contents the image or images he deems to be predictive of the future. He then asks the dreamer about the circumstances in his or her life, such as family, health, marital status, and financial problems. The interpreter then applies these data to the dream symbol(s) in order to decide the dream's significance. For example,

A woman consulted the dream interpreter Sereim: "I dreamt that the top doorjamb of my house fell down onto the lower one, causing one door to fall to the outside of the house, the other to the inside." Sereim asked her: "Do you have a husband and children?" She replied: "I do, but my husband is living in a foreign country with my son, while I have a daughter at home with me." Sereim then said: "Your husband will soon return home because of the fall of the top doorjamb, and your son with his new bride will accompany him because of the falling of one door to the inside; your daughter, on the other hand, will become attached to some man and go away because the other door fell to the outside." And the dream turned out just as he had predicted. [147]

A married woman came and consulted the dream interpreter: "I dreamt that I was walking about in public unveiled. What does this foretell for me?" He asked: "Do you have a husband?" "Yes, I do, but he is in a foreign country at the moment." He replied: "You will never see him again." And so it turned out, for the husband died abroad. [264]

Unlike Achmet (and Artemidorus), the Byzantine dreambook writers do not go to such lengths to interpret their dream symbols. As a rule, each interpretation is applicable to anyone, irrespective of factors like gender, economic means, political rank, and state of health. This is a significant departure from pagan oneirocriticism and doubtlessly is a reductivism of a rich tradition of dream interpretation to a simple key-code approach.[23] Only occasionally do we see dreams interpreted in several ways, and then in simple contrastive pairs—for example, if the dreamer is rich or poor, free or slave, sick or in good health:

Taking off one's clothes is good for sick people, but bad for all others. [Daniel 14]

Disowning oneself is good for those involved in business dealings, but bad for all others. [Daniel 21]

Having one's feet secured with shackles is good for slaves and the poor, but evil for the wealthy. [Daniel 430]

Flying without wings is good for those in foreign lands, but for the rest it is inauspicious. [Anonymous 124]

If you dream of becoming a *comes*, this is not a good sign for state functionaries and legal defendants. [Anonymous 148; see comment ad loc. for the political meaning of *comes*.]

Seeing thunderbolts is good for slaves, but for all others, especially the poor, [this dream] is bad, for it is a sign of misfortune. [Anonymous 152]

Such binary interpretations are rare, however. What we typically get is a dream symbol, followed by a universal interpretation applicable to any dreamer:

To dream that your brother or sister or some relative has died points to an additional span of life. [Daniel 15]

Sacrificing a rooster is good, provided that it is not strangled. [Daniel 16]

---

[23] Achmet himself often interprets a dream only in accordance with social status and gender, as he restricts himself to kings, noblemen, commoners, the poor, and women. The Muslim dreambook writers also outline detailed and complex methods of interpreting dreams and yet in the end do not apply them; usually they are content to establish "analogical relations or symbolic links between dream symbols and their meanings" (Lamoreaux 2002, 32), much as we see in the case of Byzantine writers.

To dream of crowing roosters: something you greatly desire will happen for you. [Daniel 17]

Dreaming of the stars signifies activity filled with happiness. [Daniel 18]

To dream of oneself as mute signifies great joy. [Daniel 22]

Anyone who speaks with the emperor remains out of work. [Germanus 8]

Eating loaves of white bread is an auspicious sign. [Germanus 9]

This simple key code in many of the Byzantine dreambooks may reflect the kind of clientele most likely to consult them. Achmet's book can be thought of "royal," insofar as it likely was "compiled for an imperial patron or at least used by an interpreter of imperial dreams" (Mavroudi 2002, 422), and it certainly would have been known to members of the Byzantine aristocracy. Manuel's dreambook, as we saw in Chapter 1, was written either by the emperor himself or by someone close to him, and would have been used by the men and women of the Palaeologan court. The writers of the other Byzantine dreambooks were seeking a broader spectrum of readership. One may even say that they were seeking an imaginary "everyman" for whom these interpretations could equally imply. This by no means denigrates the genre itself; as we have seen, Manuel's and Nicephorus's dreambooks seek higher audiences—Manuel, the court of the emperor himself; Nicephorus, an educated readership—but the Byzantine dreambooks as a whole, with their telegraphic brevity of dream interpretations, could be used profitably by anyone who could read or who otherwise had access to the books.

Now, what are the methodologies that the Byzantine interpreters or dreambook writers used when they determined certain interpretations for specific dreams? It is not reasonable to assume that they made capricious decisions, for any paying client or the purchaser of a dream manual would expect some semblance of deductive and scientific reasoning in return for the expense. Although our writers never set down their methods of interpretation, it is not difficult to recover the methods by which they interpreted the majority of their dreams. Five conscious/unconscious psychical and mental processes may be adduced here.[24]

---

[24] Guidorizzi (1980, 22) observes that the Byzantine dreambook writers used the same methods as their predecessor, Artemidorus; namely, associations based on analogy, similarity, antinomy, or phonetic and etymological clues ("[I] libri bizantini ricalcano gli schemi già utilizzati da Artemidoro: l'associazione è fondata su nessi di similarità, analogia, opposizione, su chiavi fonetiche ed etimologiche. Tutti questi schemi possono tuttavia essere ridotti a due modelli fondamentali: le interpretazioni contenute nei libri dei sogni si riconducono essenzialmente a rapporti costruiti sul principio della *similarità* o su quello della *contiguità*, ossia sui principi fondamentali che regolano le associazioni di idee"). Lamoreaux (2002, 28–32, 87–8) discusses similar methods used by early Muslim dreambook writers: etymology, association, antinomy, metaphor, the Koran, resemblance, metonymy, the time when the dream was seen, and relation of dream content with status of dreamer (occupation, religion, etc.); see also Sirriyeh 2006, 212–13. For Artemidorus's reliance on etymology, linguistic puns, juxtaposition of similarities, metaphor, and numerology, see Miller 1994, 85–90.

1. Use of traditional material and conformity of the dream symbol with culture

Some dream symbols are interpreted by association with traditional cultural material (religion, literature, folk tales, mythology, etc.). For example, a symbol's interpretation may be based on literary *topoi*, as in Manuel 24 where we find the ship of state metaphor (along with a nice pun here), so common in ancient literature:

> If [someone] dreams that [a Byzantine war vessel] was running swiftly thanks to a fair wind and was cutting across the sea in a straight direction [δι' εὐθύτητος], he will see the magistrate of his land and district—or even the prince himself—prosperous and blessed, keeping very straight [εὖ μάλα διευθύνοντα] the helms of his glory and dealing with matters of state.

Biblical imagery and allusions, as one might expect of a text written in a Christian society, account for some interpretations. At times, the association is straightforward, as in the case of two interpretations based on Matthew 25:31–5: "This [dream] is thus interpreted because goats are on the left hand of Christ the Savior, the true God" (Manuel 44), and "White sheep, when dreamt of, signify something good" (Daniel 436). In Nicephorus, Appendix I, 45, we have a clear reference to Pharaoh's dream, in Genesis 41, of cattle foretelling years of abundance and famine: "Dead oxen indicate the years of a famine." Some allusions to religious texts are less direct, for example: "Anyone who embraces a pillar should expect to receive divine grace" (Nicephorus 111, which alludes to the pillar of divine smoke in Exodus 13:21, to Byzantine iconography depicting Christ as a pillar, and perhaps to pillar saints). Or Daniel 208, "Dreaming that the sun is fixed in the same position indicates life and honor," where no doubt we have a reference to the sun standing still for the Israelite leader Joshua in his battle against the Amorites (Joshua 10:12–15). Or Anonymous 433, "To dream of having a boil on one's foot is a good sign for slaves and the poor, but a horrible sign for the wealthy," an allusion to the boils that Job, the "wealthiest man of the East," suffered.[25]

A dream may also be interpreted as foretelling something good or evil, depending on whether its images are in accordance with everyday social life and with traditional gender roles. This method is consistent with Artemidorus's methodology. Artemidorus had recommended the interpreter to use six categories in his analysis of dreams: nature, convention, habit, occupation, name, and time, each of which is to be qualified by *kata* (in accordance with) and *para* (in opposition to). The two principle categories, however, are *phusis* and *nomos*, or "nature" and "convention," with convention subdivided into unwritten rules and written rules. Generally speaking, in the Byzantine dreambooks dream images that are in accordance with nature or

---

[25] We may compare for similar religious associations Achmet 177: "If someone dreams that he was walking on top of the waters of the sea, he will receive courage, power, and friendship from the king." The interpretation is based on Matthew 14:25–33, where Peter walks on top of the Sea of Galilee as Jesus encourages him, and on the association of Jesus with king (cf. Achmet 126).

convention signify something good; those in opposition to nature or convention, some type of evil. For example,

A man plying a loom will commit adultery with a married woman. [Daniel 253; the interpretation is based on the sexual imagery of the movement of the loom as it is being plied; moreover, a man is doing the plying, contrary to cultural custom, and he will also violate social mores and the law by being involved in adultery with the wife of another man.]

Having one's feet secured by shackles is a good dream for slaves and the poor, but evil for the wealthy. [Daniel 430; a good sign because an image of slaves being shackled is consistent with everyday life, but for a freeperson such a condition would imply a drastic reversal of fortune.]

Losing your belt signifies that your dismissal from office is at hand. [Daniel 201; this interpretation is based on the wearing by Byzantine government officials of belts of different colors and types, depending on their rank and position.]

Being blind signifies hindrance. [Daniel 29; the reference is to the Byzantine custom of blinding political opponents, rebels, traitors, and religious dissenters. This practice also has biblical overtones; see the commentary below, ad loc.]

Shaving off your beard or having it fall out is a bitter sign for anyone. [Daniel 89; the reference is to the Byzantine custom of wearing beards. A beard was indicative of manliness, and the loss of it constituted a severe punishment. Moreover, since the Latins did not wear beards, having a beard was a sign of Byzantine citizenship.]

Having your head cropped short means loss. [Daniel 281; the association is based on longer hair denoting social status among the Byzantines, and on one's hair being cut as a form of punishment.]

Receiving letters of the alphabet that have been written in red ink: expect to receive very soon either an official rank of authority or death. [Nicephorus, Appendix I, 24–5; the emperor's orders were written in red ink, and so the words contain either the dreamer's death warrant or his promotion.]

2. Puns/wordplay/etymology

Perhaps the most common method of interpreting dreams in the ancient world was through puns and wordplay. Many an interpreter based his solution of a dream on the similarity of sound, resemblance between words, or a word's double meaning.[26] The Byzantine oneirocriticists, especially the authors of the metrical dreambooks, favored this method of interpretation. For example,

---

[26]   Freud indulged in similar wordplay in his *Interpretation of Dreams* (he even references Artemidorus in this regard); see Freud 1980, 237–40, 247–9, 441–2.

Being chased [διώκεσθαι] by cattle means being persecuted [διώκεται] by the *dunatoi* [the provincial aristocracy]. [Daniel 38]

Collecting stones signifies illness. [Daniel 331; the interpretation is based on λίθος, which means not only a rock but also a kidney stone or stone in the bladder.]

If you dream of becoming old [γέρων], you will have privilege [γέρας]. [Nicephorus 21; see comment to loc.]

A smashed oil lamp [κανδῆλα] dissolves scandal [σκάνδαλα]. [Nicephorus 49]

Figs [...] denote slander. [Manuel 13; a wordplay between σῦκον, fig and συκοθαντία, slander or defamation.]

If someone dreams of seeing a person riding a beautiful and healthy horse of short stature [σύντομον], he is about to hear a good but concise [σύντομον] report about his public standing, influence, and powerful actions. But if the horse was sluggish and maimed and therefore had difficulty moving, he will hear words that are odious and fraught with great danger—words that he will definitely accept. And if the dreamer is enjoying good fortune [εὐτυχής] and is held in high esteem [ἔνδοξος], he will soon become unfortunate [δυστυχήσει] and lose his honor [δόξαν]. [Manuel 11]

If someone dreams that he got a blessing from a bishop or received the Holy Gospel [εὐαγγέλιον] from him, he will hear good news [ἀγγελίαν] and useful words from a magistrate who will come from far away. [Manuel 27; perhaps also a pun between χρηστός, useful and Χριστός, Christ, which were pronounced the same at this time.]

Legumes [λάχανα] that are eaten [in a dream] point to profit by chance [λάχος]. [Manuel 16; wordplay between λάχανον and λάχος.]

If someone dreams that his penis was flaccid and in a contracted position, he will be weak and prove unsuccessful [ἄπρακτος]. [Manuel 19; the word ἄπρακτος can also mean "impotent."]

Related to the use of puns and wordplay is interpretation through etymology. This method appears often in Manuel's dreambook, a clear indication of the learned background of both author and audience. Here a dream symbol is interpreted on the basis of a word's etymological derivation. Following are four examples from Manuel:

If mice [μῦς] appear in someone's house roaming up and down, all the secrets [μυστήρια] of the homeowner will be revealed. For the mouse derives its name from the [verb] μύω—that is, to shut one's eyes [καμμύω]. [Manuel 4]

If someone dreams that he was riding a donkey, he is about to be promoted, resulting in his own gain [ὠφέλειαν] and success [προκοπήν]. For the word "donkey" [ὄνος] is derived from the [verb] ὀνεῖν, which means "to derive advantage" [ὠφελεῖν] and "to succeed" [προκόπτειν]. Besides, [a donkey is also called] ἀείδαρος [continually struck] because it is always beaten by the one who drives him with a stick. [Manuel 11]

[If someone dreams that he] saw the icons of the holy martyrs and ascetics or heard the voices of the Theotokos and the angels, he will face an even greater upheaval and tumult but he will be proved righteous in battle. The appearance of icons is interpreted through no method other than the fact that they and churches are further decorated with [the use of] tesserae [ψηφίδων], and a judgement is called ψῆφος. [Manuel 27; ψῆφος meant not only a mosaic pebble, but also the stone used in casting votes —hence, "judgement."]

If someone dreams that he became a priest, he will depart on a short trip and conduct some profitable business, for the word "priest" [ἱερεύς] is derived from [the verb] ἵημι [to send]—that is, πέμπω [to send]. [Manuel 27]

3. Antinomy

Antimony (or when the meaning of a dream is the converse of the dream content[27]) occurs more frequently in the poetic *oneirocritica* than in the prose texts. Overall, the verse dreambooks prefer puns and antinomy to all other methods combined. The reason may be that a dodecasyllabic line affords far less space for treating a dream symbol and its interpretation (one has only 12 syllables to work with, as opposed to the unlimited space of a prose sentence), and a simple binary opposition or pun is rather easy to effect. Or perhaps these two methods could be appreciated better by the general, wide readership of the poetic dreambooks; more sophisticated techniques like etymology and metonymy would be harder to detect and be noticed.

In the following dreams, the interpretation is the opposite of what one would expect on the basis of the dream's contents or the symbol's intrinsic meaning:

Laughing in a dream signifies grief. [Daniel 110]

Crying in one's dream signifies joy. [Daniel 294]

Holding gold: you will end up not getting what you want. [Germanus 255]

Eating sweets foretells bitterness for you. [Nicephorus 22a]

If you dream of being rich, you will be poor. [Nicephorus, Appendix I, 71]

4. Analogy (metonymy)

Here, the interpretation of the dream is made by literal associations.[28] The interpreter forms associations on the basis of analogies to the qualities and characteristics of a dream symbol, such as Achmet does in the case of carrots:

---

[27] Guidorizzi 1980, 22. This method is very common in Freud's *Interpretation of Dreams*; see, e.g., Freud 1980, 278–9, 321–2, 361–3, 389–91, 436–7, 470–71, 508–14.

[28] Cf. Mavroudi 2002, 187–8.

If someone dreams that he ate a carrot, he will have a little wealth along with illness: the wealth because of the sweetness, the illness because of the yellow color. If he dreams that he ate cooked carrots, he will have an illness of short duration: for carrots are quickly digested. If he dreams that he drank wine made from carrots, if he became drunk, he will have power along with toil and incur an illness proportionate to his drunkenness: if he did not, proportionate sorrow and illness. [207]

In the above series of dreams, Achmet bases his interpretations on analogies to color, taste, digestion, and intoxication to decipher the series of dreams. The Byzantine dreambook writers make similar associations for fruits, meats, drinks, and other foods. To make such interpretations requires some medical knowledge (even if rudimentary), acquaintance with the properties of foods, and an understanding of how specific drinks and foods affect the body. (This speaks favorably, I would note, of the educational background of the dreambook writers.) The following are examples:

[O]nions, garlic, leeks, and cardamom are judged [as bitter anger and wrath], for their pungency moves a person to passionate wrath. [Manuel 16]

Plums indicates the evil words of a most evil and troublesome woman. They also signify illness, since they overpower a person's tent—that is to say, his body. [Manuel 12; wordplay here between δαμάσηνον, plum and δαμάζω, overpower. The interpretation may also be based on the analogy of dried plums (prunes) "overpowering" a body, in digestive terms, when eaten in quantity.]

Handling pepper or mustard means illness, sorrow, and weeping. [Anonymous 326]

A thistle plant sprouting up points to a rising-up of one's enemies. [Daniel 23; thorns are analogous to the barbs of enemies.]

The grapevine signifies family. If [someone dreams that] a vine had white grapes that some people then picked, this means grief caused by the death of a layperson; but if the grapes were black, a monk or a nun will die. [Manuel 15; the interpretation derives from analogy—that is, the vine stem is analogous to the central family unit, and the clusters of grapes are analogous to the children with their own families. Manuel's interpretation here may also be based on an association of the grapes' black color with the black robes of the monastic orders.]

Animals are interpreted by analogy to their behavioral characteristics and physical attributes, and this too implies some knowledge of zoology and fauna on the part of the dreambook writer. So Manuel writes: "Fish are interpreted as fear and a lack of resolve, since they tremble and are easily frightened" (1); "The camel signifies difficulties and a situation that is hard to manage because of its hump and curved shape" (11); "The mule likewise is a very evil dream symbol, since its breed is a mixture of the horse and donkey and it is willfully mischievous and mean" (11). In other dreambooks, we read that rabbits, because of their proclivity to have repeated sex, signify prostitutes. Dogs, which in Byzantine hagiography symbolised the devil and were considered evil, signify enemies. Cats, which sneak about at night, denote thieves. Snakes, the biblical enemy of humanity and which bite people with their fangs, portray enemies who hurl sharp barbs. Crabs, with their shape, are analogous to crooked men, while lions, symbols of royalty ever since the Greek Bronze Age, represent powerful rulers. As for colors, white is always an auspicious symbol, while anything black—whether a person's skin, a person's face, clothing, an animal—is a horrible sign, an association based on racial prejudice. Purple (the color of the emperor) denotes royalty; yellow (a frequent color of disease), illness; green, faith.[29] Swords are a metaphor for strength, power, and manliness, while daggers represent war or the ability to wage war. Trees are judged metaphorically as men, and so we read these dream interpretations:

Breaking a branch off a tree signifies separation from a friend. [Anonymous 178]

If you dream of trees being uprooted or being cut down, this means wars and the falling of animals and people. [Daniel 123]

Very large trees are judged as noble and well-born men, and so their falling-down signifies death [for such a man]. Likewise, concerning small [μικρά] trees: these refer to insignificant [μικρούς] people and a lesser fortune and fate. [Manuel 14, with a pun on the word μικρός.]

Containers are analogous to women, since both receive fluids (wine, water, semen): "Wells, water tanks, and any vessel capable of holding liquids are interpreted as women. If someone dreams that he drank water from any of these items, he will satisfy his pleasure with a woman" (Manuel 7). We may adduce in this regard a parallel from Achmet (45, 47):

If someone dreams that he urinated into a glass vessel, if he is a king, he will impregnate a dishonorable woman with his seed, and neither she nor her child will be sound because of the fragility of glass. ... If [someone dreams that he urinated] into a silver vessel, he will have sex with the more beautiful of his young female slaves; if the dreamer is a commoner, he will rejoice together with his wife; if he is poor, he will make love to or marry a wealthy woman. ... If someone dreams that he urinated into a vessel that he owned, he will have sex with his wife; but if the vessel belonged to someone else, with another man's wife.[30]

Women are also analogous to beds, bedsheets, and mattresses, since men lay on top of all alike (e.g., "Dreaming of a well-made bed signifies a good [life] with a woman," Daniel 306). Given this same association of women with mattresses, Achmet makes a fascinating series of analogies:

If someone dreams that he got another mattress, he will get another wife. If he dreams that he fell asleep on a mattress in someone else's house, if he knows the homeowner, he will seduce that man's wife; if he does not know him, he will come into fornication. If he dreams that he went off somewhere after tying up his mattress, he will go away on a trip and leave his wife behind and on his return will discover her to have been chaste;

---

[29]   For green as a symbol of faith and godliness, see below comment to Anonymous 129.

[30]   The association of urine with semen is common in Muslim dreambooks; see Lamoreaux 2002, 24 and 87 for discussion and examples; also Mavroudi 2007, 54. Sirriyeh (2006, 220) notes a similar association in an Assyrian dreambook (Oppenheim 1956).

and if he dreams that his mattress thickened and puffed out while he was away, he will find on his return that she has become pregnant through him. If he dreams that he owned an unfamiliar mattress, he will find among strangers a woman who will be analogous to the mattress's beauty and size and to the bedspread on it. If he dreams that a familiar or unfamiliar mattress was laying on [his bed] and that he was lying on it, he will find great power and joy: for the bed under him is made of wood and wood symbolises very powerful men; and however long he was on the bed is how long he will be exalted. [222]

5. Metaphor and hypothetico-deductive reasoning[31]

This method is similar to analogy, but the correspondences are less literal and more metaphorical. A passage from Achmet may serve as an introductory example: "If someone dreams that he was burned by an oven, he will be punished by a noble who is a feeder of the people" (158). Here, the symbol "being burned by fire" is interpreted metaphorically as punishment; the "noble who is a feeder of the people" is derived from the metaphors of fire as a powerful force (like a noble) and the oven as a place for cooking foods that, in turn, are eaten by people.

Riding a horse is a metaphor for sexual intercourse: "Sitting on an unfamiliar horse means happiness with another man's wife" (Anonymous 265). We may compare Achmet 14: "If someone dreams of sitting on the Pharaoh's steed or saddle horse, if he did so with the Pharaoh's consent, the Pharaoh will give him a woman from the royal family; if without his consent, the dreamer will mount the Pharaoh's daughter from behind and this will become known." Having sex with one's wife is a good dream if one is away on a trip (Daniel 343), since the dream means that the dreamer will soon be in his own bed. The penis is deemed as a metaphor for power, and so an erect penis symbolises strength and success, while a flaccid penis denotes weakness and a loss of power (Manuel 19). A dream of having tattoos on one's body symbolises lashes from a whip, since both leave marks on the body (Daniel 95). Seeing a chariot-driver foretells quarrels (Daniel 212), an association derived from the numerous riots and fights that occurred at the Hippodrome in Constantinople. A man who dreams of being penetrated anally by a man will lose his wife (Daniel 357), since he will have no more interest in having sex with her. A short person who dreams of becoming taller will increase his wealth; but a tall person who dreams of becoming shorter will incur loss (Daniel 366). A tower that falls down in a dream means that magistrates will fall down in death (Nicephorus 100, with an a–b–a–b sequence of metaphors: πύργος πεσὼν δείκνυσι ἀρχόντων μόρον). Being hung means that one will be lifted up in grandeur (Nicephorus, Appendix II, 8, with comment ad loc).

At other times, an interpreter will use both metaphor and analogy in analysing a dream. Achmet employs these two methods in a series of interpretations dealing with mushrooms:

---

[31]   Cf. Guidorizzi 1980, 22–3.

The mushroom signifies a woman with no family: for the mushroom bears no fruit above the soil and has no roots below. If someone dreams that he found one or two or three mushrooms, he will come across [a similar number of] women of no family; if the mushrooms were up to ten in number, this means a similar [number of] women; but if the number was much more—in fact, countless—he will get from evil women money in proportion to the number of mushrooms. If someone dreams that he got a mushroom along with a small one, he will get a woman with a daughter. If someone dreams that he ate cooked mushrooms, he will get wealth from a woman, but be afflicted because of the violence of fire [which was seen in the dream]. If he ate boiled mushrooms, he too will be wealthy, but to a lesser degree because the mushrooms became watery as a result of being boiled. If someone dreams that he concealed mushrooms somewhere, if he knew the amount, he will hide away shameful women; if he did not know how many he hid, he will store up money acquired from evil women. [203]

The meanings of other dreams are deciphered, not from metaphor or analogy, but from a deductive, logical analysis of the dream symbol itself. Thus, defecating on one's bed means falling ill (Daniel 187), since one is too weak to get up and go to the toilet. Someone who dreams of becoming deaf will be free of worry (Daniel 298). Wanting to run but not being able to do so means experiencing some sort of hindrance in life (Daniel 125). Heretical Christians are judged as demons (Nicephorus, Appendix II, 3); an earthquake foretells tumults (Germanus 219); and trees filled with fruit signify profit, while barren trees foretell loss (Anonymous 55). Or this series of dreams from Daniel:

Seeing or reading imperial edicts signifies extremely successful opportunities.[Daniel 259; codicils placed in ivory diptychs appointed someone to a high office or granted him a title, and so we probably have a reference to being promoted.]

Growing your fingernails long signifies lack of care. [Daniel 407; an observation on the fact that a person who grows his fingernails long enjoys a life of leisure and does not engage in manual labor.]

Stowing away gifts in one's own house: this is good for each and every dreamer. [Daniel 134; a good dream since one is keeping property and not giving it away; cf. Daniel 135: "Giving away gifts: watch out lest you suffer loss."]

Making a will means renouncing the rights to one's own property. [Daniel 137]

The reason for some of the interpretations in our dreambooks may never be known. It is certainly perplexing to read that chickpeas signify that a person will be phallically penetrated; we may well wonder how that interpretation came about. Or the dream of eating a hot pita bread as signifying that the dreamer will fall ill with consumption—did that interpretation come from the interpreter's own experience? Or did the writer hear of that dream, and its result, from a friend? We will never know why we have certain interpretations, but some may derive from the interpreter himself either as a hearer of dreams or as a dreamer himself. Artemidorus had recommended that an interpreter should be an observer and a listener of dreams, and should write them down along with their outcomes for future reference; we can easily envision the Byzantine oneirocritic writers doing likewise. Thus, when Manuel writes that a dream of eating sesame bread foretells a year of pleasant and tolerable political exile, it may well have been that a friend of his, or a member of the imperial court, was eating this very kind of bread when he received news of his impending exile, thereby leading him to form the association of sesame bread and exile.[32]

---

[32]   Cf. Lamoreaux 2002, 87–8 on the interpretation of a snake as an enemy in Muslim dreambooks: "What is the underlying link between snake and enemy? We can only guess— perhaps because snakes are hostile to humans; perhaps because snakes 'hide' their poison; perhaps because of the scriptural accounts of primeval enemy. Even so, why did Ibn Qutaybah [an early Arabic dreambook writer] think that a white snake signifies a weak enemy, while a black snake indicates one that is strong? It might be because white snakes were thought to be less poisonous than black snakes, or it might have something to do with the symbolic associations of the colors themselves, perhaps because black was the color of the Abbasids. We can only guess: the underlying oneirocritic logic is inscribed in an ancient language, one that we are no longer fully able to understand."

Chapter 3

The Cultural, Historical, and Social Background

As mentioned at the onset of this book, the Greeks of the pre-Byzantine and Byzantine worlds believed in the reality of the dream world and in its significance for foretelling the present and future.[1] The dream was regarded as a valid indicator of a person's current physical and mental states, and as a conveyor of future information on such matters as goodness and evil, success and failure, wealth and poverty, health and illness.[2] Nearly every person, no matter his or her educational training, philosophical tenets, religion, social status, and cultural background, accepted this concept.[3]

It was commonly believed that dreams have multiple causes for their provenance. Some dreams have a naturalistic causation, in that they arise from purely physiological factors such as disease, drunkenness, and indigestion. Other dreams come from the impact of the emotions on the soul or from the repetition of waking-state thoughts. Dreams may also be sent by the gods, the dead, or demons, or they may be produced by the soul itself through its innate activity. On the following pages I will discuss ancient and Byzantine philosophical, medical, and religious sources on dreams and dream theory. I leave aside the use of dreams in literature, on the grounds that they are primarily plot devices.[4] First, philosophy.

Plato advocated various origins for dreams, but, as scholars have pointed out,[5] his thoughts on the subject progressed: from dreams being a means of receiving divine images to a philosophical gnoseology and then to enlightened theology. True dreams

---

[1]   This has been extensively documented in modern scholarship, the literature on which is massive. See G. Weber's "Bibliographische Online-Datenbank zu Träumen und Visionem in der Antike," which may be found at the website http://www.gnomon.ku-eichstaett.de/dreams/index.html. The site is continually updated, and is thorough and exhaustive. The reader is recommended to consult this bibliography for specifics on the general points of discussion made in the following paragraphs.

[2]   Ancient and medieval dream interpreters were concerned only with the here and now or with the impending future. They would have found odd the modern notion that dreams can shed light on a dreamer's past.

[3]   For a brief overview, see Oberhelman 1991, 23–38 and 1993; in detail, Van Lieshout 1980, with further references at 263–79; Holowchak 2001a; Walde 2001; Weber 1998 and 2000.

[4]   For dreams in Greek and Roman literature, see the numerous bibliographical entries in the "Bibliographische Online-Datenbank" referenced in note 1 above; cf. Miller 1994, Chap. 1. MacAlister (1996) is an excellent example of the use of dreams as a literary device.

[5]   Van Lieshout 1980, 103–36; Vegleris 1982. The classic work on Plato is now Rotonardo 1998, who offers a comprehensive bibliography.

come from gods or *daemones* (spirits inhabiting the air); the soul, in turn, reproduces these images in degrees of clarity or obscurity, depending on the person's ethico-philosophical state.[6] Other dreams arise from the movements of the body's internal organs; from the continued activity during sleep of one of the three parts of the human soul; or from the liver, which translates rational images from the intellectual part of the soul into the irrational language of the belly, or which comprehends the rational messages of the mind.[7] For Plato, dreams are symptomatic of the ethical, physical, and emotional states of the dreamer: the purer the dreamer's soul and ethical well-being, the more meaningful the dream. In other words, true dreams are the province of the educated person; other dreams are biological in origin, or the images seen by uneducated people.[8]

Aristotle attempted, through philosophy and science, to deny the metaphysical reality of dreams, but he could not wholly escape the influence of the widespread belief that some dreams may be divinatory.[9] Aristotle considered dreaming an activity not only of the faculty of perception, but also of imagination; that is, the process of dreaming is the process of imagining (*On Dreams* 458a33–9a22). These perceptions are, in reality, sensations produced in the sense organs, but whose effects remain even after perception has ceased (459a24–8). Such effects are more common during sleep, since the senses are active during the waking state and therefore cause the sensations to go unnoticed (460b28–61a8). But when sleep occurs, most of the blood descends to the heart and carries with it the movements of these sensations, or the impressions of former perceptions; there, in the center of the heart, the impressions occur as images. The master faculty, the faculty of judgement, cannot distinguish during sleep between these sensations and true perceptions, and therefore accepts all indiscriminately. A dream, therefore, is an image that occurs during sleep and arises from the movement of sensations (462a15–16).

So far, so good for a purely scientific explanation of dreams and dreaming. But Aristotle suddenly backtracks when he approaches the topic of divination through dreams. In the companion essay, *On Divination through Dreams*, Aristotle refuses to say whether the future can be determined through dreams:

> Now concerning prophecy that occurs during sleep and is said to arise from dreams, it is not easy to despise, or trust in, such a notion. For the fact that all people or many of them are aware of the opinion that dreams are significant [of the future] offers some credence that this is based on experience, and it is not unbelievable that in some instances divination through dreams may occur; indeed, this all has some reason behind it, and so one could suppose that the same obtains for all other dreams. But the fact that one cannot see any logical reason why this should be so causes one to be distrustful. [462b12–17]

Aristotle proceeds to discuss how dreams may have the appearance of being prophetic. If god-sent visions (the mention of which is another piece of backtracking) are excluded, then dreams must be causes, signs, or fortuitous accompaniments of

---

[6]   Plato, *Apology* 33c; *Symposium* 203a; *Republic* 571c–2b.

[7]   Plato, *Timaeus* 45e–6a, 70dff.; *Republic* 571aff.

[8]   Plato, *Laws* 904c–10e; *Republic* 574dff.

[9]   See Frère 1983; Kany-Turpin and Pellegrin 1989; Miller 1994, 42–4.

events (462b27–9). Some dreams may be causes of actions. Just as events in the waking state are often seen in dreams, so dreams may prompt the dreamer to some action during the day, simply because we are prepared for such action by what we saw occurring in our dreams (463a21–30). Other dreams may be signs, especially signs of what is occurring in the body. Stimuli arising from the body usually escape our attention during the waking state because the waking movements and outside sense perceptions are far too great. But in sleep, the opposite occurs: small movements from the body seem greater and thus are perceived. Accordingly, diseases at their incipient stage may be noticed during dreams because the movements of their beginnings can be grasped (463a4–21). Most dreams, however, are mere chance accompaniments of events that happen in waking life (463a31–b11).

As for deciphering dreams, this should be done through resemblances. A dream image is like a reflection in water: it is not the original, but only a reflection, a copy, of it. The good interpreter of dreams is one who can sort through, judge, and piece together the images of a dream, and thus identify the reality behind the reflections (463b5–15).

The Stoics of the third and second centuries BCE formulated a threefold classification of significant dreams on the basis of source. Dreams may come from God, from *daemones*, or from the soul itself. In the last case, the soul prognosticates the future through its connection with the Soul of the universe: the dreamer's own soul, when the senses are at rest, contemplates the coherence of all things and so knows the future. The first-century BCE Stoic Posidonius used these same categories, but also distinguished subtypes. He asserted that predictive dreams are not always straightforward and clear; instead, they may be enigmatic by containing symbolism. We find this system later in Christian literature, with the *daemones* of pagan philosophy replaced by Satan and evil demons.[10]

The revival of pagan philosophy in the third century CE in the form of Neoplatonism sparked further discussions of dreams.[11] Two Neoplatonists in particular—Synesius and Calcidius—strongly affected Byzantine literature through their writings on dreams. Synesius wrote his *On Dreams* before his conversion to Christianity.[12] Supposedly penned in one night,[13] the treatise offers Neoplatonic theories on dreams, along with a bewildering eclecticism of Stoic, Platonic, Aristotelian, and Epicurean doctrines. Synesius considered dreams one important way to commune with God, with straightforward or non-symbolic dreams especially helpful in this respect. Symbolic dreams may also be a means of divine communion, but since they require interpretation, they should be treated with caution. Symbolic dreams should never be deciphered through dreambooks or by interpreters, for every dreamer has a unique and individual dream language. Synesius recommends every person to keep

---

[10]   For the Stoic views on dreams, see ibid., 52–5.

[11]   The thoughts of the Middle Platonists are discussed in ibid., 55–9.

[12]   Del Corno 1978, 1613–15; Kruger 1992, 18–19; Le Goff 1985, 183; Miller 1994, 70–73 (with bibliography in n. 177). Text in Terzaghi 1944, 143–89.

[13]   Guidorizzi (1985, 154) thinks that Synesius's claim may be true, given the disorganised structure of the work.

a daily journal of all dreams received and the results of those dreams in order to gain an empirical understanding of his or her own particular dream language.[14]

Calcidius devoted a section of his *Commentary on Plato's Timaeus* to dreams (Chaps 250–56).[15] In his discussion, Calcidius gives three causes of dreams: God, angels or demons, and the soul (256); this classification, in other words, is a Christianised version of the Early Stoics' system. In the dreaming process, the soul may be either the active or the passive agent. In the latter case, the passions or external impressions stimulate the soul, thus yielding non-significant images. In the former, the higher, rational part of the soul produces a dream; since only God can send non-symbolic dreams, these soul-images are ambiguous in meaning and so require interpretation.[16]

Ancient physicians and medical authors contributed much to the discussion of the origin, classification, and interpretation of dreams. The earliest extant medical work on the subject is the fourth book of the Hippocratic *Regimen*. Spurious in authorship,[17] the work, which dates to the end of the fifth or the early fourth century BCE, is drawn from medical and traditional dream materials, all of which the author reshaped and rewrote on the basis of his own medical knowledge.[18] The author follows the twofold typology of dream classification then prevalent in the classical Greek period: divine dreams that prognosticate the future, and non-divine dreams, some of which are able to describe both the physical state of the body and the regimen needed to restore health.

The medically significant dream occurs when the soul, while the body is asleep, performs through its own agency all the acts of the body, such as sight, touch, perception of pain, and reflection.[19] During the body's sleep, a displacement of perception takes place: the soul's cognitive and sensory processes shift inwardly, to the body, whereby the soul perceives the conditions of the body, including diseases. These perceptions constitute the images of dreams and offer information on the dreamer's state of health.

A medical dream should be analysed according to a microcosm–macrocosm analogy. The human body is the microcosm of the universe (the macrocosm), and so the circulations in the outer, middle, and hollow parts of the body are analogous to the outer, middle, and hollow circuits (the stars, sun, and moon).[20] Thus, according to this model of analogy, if someone dreams of a star (outer circuit) disappearing or suffering some sort of harm, this means that a moist and phlegm-like secretion has fallen to the body's outer circulation; the dreamer must then undergo a medical regimen to remove the excess moisture from his body (this would be done by inducing perspiration). Dream images involving terrestrial phenomena are applied

---

14   Ibid., 154–5.
15   See Waszink's (1964) extensive commentary. See also Kruger 1992, 24, 29, 30–31.
16   Le Goff 1985, 184.
17   See Cambiano 1980; Joly 1960 and 1984; Oberhelman 1993.
18   The now authoritative work on the *Regimen* 4 and dreams is Van der Eijk 2004. See also Holowchak 2001b, 386–95; Joly 1984; Oberhelman 1993, § I; Palm 1933.
19   Cambiano 1980, 92–5.
20   Joly 1960, 171–6 and 1984, 19–20.

to the human body. For example, the earth is analogous to the dreamer's skin; a tree, to the penis; cisterns, to the bladder; rivers, to the blood's circulation and quantity. Thus, a dream of seeing the earth flooded with water indicates that the body is excessively moist, and the patient must take steps to promote drying.[21]

The early third-century BCE physician Herophilus relied on a threefold classification: god-sent (*theopemptoi*) dreams; dreams arising from the soul's ability to predict (*phusikoi*); and mixed (*sunkrimatikoi*) dreams, which reflect the physical condition of the body. What Herophilus (or his source) did was to incorporate into the twofold system of the *Regimen* (god-sent dreams and medical dreams) the Early Stoics' belief that the soul, through its connections with the divine, can foretell the future.[22]

Of the Eclectic physicians, we know only the theories of Rufus of Ephesus and Galen. The second-century CE Rufus, like the writer of the Hippocratic *Epidemics* (1.23), insists that a physician should take into account a patient's dreams: "And you should also ask … whether the patient has had any vision or dreams, since from these a doctor can also make his inferences."[23] The images of the dream are to be applied to the humors of the body on the basis of the microcosm–macrocosm analogy. Rufus gives three illustrative dreams, each of which he interprets along the methodology in the Hippocratic *Regimen*. A wrestler dreamt that he spent the night in a black marsh of fresh water; the dream indicated the need of a massive evacuation of blood. A feverish patient dreamt of violence and fighting; this meant that he needed to be bled. Another patient, who had excessive moisture in his body, dreamt of swimming in a river.

Dreams exerted considerable influence on the life of Galen, another second-century CE physician: from his education and training to his military service, literary production, and even his surgical procedures and therapeutic practice.[24] Although Galen reports that he wrote a treatise on dreams, the only extended discussion extant in the Galenic corpus on this subject is a short fragment entitled *On Diagnosis from Dreams*.[25] As Guidorizzi has demonstrated, this fragment is actually a loose, haphazard collection of passages extracted from Galen's lost commentary on the Hippocratic *Regimen*; the collection was compiled in the early Byzantine era and was intended for a reading audience of physicians and savants.[26] In the text, Galen adduces four sources for dreams. Some images are daytime thoughts that reappear in a dream; this occurs most frequently when a person is overly concerned or anxious. Other images merely reproduce what one habitually does in the daytime; thus, a baker will dream of making bread, a sailor will dream of sailing, and an artist

---

[21] For all this in considerable detail, see the masterful study of Van der Eijk 2004. For analogy in medical dreams, see Holowchak 2001b; Oberhelman 1981, 420–23; 1983, 42–3; 1987, 59–60. Cf. Cambiano 1980, 95–6.

[22] See in detail Von Staden 1989, 307–10 (Greek text on 386); cf. Stewart 2002, 289 and Holowchak 2001b, 395–6 with n. 37.

[23] See Rufus, *Medical Questions* 5; Holowchak 2001b, 398; Oberhelman 1983 and 1993, § II.

[24] Guidorizzi 1973; Holowchak 2001a, Chap. 3 (with Appendices B and C).

[25] Guidorizzi (1973) is the authoritative edition, superseding Kühn 1964–65, 6:832–5.

[26] Guidorizzi 1973, 99–100.

will have dreams pertaining to the arts. Dreams also arise when the soul, through its inherent power, foretells future events—a theory that the Stoics had developed. Finally, dreams can give a clue to the dreamer's medical condition by portraying in symbolic images the state of the humors in the body.

Galen's views on medical dreams derive from Aristotle and the pseudo-Hippocratic *Regimen*. While the body is asleep, the soul sinks into the interior of the body and is there removed from outside sensory perceptions. The soul then forms images from residues of waking-state thoughts and through its own prognosticative ability; it also receives images from the various parts of the body. All these images are influenced by the dreamer's physical condition and the balances of the four bodily humors.

Galen uses various methods of interpretation, but the one most preferred was the Hippocratic microcosm–macrocosm analogy.[27] Galen refined this system by also taking into account the symbolic similarity between dream images and the various mixtures of the humors and elements. Thus, if someone dreams of snow or ice, he is ill from an excess of phlegm, since this humor is cold and wet. A dream of deep darkness means disease from black bile, for this humor is dry and cold. A fire in a dream indicates yellow bile, as this humor is hot and dry like fire. As per the *Regimen*'s microcosm–macrocosm analogy, excess blood in the body will cause an image of standing in a cistern of blood; a fever on the verge of crisis, an image of swimming or bathing in hot water; too much sperm, an image of sexual intercourse; a large quantity of feces or foul humors, an image of sitting amid filth and dung; a plethora of humors, the impression that one is carrying a heavy burden or is scarcely able to move.[28]

Healing dreams were the purpose of the ritual of religious incubation, which was the practice of sleeping within the precincts of a temple (or similar places) in order to receive a visitation from a deity. During the suppliant's sleep, a god directly applied a cure, or revealed in a dream a curative remedy (drug, regimen, or poultice), or gave an oracular response.[29] Incubation, attested to as early as mid-second millennium BCE Egypt, was inexpensive and simple as practiced at Greek and Roman sanctuaries,

---

[27]   Oberhelman 1987, 54–60.

[28]   Why this emphasis on the microcosm–macrocosm analogy among physicians? The reason may be that this method of interpretation had the greatest similitude to scientific procedure and was the least connected to popular lay methods. Furthermore, doctors could claim that they alone possessed the specific training to use this method; for if success of the microcosm–macrocosm analogy depended on thorough knowledge of the internal processes and anatomy of the body, and if cures could be effected only through countering imbalances and disturbances in the body's conditions, then no one but a well-trained physician could interpret the medical dream for proper diagnosis and treatment of disease. Prof. Mavroudi points out that ancient physicians were trained in philosophy, and the microcosm–macrocosm understanding of the universe was founded on the philosophical notion of *sympatheia*, or the affinity of all creation.

[29]   Deubner 1900 (old, but useful for primary sources); Edelstein and Edelstein 1945; Van Lieshout 1980, 277–8 (for bibliography). The bibliography on Aelius Aristides, a second-century CE orator who kept a journal of his cures and dreams at the hands of Asclepius, is vast. Good starting-points are Behr 1968; Del Corno 1975, 1615–18; Le Goff 1985, 181ff.; Michenaud and Dierkens 1972; Miller 1994, 184–204; Pearcy 1988.

especially the worship centers of the healing-god Asclepius. Incubation was available to everyone; only those in childbirth or at the point of death were turned away, and this was because of pollution taboos. After certain preparatory steps such as bathing and the offering of sacred cakes of honey and cheese, a suppliant went at night to the *abaton* (sleeping-room) and fell asleep on a bench or pallet. The god then approached the patient and healed him directly, or appeared in a dream and gave directions for medical treatments and regimens. The next morning, the patient, either healed or in possession of his course of treatment, performed a thanksgiving to the god and departed for home.

The proceedings at these healing sanctuaries were very much a fact of life for the ancients. It was the Greek or Roman who did not believe in the reality of incubation dreams that was the exception. Even physicians acknowledged the power and medical reality of Asclepius, and they themselves readily followed the cures and admonitions he gave them.[30] Moreover, the Asclepian cures preserved in ancient sources are not inconsistent with the pharmacology, regimens, and courses of treatment of Greek medical practice.[31] We also cannot ignore the simple fact that many people were cured at the Asclepian sanctuaries for over a millennium, and that charges of fraud were never leveled against the god or his healing centers.[32]

The old notion that the Asclepian sanctuaries were in reality medical hospitals, with the priests functioning as doctors, has long been discarded: there is no evidence to think anything other than the priests simply were officials in charge of attending to the god's temple and sanctuary. It was the responsibility of the dreamer, if not miraculously cured on the spot by the god, to decipher the import of the vision that was received. It is reasonable to assume that the majority of people took their dreams at face value—that is, they considered them straightforward and void of symbolism. In the case of dreams that seemed ambiguous, some patients would have consulted a professional interpreter, while others would have relied on their own experience and knowledge in oneirology and medicine.[33]

Dreams had a checkered history throughout the formation and growth of Christianity. Although the Church hierarchy may have wanted to remove dream interpretation from the life of their flocks, they could not; instead, they grudgingly and gradually assimilated into orthodox Christian thought their new converts' pagan views on the divinatory nature of dreams. This evolution of quasi-official acceptance of dreams explains to some extent the publication and widespread acceptance of the Byzantine *oneirocritica*.

Dreams frequently appear in the Hebrew Bible and, along with visions, constitute one of God's primary means of revealing His word and will.[34] Prophecy and dreams

---

[30]   See Oberhelman 1983, 37–9 for examples.

[31]   Michenaud and Dierkens 1972, 22–57; Oberhelman 1990 and 1993, § III.

[32]   See Oberhelman 1993, 151–5 with notes and bibliography.

[33]   See the discussion in Oberhelman 1990.

[34]   For dreams in the Hebrew Bible, see Bar 2001; Guillaume 1950, 224–79; Husser 1999; Le Goff 1985, 172–5; Oepke 1954, 228–33; Richter 1963. See too the massive bibliography on dreams in the Hebrew Bible and the Talmud at http://faculty.washington.edu/snoegel/dreamsanddreaminterpretatio.htm.

are intimately connected, as we read in 1 Samuel 28:6 and 15, Jeremiah 23:25–32, and Joel 2:28. Such revelation, however, was considered inferior to the sort of direct contact that Yahweh had with Moses, to whom He spoke directly and without ambiguity. We read in Numbers 12:6–8,

> And [the LORD] said: "Hear my words: If there is a prophet among you, I the LORD make myself known to him in a vision, I speak with him in a dream. Not so with my servant Moses: he is entrusted with all my house. With him I speak mouth to mouth, clearly, and not in dark speech; and he beholds the form of the LORD."

This passage, as Le Goff (1985, 173) observes, implies a hierarchy of dreams wherein one's closeness to God will affect the type and clarity of one's dream ("une hiérarchie de rêveurs définie par le caractère plus ou moins clair des messages oniriques divins selon la plus ou moins grande familiarité des rêveurs avec Dieu"). Thus, Moses and the patriarchs experience visions that are clear and non-symbolic in content, while other people, depending on their familiarity with God (e.g., Samuel, Isaiah, Nathan, Zechariah), receive more or less obscure dreams and visions.[35]

Both straightforward and symbolic dreams appear in the Hebrew Scriptures, although the latter are usually seen by pagans.[36] Humans do not possess an inherent skill for interpreting dreams; rather, God gives this skill to those whom He favors.[37] Thus, Pharaoh's dreams can be interpreted only by the pious Joseph, Nebuchadnezzar's by the faithful Daniel.

Dreams are not always viewed favorably in Jewish sacred texts, however; in fact, they often are the object of mistrust for many reasons. The Hebrews were instructed by God not to consult dreams to find out the future, since pagans had such divinatory practices (Deuteronomy 13:1–3; 18:9–14). Often we read of Yahweh warning the people not to listen to prophets who recommend a course of action based on their dreams (see, e.g., Jeremiah 27:9 and 29:8). Some dreams may be nightmares and therefore can inflict physical and mental distress (Job 4:12–16, 7:13–14). Later, under the influence of Greek philosophy, the Jews came to view dreams as vain (Ecclesiastes 5:3, 7) or as derived from the reoccurrence of waking-state concerns (Ecclesiasticus 40:5–6). The prophetic tradition most strongly attacked dreams, however, because of the potential for deception and deceit by false prophets.[38] Parts of the Old Testament Apocrypha reflect this hostility. The wisdom literature—e.g.,

---

[35]   Dreams as recounted in the Hebrew Bible differ from those in Greek sources, in that a dream's prophetic value is usually intended for the Jewish nation or people collectively, not for individuals. We do not find in the Hebrew Bible (or in the Christian New Testament) dreams foretelling personal power or personal wealth for the faithful; such dreams are reserved for pagan personalities.

[36]   Ehrlich 1953, 125–36.

[37]   Dulaey (1973, 35) points out that in the eyes of the Jews oneiromancy was not a human science but rather a gift from God, a fact that explains why Joseph and Daniel were superior interpreters to any pagan ("[P]our un Juif, l'oniromancie n'est pas une science humaine: elle est un don de Dieu. C'est pourquoi Joseph et Daniel surpassent tous les onirologues païens").

[38]   See Oepke 1954, 230–31; Le Goff 1985, 175. Biblical passages include Jeremiah 14:14, 23:16–32, 27:9–10, 29:8–9; Zechariah 10:2.

Ecclesiasticus and the Wisdom of Sirach—are especially harsh in their criticism of dreams.[39] Other books, however, show a very favorable attitude toward dreams. The author of Second Maccabees, for instance, believed strongly in the reality of dreams and recorded many of them,[40] while the apocalypses, most notably the visions of Enoch and Esdras, are filled with visions and ecstatic dreams.

Rabbinic Judaism at first attempted to dissuade people from divination through dreams on the grounds that it was a pagan practice and because it was difficult to know the meaning and significance of dreams that were not straightforward visions.[41] Soon, however, oneirocritic theories were developed. The tractate Berakot, in the Babylonian Talmud, contains a lengthy discussion of dreams and dream interpretation. Here we read that God sends true dreams to believers, for even though prophecy may have ceased with the destruction of the First Temple, God did not cease communicating with His people. Thus, a kind of prophecy can occur through dreams, although this is a lower form of revelation (Berakot 57b). Not all dreams are significant, however, in that demons can be the source of false dreams (Berakot 55b). Certain rabbis, evidently inspired by current philosophical thought, advocated a psycho-biological genesis of other dreams. During sleep, the mind is not completely shut down: the imagination remains active and creates images that are perceived as actually happening, but are in fact false sensations or images.[42] Still other dreams are simply expressions of fears or desires, or are reflections of what we think of in the daytime, another common Hellenistic philosophical thought (Berakot 55b).

According to the Talmud, dreams require interpretation. The third-century rabbi Rav Chisda stated that a "dream that is not interpreted is like a letter that is not read" (Berakot 58a). But because people cannot interpret dreams on their own and so need help, a trade of professional dream interpreters arose. We are told that the rabbi Benaa had a dream and, seeking an interpretation, consulted the dream interpreters in Jerusalem; there were 24 of them and, to his dismay, each of them gave him a different interpretation (Berakot 55b). Berakot (55a–7b) and other tractates preserve some of these interpretations. As in the case of Artemidorus and other oneirocritic writers, these interpreters decoded dreams on the basis of analogy and metaphor, wordplay and puns, scriptural references, and what were probably folklore associations ("A red horse is a sign of evil, while a white horse foretells goodness": Sanhedrin 93a).[43]

In the writings of the canonical Christian New Testament, little distinction is made between dream and vision. Equal importance is assigned to Paul's visions (e.g., Acts 18:9) and to his dream at Troas (Acts 16:9–10), while Peter, who himself received visions, referred to Joel and dreams and visions in his sermon on Pentecost (Acts 2:17): "And in the last days it shall be, God declares, that I will pour out my Spirit upon all flesh, and your sons and your daughters shall prophesy, and your young men

---

[39]   See, e.g., Wisdom of Sirach 34:5–8, 40:5ff.

[40]   First Maccabees makes no mention of dreams, omens, and portents.

[41]   For a quick introduction, see Lorand 1957; Parry 2004; Zeitlin 1975.

[42]   Parry 2004, 147–8.

[43]   See the detailed analysis in Bar 2001, 101ff., who comments that the passage in Berakot on dream interpretation "constitutes a miniature dreambook."

shall see visions, and your old men shall dream dreams." The gospels themselves contain only a few references to dreams and dream visions.[44] Matthew records five dreams, four of which involve Jesus' birth and early life (1:20ff.; 2:12; 2:13ff.; 2:22), with the fifth being the troubled dream of Pilate's wife (27:19). All these dreams occur in Matthew's special source material that literary critics have labeled "M," and do not occur in Matthew's primary source material (Mark's gospel and "Q," which is the hypothesised collection of Jesus' sayings that Matthew and Luke both used).[45] This emphasis in "M" on miraculous dreams affecting human actions and destinies may be either Gentile or Jewish in origin, although these dreams best reflect the tradition of dreams as active in Jewish salvation history that we see in the Hebrew Bible and in Second Maccabees. In his gospel, Luke does not mention dreams but only visions. Depicted as direct revelations of angels and God, these visions are connected with his birth stories (1:5ff.; 1:26ff.; 2:8ff.) and are connected to Luke's special sources, collectively called "L" by literary critics.[46] The two remaining canonical gospels, Mark and John, record neither dreams nor visions. The only other dreams in the canonical New Testament (beyond Revelation) appear in Acts and involve Paul: his call to Macedonia (16:9–10); God's command to preach at Corinth without fear (18:9ff.); Jesus' words of encouragement to the apostle and his prediction of his journey to Rome (23:11); and the appearance of an angel during the voyage to Rome (27:23ff.). The earliest written material of the New Testament—the letters of Paul—contains no full record of a vision, nor does Paul make use of his own dreams or visions, which Luke records in Acts (see, e.g., Paul's vision on the road to Damascus: Acts 9:1ff.).[47]

A reading of the canonical New Testament yields the impression that dreams are not emphasised because they are inferior to waking state contact with God (cf. the Numbers 12:6–8 passage discussed above). There is certainly no example of dream interpretation in the New Testament, for God always speaks unambiguously in the dreams and visions He sends; His instructions to the dreamer are very clear as to what he or she must do, or regarding the events that will transpire.[48] Finally, we may note that dreams and visions are absent from our earliest material—Paul's letters, Mark, and "Q"—, but present in later material—"M," "L," and Acts. It would seem, then, that the Early Church could not refrain from adding miraculous dreams and visions to the *kerygma* (the original proclamation of the gospel) and the earliest written accounts of Jesus' life. Perhaps the impetus for their addition was the fact that both Jewish-Christian and Gentile-Christian audiences appreciated such otherworldly phenomena and anticipated reading about them in their holy books. Cultural appreciation of dreams may also explain the repeated use of dreams and

---

[44]   See Hanson 1980; Wilkenhauser 1939 and 1948. I omit from discussion here the apocalypse attributed to John, since its genre is the traditional Jewish apocalypse, commonly found in the Old Testament apocrypha and pseudepigrapha.

[45]   For "M," see Brooks 1987 and Harrington 1991; for "Q" (the subject of intense scholarly debate), Mack 1993 and Tuckett 1996.

[46]   For "L," see Paffenroth 1997 and Van Voorst 2000, 136–40.

[47]   So Hanson 1980, 1421. In the Book of Acts, many people besides Peter and Paul, e.g., Ananias (9:10–16), receive visions.

[48]   See Dulaey 1973, 34 for discussion.

visions in the New Testament apocrypha and pseudepigrapha, works that were meant for a wide-reading, popular audience, primarily Gentile in background.

The 27 books that make up the canonical New Testament comprise a late fourth-century formulation of the Third Council of Carthage (397) and the Council of Hippo (419). These texts, however, did not comprise the canon of earlier patristic writers such as Origen and Eusebius or the Marcion (*c.* 140), Mauratorian (*c.* 170), and Cheltenham (*c.* 360) canons.[49] In fact, some Christians, particularly those who did not adhere to mainstream orthodox beliefs, did not even bother with these texts; rather, they used and read non-orthodox or non-canonical writings, some of which have survived. Because these writings are important for demonstrating the pervasive role of dreams in the culture of late antiquity and the early Byzantine period, it is to them we now turn.

Just as many important people of primitive Christianity received visions and the gift of prophetic dreams, so too did leading figures of non-orthodox forms of Christianity. Many Gnostic movements were based on revelatory visions,[50] and special dreams were claimed by the founders and adherents of splinter movements of Christianity such as Montanism. The Orthodox Church attacked these revelations, claiming that they were inspired by the devil and riddled with deceit and lies—even as it believed that its own revelation and visionary literature were divinely inspired. One person's dream vision from God, it would seem, is for another a satanic lie.

As might be expected, most of the writings produced by non-orthodox Christians did not survive Church censorship; only chance finds, such as those recovered from the sands of Egypt, have emerged. Perhaps the most important collection of texts is the Nag Hammadi Library, consisting of 13 papyrus codices that were buried around 400 CE at the foot of Gebel-et Tarifin in Upper Egypt and containing 52 tractates written in Coptic. The tractates include religious texts ranging from Christian Gnosticism (in its many various forms) to Neoplatonism and Hermetica. Many of these works use dreams and visions as a means to achieve revelatory or religious experiences,[51] but therein lay a serious problem for the Church. The Orthodox Church[52] asserted its primacy, and privileged position as the sole avenue to salvation, on the basis of knowledge that Jesus and His disciples revealed and then in turn (so the Church insisted) transmitted faithfully. Each non-orthodox belief system, such as Sethian Gnosticism, Valentinian Gnosticism, Neoplatonic Gnosticism, or Montanism, claimed that it possessed unique knowledge, or *gnōsis*, of salvation on the basis of its own special set of revelations. And if that *gnōsis* came through visions and revelatory dreams, who could argue? The Orthodox Church was hardly in a position to refute these "heretics," given the role of dreams and visions in the Hebrew Bible

---

[49]   For the growth and formation of the New Testament canon, see Bruce 1988; Dunbar 1986; Metzger 1987.

[50]   For these and subsequent Gnostic movements, see Bauer 1964 and Foerster 1972–74.

[51]   See the discussion, with examples, in Oberhelman 1991, 47–9.

[52]   When I use the term *Orthodox Church*, I am not referring to any denomination of Christianity (e.g., the Greek Orthodox Church), but to the Church wielding power at that moment in time. See Bauer 1964, 2, 231–4 for discussion of the terms *orthodoxy* and *heresy*.

and in its canonical New Testament.[53] When confronted with dreams espoused by those Christian movements it deemed heretical, the Church pursued its only course of action: it went on the offensive. Dreams and visions were now viewed with extreme suspicion because they circumvented the control that the Church wanted over the spiritual life of its faithful.[54] Dreams and visions were still accepted as revelations from God, *but only if the orthodox hierarchy granted official approval.*

The Orthodox Church did not trust dreams for reasons other than fear that heretics could use them to advance and validate their false doctrines and theology. First, it was widely believed that Satan and demons could send false dreams and thereby deceive Christians. Augustine and Tertullian, for example, both were alarmed at the way that demonic powers could attack even the righteous.[55] The Church was also troubled by the lack of reliable and absolute criteria for distinguishing between God-sent dreams and demon-inspired dreams,[56] as well as between prophetic dreams and insignificant dreams. Some Church Fathers did acknowledge that dreams could arise from a multiplicity of causes. Gregory the Great, for example, divided dreams into six types, ranging from malevolent to benevolent and attributable to such sources as God, demons, the mind, and physiological factors.[57] Tertullian likewise wrote that dreams could arise from the soul's own activity or could be sent by God and evil forces.[58] Herein the problem: if dreams may or may not be prophetic, and if they can have multiple causes, what guidelines does one use to distinguish between them? Augustine stressed the importance of the holiness of the dreamer (Joseph and Daniel are prime examples), and he and Origen both argued that dreams must be interpreted allegorically, much as scriptural texts are to be approached.[59] But not everyone had the intellectual and spiritual abilities to indulge in the allegorical and associative processes required to interpret dreams properly. What could the normal layperson do? To compound the matter, the Church had come to view divination through dreams (oneiromancy, not prophecy) as a mark of paganism, and so it had officially condemned popular dream interpretation as early as 314 CE.[60] Dreams were also mistrusted because through their sensual imagery they could induce seminal emissions; such "nocturnal pollutions" were a source of great concern to the Church.[61] Finally, dreams were feared because some could become nightmares and so trouble a faithful Christian's soul.[62]

---

[53] For visions in the Christian Church, see Dinzelbacher 1981 and 1989.

[54] Le Goff 1985, 196–7.

[55] Augustine: Kruger 1992, 47–8, 50–52. Tertullian: Kruger 1992, 49–50; Miller 1994, 67–70; Stewart 2002, 289.

[56] See Dulaey 1973, 109–30; Le Goff 1985, 193, 196.

[57] Kruger 1992, 45–8.

[58] Ibid., 44–7.

[59] See Miller 1994, 91–105 for an excellent discussion.

[60] Dulaey 1973, 188–9, 200; Guidorizzi 1985, 152; Kruger 1992, 7, 11–13, 138.

[61] Dulaey 1973, 135–9. See now Stewart 2002, 289–90. Stewart discusses the late fourth-century monk Evagrius, who writes on how demons can cause erotic dreams.

[62] Dulaey 1973, 132–5.

Despite these deep reservations and concerns, the Church continued to connect dreams intimately with conversion, martyrdom, and contact with God.[63] Origen, writing in the early third century, observes in his *Against Celsus* (1.48) that many people converted to Christianity because of a dream or vision. The strength of these converts' dreams, Origen states, was so powerful that they willingly died for their faith. And according to Christian tradition, many of the great spiritual leaders of the Church—Arnobius, Gregory of Nyssa, Evagrius of Pontus, and Basilides, to name a few—were converted through dreams, while the parents of Gregory of Nazianus and Augustine foresaw in dreams their sons' conversions.[64]

Dreams were also thought to impart knowledge of God to the faithful. Tertullian went so far as to assert that "nearly the majority of people get their knowledge of God from dreams."[65] Cyprian also tells us that contact with God is made possible through dreams and visions.[66] Cyprian, however, restricted the privilege of receiving such dreams to ecclesiastical authorities like himself, since he wanted the Orthodox Church to retain control over dreams and visions, and prevent heretics from manipulating them for their purposes.[67] A young Montanist woman of Carthage, Perpetua, while she was awaiting martyrdom, recorded her dreams in a personal diary.[68] Perpetua recounts that she spoke directly with Jesus and received a prophetic vision of what would happen to her.[69]

Dreams occur frequently in the hagiographic accounts of the holy martyrs.[70] Because of their spiritual excellence, martyrs were deemed most susceptible to receiving visions of God and messages about the future; Polycarp and Cyprian both received dream visions before their martyrdom.[71] Indeed, not only are martyrs worthy of such dreams, but they possess the right to demand them. In the five dreams of Perpetua and her companion Satura in the *Martyrdom of Perpetua and Felicitas*, we read how these martyrs, in full knowledge of their ability to converse directly with God, requested, and received, prophetic dreams.[72]

---

[63]   To Dulaey's (1973) and Le Goff's (1985 and 1992) discussions on this topic, add Keskiaho 2005 (heavily documented); Kruger 1992; MacAlister 1996; Miller 1994; Moreira 2003 (extensive bibliography).

[64]   Dulaey (1973, 152–65) is rich in details.

[65]   See Miller 1994, 66–70.

[66]   Le Goff 1985, 186.

[67]   For dreams in other patristic fathers, see Dulaey 1973, esp. 56–84; MacAlister 1996, 84–6; Miller 1994, 92–5, 129–30 (Augustine), 205–13, 230–31 (Jerome), 232–6, 245–9 (Gregory of Nazianus), 47–51, 232–41 (Gregory of Nyssa).

[68]   Miller (1994, 148–83) is a superb study of these dreams. Miller discusses Perpetua's dreams not solely as premonitory warnings, but also in the context of self-identity and sexual politics.

[69]   Miller 1986, 154–6.

[70]   Dulaey 1973, 52–4; MacAlister 1996, 101–5.

[71]   Miller 1994, 250 n. 15.

[72]   We must keep in mind that all the while the Church Fathers were working through their theories on dreams, the laity was dreaming. A scholarly debate has arisen over the extent to which the Church controlled laypeople's dreams. Le Goff (1985, 211) argues that ordinary Christians had no tools for dealing with dreams; saints and monks were accorded the right to

During the Byzantine period, the Eastern Greek Church held, at first, a very favorable attitude toward dreams for several reasons: dreams were too much a part of Greek cultural heritage to be dismissed out of hand; they played an important role in the Bible; and they refuted the body/soul dualism that the Gnostic heresy advocated.[73] The Church, therefore, was initially quite tolerant, and under its auspices a dream theory evolved that was similar to the tripartite typology then in vogue in the West: dreams sent from God, dreams caused by demons or the devil, and dreams that arise from the dreamer's own body or soul.[74] The Church did disapprove of oneiromancy, since it was associated with pagan practices, and civil decrees were enacted against it.[75] But the Church could not, and would not, condemn the dream itself, since dreams had scriptural authority and had played too great a role throughout the growth and development of Christianity.[76] Eastern hagiographical literature depict many holy men and women receiving revelations and visions, and having their lives directed through dreams.[77] Hence the Church ended up embracing what Kruger (1992, 7, 15–16) has called the "simultaneous caution and enthusiasm." Distrustful of dreams because of their association with paganism, demonic powers, and sex, and yet accepting of dreams because some could be divinely inspired and could reveal the future as the scriptures proved, "the same social groups, even the

---

have significant dreams, but ordinary Christians were told that their dreams had no value; the Church strictly censured dreaming and exercised a tight control over what was dreamt and how it was interpreted. Moreira (2003) has pointed out that until 813–40 there was no prohibition against dream interpretation in the West and that the clergy were not much interested in the laity's dreams. Moreira argues that the clergy simply did not have the "manpower" to invest the time and effort needed to deal with everyone's dreams; the sacraments and liturgy were much more important to the clergy. For Moreira, the laity was "free to make of their dreams as it would" (642). Keskiaho (2005) likewise asserts that there was no top–down control of dreams, at least in the West, through the eighth century. Monastic and clerical texts bestow on spiritual leaders a unique status as interpreters of dreams, but laypeople were allowed to interpret symbolic dreams through whatever tools they could find.

[73]   Dagron 1985, 38. For oneiromancy and divination during this period, see Koukoules 1948–57, 1.2: 139–229, although Koukoules views these practices very negatively.

[74]   Dagron 1985, 38–9. Mavroudi (2002, 238) discusses similar causations of dreams in Christian Syriac dreambooks. See Lamoreaux 2002, 154–67 for a dreambook written by a Christian Nestorian living in Iraq in the tenth century; the writer, Bar Bahlul, divided dreams into eight types: four that arise from imbalances of each of the four bodily humors; the dream that comes from one's fixation on thoughts of the previous day; the dream arising from the soul; the dream caused by ingestion of bad food; and dreams sent by the angel of dreams.

[75]   See Calofonos 1984–85, 217–19; Guidorizzi 1980, 12–13; MacAlister 1996, 105–6.

[76]   So Dagron 1985, 40 ("Le rêve reste donc un domaine à part, impliqué partiellement dans le rejet du paganisme, protégé par de solides références scripturaires, magnifié déjà par le rôle que la littérature chrétienne lui a fait jouer dans la conversion des princes ou des saints, et dans la connaissance des mystères de l'au-delà").

The early Byzantine emperors banned dream interpreters, although their legislation merely replicated earlier Roman edicts; see Calofonos 1984–85, 217 (with bibliography); Kruger 1992, 139 with n. 19. The laws, however, were ignored.

[77]   Le Goff 1985, 205–13.

same individuals, were drawn toward and, at the same time, backed away from a belief in the predictive significance of dreams" (Kruger 1992, 16).[78]

A most visible sign of the Church's acceptance of dreams in the early Byzantine period was the continuation, and even enthusiastic embracing, of incubation. The difference now was that the places of incubation were not pagan temples and Asclepian sanctuaries, but churches, shrines of martyrs and saints, and pagan centers converted into Christian holy sites.[79] The church of Cosmas and Damian in Constantinople was the site of numerous miracles and cures accomplished through the faithful sleeping in its porticoes and atrium.[80] Justinian the Great himself was cured through a dream vision at this church.[81] Cosmas and Damian's fame spread throughout Greece and Crete, with even the Asclepian sanctuary on the south slope of the Athenian acropolis converted in the fifth or sixth century into a healing shrine for the pair.[82] The saints conducted business just as Asclepius had done, in that they came to a suppliant in dreams; they either cured the suppliant with unguents and medical instruments, or gave instructions for a cure that he was to follow the next day. Another famous

---

[78]   See also Lamoreaux 2002, 136–8 for the conflict in the writings of the early seventh-century monk Antiochus. To Antiochus, dreams are dangerous images of a mind being led astray by demons, and so a Christian must pray to escape them; and yet because the Bible contains God-sent dreams, not every dream should be rejected.

An analogous problem for the Byzantine Church was divination and magic (for which see Koukoules 1948–57, 1.2:155–226; *ODB* 1:639–40). The Church of course condemned all forms of divination and sympathetic magic, but the Bible and popular religious practices seemed to contradict this stance. The Bible contains examples of celestial phenomena influencing events or predicting future events (one thinks, for example, of the Magi and the star), and so Church edicts against astrology must have seemed perplexing (see *ODB* 1:214–16). Likewise, religious people believed that holy objects like relics, icons, and liturgical objects had special power, and that dead saints and living holy men and women possessed supernatural abilities (*ODB* 2:1265). Is this, or is this not, sympathetic magic? It would seem that it was magic whenever pagans or heretics used amulets or sacred objects, but good religion when godly people are involved. Thus, carrying a protective amulet was magic, but wearing an encolpion for protection was what a good Christian would do. Or, if someone paraded around a *pharmakos* (scapegoat) and then expelled him from the city as part of a vegetation festival (the Thargelia), this was apotropaic magic. But it was not magic when a Christian erected a cross in a field to turn away drought or locusts (*ODB* 1:551). The boundaries between pagan and Christian behavior and practices were obviously very blurred. See the excellent 1995 article by Greenfield on the tension between orthodox and non-orthodox practices in Byzantine religion and magic.

[79]   See Dagron 1985, 41–2; Deubner 1900; Delehaye 1925; Dulaey 1973, 181–8; Vikan 1984; and especially Gregory 1986 and Talbot 2002. In the Byzantine period, there were two ways for a person to be healed: physicians and faith healing (*ODB* 2:905). People often rejected the former because of cost and incompetence, and so sought out faith healing, which consisted of not only incubation, but also visiting shrines of saints, touching relics, and using objects like amulets.

Talbot (2002, 154–67) offers a lengthy and impressive list of healing shrines throughout the Byzantine world; on pp. 155–67, she surveys the newest excavations.

[80]   See *ODB* 2:1151; Krueger 2005, 307–8; Lascaratos 2004.

[81]   Krueger 2005, 306–7; cf. Keskiaho 2005, 237 n. 50.

[82]   Dagron 1985, 41 n. 17; Deubner 1900, 68–79; Deubner 1907.

healing pair, Cyrus and John, also called the *anarguroi*,[83] healed worshippers through personal touch or by prescribing remedies in dreams. The cult was originally based in Egypt, but after that country fell to the Arabs in the seventh century, it moved to Rome and Constantinople.[84] The Greek writer Sophronius records 70 miracle cures performed by the two saints.[85] Other famous sites of incubation were the shrine of Artemius, whose specialty seemed to have been male genital ailments, at the church of John Prodromus in Oxeia;[86] the shrine of Saint Simeon the Younger, near Antioch;[87] and the shrine of Thecla at Seleucia.[88] These places, and the many others documented in Talbot 2002, demonstrate that healing through dreams was a very important component of both religion and society.

In the sixth century, a hostile attitude toward dreams emerged in ascetic literature and theological texts, an attitude that Dagron has called "une défiance systématique."[89] Buttressing their arguments with ancient theories on physiology and with Christian views on demonology, Eastern Church Fathers like John Climacus now claimed that dreams were in the main demon-inspired torments; those few dreams not sent by evil forces were irrelevant images of mental illusion or were warnings sent by God to sinners to beware of judgement and punishment. It was even argued that images of Jesus, angels, and the saints could not be trusted, since Satan and demons are able to disguise themselves as heavenly beings in order to destroy a dreamer's peace of mind.[90] The dream, therefore, has now become the devil's deceit or an invasion of a person's rest through its tormenting and disturbing images. To compound matters, Iconoclasm soon broke out and, with the resulting attacks on images of cult, dream imagery became thoroughly mistrusted.[91]

It is in the second half of the ninth century, after the demise of Iconoclasm, that the hostility of the previous two centuries toward dreams began to cease and it became safe once again to produce literature on this subject, or at least we find open

---

[83] The title distinguished these and other healing saints from pagan gods and physicians: *ODB* 1:85.

[84] Vikan 1984, 66.

[85] Deubner 1900, 80–98; Duffy 1984.

[86] Gregory 2005, 174–5; Krueger 2005, 307; *ODB* 1:194.

[87] Vikan 1984, 73.

[88] Dagron (1978) details the miracles; cf. *ODB* 3:2033–4.

[89] See Dagron 1985, 43.

[90] Ibid., 46.

[91] See Guidorizzi 1980, 10–11; for Iconoclasm, see Chapter 1 above. We must keep in mind that there is always a divide between what is written and believed at the top hierarchical level, and what is practiced at the lower levels. Although there were Church canons and even imperial edicts against dreams, that did not stop people from interpreting their own dreams; see note 72 above. Paganism was very slow to disappear. The Brumalia (Feast of Dionysus) was celebrated even as late as 700 (*ODB* 1:327–8; Gregory 2005, 162), as were other pagan festivals (Treadgold 1997, 125). See Brown 1988, passim (e.g., 319, 430); Greenfield 1995; Gregory 1986. Krueger (2005, 305–6) discusses sixth-century Christians using binding spells, curse tablets, amulets, and different methods of conjuring spirits.

discussions of dreams.[92] It is precisely at this moment that we see new *oneirocritica* being penned. As we saw in Chapter 1, the Daniel dreambook, which in its Greek form is best placed in the fourth century, is the only dreambook we know of until the Nicephorus dreambook, which appears in the second half of the ninth century. Three reasons seem likely for the re-emergence of dreambooks during this timeframe.

1. Warren Treadgold has posited a cultural and literary revival in the period from the mid-ninth century through *c.* 1025.[93] This "renaissance" was led by iconophiles who perceived quite quickly that learning could be useful in defending their beloved icons. Dreams were very useful in advancing the iconophiles' agenda. Because dreams were authenticated by scripture and Church tradition as gifts of God's grace and mercy, they could help prove iconophiles' arguments for the validity of images. Dreams could even be used to rehabilitate iconoclast personalities. A striking example is Theophilus, the last iconoclast emperor (829–42). In late ninth- and tenth-century texts, his reputation was restored through references to dreams in hagiographical texts.[94] In the *Life of Theodora*, this empress dreamt that Theophilus was being beaten for his support of Iconoclasm by angels in the presence of the Virgin Mary (Theotokos), who was holding the Christ child; Theophilus then recognized the errors of his ways and found peace while giving veneration to the encolpion of the logothete Theoctisthus. Two other dreams concerning Theophilus are recorded in the *On the Absolution of the Emperor Theophilus*. In one dream, Theodora sees Theophilus being beaten and dragged before a man enthroned before the Chalke Gate (the main entrance to the Great Palace of Constantinople). The man is none other than God, who then forgives the emperor for his actions against icons.[95] A second dream centers on the patriarch Methodius, who dreams of an angel announcing that Theophilus has been forgiven; on awakening, Methodius rushes to the church where, sure enough, Theophilus's name has been removed from the list containing the names of heretics.[96] Clearly it was in the late ninth and early tenth centuries that dreams, after being the object of intense distrust and after disappearing from vernacular and religious literature, were now accepted by ecclesiastical and political figures alike. They now carried so powerful a validity that they could

---

[92]   Guidorizzi 1980, 11; cf. Dagron 1985, 47–8; Lamoreaux 2002, 140; MacAlister 1996, 106–7.

[93]   See Treadgold 1997, 558–65, and, among others, Speck 1998, 80–84; Mavroudi 2002, 392.

[94]   For these dreams, see the excellent article by Markopoulos (1998).

[95]   The Chalke Gate was a very appropriate place for this dream. On the façade of the main door was an icon of Christ. Leo III, in his first great act of Iconoclasm, had it removed. The icon was then restored by the empress Irene, but then taken down by Leo V in his wave of Iconoclasm. The icon was placed up yet again in 843. See *ODB* 1:406, with bibliography.

[96]   As Markopoulos (1998, 46 with n. 52) points out, Theophilus also appeared to Saint Symeon in a dream, wherein he asks three times for the saint to help him.

be used to rehabilitate iconoclast emperors and underpin the propagandistic arguments of iconophile writers.

2. Another reason for the re-emergence of dreambooks in the late ninth century, in the midst of this renaissance, was the Byzantines' reappropriation of Greek culture.[97] The Arabs had "learned, copied, collected or translated what they could find and maintained that they could do it better than the Romans (i.e. the Byzantines)" (Speck 1998, 80). That is, the Byzantines realised that the Arabs were appropriating what they, the heirs of Hellenism, had lost in the dark centuries before. Their reaction was to demonstrate that they, not the Arabs, were the true heirs of what antiquity had to offer. Perhaps it is not too far a stretch to think that the authors of dreambooks like the Nicephorus and Germanus were in part attempting to recapture the oneirocritic tradition of Artemidorus and other Hellenistic oneirocriticists. The Arabs already possessed a translation of Artemidorus, and Arabic writers consulted this translation.[98] Moreover, all the while the Byzantines were quiet on the oneirocritic front, the Arabs had been publishing dreambooks at an astonishing rate. Toufic Fahd (1966) identified 158 Arabic dream manuals, while John Lamoreaux (2002) has located 60 additional treatises from early Islam.[99] Perhaps in reaction to this perceived loss of their oneirocritic heritage, some Byzantines began to reassert their cultural heritage through their penning dreambooks for the people of the capital. Granted, the Byzantines came nowhere close to the immense output of the Arabs, but it cannot be coincidence that nearly all of our extant Byzantine *oneirocritica* date to this very time of Arabic activity in dreambook writing.

3. This leads us to consider Maria Mavroudi's (2002) discussion of the Arab and Byzantine exchange and crossover of cultural ideas and thoughts which were transpiring along the borders between the Arabic and Byzantine empires at this moment (the tenth century).[100] At first, the exchange was one-sided, as Arabs translated Greek texts, thanks to an aggressive patronage system by Abbasid rulers and aristocrats.[101] The Byzantines at first did little in terms of translating Greek texts. But during the tenth century we have Arabic texts being translated for Greek readers, as Byzantines sought to fill the gaps in their own knowledge. When it came to dreams, the dreambook of Artemidorus and the dreambook of Daniel, at least in its original form, would have been too pagan for authors to use. The Arabic manuals were a different matter, as they were grounded in a monotheistic religion, and so they would have been more in line with Byzantine religious views and easier to adapt for a

---

[97]   Here I am following Speck 1998, 80–84; cf. Mavroudi 2002, 390: "[This] 'Macedonian Renaissance' ... has been viewed as a Byzantine return to classical and late-antique models."

[98]   See above Chapter 2, note 15.

[99]   Lamoreaux (2002, 1–2) wonders whether this is merely a small representative number of manuals existing in libraries and collections throughout the Near and Middle East.

[100]   Lamoreaux (2002, 152–4, 165) makes a similar argument. Mavroudi's and Lamoreaux's books appeared, by a quirky twist of fate, at nearly the very same moment.

[101]   Mavroudi 2002, 392–429, esp. 419–20; see now Mavroudi 2007, 50–52.

Christian audience.[102] This explains Achmet's use of the Arabic translation of Artemidorus (and not Artemidorus's Greek text) and other Arabic dream manuals (although he was required to Christianise some portions of these texts). In the midst of such exchanges of ideas and materials on dreams perhaps came the stimulus to produce for Byzantine audiences *oneirocritica* with authorships assigned to solidly reputable patriarchs. Such a scenario may be speculative, but it is a fact that at the time when dreams reappear in the works of theologians, philosophers, and hagiographers, they also became the focus of attention at the imperial court. Leo VI (886–912) was intensely interested in dreams and divination in general, so much so that Mavroudi (2002, 61) hypothesises that Achmet's dreambook was commissioned for Leo. Leo even went so far as to remove dream interpretation from the list of evil practices,[103] and in Constantine VII Porphyrogenitus's *On Ceremonies*, dreambooks are mentioned as being among the few books that an emperor should carry with him while on military campaigns.[104] Oneiromancy had never died out, of course. Guidorizzi describes its survival among the non-literary classes and among diviners who practiced dream interpretation while wandering from village to city to festival;[105] and as we saw in Chapter 1, the *oneirocriticon* of Daniel continued to stay in circulation after its composition around the fourth century (though mainly in a Latinised form). But it was not until after 900 that the climate for dreambooks became ideal.

The Nicephorus dreambook, inspired by and drawing on the *oneirocriticon* of Daniel, appeared first, followed very shortly afterwards by Achmet's Christianised edition of Arabic dream treatises. These two dreambooks stimulated the production of more dreambooks down to the fall of Constantinople. The authorships were, as we have seen, falsely attributed to renowned patriarchs, biblical personalities, and emperors in order to create the semblance of authenticity and authority. The dreambooks were of two types: short alphabetical manuals in prose or verse, and longer treatises with subject matter arranged according to topics and with some attempt at dream theory. The former is the dream key manual. Symbols are listed in alphabetical order, followed by an interpretation applicable to all dreamers or, less commonly, to binary pairs or classifications of dreamers (rich and poor, slave and free, male and female, healthy and ill). In the longer treatises dreams are interpreted in greater detail, usually in accordance with the individual circumstances of the dreamer. The shorter manuals would have been handy, easy-to-use dream keys that anyone, of any background, could consult. The Nicephorus dreambook was intended for a learned audience, but even the "man on the street" could profitably use it. The

---

[102]   Mavroudi 2002, 421; and above Chapter 2, note 15. The Arabic translator of Artemidorus purged the book of its polytheism and its more offensive aspects; see Sirriyeh 2006, 209.

[103]   Calofonos 1984–85, 219 and 1990, 450 n. 17; MacAlister 1996, 107; Mavroudi 2002, 61 (with n. 236).

[104]   Calofonos 1984–85, 219 with his n. 22; Mavroudi 2002, 424.

[105]   See Guidorizzi 1980, 9–10, 13–14; also Calofonos 1984–85, 218–19.

longer treatises (Achmet and Manuel) served the imperial court and were read by emperor, courtier, and aristocrat alike.

Peasant, merchant, baker, theologian, philosopher, imperial secretary, King of the Romans—each of them we can easily envision searching diligently (even with some trepidation) his *oneirocriticon* for an answer to what the future held in store. In an age where anxiety and fear were pervasive, each person could take comfort in knowing that every event that would befall him, his family, his friends, even his city and king, could be revealed beforehand, provided he interpret his dreams correctly.[106] Beset everywhere by plague, famine, drought, invasion, and political instability and turmoil, the Byzantine, armed with his *oneirocriticon*, could face the future with a degree of certainty and security he could not otherwise feel.

---

[106] Brodersen (2006, 23) observes how the Byzantine dreambooks can offer a "glimpse into the everyday aspirations and anxieties" ("einen Blick auf die alltäglichen Hoffnungen und Ängste") of the person of Byzantium. The frequent use of second-person singular verbs served to reassure the reader, for it told him that the interpretation was his very own and foretold for him his personal future.

Chapter 4

The *Oneirocriticon* of Daniel
The Dreambook of the Holy Prophet Daniel with the Help of Holy God, according to the Alphabet

[Beginning of the Letter A]

1. To dream of statues of men signifies friends and loved ones.[1]
2. To dream of silver or gold points to an impeding situation.[2]
3. To dream of a cloudy sky signifies that you will be hindered.[3]
4. Seeing or handling[4] silver or gold vessels signifies losses.[5]
5. To ascend a high place signifies something good.[6]

---

[1]   There is a probable pun on the word ἀνδρίας, which not only denoted a statue (of a man, not of a god), but was also a term of endearment (for which see Liddell and Scott 1968—hereafter, "LSJ"—, s.h.v.). Artemidorus (3.63) interprets statues as symbolising the leading men of a city (an obvious analogy).

[2]   Achmet consistently interprets silver as a woman, and gold as sorrow; see, e.g., 12, 45, 150, 217, 236, 255, 256. Gold and silver have both negative and positive interpretations in Artemidorus; see, e.g., 1.50, 1.66, 2.39, 2.58, 3.30. Silver was the second most precious metal (after gold) in Byzantium; Schilbach (1970, 125) estimates that the proportion of silver to gold was 14 to 1. See also *ODB* 1:853, 3:1898–9; Rautman 2006, 100–101. Gold was used mainly for coins, jewelry, and the imperial plate; silver, more for plate than for coins and jewelry: *LAnt* 576. Matschke (2002a, 115–18) discusses the mining of gold and silver in the Byzantine Empire.

[3]   Cf. *Somniale Danielis* ("Beiträge, V") 10: *aerem turbolentum vel nebulosum videre, aliquam petitionem significat*; cf. Artemidorus 2.8. But in Achmet 166, this dream means illness and sorrow. There were in Byzantine times a group of people called "cloud-drivers," who predicted the future from the shapes of clouds and used incantations to cause rain. Although proscribed by law, they were consulted frequently. See *ODB* 3:1699.

[4]   Drexl (1926, 292 ad loc.) comments on this verb: "ἐγγίσαι = berühren (ngr.)."

[5]   So too Achmet 45. But cf. Artemidorus 1.66: "But, indeed, we must also consider this: gold, and silver, and earthenware drinking vessels are auspicious for everyone and symbolize great safety. The first two, because they are fashioned from solid matter...."

[6]   Cf. the dream of climbing trees in *Somniale Danielis* ("Beiträge, V") 8: *arbores ascendere, nuntium bonum significat*. Artemidorus (2.28) considers climbing a height a sign of evil.

6.   Quickly riding up to the top of a hill on horseback signifies freedom for
      slaves[7] and something good for all others.[8]

7.   To dream of oneself beheaded signifies getting rid of great oppression.[9]

8.   Jumping from a ship onto dry land signifies a change of residence.[10]

9.   Gazing about from a high place points to the cementing[11] of a friendship, and
      a powerful one at that.[12]

10.   Coming down from a high place is terrible for all [dreamers].[13]

11.   To dream that a child has become old signifies loss of capital.[14]

---

[7]   Slavery existed throughout Byzantium and was tolerated by the Church. The most
common source of slaves was prisoners of war. Slavery was mostly an urban phenomenon,
as peasants did the work in the country, but it declined in the eleventh and twelfth centuries,
practically disappearing in the thirteenth. See Dagron 2002, 420–21; Köpstein 1966; Morrisson
and Cheynet 2002, who discuss the price of slaves; *ODB* 3:1915–16; Rautman 2006, 21–2, 34.

[8]   So too Achmet 154: "If someone dreams that he was riding his horse on a swift and
straight course and ascended a hill with the horse obeying his commands, he will find joy and
obedience in his household, as well as power, by analogy to the horse's gait and straightness of
direction." Cf. Manuel 11 below. The interpretation here may be based not just on the analogy
of commanding a horse well, but also on the various meanings of ὕψος (literally, a "summit"
or "height," but figuratively "honor" or "grandeur"). Byzantine legal codes, I may note, denied
Jews the right to ride horses: *ODB* 1:122.

[9]   Cf. *Somniale Danielis* ("Beiträge, IV") CCLVI: *decollare se videre, lucrum significat*; so
too Achmet 120. Artemidorus (1.35) interprets this dream as a positive sign for everyone except
"bankers, usurers, men who have to collect subscriptions, shipmasters, merchants, and all who
collect money, [since] it signifies loss of capital, because the word for 'capital' is derived from
the word for 'head.'" See the Arabic interpretations in Mavroudi 2002, 194–8; Mavroudi argues
for an Arabic, not Artemidorean, provenance for Achmet's interpretations of decapitation.

[10]   The interpretation perhaps derives from an analogy between disembarking onto land
and moving from one place to another.

[11]   For this unusual word, see Stephanus 1954, s.v. "συνδύασις."

[12]   According to Achmet 142, a height symbolizes a powerful man: "If someone dreams
that he owned a flat and level tract of land, in the middle of which a mountain projected upwards,
the mountain symbolizes a man whose exaltation is proportionate to the mountain's height, while
the area around the mountain signifies that man's wealth; moreover, the dreamer either will lord
over this noble and his property [because he owned the land in the dream] or will follow and live
with an exalted man and be well treated by him for his complete obedience."

[13]   The interpretation would seem to be based on the analogy of coming down from a
height (ὕψος) as a reflection of a fall from power (ὕψος). This dream has a good interpretation,
however, in Artemidorus 2.28. An analogous dream to the one above is in *Somniale Danielis*
("Beiträge, V") 123: *quadrigas descendere vel de eis cecidisse, honores perdere vel seniores
offendere*.

[14]   Cf. Artemidorus 1.50: "And if someone dreams that his own small child has become a
man, it means that the child will die. It is also unlucky if an old man is transformed into a child,
since it signifies death for him. But it is auspicious for a grown man to change into a young man,
or for a young man to change into a child. For each of these is changing into a more youthful
period of life. It is also auspicious for a child to change into a young man, for a young man to
change into a grown man, or for a man to change into an old man. For each of these is changing
to a more honored time of life."

12. A dream of lightning signifies unexpected profit.[15]

13. Dreaming of oneself barefoot points to loss.[16]

14. Taking off one's clothes is good for sick people, but bad for all others.[17]

15. To dream that your brother or sister or some relative has died points to an additional span of life.[18]

16. Sacrificing a rooster is good, provided that it is not strangled.[19]

17. To dream of crowing roosters: something you greatly desire will happen for you.[20]

18. Dreaming of the stars signifies activity filled with happiness.[21]

19. Dreaming of being beltless points to distress.[22]

20. Dreaming of becoming ill spontaneously[23] signifies distress.[24]

---

[15] Cf. Artemidorus 2.9. Lightning storms caused a significant loss of human life and property in Constantinople in the years 548, 555, and 556; see Croke 2005, 71.

[16] *Somniale Danielis* ("Beiträge, IV") CLXXXIX: *nudis pedibus ambulare, dampnum significat*; *Somniale Danielis* ("Beiträge, V") 103: *nudis pedibus ambulare vel nudum se videre, tristitias et labores magnas significat.* The interpretation above is probably based on the fact that one went barefoot while doing penance (*ODB* 1:203, 2:796) or, more likely, on the fact that slaves did not wear shoes.

In Byzantium, profit (κέρδος) was disapproved of if sought by nobles or if procured through commercial activities; profits in fact were fixed and regulated. See *ODB* 3:1728.

[17] Cf. Achmet 118 and 119. Artemidorus (2.3) comments: "The loss of … garments is in no way auspicious, except perhaps for poor men, slaves, prisoners, debtors, and for all those who are in a difficult situation. For the loss of these garments signifies that the evils that surround a person will disappear. For other men, being naked or losing one's clothes is not good. For if signifies the loss of everything that pertains to the embellishment of life."

[18] I take ζωή as meaning "life," not "one's livelihood" as Brackertz (1993) takes it. He translates: "Wähnt einer, der Bruder, die Schwester oder irgendein Verwandter sei gestorben, dessen Hab und Gut wird sich vermehren."

[19] Cf. Artemidorus 2.33. Sacrificing a rooster to the healing-god Asclepius was part of the popular Eleusinian Mysteries of antiquity. The most famous reference to such a sacrifice appears in Plato, *Phaedo* 118a (although there is much debate over the significance of Socrates' words). Byzantine canonical law forbade eating animals that had been killed by strangulation (*ODB* 2:1326; *LAnt* 409). In modern Greece, it is common to kill a rooster over the foundations of a new house: see Gage 2004, 89.

[20] Roosters signify the master of a house or the house steward according to Artemidorus 2.42.

[21] Cf. *Somniale Danielis* ("Beiträge, IV") CCXXVIII: *stellas cum plures viderit, letitiam significat.* But stars symbolise people according to Achmet 166 and 167. For the Byzantines' knowledge of the stars, see Tihon 1981; *ODB* 1:216–17; Rautman 2006, 296–8.

[22] For discussion of the interpretation, see the comment to 199 below, and cf. Achmet 242. I would add that Christians and Jews living in Muslim lands were required to wear a belt as one means to maintain recognisable distinguishing marks between Muslims and non-Muslims: *LAnt* 339.

[23] So I translate αὐτομάτως, which Brackertz (1993) translates as "zufällig."

[24] Cf. Artemidorus 3.22.

21. Disowning [ἀθετεῖν] oneself is good for those involved in business dealings, but bad for all others.[25]

22. To dream of oneself as mute signifies great joy.[26]

23. A thistle plant sprouting up points to a rising-up of one's enemies.[27]

24. Dreaming of a grapevine ready for harvest signifies joy[28]<, while walking in a vineyard signifies a horrible[29] omen>.[30]

25. Dreaming of an unripe[31] grapevine signifies a decree.[32]

26. Using or receiving from someone a wineskin or some other marketable commodity[33] signifies sorrows and quarrels.[34]

---

[25]　The word ἀθετεῖν (which Brackertz 1993 translates as "verleugnen") was routinely used to denote breaking one's word in a business agreement; the verb in modern Greek still retains the idea of violating a pact or agreement. This meaning would explain the reference to business dealings in the interpretation.

[26]　But cf. Achmet 63.

[27]　See Achmet 211. The Greek oneirocritic tradition and Achmet consistently associate thorns as symbolising the barbs of enemies—a rather straightforward analogy.

[28]　*Somniale Danielis* ("Beiträge, IV") CCXL: *vites maturas plenas viderit, letitiam significat.* See also Achmet 151 and 253. Laiou (1977, 174–5) estimates that up to 96 per cent of peasants owned a vineyard, while Kazhdan (1997, 50) remarks that vineyards could be found everywhere throughout Byzantium; cf. Koukoules 1948–57, 5:280–95; Lefort 2002, 249–50, 254–6; *ODB* 3:2169–70. Morrisson and Cheynet (2002, 832–3) give the price for vineyards in Byzantium.

[29]　Perhaps a pun on σαπρός, which was often used to describe wine: Dalby 1996, 100–101.

[30]　Drexl (1926, 293 ad loc.) brackets this phrase, commenting, "Kann ich nicht belegen." But we may adduce as a parallel *Somniale Danielis* ("Beiträge, IV") CXLV: *in pomerio ambulare, anxietatem gravem significat.*

[31]　According to Hesychius, s.v. "στυγνόν," this word is equivalent in meaning to ὠμόν. Brackertz (1993) translates as "verkümmerter."

[32]　I take ὁρισμός in the typical Byzantine meaning of "decree" or "command" (a meaning consistent with modern Greek usage). There could be a pun in that the word also meant "boundary of one's crops"; see the papyrological references in LSJ, s.h.v.
Brackertz takes the word as referring to legal proceedings. He writes (1993, 251 ad loc.): "Griech. *horismos* = Prozeßwette, d.h. Niederlegung einer Geldsumme vor Gericht, die derjenige verlor, welcher verurteilt wurde." From the eleventh century on, the *horismos* denoted either an imperial decree or the correspondence of the governor of a territorial province; see *ODB* 2:946.

[33]　Drexl (1926, 293 ad loc.), citing Stephanus 1954, translates πρατόν as "verkauft"; however, he believed the reading to be corrupt ("scheint verderbt"). Brackertz (1993) does not translate, instead marking the word with an ellipsis.

[34]　The interpretation probably derives from the association in Byzantine oneirocritic texts of wine with quarrels.

27. A bear noiselessly[35] approaching you signifies grief and dishonor.[36]

28. Dreaming of a grapevine sprouting in some place signifies exceedingly good [opportunities].[37]

29. Being blind[38] signifies hindrance.[39]

30. Seeing a grapevine in some place signifies a good opportunity.[40]

31. Scaling a high place signifies something good.[41]

32. Seeing the constellations or drawing close to them indicates a time of happiness.[42]

---

[35] Drexl (1926) suggests emending ἄχρωμος to ἄβρομος; this emendation makes better sense and so I have adopted it here. Perhaps αὐστηρος is meant (cf. 185, 322, and 323 below; and cf. Germanus 16), although this would be hard to justify on paleographical grounds. Brackertz (1993) translates as "brummend," although he does place the word in parentheses.

[36] *Somniale Danielis* ("Beiträge, IV") CCXLV: *ursum ad se infestare viderit, inimici seditionem significat.* But cf. Achmet 272: "The bear signifies an enemy who is wealthy, powerful, daring, but without intelligence." See also Artemidorus 2.12.

[37] I assume the word καιρούς with καλούς, on the basis of 30 below. For the dream, cf. *Somniale Danielis* ("Beiträge, IV") CCXLI: *vindemiare, hilaritatem vite significat.*

[38] The phrase ἀπὸ ὀμμάτων equals the Latin *caecus*; see Stephanus 1954, s.v. "ὄμμα." In Byzantine Greek, ἀπό often denoted the privative ἀ–. Drexl (1926, 293 ad loc.) hypothesises: "Sollte ἀπὸ ὀμῆτων in ἀπομύτων (= ohne Nase) geändert werden?" But it does not seem necessary to change a dream of being blind to one of being without a nose. Brackertz (1993) translates along my lines: "Träumt einer, er sei erblindet ...."

[39] *Somniale Danielis* ("Beiträge, IV") XLI: *cecum qui se viderit, inpeditionem significat.* But cf. *Somniale Danielis* ("Beiträge, V") 30: *cecum se videre, in peccatis cadere significat.* This interpretation is similar to Achmet 52: "The eyes symbolise faith, reputation, and spiritual illumination. If someone dreams that he was completely blind, he will lose his faith and have a short life. If someone dreams that he was blind in one eye only, he will lose half of his faith and be put to shame before many people. If someone dreams that he was bleary-eyed, he will sin greatly but later repent." Cf. Artemidorus 1.26.

Byzantine kings often inflicted blinding on political rivals, rebels, traitors, and religious dissenters: *ODB* 1:297–8; Treadgold 1997, passim, e.g., 343, 358, 364, 422, 429, 460–63, 526, 588, 597, 619, 654, 656, 722 (some victims died from their wounds: see Treadgold 604 [the emperor Romanus] and 780). The practice was common among the ancient Israelites: see, e.g., 1 Samuel 11:2; 2 Kings 25:7; Judges 16:21. The most notorious episode in Byzantine history perhaps occurred in 1014, when Basil II captured a large number of Bulgarians; he blinded 15,000, although he spared a few so that they could guide the others home: Treadgold 1997, 526. For mutilations like slitting noses and tongues, see Gregory 2005, 171, 177; Treadgold 1997, 310, 329, 339, 352, 392, 422; *ODB* 2:1428. The mutilation of an emperor's relatives was a common means to deter them from committing high treason; cf. *ODB* 3:2110–11.

[40] This dream is basically the same as 28 above; such replication shows the author's use of several sources.

[41] This dream and interpretation are the same as 5 above; the difference is the verb in the dream symbol (ἀνελθεῖν versus ἀναβῆναι). Brackertz (1993) translates τόπος as "hill," but we cannot exclude the possibility that some other high point is intended (a wall, tall tree, multistory building, etc.).

[42] Cf. Artemidorus 2.36.

33.   Dreaming that one is sick signifies oppressive difficulties.[43]

34.   Dreaming of being swept away by a river's current: be on your guard lest something you have done well turns out adversely.[44]

35.   Blood trickling out of your mouth points to danger.[45]

36.   Being beaten by a dead person points to illness.[46]

37.   Receiving a kiss from a dead person signifies life.[47]

38.   Being chased [διώκεσθαι] by cattle means being persecuted [διώκεται] by the *dunatoi*.[48]

39.   If you dream of wearing armor, this means strength.[49]

40.   If you dream that you yourself have been beheaded, this means the death of your sperm—that is, your seed.[50]

41.   If you dream that someone is dying, you will come into a state of no worry.[51]

---

[43]   Cf. *Somniale Danielis* ("Beiträge, V") 76: *Hegrotum se videre, aliquam accusationem significat*.

[44]   Cf. Artemidorus 2.27; Achmet 173 and 174. Rivers in the Byzantine Empire were typically dry in the summer and susceptible to flooding after heavy rains or the melting of the winter snow. Moreover, most rivers were not capable of navigation, the exceptions being major rivers like the Euphrates: *ODB* 3:1797–8.

[45]   Cf. *Somniale Danielis* ("Beiträge, V") 134: *sanguinem de corpore cadere, dampnum significant*; *Somniale Danielis* ("Beiträge, IV") CCXXIX: *sanguinem de suo latere distillare, dampnum significat*. Blood flow as a symbol of loss appears in Artemidorus (1.33 and 2.36) and Achmet (passim, e.g., 32, 33, 47, 67, 103, 104, 105); cf. *ODB* 1:298.

[46]   So too Artemidorus 1.60; Achmet 132. But see Artemidorus 2.48 for benefits derived from this dream.

[47]   *Somniale Danielis* ("Beiträge, IV") CLXXVIII: *mortuum osculari, vitam vivendi significat*. So too Achmet 131; Artemidorus (2.2), however, offers a negative interpretation (death will occur).

[48]   Cf. Artemidorus 2.12; Achmet 236. For *dunatoi* meaning the aristocracy, especially the provincial aristocracy, see Gregory 2005, 230; cf. Rautman 2006, 20; *ODB* 1:160, 169–70, 667–8.

[49]   Cf. *Somniale Danielis* ("Beiträge, IV") CCLXXVII: *si videris, quod gladio eris ciinctus* [*sc.* for *cinctus*], *securitatem significat*; Artemidorus 2.31.

[50]   I take σπόρος and καρπός figuratively, as referring to a person's lineage, not to one's crops (i.e., livelihood). Brackertz (1993) translates: "Scheint es dir, du seist geköpft worden, wird die Aussaat oder die Ernte verhageln." For numerous interpretations of the dream of decapitation, see Artemidorus 1.35.

[51]   But cf. Artemidorus 2.57: "Simply to see the dead without doing or suffering anything noteworthy signifies that the dreamer will be affected in a way that corresponds to the relationship that existed between the dreamer and the dead while they were alive. For if they were pleasant and generous, it means good luck and it indicates that the present time will pass pleasantly. Otherwise, it means just the opposite." Cf. *Somniale Danielis* ("Beiträge, IV") CLXXVII: *mortuum viderit, gaudium significat*.

42.   Dreaming of birds made of gold or silver signifies an untimely quarrel.[52]

43.   Handling flour signifies gain.[53]

44.   If you dream of eating the midday meal, this signifies great sorrow.[54]

45.   Seeing or eating sun-dried[55] pork signifies profit at some point in time.[56]

46.   To be looking around in a vineyard signifies joy and life.[57]

Beginning of the Letter B

47.   Dreaming of altars points to good opportunities.[58]

48.   Dreaming that you are being carried by someone means vexation and shameful business dealings.[59]

49.   If you dream of traveling while sitting down, this signifies useless effort.[60]

50.   A dream that you have lost your arms: watch out for your business ventures.[61]

---

[52]   Cf. *Somniale Danielis* ("Beiträge, IV") I: *aves in somniis qui viderit & cum ipsis pugnaverit, lites aliquas significat.*

[53]   So too Achmet 208; *Somniale Danielis* ("Beiträge, IV") XCVIII: *farinam in somnis trectare, incrementum negotii significat.*

[54]   The verb ἀριστάω means to have the midday meal (ἄριστον). In early Greece, the ἄριστον was a breakfast eaten at daybreak (two main meals occurred later in the day); but later it became the light lunch. Among the Byzantines, lunch was like supper in that both meals had several courses (appetizers, meat or fish or poultry dish, vegetables), along with wine and sweets; of course, this type of full meal was eaten primarily by members of the upper class. See *ODB* 1:170.

[55]   So Drexl (1926, 294 ad loc.), who comments: "αἰφίλια wohl = ἐφήλια (an der Sonne getrocknet)." Perhaps the word is related to ἐφῆλιξ (young), and so the phrase αἰφίλια χοίρεια could mean "meat from young pigs." According to Pseudo-Caesarius (PG 38:928), shepherds used to place meat in a glass vessel and then enclose the vessel in dried dung, leaving the vessel in the sun. Dagron (1974, 447) mentions that cured pork formed part of the rations of soldiers on campaign. (I owe both references to *ODB* 2:1326.) See *LAnt* 454 for other sun-dried meats.

[56]   So too Achmet 279, where eating pork symbolises money and wealth; this dream also has a very positive interpretation in Artemidorus 1.70. Morrisson and Sodini (2002, 199–200) discuss pork as a dietary supplement in Byzantium.

[57]   Cf. the dream of gathering grapes in *Somniale Danielis* ("Beiträge, IV") CCXLI: *vindemiare, hilaritatem vite significat.*

[58]   The auspicious interpretation is probably based on the purpose of ancient sacrifice—namely, to procure the gods' favor, to thank them for past favors, or to garner their assistance in fulfilling requests. For altars in Byzantine culture, see Braun 1924; *ODB* 1:71.

[59]   See Artemidorus 2.56.

[60]   It was common for rich people to be carried on a litter by slaves: *ODB* 3:2109.

[61]   Cf. Artemidorus 1.42; Achmet 70 and 71. But cf. *Somniale Danielis* ("Beiträge, IV") CCXCIII: *si videris brachia tua truncata, bonum significat.*

51. Dreaming of having powerful but soiled arms points to friends along with deceit.[62]

52. Having beautiful arms signifies a great friendship.[63]

53. Sacrificing a cow indicates something good for you.[64]

54. Sitting on cattle signifies a great friendship.[65]

55. [Dreaming of] cattle ploughing and of sitting on them points to friends and foresight.[66]

56. Seeing white cows or sitting on them indicates honor from a position of authority.[67]

57. A dream of grazing cattle signifies negligence in your actions.[68]

58. Wearing a monk's robe[69] means freedom in your actions.

59. Sitting in a closed litter[70] signifies failure in your actions.

---

[62] Cf. *Somniale Danielis* ("Beiträge, IV") XXVII on having strong arms: *brachia valida habere, incrementum significat*. Also Artemidorus 1.42; Achmet 70. The negative interpretation above is perhaps based on the dirt appearing on the arms.

[63] Cf. *Somniale Danielis* ("Beiträge, V") 24: *brachia magna habere, potestates tibi accrescunt*. Cf. ibid., 25: *brachia parva habere, dissolutionem significat*.

[64] Cf. ibid., 18: *ad sacrificium accedere vel sacrificare, letitiam magnam significat*. For a dream of slaughtering a cow as indicating future wealth, see Achmet 237. See Conybeare 1901, 109 for a prayer for sacrificing an ox (εὐχὴ ἐπὶ θυσίας βοῶν), which dates to the eighth century. For the continuation of animal sacrifices in the Greek Orthodox Church, see Håland 2004, Chaps 3–4. There were penalties against sacrifices, but people did not always follow Church rules in this regard: *ODB* 3:1699.

[65] Cf. Achmet 236.

[66] Cf. ibid., 236. Horses replaced cattle for ploughing in the tenth century, when the system of harness changed: *ODB* 2:948. For brief but good discussions of ploughing in Byzantium, see Bryer 2002, 107–8; Kazhdan 1997, 47–8; Lefort 2002, 235; *ODB* 3:1686–7; Rautman 2006, 178 (with n. 14 on 196).

[67] According to Achmet 236, sitting on a rose-colored cow is equivalent to power, while sitting on a black cow means mastery over a wealthy magistrate.

[68] *Somniale Danielis* ("Beiträge, IV") XXXVI: *boves pascentes viderit, agoniam negotii significat*. Cf. Achmet 236: "If [a king] dreams that he sent herds of non-working cows to graze on his land, he will colonise his land with foreigners." For pasturage in Byzantium, see Lefort 2002, 263–7. Rautman (2006, 185–6) mentions how a few cattle or oxen would have represented for many peasants their heaviest investment (excluding, of course, their houses and fields).

[69] DuCange 1688 (s.v. "βερνίδιον") calls this a monk's robe; cf. Brackertz's (1993) "Mönchskleid." Drexl (1926, 295 ad loc.) comments: "βερνίδιον, offenbar ein Kleidungsstück, scheint verwandt zu sein mit βηρίον, was nach Ducange Sp. 204 ein mönchisches Kleidungsstück bedeutet."

[70] Βαστέρνιον = the Latin *basterna*, or a litter used to carry women and pulled by two mules. The negative dream interpretation is probably due to the mules, which were considered a bad sign in dream literature; see Manuel 11 below.

60. Wearing a *berinon*—that is, a white woolen cape[71]—indicates a good opportunity.

61. Dreaming of breasts filled with milk signifies profit.[72]

62. Dreaming that your breasts have been cut off is a bitter [sign].[73]

63. Dreaming that the meshes of your nets have fallen out indicates [that you will fail just as the meshes did].[74]

64. Receiving a palm leaf signifies honor.[75]

65. Dice falling from your hands signifies loss of livelihood.[76]

66. Seeing a very large number of dice or picking them up signifies a life full of changes.[77]

67. Dreaming of beautiful cattle signifies great friendships with profit.

68. Dreaming of cattle that are standing still: [this has] the same [interpretation].

69. Dreaming of running cattle signifies great joy.

70. Dreaming of fighting cattle means struggle in your actions.[78]

---

[71] Βέρινον = βηρίον (for which, see DuCange 1688, s.h.v.) = the Latin *birrus/burrus*, which was a cape worn over the shoulders and typically made of sheep's wool; see Mihăescu 1981; *LAnt* 381. Cf. *Somniale Danielis* ("Beiträge, IV") XXXII: *byrrum album habere, letitiam significat*. For white clothes as a very auspicious dream symbol, see Achmet 156.

[72] Cf. Achmet 128: "If someone dreams that he grabbed hold of [a beautiful woman's] breasts and squeezed out milk, he will receive great joy in that very year, and the woman will have a great share in this happiness; if the dreamer is a commoner, he will acquire wealth for one year in his business; if a slave, he will soon be set free; if a poor man, he will become rich." Achmet's interpretations come from Arabic sources: Mavroudi 2002, 462–4.

[73] Breasts symbolise daughters according to Achmet 80; cf. Artemidorus 1.41.

[74] A hopelessly confused sentence. The sentence merely reads: Βρόχους ἰδεῖν ἐκπεσόντας μετ᾽ ἐκείνους δηλοῖ. I have placed within the square brackets my own guess as to the meaning. Brackertz (1993) translates with an ellipsis: "Schlingen, die abfallen, bedeuten ...."
An unfavorable interpretation is obvious, in any case, from the dream and interpretation of fish-nets in 136 below. For negative interpretations of fishing nets, see Artemidorus 2.11 and 2.14.

[75] *Somniale Danielis* ("Beiträge, V") 117: *palmam accipere, honorem significat*. So too Achmet 197, although the wealth will come from a woman of royal blood.

[76] Cf. Artemidorus 3.1: "If a person dreams that he is playing at dice, it signifies that he will quarrel with someone over money. For the dice contain numbers and those which players use are called 'counters.'" See Koukoules 1948–57, 1:185–219 for dice used in various Byzantine games; *ODB* 2:820–21, where it is commented that while the clergy were prohibited by canon law from playing such games, laypeople were zealously devoted to them.

[77] The assocation of casting dice with uncertainty in one's life was a common *topos* in ancient literature; see the examples in Lewis and Short 1879, s.v. "*bolus*."

[78] The interpretation may be based on fighting as a metaphor for struggle, and on cattle as a metaphor for property or livelihood.

71. Seeing a bathtub[79] or bathing in one signifies an unexpected state of confusion.[80]

72. Sitting on a young mule means untimely toil.[81]

73. Owning trousers[82] with belt fittings[83] signifies freedom from care.[84]

74. Building a bathtub signifies distress.

---

[79] I take βαλάνιον as equivalent to βαλανεῖον. Drexl (1926, 295 ad loc.), on the other hand, comments: "βαλάνιον bedeutet hier den 'Laubaderaum' = suppositorium." Brackertz (1993) translates: "Wer einen Laudaderaum erblickt oder darin badet, hat eine plötzliche Aufregung zu gewärtigen." But I think that the subsequent phrase, λούσασθαι ἐν αὐτῷ, and the οἰκοδομεῖν in 74 below, are better understood if βαλάνιον denotes a bath; also cf. the Latin Daniel dream cited in the next note.

The large bath complexes, famous during Greek and Roman times, disappeared in Byzantium after the sixth century, when personal tubs and hip-baths came to be used; see *LAnt* 241 for private bath-houses in the houses of the rich. The change may have been due to a greater sense of modesty associated with Christianity (nakedness is a terrible dream symbol in the Byzantine dreambooks); for Byzantine attitudes to the naked body, see *ODB* 1:539 and 2: 763; cf. Holum 2005, 103–4 (with nn. 37–8 on 111), although perhaps a greater consideration for the decline of the bath complexes was the large costs associated with their construction, maintenance, and upkeep; for this, see Berger 1982; Bouras 2002, 525–6; Kazhdan and Epstein 1985, 79–80; *LAnt* 338; *ODB* 1:271–2; Rautman 2006, 49, 76–7; Treadgold 1997, 280.

[80] Cf. *Somniale Danielis* ("Beiträge, IV") XXX: *balneo se lavare, anxietatem significat.* But Artemidorus (1.64) offers a very favorable interpretation: "In our time, indeed, some people do not eat unless they have taken a bath beforehand. Others, moreover, also bathe after they have eaten. Then they wash when they are about to take supper. Therefore, in our day, the bath is nothing but a road to luxury. And thus washing in baths that are beautiful, bright, and moderately heated is auspicious. It signifies wealth and success in business for the healthy and health for the sick. For healthy people wash themselves even when it is unnecessary." Artemidorus's interpretations are positive perhaps because he wrote in a period when nakedness and the display of the human body were normal and when the public baths were in full use.

[81] Cf. Achmet 232: "If someone dreams that he was riding a young mule, he will voluntarily undertake a journey and derive from it vexation and constraint: for all mules, both male and female, represent for any dreamer the upsetting of any particular matter, since the mule is incapable of having children." Cf. *Somniale Danielis* ("Beiträge, IV") XXV: *bordore sedere deceptionem negotii significat.*

[82] For βρακία, see Sophocles 1975, s.h.v. Brackertz (1993, 252 ad loc.) comments: "Die Byzantiner trugen im Gegensatz zu den Römern Hosen, eine Sitte, die sie von den Barbaren übernommen hatten. Nach der Niederlage, die Manuel I. (1143–1180) durch die Seldschuken erlitt, soll ein Krieger dem Kaiser empört zugerufen haben: »Zeig doch den Türken, daß du Hosen anhast«, d.h. daß du »ein Mann bist«." See also Kazhdan 1997, 60; *ODB* 3:2125.

[83] This is how I attempt μετὰ χεῖρας, which I am at a loss to translate. (Χέρι in modern Greek can mean "handle" or "grip," hence my translation above.) For belt fittings, see *ODB* 1:280. Brackertz (1993) prefers to ignore the phrase, and so simply translates as "Hosen anziehen besagt ohne Sorgen sein."

[84] Cf. Achmet 242; *Somniale Danielis* ("Beiträge, IV") XXIV: *bracas in somnis viderit, securitatem significat.*

75. Eating butter signifies good news.[85]

76. Gathering and eating acorns means freedom in your activities along with profit.[86]

77. Hearing thunder signifies good news.[87]

78. If you dream of becoming emperor, you will be deemed hereafter as worthy of great honor.[88]

79. Holding or receiving a book: you will receive an office of honor.[89]

80. Sitting on a donkey[90] [means] idleness.[91]

---

[85] Ibid., XXXV: *butirum edere, nuntium bonum significat.* Achmet 237: "If someone dreams of eating butter, he will have sweet and long-lasting wealth."

Brackertz (1993, 252 ad loc.) comments that butter, common in Byzantium, was originally a Greek import from Scythia: "Die Butter ist ein Produkt der Skythen, von welchen die Griechen sie bezogen." Butter was used in ancient Egypt, and a version of it (perhaps curdled milk) appears in the Hebrew Bible.

[86] Artemidorus (1.73) considers nuts indicative of troubles.

[87] *Somniale Danielis* ("Beiträge, IV") CCXXXIII: *tonitruum audire vel videre, nuntium bonum significat.* For thunder as a divinationary sign, see Koukoules 1948–57, 1.2:218–19; *ODB* 1:326.

[88] *Somniale Danielis* ("Beiträge, IV") CXXXII: *imperatorem se factum, aliquem honorem significat.* But cf. Artemidorus 2.30: "Dreaming that one is a king portends death for a sick man. For only a king, like a dead man, is subject to no man. But for a man in good health, it signifies the loss of all his relatives and separation from his companions. For monarchy is not shared. But for a criminal, it signifies that he will be imprisoned and that secret deeds will be brought to light. For the king is in the spotlight and has many to watch over him. … If a poor man dreams that he is a king, he will accomplish many deeds that will bring him fame but no profit. If a slave dreams that he is a king, it foretells his freedom. For it is altogether necessary that the king be free. But it is best for philosophers and prophets to dream that they are kings. For we maintain that there is nothing freer or more majestic than a sound mind."

[89] But books signify the lives of dreamers according to Artemidorus 2.45. In *ODB* 1:305, 308–9, we read that books in Byzantium were expensive and rare (due to the cost of materials and the time involved in copying manuscripts). This explains why friends and fellow scholars exchanged books so extensively. Mango (1975, 38–9) has determined that a book of 400 folia would cost 15 to 20 *nomismata*, an amount equivalent to six months' salary for a civil servant. Wilson (1975) notes that although paper did cut costs somewhat, books remained the province of the wealthy and institutions such as the Church. But see Cavallo 1981 for a good study of the "bookish mentality" of the Byzantines. Also Kazhdan and Epstein 1985, 41–2 (on the active book production in the eleventh and twelfth centuries); *LAnt* 345–7; Rapp 2005, 377–9; Rautman 2006, 267–70 (with nn. 12–14 on 279), 287–9 (with nn. 7–9 on 308).

[90] So I take βαδιστής (for which, see LSJ, s.h.v.). Hesychius (Schmidt 1965) and Sophocles (1975) (both s.h.v.) translate as "trotting horse." Brackertz (1993) offers as translation of this line: "Unterwegs sein und dann ins Gras strecken zeigt vergebliche Mühe an."

[91] But this dream means success in Achmet 233 if the donkey is tame and walks well; see also Artemidorus 2.12 for a favorable interpretation. Riding horses were the mark of high officials and the military, since most people rode donkeys (*LAnt* 498). Morrisson and Sodini (2002, 200) point out that in Byzantium, donkeys were more important than horses as draft animals.

81. Dreaming of cattle giving birth signifies negligence in your actions.[92]

82. Dreaming of agitated cattle indicates the purchase of goods.[93]

83. Dreaming that a cow has been [offered] as a sacrifice[94] is good.

84. Dreaming of shaking acorns from an oak tree: watch out lest you fall into evil situations.[95]

85. If you see or approach dung, this signifies quarrels or shame and sorrows.[96]

86. Dreaming of an emperor signifies great tumult.[97]

87. A dream of rain points to profit earned from poor people.[98]

---

[92] So I take ἀμέλειαν πραγμάτων. Brackertz (1993) translates as "ein Leben ohne Sorgen."

[93] The sentence reads, Βόας σαλεύοντας ἰδεῖν ἀγοράσαι πράγματα δηλοῖ. I take ἀγοράσαι with the interpretation, not with the symbol, since the writer of this dreambook prefers to end the symbol with ἰδεῖν. (We may even translate ἀγοράσαι πράματα as "business purchases.") Brackertz (1993), on the other hand, takes the infinitive with the symbol and thus offers a different interpretation: "Träumt man, unruhige, schwankende Rinder zu kaufen, stehen einem arge Schwierigkeiten bevor."

I take σαλεύω as roughly equivalent to παλαίω (for which, see 70 above) and so translate as "agitated." Drexl (1926, 296 ad loc.) points out this equivalence as well: "82 ist 70 auffallend ähnlich."

[94] I take the phrase βοῦν ἐπὶ θυσίαις ἰδεῖν as indicating an animal sacrifice, not butchering a cow (see 53 above, with comment). Cf. Brackertz's (1993) translation: "Schaut man, wie ein Rind geschlachtet wird, ist das ein glückbringendes Zeichen" ("Schlachten" means "to immolate" as well as "to butcher").

[95] Cf. Achmet 151: "If someone dreams that he owned an oak tree under which he was sitting, he will meet a powerful but fickle man, and his happiness with him will be accompanied by pain and trouble because of the inedible nature of acorns."

[96] Artemidorus 2.26: "Cow dung means good luck only for farmers, which is also true of horse dung and all kinds of excrement except for human feces. But for other men, it signifies sorrows and injuries and, if it stains, it means sickness as well. It signifies benefits and has been observed to indicate success only for those who are engaged in lowly professions." Cf. Achmet 105. For the removal of dung from latrines and family cesspools in Constantinople, see Rautman 2006, 76.

[97] Cf. *Somniale Danielis* ("Beiträge, V") 125: *reges videre, de seculo migrare significat*; cf. Artemidorus 2.30.

[98] Cf. *Somniale Danielis* ("Beiträge, V") 113: *pluvias videre, habundantiam et letitiam significat*; cf. *Somniale Danielis* ("Beiträge, IV") CXCVII and Achmet 170; rain has a negative interpretation in Artemidorus 2.8. Drought was always a concern for the Byzantines; we have records of processions conducted to procure rain: Krueger 2005, 301.

The word "poor" (πτωχός) denoted a legally defined class of people, namely those who had less than 50 *nomismata*; these included not only the destitute, but also underemployed city workers and small farmers who could not make a profit from their work: *ODB* 3:1697–8. This was not a very large group, perhaps about 5 per cent of the total population. See Patlagean 1997 for extended discussion, with full bibliography.

Beginning of the Letter Γ

88. Having a dirty beard is good for those involved with the lawcourts,[99] but bad for all others.

89. Shaving off your beard or having it fall out is bitter for anyone.[100]

90. Eating sweets: [you] will fall into many evils.[101]

91. Plucking out one's own beard is a harsh sign for anyone.[102]

92. Drinking milk signifies a happy life.[103]

93. Seeing gold or silver letters of the alphabet in any place is good for craftsmen,[104] but evil for all others.[105]

94. Dreaming of a woman's hair points to the disappearance of one's goods.[106]

---

[99] Perhaps the interpretation refers to the ancient rhetorical ruse of assuming a sordid appearance when appearing in trials. For lawcourts in Byzantium, see *ODB* 1:543, 3:2113–14; in late antiquity, *LAnt* 530–31, 540.

[100] Cf. *Somniale Danielis* ("Beiträge, V") 23: *barbam radere, damnum significat*; and *Somniale Danielis* ("Beiträge, IV") XXIII: *barba sibi tondi, dampnum significat*. Artemidorus 1.30: "If a man dreams that his beard has fallen off, or that it has been shaved off or forcibly ripped off by anyone, it signifies, in addition to the loss of his blood relations, harm together with shame." Cf. Achmet 21, 22, 34.
The Byzantines considered the beard a mark of manliness (eunuchs, for example, were beardless), and so being deprived of one's beard was a severe punishment: *ODB* 1:274. Since the Latins did not have beards, having a beard was a mark of Byzantine citizenship, although as Rautman (2006, 47) points out, fashion did change during the Empire. For the Hebrew background, see 2 Samuel 10:4–5.

[101] Cf. *Somniale Danielis* ("Beiträge, IV") LXXXIV: *dulcia edere, in multis criminibus opprimitur significat*. A positive interpretation is in Achmet 241; cf. Mavroudi 2002, 231 for Arabic parallels. For sweets in the Byzantine diet, see Koukoules 1948–57, 5:110–21.

[102] Cf. Achmet 34 for a dream where other people pull out the dreamer's beard: "If someone dreams that [some people] plucked out the hairs of his beard, he will lose his wealth amid pain and punishment and come into disgrace."

[103] Ibid. 237: "If someone dreams that he was milking a cow and then drank some of the milk, if he is a slave, he will be set free and will possibly inherit the house of his master or get ownership of it; if a commoner, he will find joy and greater exultation; if a king, the same results will occur for him as for a commoner." Cf. Artemidorus 4.62.

[104] In Byzantium, the word τεχνίτης denoted skilled craftsmen or people involved in construction: *ODB* 3:2020.

[105] Cf. Achmet 161 and 169. For letters of the alphabet, Artemidorus 3.34: "The vowels signify fears and confusion. As for the semi-vowels, though they do not signify unemployment, they do indicate fears. The consonants signify neither fears nor business transactions." Artemidorus then demonstrates how a single word may symbolize different objects or persons by determining the numerical value of each of its letters. (In Greek, each letter stands for a certain number: alpha = 1, beta = 2, etc.: *ODB* 3:1501.) See Rautman 2006, 304 for the supernatural power of words through the invoking of their numerical totals (the number 99, for example, represents "amen"); cf. *ODB* 3:1502; *LAnt* 413. See note 111 below for an example.

[106] Artemidorus (1.19) interprets hair as an evil sign only if it is in a mess: "Long hair that is dishevelled, so that it gives the impression not of hair but rather of a confused mass of tufts, indicates griefs and pains for all. For to groom and comb one's head is to take care of one's

95.   Dreaming of letters tattooed on one's own body signifies [cuts from] whips.[107]

96.   If a woman dreams of having sex with a man other than her husband,[108] this signifies illness.[109]

97.   If a woman dreams of being a virgin, this means gracefulness.[110]

98.   Weasels, when dreamt of, signify profit.[111]

99.   Seeing oneself naked or walking around barefoot signifies dangerous loss.[112]

100.   Throwing a wedding feast[113] means loss fraught with danger.[114]

101.   Dreaming that you are born: you will soon die.[115]

---

person, but unkempt hair grows in periods of distress." Cf. *Somniale Danielis* ("Beiträge, IV") CLXXIV: *mulierem sparsis crinibus se viderit, seditionem significat.*

[107]   The marks on the body from the tattooing are analogous to the marks inflicted by the whip.

[108]   In all the dreams that Achmet records regarding sex (and this includes two chapters on bestiality—for the Byzantine attitudes toward which, see *ODB* 1:286), the dreamer is always a man; women do not dream of sex, although their fornication is constantly predicted in men's dreams. See also Mavroudi 2007, 57–9.

[109]   One could take ἀρρωστία (illness) in its metaphorical sense—namely, "moral weakness." If so, then the "weakness" above would refer to the husband's inability to control the actions of his wife.

A parallel to the above dream is *Somniale Danielis* ("Beiträge, V") 92: *mulier que secum aliquem viderit nubere, gravem languorem significat.*

[110]   So I take the word ἐλαφρότης (Brackertz 1993 translates as "wird sie leicht gebären"). I reject the classical meaning of "lightness," as well as the often Byzantine and modern Greek sense of "frivolity" or "superficiality," and take the word in the sense of "mildness" or "gracefulness" (the adjective ἐλαφρός can mean "gentle"; see LSJ, s.h.v.). The interpretation, in any case, would have to be positive, given how Christian literature deemed virginity the highest state of human life. See Lampe 1976, s.v. "παρθενία," for numerous references; also the recent discussion, with bibliography, in Cooper 1996; cf. Rautman 2006, 50 and *LAnt* 366.

[111]   Cf. Artemidorus 3.28: "A weasel signifies a cunning, treacherous woman and a lawsuit. For the word δική [lawsuit] is equal in numerical value to the word γαλή [weasel]. A weasel also means death. For whatever a weasel catches, it causes to rot. It also signifies profits and success in business. For some people call it a fox [κερδώ]." There is a pun here between κερδώ and κέρδος (profit); cf. Achmet 275.

The weasel was portrayed as a symbol of bad luck in classical Greek literature; see Theophrastus, *Characters* 16.3.

[112]   Cf. *Somniale Danielis* ("Beiträge, V") 103: *nudis pedibus ambulare vel nudum se videre, tristitias et labores magnas significat.* The Byzantines did not portray the nude body except occasionally in iconography (and then in biblical scenes): *ODB* 3:1500–1501; this explains the everyday use of trousers, sleeves, and long cloaks. Cf. *LAnt* 615–6. See also note 79 above.

[113]   For the phrase γάμους ποιεῖν, see Arndt and Gingrich 1958, s.v. "γάμος."

[114]   Cf. *Somniale Danielis* ("Beiträge, V") 150: *xsponsalia facere, dampnum significat; Somniale Danielis* ("Beiträge, V") 101: *nuptias facere vel cantratrices videre, planctum et laborem significat;* Artemidorus 2.49; Achmet 129 and 130.

[115]   A typical dream interpretation based on antinomy. As for death in Byzantium, Laiou (1977, 276), analysing data from Macedonia, calculates that life expectancy was about 22–23 years for males and females. Laiou more recently (2002b, 52) has shown that if a child survived

102. Having two tongues is [good] for lawyers[116] [or] curators,[117] but evil for anyone else.[118]

103. Dreaming of a woman who is beautifying her face or is simply walking around points to adultery.[119]

104. Having sex with a woman you know, even if she is married to someone else: this signifies illness.[120]

---

the first year of life, then its life expectancy was 33 years; if the child made it past the fifth birthday, then 47 years. Forty-nine per cent of Byzantine children died before the age of five years, with the highest mortality in the first year of life (Laiou 1977, 292–4). See also Rautman 2006, 8–9; *ODB* 1:608, 2:1226. On a sidenote, no Byzantine oneirocritic text, including Achmet, refers to suicide; this is in keeping with Byzantine attitudes; as noted in *ODB* 3:1974–5, documented instances of suicide are extremely rare.

[116] Brackertz (1993, 252–3 ad loc.) comments on this word: "Griech. *scholastikos*; eigentlich einer, der Lehrvorträge (*scholas*) hält oder anhört, ein Professor oder Student, dann auch Angehöriger eines akademischen Berufes, ein Arzt, Rechtsanwalt." Σχολαστικός (or συνήγορος) was equivalent to the Latin *advocatus*, but was also used generally of any well-educated person who appeared in a lawcourt or in public; see Rapp 2005, 382, 393. The term is not used after the ninth century: *ODB* 3:1852.

[117] For the office of *curator*, see Hornblower and Spawforth 2003 (hereafter, "*OCD*³"), s.h.v. In Byzantium, the word could also denote a manager of imperial estates: *ODB* 2:1155–6; cf. Oikonomides 2002, 989.

[118] For the interpretation of tongues as a good dream symbol for people involved in lawcourts, see Achmet 62; cf. Artemidorus 1.32.

[119] Cf. 112 below for censure of a woman's activities, even in a dream. Women were continuously trapped in a maze of gender-appropriate codes of behavior, and how they acted determined how others perceived them; see the comments in Brubaker 2005, 438–40. Justinian I in 540 issued a list of misbehaviors by wives—for example, eating with other men, hunting wild animals, and going to games and theaters (*ODB* 1:640). Dreams helped regulate proper sexual conduct by warning women not to overstep boundaries or to beware of the consequences of impropriety. A dream of what may seem an innocuous enough action can foretell a horrible fate; for example, Achmet 132: "If a woman dreams that she went into a graveyard or that she spoke with a dead man, this signifies deceit toward her husband; if she is not married, she will spend her whole life in fornication." Given the horrible outcomes (divorce, prostitution, death) that could befall a Byzantine woman simply because of a dream that she (or her husband or child) might have—for example, as we read in the Daniel dreambook, a dream of a woman dancing (see 112 below), applying cosmetics, or simply talking to another person; or, as we read in Achmet, a child's dream that his mother was eating raw or roasted beef—many a woman must have been anxious after she and her family woke up and dreams were discussed at the breakfast meal. See too Mavroudi 2007, with bibliography.

As for adultery, some Byzantine authors, especially those connected with the Church, distinguished it from fornication (πορνεία), which denoted any sort of illicit sexual intercourse. The distinction was based on whether legitimacy of children was at issue: Brubaker 2005, 437–8. There were severe legal penalties against adultery, but they usually were not enforced. See Zhishman 1964, 578–600; *ODB* 1:25.

[120] Cf. the comment above to 96. For the dream, cf. *Somniale Danielis* ("Beiträge, IV") CCXCIX: *si videris, quod concupiscas uxorem proximi tui, malum dolorem in corpus significat*; Achmet 127. But see the favorable interpretation in Artemidorus 1.78.

105.   If [a woman dreams of] marrying a man who already has a wife,[121] this signifies widowhood.[122]

106.   Carrying dirt or digging it up signifies distress.

107.   Having sex with a prudent[123] woman means something good.

108.   Dreaming of oneself being married: let him have a wife.[124]

109.   Carrying a woman points to distress.

110.   Laughing in a dream signifies grief.[125]

111.   Walking around with bare feet indicates loss.[126]

112.   If you dream that a woman is dancing or jumping about, this indicates adultery.[127]

113.   Dreaming of a desolate stretch of land signifies bad luck and hindrance.[128]

Beginning of the Letter Δ

114.   Wearing a silver ring: you will be released from every evil.[129]

---

[121]   So I take γαμεῖν ἔχοντα γυναῖκα. One could also translate as, "If a man who is already married dreams of getting married ...." Brackertz (1993) translates: "Wähnt ein Verheirateter, er feiere Hochzeit, wird er Witwer werden."

[122]   For death and marriage, see Artemidorus 2.49 and 2.65; cf. Achmet 124. Achmet's chapters on marriage (129 and 130) come before those on death (131 and 132). For a dream similar to the one above, Artemidorus 1.65: "If a woman who has a husband dreams that she is marrying another man, she will, as early writers tell us, bury her husband or be separated from him in some other way. I have observed that this is not always the case. It is only true when the wife is not pregnant or childless or has nothing for sale."

Laiou (1977, 273) observes that Byzantine males married at 20 years of age, and females at 15 years. She also estimates (89–94) that about a fifth of late Byzantine households were headed by a widow; see also *ODB* 3:2195. Remarriage was permitted, although some Church Fathers condemned it. For a general introduction to marriage in Byzantium, see Rautman 2006, 40–42 (with n. 1 on 57); *ODB* 2:1304–5.

[123]   For γνωστική (which Brackertz [1993] translates as "bekannt"), see Lampe 1976, s.h.v.

[124]   This dream is usually interpreted as a symbol of death.

[125]   *Somniale Danielis* ("Beiträge, IV") CCXVII: *ridere aut stridentes viderit, tristitiam significat.* For Byzantine attitudes to laughter, see *ODB* 2:1189.

[126]   This is an abbreviated version of 99. The interpretation is based on an analogy to a servile status (slaves went barefoot).

[127]   Cf. Artemidorus 1.76: "We have observed, however, that [a dream of dancing] is good neither for a rich or a poor woman. For they will be involved in great and notorious scandals." Dancing, the object of condemnation by the Church, was performed only at certain court festivals or among the lower classes. See the discussion in *ODB* 1:582.

[128]   Achmet (142 and 143) interprets stretches of good land as wealth and power.

[129]   Cf. Artemidorus 2.5.

115. Wearing a ring made from any type of bone signifies the surety of one's goods.[130]

116. Having a tin[131] ring means perdition—that is to say, treason.[132]

117. Giving away one's ring indicates poverty in one's business.[133]

118. Receiving a ring means a lack of worry over one's affairs.[134]

119. Wearing an iron ring signifies that a woman will entrust her capital to you.[135]

120. Having more fingers signifies additional livelihood.[136]

121. Dreaming of a fruit-bearing tree signifies profit.[137]

122. Dreaming of barren trees signifies bad luck, especially loss, but profit for a slave.[138]

123. If you dream of trees being uprooted or being cut down, this means wars and the falling of animals and people.[139]

---

[130] I use Brackertz's (1993) translation here for πίστιν ἀγαθῶν: "Ein Ring aus irgendeinem Gebein deutet auf Bürgschaft für Hab und Gut."

[131] Or "peuter." Tin was imported from the Taurus and even Britain: Haldon 2005, 33, 35.

[132] Καθοσίωσις in Byzantine Greek was equivalent to the Latin *maiestas*; see Sophocles 1975, s.h.v. The word has the same meaning in modern Greek. In Byzantium, the penalty for treason was death, confiscation of property, denial of proper burial, and erasure of one's memory: *ODB* 3:2110–11.

[133] Cf. *Somniale Danielis* ("Beiträge, V") 15: *anulos aut armillas dare vel perdere, dolorem significat.*

[134] Cf. ibid., 14: *anulos vel armillas accipere, aliquam securitatem significat;* see 115 above and cf. Achmet 257. Byzantine rings were not used as seals, since they did not contain titles or family names; see *ODB* 3:1796.

[135] Cf. Artemidorus 2.5: "Iron rings are auspicious, but they signify that the good things will not come about without some effort. For the poet [Homer] himself describes iron as 'wrought with much toil.'" Iron was the most common metal in Byzantium for making weapons and implements: *ODB* 2:1010–11; Haldon 2005, 33.

[136] Cf. Artemidorus 1.42: "To have more than the normal number of fingers means the opposite of dreaming that one has fewer [where the interpretation is harm and the loss of underlings]. For fingers that are added to those given to us by nature, besides being useless themselves, make those from which they have sprung useless as well. Some people have erroneously maintained that this dream is auspicious." Achmet 72: "If someone dreams that he had more fingers on his hand, he will add to his prayers and be strong in his faith"; for Achmet's reliance on Arabic sources for this interpretation, see Mavroudi 2002, 335–7.

[137] *Somniale Danielis* ("Beiträge, V") 7: *arbores cum fructibus videre, lucrum expertum significat.* See too Artemidorus 1.73; Achmet 213. The Byzantines had many fruit trees in their gardens or on their country estates; even peasants had trees such as the pear, fig, apple, cherry, almond, and mulberry. See Kazhdan 1997, 46; Laiou 1977, 29–30, 32–3 (size of gardens), and 2002b, 327; Lefort 2002, 248, 253–4; *ODB* 2:807–8; Rautman 2006, 176. Dagron (2002, 447–9) points out that small garden plots existed in the city of Constantinople (e.g., in the open spaces near the city walls); cf. Matschke 2002b, 466; Rautman 2006, 75, 91–92.

[138] See Artemidorus 2.15.

[139] Cf. Achmet 164: "If someone dreams that a worldwide or local wind was blowing, the king will be the cause of fear; and if he dreams that the wind tore down trees, the king's anger will cut down nobles by analogy to the trees." Cf. Artemidorus 2.10 and 2.25.

124. Wearing or receiving rings of any sort in a dream is good; but if one gives them away for any reason, this means unsuccessful actions.[140]

125. Wanting to run but not being able to do so means an impediment to one's actions.[141]

126. Wanting to run quickly signifies profit.[142]

127. Dreaming of a tree in full blossom is good for anyone.[143]

128. Dreaming of a large serpent signifies distress.[144]

129. If you dream of a large serpent that is chasing you, this signifies at first fear and then honor.[145]

130. Seeing a dolphin in the distance signifies good news.[146]

131. Having two heads signifies a union of friends.[147]

132. Sitting in a two-wheeled carriage[148] signifies illness.[149]

133. Dreaming of a demon means anxiety and unceasing labor.[150]

---

[140] Cf. *Somniale Danielis* ("Beiträge, IV") XIV: *anullum in somniis viderit, locum exsperatum significat*; XV: *anullum in somnis accipere, securitatem significat*; XVI: *anullum dare, dampnum significat*. Cf. Achmet 257.

[141] A straightforward analogy. Cf. *Somniale Danielis* ("Beiträge, IV") LXIII: *currere qui se viderit & non potest, inpeditionem significat*; Artemidorus 2.2.

[142] So I translate Δραμεῖν θέλειν ἐν τάχει κέρδος σημαίνει. The phrase ἐν τάχει may be taken with δραμεῖν, with κέρδος ("Wanting to run means that profit [will come] in a hurry"), or with both.

[143] See Achmet 200.

[144] Or, "dreaming of a dragon ...." The interpretation differs in *Somniale Danielis* ("Beiträge, IV") LXXXVI: *dracones viderit, aliquam dignitatem significat*; Achmet 281. Many saints—e.g., Theodore Stratelates and Theodore Teron—are recorded in their hagiographies as having slain a dragon.

[145] Cf. Achmet 281.

[146] Artemidorus 2.16: "If a man dreams of any sea creature, with the exception of a dolphin, in the sea, it signifies benefits for no one. Seeing a dolphin in the sea is a good sign and signifies that a favorable wind will blow from wherever it is seen swimming."

[147] Achmet (39) states that a head (κεφαλή) signifies a man (an association evident here). But Achmet states that if a woman is the dreamer, the head symbolizes her husband (an interpretation based on Paul's dictum in Ephesians 5:23). Κεφαλή was also the fourteenth-century title of the top civil and military administrator of a province: *ODB* 2:1122.

[148] Δίτροχος = the Latin *birota*, which was a lightweight carriage used to carry passengers.

[149] The interpretation is perhaps based on the analogy of sitting (riding in a carriage) and not being active. Cf. *Somniale Danielis* ("Beiträge, IV") CCXXXII: *sedere in somniis, infirmitatem significat*.

[150] But see Achmet 111 for a positive interpretation. Demons were pervasive in Byzantine culture and were always considered evil. Byzantines feared them so much that they used amulets and talismans to ward them off and resorted to exorcisms (cf. *ODB* 1:82–3). Demons were thought to live in dark places like tombs and caves, and to be responsible for drought, famine, crop failures, and other disasters: *ODB* 1:609. On the other hand, demons were purposely solicited through so-called curse tablets to cause illness and induce love; see Gager 1992.

134. Stowing away gifts in one's own house: this is good for each and every dreamer.[151]

135. Giving away gifts: watch out lest you suffer loss.

136. Spreading out fish-nets signifies evildoing and hindrance to your actions.[152]

137. Making a will means renouncing the rights to one's own property.[153]

138. Being a slave means profit in whatever one does.[154]

139. Walking on coals[155] points to distress.

140. Seeing two suns signifies life.[156]

141. Dreaming that a large serpent is entering your house is good for anyone.[157]

Beginning of the Letter E

142. Falling to the ground signifies evildoing.[158]

143. Falling into the sea signifies great joy.[159]

---

[151] Interpreted as good since one is keeping property and not giving it away (cf. the negative interpretation in the next dream).

[152] See Artemidorus 2.14.

[153] The basis for the interpretation is clear. But cf. *Somniale Danielis* ("Beiträge, IV") CCXXXVII: *testamenta facere, tutamentum significat.*

[154] See Artemidorus 4.30. Perhaps the interpretation is based on the fact that slaves produce profit for their masters.

[155] The word δαμπρόν does not exist. There are four possible solutions. (1) We can make a best guess as to the meaning of the word and place it in brackets or parentheses. Brackertz does the latter, translating the phrase as "Über (Kohlen) zu gehen sagt Bedrängnis an," and then comments (1993, 254): "Die Überlieferung ist hier unsicher." (2) We can take the word as equivalent to ἄνθρακες. So Drexl 1926, 298 ad loc.: "Soll das erste Wort vielleicht Λαμπρούς (= ἄνθρακας) heißen?" Cf. Brackertz's translation just given. (3) We can take the word as an error for λαμπρόν (= πῦρ); this, however, would necessitate changing ἀναπατεῖν to ἀνάπτειν. (4) We can read the word as δρομαίως, as Drexl (ibid., ad loc.) suggests, although I do not understand why we should take it so. Option 2 seems best, especially since this reading makes the verse equivalent to Nicephorus 4, Astrampsychus 58, and Germanus 13.

[156] The sun is symbolic of a king in other dreambooks—e.g., Achmet 166 and Artemidorus 2.36.

[157] But in Achmet 281 this dream means that a hostile king will come to the dreamer's land.

[158] Cf. *Somniale Danielis* ("Beiträge, IV") CCLXXII.

[159] Cf. ibid., CXXXIX: *in mare cecidisse, lucrum significat.* But cf. the dream in Artemidorus 5.53: "Someone dreamt that he fell into the sea and was carried out into the deep. He felt that he was being carried out a long time, until, finally, he was awakened by his fear. He married a prostitute, migrated with her, and spent the greater part of his life in a foreign country." See Rautman 2006, 153–4 (with n. 22 on 156) for the Byzantines' fear of the sea.

144. Finding yourself in your homeland or in your own house points to escape from great danger.[160]

145. Eating venison means something good.[161]

146. Seeing or hunting red deer means fear without danger.[162]

147. Touching a red deer in a dream signifies profit.

148. Seeing or eating or, in short, handling eels means a great disturbance.[163]

149. Seeing elephants or being chased by them signifies being overpowered by enemies.[164]

150. Sitting on an elephant signifies great honors.[165]

151. Dreaming of removing one's clothes is good for the sick, but bad for all others.[166]

152. Reading an epistle signifies great joy.[167]

153. Dreaming that a conflagration is occurring in some place signifies danger.[168]

---

[160]   The interpretation is based on a feeling of security that the dreamer would have by being in familiar surroundings. Cf. Artemidorus 4.30.

[161]   So Achmet 240; cf. Artemidorus 2.12. The Byzantines ate venison during the cold months, but considered the meat poisonous during the summer months: *ODB* 1:598.

[162]   Cf. *Somniale Danielis* ("Beiträge, V") 143: *venationes facere, aliquam adquisitionem significat*; Achmet 240. In Byzantine religious symbolism, the deer represents Jesus, since it kills snakes, which signify the devil: *ODB* 1:598–9.

Hunting was a very popular sport among the upper classes: Koukoules 1948–57, 5:387–423. Three emperors, in fact, died from injuries that they had suffered while hunting: *ODB* 2:958; Treadgold 1997, 461 (although Basil's death may have been due to assassination; primary account published in Kazhdan and Epstein 1985, 244) and 636 (John II Comnenus supposedly pricked himself with a poisoned arrow while on a hunt). Spears, as well as nets, dogs, and hawks, were used to kill such game as bears, boars, rabbits, and deer. Peasants also hunted, but did so for food and to destroy animals that attacked their flocks: Kazhdan 1997, 55; Lefort 2002, 262–3; Rautman 2006, 95, 110, 170, 214.

[163]   For a similar negative interpretation of eels, cf. Artemidorus 2.14: "All long cartaginous fish signify that one's efforts will be in vain and that one's expectations will not be fulfilled, since they slip away through the hands and have no scales, which surround the bodies of fish just as property surrounds men. To this group belong the moray, the eel, and the conger-eel."

[164]   Achmet 240 and 241 (with Mavroudi 2002, 234–5); cf. *Somniale Danielis* ("Beiträge, IV") XCV: *elephantum viderit infestum, aliquam accusationem significat*. Cf. *Somniale Danielis* ("Beiträge, V") 11: *a bestiis qui se viderit infestare, ab inimicis suis superabitur*.

Elephants were often used in war into the sixth century, but very rarely after that. Nicephorus I the Patriarch describes how the emperor Heraclius made a triumphal entrance into the city in a chariot drawn by four elephants. See *ODB* 1:684, from which my Nicephorus reference is taken.

[165]   So too Artemidorus 2.12; Achmet 268.

[166]   Cf. ibid., 119.

[167]   But cf. *Somniale Danielis* ("Beiträge, IV") LX: [*c*]*artam scribere aut legere nuntium fedum significat*. Cf. Artemidorus 3.44.

[168]   *Somniale Danielis* ("Beiträge, IV") CXXXIV: *incendia in quocumque loco viderit, aliquod periculum significat*; cf. Artemidorus 2.9. Constantinople suffered many conflagrations

154. Walking around in a garden signifies good profit.[169]

155. Bathing in a river signifies distress.[170]

156. Bathing in the sea indicates happiness.[171]

157. Bathing in hot water [signifies] the same thing.[172]

158. Bathing in dirty water points to constant involvement in business.[173]

159. If you dream of living overseas, you will have a long life.

160. Bathing in a fish pond[174] signifies joy.

161. Falling into a spring indicates evildoing.[175]

162. Bathing in a spring signifies unexpected profit.[176]

---

in its history; Schneider (1941) lists 39 during the Byzantine era (I owe this reference to *ODB* 2:786).

[169]   Achmet 151; but cf. *Somniale Danielis* ("Beiträge, IV") CXLV: *in pomerio ambulare, anxietatem gravem significat*; and Artemidorus 4.11: "In itself, a garden is auspicious for brothel-keepers because of the many seeds and the seasonal nature of work in a garden. But to all women it signifies that they will be slandered for indecency and lewd behavior."

Gardens provided fruit and vegetables (cabbage, leeks, carrots, garlic, onions, courgettes, melons, cucumbers, etc.) for the Byzantine family. For a discussion of different kinds of vegetables, see Dalby 1996, 82–5 and Koukoules 1948–57, 5:88–96. Even most peasants had a vineyard and a small garden plot—see Haldon 2005, 31; Kazhdan 1997, 46; Laiou 1977, 29–33; *ODB* 2:822; Rautman 2006, 135, 172, 175–6. For the imperial gardens (and their ideology), see Littlewood 1997.

[170]   But cf. *Somniale Danielis* ("Beiträge, IV") CCLX: *in flumine lavare, gaudium significat.* Cf. Achmet 174: "If someone dreams that he was swimming in a river in order to cross it or to bathe in it, if he did cross it, he will overcome with his own hand the person with whom he is struggling; if not, the opposite; and if he was swimming to wash off his dirt, he will cast off his sorrow through a very powerful man by analogy to the river." For Artemidorus 2.64, this dream is positive or negative depending on the clarity of the water.

[171]   *Somniale Danielis* ("Beiträge, IV") CXXXVII: *in mare se lavare, letitiam significat.* So too Achmet 177; but cf. 119: "If someone dreams that he took off his clothes to swim in the sea, he will make a request of the king: and if he swam well, the king will fulfill it; if not, the opposite."

[172]   This positive interpretation is surprising, since hot water is usually interpreted by oneirocritic writers as a bad sign (cold water, on the other hand, is a good sign). Cf. *Somniale Danielis* ("Beiträge, IV") CCLXXXVIII: *si videris te in calida aqua lavare, dampnum corporis significat*; also Achmet 183 and 184; Anonymous 419; Germanus 89.

[173]   Dirty water is always a bad sign in Achmet's dreambook; see, e.g., 170 and 191; cf. Artemidorus 1.64, and *Somniale Danielis* ("Beiträge, IV") CXXXVIII.

[174]   *Somniale Danielis* ("Beiträge, IV") CCLIX: *in piscario lavare, iocunditatem significat.* For the meaning of φισκίνη, see DuCange 1688 and Lampe 1976, both s.h.v. The other word for fish pond, βιβάριον, denoted any place used to keep fish generally, whether a pool, a riverbank, or a marsh: *ODB* 3:2183.

[175]   Cf. *Somniale Danielis* ("Beiträge, IV") CCLXI: *in fontem cecidisse, aliquam accusationem significat.*

[176]   Cf. *Somniale Danielis* ("Beiträge, V") 81: *in fontem lavare aut in claro flumine, letitiam cum lucro significat.*

163. Falling into a river [signifies] the same thing.[177]

164. Someone who dreams of being in prison or placed in bonds will be amid many evils.[178]

165. Sitting in a wagon signifies grief and hatred.[179]

166. Falling into the sea or a river and not being able to get out points to sorrows.[180]

167. Being in a foreign place signifies unforeseen profit.

168. Walking in mud: be on your guard lest you experience something evil.[181]

169. Walking on a good road points to freedom in your actions.[182]

170. Pouring oil on yourself or anointing yourself with it signifies good opportunities.[183]

171. Handling olives means spiritual distress.[184]

---

[177] But cf. Artemidorus 2.27.

[178] So ibid., 3.60; cf. *Somniale Danielis* ("Beiträge, V") 37: *custodias introire, deceptionem significat*; *Somniale Danielis* ("Beiträge, IV") XLVI: *carcere qui se viderit, aliquam sollicitudinem vel calumpniam significat*. In Byzantium a prison could be a part of the palace, a self-standing building, or even a monastery; Constantinople had many prisons, six alone in the Great Palace: *ODB* 3:1723.

[179] This is a negative dream symbol also in Achmet 238; but see Artemidorus 3.19. The cart or wagon (ἅμαξα) was a heavy, single-axle vehicle used for transporting farm produce and usually drawn by a pair of oxen. See Bryer 2002, 112; *ODB* 1:383–4; Rautman 2006, 147–8.

[180] Cf. Achmet 177; *Somniale Danielis* ("Beiträge, IV") CCXXII.

[181] So ibid., CC; Achmet 172 (with Mavroudi 2002, 441).

[182] A muddy road has a bad interpretation in *Somniale Danielis* ("Beiträge, V") 148: *viam lutosam amb<ul>are, periculum significat*; *Somniale Danielis* ("Beiträge, IV") CCXLVIII: *via lutosa ducere vel ambulare, molestias graves signficat*; cf. Achmet 211.

There were different kinds of roads in the Byzantine Empire: public, local, and private. Some were excellent (usually the imperial roads), while some were no more than wagon pathways: *ODB* 2:1798. See also Koukoules 1948–57, 4: 318–36; Avramea 2002, 57–90 (with full bibliography), who offers a survey of roads throughout the Empire. Cf. Haldon 2005, 33–4; Rautman 2006, 141–2, 146–8.

[183] Cf. Achmet 23; but cf. *Somniale Danielis* ("Beiträge, V") 141: *unguentem facere, angustias significat*; Artemidorus 1.75. The interpretation above may be based on an association with the anointing that occurred in the coronation ceremony of the Byzantine emperor; see Nicol 1976.

Olive production was not a major fixture in Greece during the first half of Byzantium, as olives were grown in Syria and North Africa: *ODB* 3:1522–3. But after the loss of these lands to the Arabs, olive trees came to be cultivated throughout Greece; so Kazhdan 1997, 49–50, with primary sources; Lefort 2002, 248, 256–7. See Morrisson and Cheynet 2002, 837–8 for prices of olive trees and olive oil in thirteenth-century Turkey. For olive oil presses, see Morrisson and Sodini 2002, 198; Rautman 2006, 180–81. Rautman (175) mentions that the annual consumption of olive oil by a single person averaged between 5 and 13 gallons.

[184] But cf. *Somniale Danielis* ("Beiträge, IV") CXCIV: *olivas trectare, lucrum significat*; cf. Artemidorus 4.11; Achmet 198: "If someone dreams that while lifted up into an olive tree he was harvesting olives, he will receive from a gentle and gracious man bitterness and sorrow

172. Vomiting means loss.[185]
173. If you dream of being on a lofty place, this signifies loss.
174. If you dream of being kicked by some animal, this signifies trickery.[186]
175. Eating young goats signifies something good.[187]
176. Being entrusted with the care of young goats indicates profit.[188]
177. Approaching the heavens indicates honor.[189]
178. Seeing or eating eels signifies a great amount of profit.[190]
179. [Seeing oneself] in a court of law signifies hindrance.[191]
180. If you dream of falling into a pond, this signifies danger.[192]
181. Dreaming of entering a tomb and being abandoned[193] there signifies coming before a tribunal.[194]

---

because of the olive's astringency; and if he ate some of the olives, he will endure sorrowful and evil days in proportion to the number of olives."

[185] *Somniale Danielis* ("Beiträge, IV") LXI: *cibum vomere, dampnum significat.* Cf. Artemidorus 1.33; Achmet 114, 137, 140; cf. 138: "If someone dreams that he vomited food, there will be strife in his house because of money: for whatever the stomach contains signifies the house's wealth. If someone dreams that he vomited blood, he will be fined an amount of money proportionate to the amount of blood; if he vomited only water, this too means a fine of gold; if he vomited bile, he will be released from illness, but will pay out money; if he vomited chyme along with his food, this too means a fine of gold."

[186] Achmet 236.

[187] But Achmet (240) interprets raw goat meat as illness and punishment from the authorities. Goats provided the Byzantine household meat, milk, cheese, and wool. A household could have up to 100 sheep; larger estates, thousands of them (up to 70,000): *ODB* 2:857. For the discrepancies in holdings of sheep and goats between the small peasant farm and the large estate, see Laiou 1977, 30–31, 173–4, and 2002b, 348–57; cf. Morrisson and Sodini 2002, 199. Lefort (2002, 246) describes the typical holdings of a peasant in Thessalonica in the fourteenth century as follows: a cow, a pig, four goats or sheep, poultry, and beehives (which yielded sugar and wax for candles), in addition to olive trees and some vines; see also Laiou 2002c, 346. Dalby (2003, 197) gives a recipe for cooking a fatted kid stuffed full of garlic, onion, and leeks, and then drenched in fish sauce.

[188] So too Achmet 240; but cf. Artemidorus 2.12.

[189] So too Achmet 161.

[190] This line is another proof that the author of this version of the Daniel dreambook drew from several sources. In 148 above, we read ἐγχέλους and an interpretation of evil; but here we read ἐχέλυα and an interpretation of goodness. The type of eels referred to here (ἐχέλυα) may be the eels taken from Lake Copais in Boeotia, for which see Dalby 1996, 69.

[191] Cf. *Somniale Danielis* ("Beiträge, IV") CLXVII: *litigare in somniis, negotii incrementum significat*; Artemidorus 2.29.

[192] Cf. Artemidorus 2.27.

[193] I do not know how to take ἀναγευόμενον. I follow Brackertz (1993), who translates as "verlasse." Perhaps we can read instead ἀναγόμενον (being carried [into a tomb]), or even ἀναγεγραμμένον (having your name inscribed [on a tomb]).

[194] Also a very inauspicious interpretation in Achmet 131 and 132. The interpretation above is based perhaps on an analogy between the tribunal and the final judgement that will occur at

182. Dreaming of being shut up inside a fortress:[195] you will experience many evils.[196]

183. Drinking olive oil in a dream signifies illness.[197]

184. Saying prayers in a dream signifies something good.[198]

185. If you dream that reptiles are approaching you in a hostile manner, this signifies a rising-up of enemies.[199]

186. Wearing an olive or laurel wreath[200] means a journey with toils.[201]

187. Dreaming of defecating on your bed means weakness.[202]

188. Dreaming that you are in the heavens: whatever you want will happen.[203]

---

the Lord's return. For Byzantine tombs, see Bouras 2002, 527; Koukoules 1948–57, 4:198–203; *ODB* 2: 2092.

[195] Κάστρον = the Latin *castrum*, which in the Byzantine Empire meant a fortified hill or castle above a city: Bouras 2002, 505; Laiou 1977, 36–7; Rautman 2006, 127, 161, 204, 223. *Kastra* were erected especially in Turkey for protection against the Arabs and Turks; see Rosser 2001, s.v. "*kastron.*" The local population was expected to build and maintain these fortresses: *ODB* 2:1112. The commander, the καστροφύλαξ, was appointed by the emperor; see Kazhdan 1997, 74.

[196] The interpretation is based perhaps on the dangers and griefs associated with sieges. As Lee (2005, 123–7) writes, the horrors caused by siege were extensive; according to our primary sources, starving people ate acorns, grass, mice, and even excrement. For Byzantine siege warfare, see Rautman 2006, 223–6.

[197] So too Artemidorus 1.66; Achmet 198. Cf. *Somniale Danielis* ("Beiträge, V") 105: *oleum accipere, letitiam significat*; *Somniale Danielis* ("Beiträge, IV") CCLXIV: *oleum videre, letitiam significat.*

[198] Cf. ibid., CCCI: *si videris te orare ad dominum, grande gaudium tibi advenisse significat.*

[199] So Artemidorus 2.13; Achmet 281.

[200] For wreaths, see Baus 1940. In Byzantine Christian art, wreaths symbolised immortality and victory over death and thus were placed on the heads of Jesus, martyrs, and saints: *ODB* 3:2205.

[201] Perhaps there is an association with the toils that come from competing in athletic games, where victors were crowned with wreaths.

[202] Artemidorus 2.26: "It is also inauspicious to defecate while one is still in bed, for it portends lingering illness, since those who are unable to raise themselves up and those who are close to death discharge their waste in bed." Cf. Achmet's series of analogies on defecation in a toilet: "If anyone dreams that he defecated in his own toilet, he will spend money on his house: for the toilet is the place of discharges [a pun on ἔξοδος, which means 'a payment of money' and 'a bowel discharge']. And if the feces was hard and dry, the expense will be small; but if it was moist and soft, it will be considerable. If someone dreams that he defecated in someone else's toilet, he will spend money on a stranger; but if he simply defecated on the ground, the money will be spent on women and a trip abroad [analogies of earth ~ mother/woman, and earth ~ travel]. If he dreams that he was defecating repeatedly with such force that he became injured, if he is a king, he will be forced to empty out his treasuries to pay his army; if a commoner, he will be forced to take away from his money; if a poor man, he will experience hunger and violence: for however much a human or animal defecates signifies [a proportionate amount of] a person's property" (105).

[203] Achmet 160.

189. Leaning over and looking about from a high place signifies freedom from anxiety.[204]

190. Walking around in white clothes signifies something good for a slave, but censure for free people.[205]

191. To have fallen into a fire points to an accusation.[206]

192. Bathing while fully clothed signifies prosecution.[207]

193. Dreaming of beautiful garments signifies profit.[208]

194. Bathing in a well[209] signifies profit.

195. If you dream of being fully armed, this signifies sudden fear.[210]

196. If someone is searching for you, [this means] utterly unexpected[211] gain.

197. Eating olives points to profit.[212]

198. Dreaming that one is covered with hair signifies profit.[213]

Beginning of the Letter Z

199. A dream of being girded signifies gain.[214]

---

[204] The interpretation may be based on the dreamer's ability to lean over with a sense of security.

[205] But cf. *Somniale Danielis* ("Beiträge, IV") XXI: *alba aut splendida se vestire, iocunditatem significat*. However, see the cautionary remarks in Artemidorus 2.3.

Colors played a significant role at the Byzantine imperial court in that they denoted ranks. Specific rules were laid down for the colors of everything, from shoes to hats to cloaks: *ODB* 1:482; Piltz 1997, 48–50. For colors of Byzantine textiles generally, see Rautman 2006, 267.

I here take the word ἐλεύθεροι (free) in a general sense. The term denoted in later Byzantium peasants who were exempt from paying taxes to the state; usually, they were poor settlers. See Kazhdan 1997, 43; Laiou 1977, 34, 213–14, 245–7, 255–8; *ODB* 1:685.

[206] So too Achmet 158. The interpretation is surely based on the association of fire with hell (a common theme in patristic literature: see Lampe 1976, s.v. "πῦρ"), or fire that tested and purified metals (a very frequent biblical image).

[207] Cf. Artemidorus 1.64: "If a man enters the hot baths with his clothes on, it signifies sickness and great anguish for him. For the sick enter the baths clothed and, furthermore, people who are anxious about important affairs sweat in their clothes."

[208] Cf. *Somniale Danielis* ("Beiträge, V") 146: *vestimenta formosa habere, gratiam in publico significat*; Achmet 157.

[209] I take φρέαρ in the ancient and patristic, as well as modern, Greek sense of "well." In Artemidorus 2.27, a well is a favorable symbol.

[210] But this dream means fearlessness in Achmet 247; cf. Artemidorus 2.31. Perhaps the interpretation above is based on the fear that people feel when going off to war.

[211] The adjective ἐξανέλπιστος is an intensification of ἀνέλπιστος.

[212] But cf. Achmet 198. See Dalby 2003, 75–6 for recipes of olive dishes.

[213] So too Achmet 43 and 44 (for which see Mavroudi 2002, 389–90); cf. *Somniale Danielis* ("Beiträge, V") 114: *pilosum se factum videre, fortitudinem significat*.

[214] Cf. Achmet 242. Brackertz (1993, 255 ad loc.) refers to belts as a mark of Byzantine government officials: "Unter *zone* = Gürtel ist der Beamtengürtel zu verstehen (lat. *cingulum*),

200. Wearing a belt signifies the same thing.[215]

201. Losing your belt signifies that your dismissal from office is at hand.[216]

202. Taking off your belt: you will fall from great honor.

Beginning of the Letter H

203. Dreaming of clear sunlight signifies gain.[217]

204. Seeing two suns means getting a great deal more power.[218]

205. If you dream that the sun and moon are taking the same trajectory, this indicates displeasures and quarrels.[219]

206. [Dreaming that] the sun is rising from the east signifies all good things.[220]

207. Dreaming that the sun is running a course below the clouds indicates profit and a good deed.[221]

208. Dreaming that the sun is fixed in the same position indicates life and honor.[222]

209. [Dreaming that] the sun and moon are running about here and there points to the separation of husband and wife.

210. [Dreaming that] the moon has fallen from the sky signifies something good for the dreamer, but evil [for the emperor].[223]

---

der als Kennzeichen der byzantinischen Staatsbeamten galt." Sommer (1984) mentions how every official, except for the empress, wore a belt, with different colors and forms distinguishing the various ranks. Belts could be made of cloth or leather and typically had buckles (*ODB* 1:280); they were used to hold up trousers and were worn over tunics. See also the discussion in Koukoules 1948–57, 5.2:50–55.

[215] So too Achmet 256.

[216] An obvious interpretation here and in the next dream, given Brackertz's (1993) comments and the bibliography in note 214 above. For the dream, cf. Achmet 242.

[217] Cf. *Somniale Danielis* ("Beiträge, V") 130: *sol splendidum videre, stabilitatem significat*; Artemidorus 2.36.

[218] See 140 above with comment ad loc.

[219] Cf. *Somniale Danielis* ("Beiträge, V") 133: *sol cum luna videre, nuntium pessimum significat*. A favorable interpretation is offered in Achmet 166.

[220] A dream that always has good implications, according to Achmet 166.

[221] Ibid., 166.

[222] Perhaps a reference to the sun standing still for the Israelite leader Joshua in his battle against the Amorites; see Joshua 10:12–15.

[223] The phrase τῷ δὲ ἄνακτι is Drexl's (1926) emendation (ad loc.) for the manuscript reading of τοῖς δὲ λοιποῖς (for everyone else). But cf. *Somniale Danielis* ("Beiträge, V") 85: *lunam de celo cadere, laborem maximam significat*. A somewhat similar interpretation of falling heavenly bodies as symbolising evil can be found in *Somniale Danielis* ("Beiträge, V") 132: *stellas de celo cadere, populus in prelio cadet*.

211. Gathering[224] or driving in nails means loss.[225]

212. Dreaming of a chariot-driver indicates quarrels with one's neighbor.[226]

213. Seeing the sun a blood-red color means harm.[227]

214. Dreaming that the sun is [not] rising or shining points to danger.[228]

215. Dreaming that the sun and moon are both shining indicates displeasures and quarrels.[229]

216. Seeing many suns in the sky points to misfortunes and quarrels.[230]

217. Dreaming that the sun is in a lake indicates loss.[231]

Beginning of the Letter Θ

218. Seeing wild animals and associating with them signifies a disturbance caused by enemies.[232]

219. Dreaming of wild animals fighting each other means fear without danger.[233]

---

[224] Drexl (1926, 302 ad loc.) takes the verb συνάξαι differently: "Man könnte auch an συνᾶξαι = 'zerbrechen' denken."

[225] Cf. *Somniale Danielis* ("Beiträge, IV") LI: *clavos colligere vel facere, laborem significat.*

[226] *Somniale Danielis* ("Beiträge, V") 12: *aurigam currentem videre, cum propinquis tuis iram significat.* Brackertz (1993, 256 ad loc.) references the mania that characterised the Hippodrome in Constantinople (especially with respect to the Nica revolt in 532). The classic discussion on this subject remains Cameron 1976; cf. Croke 2005, 71–2 (with n. 79 on 83); Gregory 2005, 121–3, 126–8, 154–5; Ostrogorsky 1969, 66–7. The Church condemned chariot races, and we find such entertainment after the seventh century only in Constantinople itself (where it continued into at least the twelfth century: *LAnt* 493–4): *ODB* 1:412. Dagron (1974, 320–47) discusses the Hippodrome and its significance in Byzantine political and cultural thought; cf. Rautman 2006, 110–13; Treadgold 1997, 165, 169, 171, 181–2, 256, 280, 288, 363–5.

[227] Artemidorus 2.36.

[228] I add "not" on the basis of 203 above and the parallel dreams of Anonymous 94 and *Somniale Danielis* ("Beiträge, V") 131: *sol tenebrosum videre, periculum significat.* A solar eclipse caused great fear and was considered an omen of doom; see John Lydus, *On Omens* 9, and Hephaestion of Thebes, *Astrological Effects* 1.20–22. (I owe these two references to *ODB* 1:672, which discusses eclipses and late Byzantine interest in them.)

[229] This is a variation of 205 above. Cf. *Somniale Danielis* ("Beiträge, V") CCXXVII: *solem vel lunam viderit, letitiam iudicii significat.*

[230] But cf. 204 above.

[231] See Artemidorus 2.36; cf. Achmet 169 on stars falling into the sea (itself a symbol of a king): "If someone dreams of stars falling into the sea, this means destruction of men at the hands of the king; if a king is the dreamer, he will behold deaths of his grandees and subjects."

[232] Cf. *Somniale Danielis* ("Beiträge, IV") CCXIV: *quadrupedem quicumque viderit, anxietatem significat.*

[233] The reason, of course, is that the fighting generates fear in the observer who, however, safely watches from a distance. Perhaps the dream is a reference to animals in the arena. Even

220. Dreaming of wild animals running indicates tumult.[234]

221. Looking at the sea [while standing] on the coast means freedom from spiritual anxiety.[235]

222. Dreaming of the sea being swept by heavy waves indicates confusion and distress.[236]

223. Making an artistic representation of God[237] signifies profit.[238]

224. Dreaming that wild animals are talking points to confusion.[239]

225. Seeing wild animals and going around with them will cause friendship with enemies.[240]

226. Domesticating wild animals indicates becoming friends with enemies.[241]

227. Calling upon God or worshipping Him [means] being set free from every kind of evil situation.[242]

228. Kissing God in your dreams: you will be held accountable for something that you do not expect.

229. Seeing God in any[243] place indicates freedom from spiritual anxiety.[244]

---

though gladiatorial games were prohibited, Byzantines still enjoyed watching animal combats (examples even from the twelfth century): *ODB* 1:101.

[234] Cf. *Somniale Danielis* ("Beiträge, IV") XXIX: *bestias currentes viderit, aliquam turbationem significat.*

[235] Achmet (177) interprets this as denoting the opposite.

[236] *Somniale Danielis* ("Beiträge, V") 89: *mare tempestativum videre, anxietatem grandem significat*; Achmet 177. Artemidorus (2.23) gives a favorable interpretation.

[237] So I take the phrase θεὸν ποιῆσαι. Brackertz (1993) translates similarly: "Gott im Bild darzustellen bringt Segen."

[238] See Achmet 150 for dreams involving icons; for Byzantine icons and their adornments, see Cutler 2002, 565–9; *LAnt* 506–7; Rautman 2006, 260.

[239] Cf. *Somniale Danielis* ("Beiträge, IV") XXXVIII: *bestias loquentes viderit, molestias graves significat*. But Achmet (214) interprets this dream as a good sign; cf. Artemidorus 2.12: "Animals whose tongues have been loosened and that are endowed with human speech signify great good fortune, especially if they say anything auspicious or pleasant. But whatever they say is always the truth and one must believe it. If their message is plain, a man must take heed immediately. If they have spoken in riddles, one must attempt to interpret them."

[240] But cf. 218 above for the opposite interpretation (another example of the author's conflation of different sources).

[241] An obvious analogy; so too *Somniale Danielis* ("Beiträge, IV") XXVIII: *bestias domare qui se viderit, gratiam adversariorum significat*. But cf. *Somniale Danielis* ("Beiträge, V") 26: *beluas vel elefantos domare, molestiam gravem significat*; Artemidorus 4.56.

[242] *Somniale Danielis* ("Beiträge, IV") CCCI.

[243] Perhaps instead of παντὶ we can read πλατεῖ, which is the reading of Anonymous 108.

[244] For a different interpretation, see Achmet 150 (with Mavroudi 2002, 275–6). If we substitute Heracles for God, we have the following dream in *Somniale Danielis* ("Beiträge, IV") CXXX: *Herculem viderit, amicitiam iungit.*

230. A warm[245] sleeveless tunic:[246] this too [signifies] disturbance.

231. Burning incense means bitterness.[247]

232. If [you dream that] the door of your house collapses or is taken off its hinges, you will lose your wife.[248]

233. Dreaming of having harvested, or being in the process of harvesting, the summer crops indicates a good deed.[249]

Beginning of the Letter I

234. Collecting or eating dried figs signifies a very great deed.[250]

235. Dreaming of a textile being woven without a man or woman [operating the loom] means good news.[251]

236. Sitting on a white horse indicates additional capital.[252]

---

[245] It is not clear how θερμός works here; perhaps we can translate as "for use in the summer."

[246] Brackertz (1993, 256 ad loc.) glosses κολόβιον as follows: "Kolobion: eine ärmellose Tunika, die als Obergewand diente." This tunic could be short-sleeved and colored with stripes. Oppenheim (1931, 95–103) associates it with Egyptian monks.

[247] Cf. Achmet 130.

[248] Artemidorus 2.10: "Burning doors portend the death of a wife and signify that the dreamer's life is in danger. Of these, the door with the bolt-pin signifies a free-born wife, whereas the door that is held signifies a slave." Achmet 145: "If someone dreams that after an earthquake there was a falling of doors and a breaking of wood or a collapse of the wall enclosing the house …, the fall of the door denotes the death of the legitimate wives of the master of the house."

[249] See Achmet 200. For harvesting methods in Byazantium, see Haldon 2005, 32; Rautman 2006, 173–4, 178–80.

[250] See Artemidorus 1.73; cf. Achmet 241: "If someone dreams that he was gathering ripe figs from a fig tree, he will receive from an exceedingly wealthy man money and wealth in accordance with the number of seeds inside the figs; but if the figs were not ripe, he will receive strife and a lawsuit from such a man." A negative interpretation for figs appears in *Somniale Danielis* ("Beiträge, IV") CXII and CXIII. Brackertz (1993, 256 ad loc.) comments how figs were considered conducive to dreaming. Dalby (2003, 200) records a directive of eating dried figs with walnuts and rue before eating a main meal as a protection against poisoning; see also Dalby 1996, 79 for figs as a metaphor for the sexual organs.

[251] Cf. Artemidorus 3.36: "A loom that stands in a vertical position signifies movements and trips abroad, since a woman who plies this loom must ply back and forth. A horizontal loom is a symbol of delay, since the women who ply this loom are seated. It is always better to see a loom on which the yarn is just beginning to be spun than one on which the cloth is ready to be cut. For the loom resembles life. And so a loom that is just beginning to be plied suggests a long life. A loom that has cloth which is ready to be cut indicates a short life."

For Byzantine looms, see *LAnt* 746–7, where two types are discussed: the horizontal loom with horizontal warp (used for complicated patterns), and the upright loom with vertical warp (this type was either a warp-pointed loom or a two-beam upright loom). The vertical loom is described in Judges 16:13. See also Muthesius 2002, 152–8; Rautman 2006, 106, 192–3.

[252] *Somniale Danielis* ("Beiträge, IV") LXXXVII: *equo albo sedere, eventum bonum significat*; cf. *Somniale Danielis* ("Beiträge, V") 55: *equos albos habere vel sedere, iocunditatem*

237. Sitting on a reddish-brown horse means unexpected profit.[253]

238. A dream of catching fish means scaring up an enemy.[254]

239. Wearing or seeing clothes made entirely of silk means envy.[255]

240. Owning different kinds of clothes points to the same thing.

241. Washing clothes signifies release from shame.[256]

242. Dreaming of having or touching soiled clothes indicates something evil.[257]

---

significat. Achmet (231) considers the king's white horse symbolic of the queen. Brackertz (1993, 245 ad Germanus 100) refers to the use of white horses in Roman triumphal processions and in Greek religious processions. For Byzantine imperial triumphs, see Croke 2005, 78 (with nn. 140–43 on 85); *ODB* 3:2121–2; Ousterhout 1998, 115 (with nn. 1–3); Rautman 2006, 109; Treadgold 1997, 108. Horses and mules were raised for the essential services of the Empire (public postal system, army, transport system): Haldon 2005, 32; *LAnt* 498–9.

[253] Cf. *Somniale Danielis* ("Beiträge, V") 56: *equos rufos vel baios habere, bonum nuntium significat*.

[254] Probably an analogy to how fish are scared at nets thrown into the water (cf. Manuel 1 below). This is also a favorable dream in Artemidorus 2.14 and 2.18. But cf. Achmet 177: "If a king dreams that he was catching fish or was drawing them up with nets from the bottom of the sea or gave fish to some people or even stored them somewhere, he will enrich those under his sway or will pile up [his wealth]."

The word for fish (ἰχθύς) and its pictorial representation played a very extensive role in Christian iconography, appearing, e.g., on sarcophagi, gravestones, and paintings: *ODB* 2:788. The word was thought to be comprised of a series of five words, Ἰησοῦς Χρίστος Θεοῦ Ὑιὸς Σωτήρ (Jesus Christ, the son of God, Savior). Fish were an important part of the Byzantine diet; those taken from streams and rivers were much preferred over those drawn from the sea. See Croke 2005, 70; Dagron 2002, 447, 457–9; Dalby 1996, 66–75; Kazhdan 1997, 55; Koukoules 1948–57, 5:79–86 (331–43 for methods of fishing); Lefort 2002, 263; Morrisson and Sodini 2002, 200; Rautman 2006, 103, 171–2.

[255] But this dream means wealth in Achmet 219. See Brackertz's discussion (1993, 256–7 ad loc.) of silk as the object of praise in Constantinople; for the importation of silk from China, *ODB* 3:1896–7, 1898. Fuller treatment in *LAnt* 241–2 (wealth could be publicly displayed through patterned silks) and 695–6, with bibliography; more recently, Dagron 2002, 438–41; Muthesius 2002, 147–52, 165–6; Rautman 2006, 48, 106–107. After Justinian smuggled silkworm eggs from China (recorded by Theophanes of Byzantium and Procopius of Caesarea: *ODB* 3:2063), silk production became a privatised, state-run industry; see Lopez 1945; cf. *ODB* 3:1898 (silk routes) and Rautman 2006, 186. The interpretation of the dream here is based on the fact that Byzantine silk was coveted both in Byzantium and abroad, with silk garments serving as valuable gifts in diplomacy. Thebes was the center of the silk industry in Greece itself: Treadgold 1997, 703 (with n. 31 on 962). Theban products were highly prized; for example, the Seljuks insisted on only these silks (*ODB* 3:2032).

[256] Achmet 229. But cf. *Somniale Danielis* ("Beiträge, IV") CLVIII: *linea vestimenta lavare videre, dampnum significat*. Artemidorus 2.4: "If a man dreams that he is washing his own clothes or the clothes of others, this signifies that he will shake off some difficult situation in his life, since the clothes are also throwing off their dirt. It signifies, moreover, that secrets will be revealed and learned." For the washing of garments in Constantinople, see Rautman 2006, 49–50.

[257] Achmet 156; cf. 172.

243. Flying without wings is good for those living abroad, but unfortunate for anyone else.[258]

244. Dreaming of oneself as strong means profit in one's activities.[259]

245. Catching sight of a horseman means quarrels and displeasures.[260]

246. Sitting on a black horse signifies loss.[261]

247. Sitting on an Arabian steed[262] signifies loss.[263]

248. [Dreaming that one is] running with horses and being pursued by them means untimely quarrels.[264]

249. Being dressed in beautiful clothes signifies delight.

250. Owning silk or purple clothes means envy.[265]

251. Owning [or] wearing clean clothes means good [opportunities].

252. A loom that is being plied means good news.[266]

253. A man plying a loom will commit adultery with a married woman.[267]

---

[258] Cf. Artemidorus 2.68; Achmet 161; *Somniale Danielis* ("Beiträge, V") 144: *volare qui se viderit, locum mutare significat.*

[259] See Achmet 70.

[260] Artemidorus (1.56) also considers this an evil dream, provided the rider is coming out of the city.

[261] *Somniale Danielis* ("Beiträge, V") 57: *equos nigros vel fallicios sedere, anxietatem cum dampno vel detrimentum significat*; cf. Achmet 231.

[262] Drexl (1926, 303 ad loc.) glosses as follows: "Ich ziehe ψαρῷ als Gegenüberstellung zu μελανῷ in 246 vor, obwohl es ψάρας = ,arabisches Pferd' gibt." It is not clear whether the Byzantine term "Arabian horse" meant a breed of horse or animals that were imported from the caliphate: *ODB* 2:948. In modern Greek ψαρός means "grey," and so it is not certain how the word should be translated here. Below, in Anonymous 115, I use the translation "grey" because of the lateness of the manuscript; here, if we assume an earlier date for Daniel, "Arabian" may be more appropriate.

[263] Perhaps the interpretation is based on the numerous losses that the Arabs inflicted on the Byzantines.

[264] Horses assumed an ever-growing role as the Byzantine period progressed. This was due to the increased importance of calvary as opposed to infantry, and to the fact that horses supplanted oxen and mules in ploughing, working in mills, and pulling wagons and carts: *ODB* 2:948.

[265] But cf. Artemidorus 2.3 and Achmet 157. For purple and its role in Byzantine life, see Muthesius 2002, 158–60 (on the purple dye industry); *ODB* 2:1759–60; Reinhold 1970.

[266] Cf. Achmet 161.

[267] The interpretation could be based on the sexual imagery of the loom moving while being plied. Moreover, a man is doing the plying, which is contrary to cultural practice. Artemidorus wrote that custom is one of the six elements that an interpreter must analyse, and then with respect to conformity with or contrariness to culture.. Since the action in the dream above is contrary to custom, we have a negative interpretation, with the sexuality based perhaps on the dream action. In Genesis, Chapter 40, the dreams of the cupbearer and the baker were both consistent with their everyday activities, and so it was easy for Joseph to associate the contents of their dreams with the interpretation. See also Oberhelman 1993, 141–2.

Beginning of the Letter K

254. For one to be on fire without smoke signifies love for a female prostitute along with profit.[268]

255. Seeing one's clothes on fire signifies unexpected profit.[269]

256. Being beaten is good.[270]

257. Eating parsley[271] points to a shameful piece of news.[272]

258. Eating gourds means illness.[273]

259. Seeing or reading imperial edicts[274] signifies extremely successful opportunities.[275]

260. Drinking spiced wine signifies bad luck.[276]

---

[268] But Achmet (158) interprets this dream as gold gained through wrongdoing.

[269] But an evil dream in Achmet 158; cf. *Somniale Danielis* ("Beiträge, V") 145: *vestimenta combusta videre, deceptionem significat.*

[270] *Somniale Danielis* ("Beiträge, IV") CCXLII: *vapulare in somnis, bonum prosequitur.* But Artemidorus (2.48) reverses this: "It is only auspicious to strike those over whom one rules, with the exception of one's wife. For if she is beaten, it means that she is committing adultery. But when other men are beaten, it indicates benefits for the person who is dealing the blows." Achmet (211) agrees with Daniel; cf. 218: "If someone dreams that a friend beat him with whips, he will have a profitable amount of gold coins in proportion to the number of blows; and if the person who beat him is a person of power, the dreamer will get some of his power. If a king dreams that he ordered someone to be beaten with whips, that person will find great joy and wealth in accordance with the number of blows. If the king dreams that he himself beat someone with straps or whips, that man will receive from the king very great and distinguished honor over and beyond boasting. If the king dreams that he personally beat someone with his staff, that man will receive happiness and power from the king's first minister with the king's knowledge and consent." For this line of interpretation in Arabic texts, see Mavroudi 2002, 318.

[271] For κοδίμε<ν>τον, see DuCange 1688, s.v. "κοδίμεντα"; Drexl (1926) translates as "Petersilie." Cf. Dalby 2003, 205.

[272] But a favorable interpretation in both Artemidorus 1.77 and Achmet 204.

[273] Cf. Artemidorus 1.67; Achmet 201.

[274] Brackertz (1993, 257 ad loc.) comments on this word: "Griech. *kodikellos*, eine Urkunde, die jenen Ehrenämtern beigegeben wurde, welche die byzantinischen Kaiser verliehen." Codicils that appointed someone to a high office or granted him a title were placed inside ivory diptychs: *ODB* 1:475–6. This practice may explain the interpretation here.

[275] *Somniale Danielis* ("Beiträge, IV") LXXI: *codicellos cuiusque rei accipere vel legere aut legente audire, felicitatem temporis significat.*

[276] But cf. Artemidorus 1.66; Achmet 244: "If someone dreams that he drank wine spiced with cinnamon, he will find harsh but noble power in proportion to how much he drank; and if he became drunk, he will find wealth." It was common for Byzantines to conclude a meal with spiced wines, since these drinks were thought to aid digestion: Dalby 2003, 25, 51, 180–82 (12 recipes for various kinds of spiced wines); cf. Dalby 1996, 192–5; Koukoules 1948–57, 5:130–35; Rautman 2006, 103. Wine could also be made from honey, dates, apples, and pears: Dalby 2003, 86–93; *LAnt* 455. For the wine merchants in Constantinople, see Dagron 2002, 459–60; Rautman 2006, 103–5, 181. Morrisson and Cheynet (2002, 833–5) give the prices for wine from the year 301 to 1439. The interpretation here resembles the one in *Somniale Danielis* ("Beiträge, IV") CCXLVI: *vinum bibere, infirmitatem significat.*

261. Playing cymbals or citharas means quarrels.[277]

262. If you hurl a javelin by hand, take care lest you suffer something evil.

263. Sitting on a camel signifies profit.[278]

264. Dreaming of screeching crows or ravens points to a profitable action.[279]

265. Playing the cithara[280] indicates an unlucky day.[281]

266. Seeing or having red cherries is good for merchants,[282] but evil for anyone else.[283]

267. Seeing or handling rabbit meat: you will get someone else's property.[284]

268. Seeing or handling beef means displeasure and sorrow.[285]

269. Crying in one's dream means something good.[286]

The Byzantines used extensively spices such as parsley, white pepper, mustard, sage, ginger, cinnamon, cumin, mint, and fennel. For fuller lists, see Dalby 1996, 85–7, 137–42, and 2003, 38–52 (including a discussion of how spices were used in conjunction with medical humoral theory); *LAnt* 454; *ODB* 3:1937–8; Rautman 2006, 95–6, 105 (with n. 30 on 118).

[277]   Achmet 129; cf. *Somniale Danielis* ("Beiträge, V") 39: *citharam cum cymbalis audire, verba inania et otiosa significat*; *Somniale Danielis* ("Beiträge, IV") LXXIV: *cimbala aut salteria aut corda tangere, lites significat*. Cithara players were denied baptism and even excommunicated: *ODB* 2:1427.

[278]   But cf. Achmet 234 and 235, where mercantile camels are considered a symbol of acquiring power and slaves. *LAnt* (361) comments: "To be paraded on camel-back through the city was a common punishment, the height of the animal providing visibility and its awkward stride inflicting exquisite humiliation on those accustomed (in the west) to showing their status by riding on horseback." See also Cavallo 1997b, 6 (for the humiliation of Andronicus I Comnenus); cf. *ODB* 1:368.

The one-hump camel came to dominate the camel industry, thanks to Arab traders who crossbred one- and two-hump camels in order to produce strong camels for the Silk Route (the interpretation above is perhaps based on an association of camels with commerce and trade): *LAnt* 361. See this same entry for a discussion of the impact that camels had on urban city-planning (camels could navigate narrow winding streets, versus the broad and straight streets needed for horse- and ox-drawn wagons).

[279]   But Achmet (290) considers crows and ravens symbolic of liars, extorters, and greedy foreigners.

[280]   I emend καθαρίζειν to κιθαρίζειν, as we read in Anonymous 141.

[281]   Also an unfavorable sign in Achmet 252.

[282]   LSJ (s.h.v.) translates πραγματευτής as "business representative," equating it to the Latin *actor*; cf. Lampe 1976, s.h.v., whom I follow.

[283]   But cf. Artemidorus 1.73.

[284]   Achmet (276) says that the wealth will come from a prostitute or a woman "plastered with cosmetics".

[285]   But cf. Artemidorus 1.70, where beef, since it is so cheap, symbolises small businesses; and Achmet 237, where it is interpreted as wealth that will come to the dreamer from a very great man and as the begetting of a son. For beef as a part of the Byzantine diet, see Morrisson and Sodini 2002, 199.

[286]   *Somniale Danielis* ("Beiträge, LV") CCII: *plorare in somniis, gaudium significat*.

270.　Seeing or eating roasted meats indicates loss.[287]

271.　Holding κατάφανα[288] signifies something good.

272.　Eating red cherries means illness.

273.　Being hailed in a dream but [not] being able to answer back means hindrance; but if you do answer back, this is good.

274.　Seeing an obstacle in a dream is good.[289]

275.　Beautifying or washing oneself is good for anyone.[290]

276.　A dream of lit wax candles signifies good opportunities.[291]

277.　Seeing or sitting on camels or being chased by them indicates violence at the hands of *dunatoi*.[292]

278.　Chasing after camels signifies quarrels.

279.　Dreaming of having a hernia: you will fall into many evils.[293]

280.　Dreaming that one has long flowing hair signifies profit.[294]

281.　Having your head cropped short means loss.[295]

---

[287]　So too Achmet 158; but Artemidorus (1.70) considers it a favorable sign. People of all social classes ate meat (Dagron 2002, 446–7), although consumption was highest among the upper classes and involved lamb and mutton, followed by goat and beef; pork and lard were considered the food of the lowest classes. See Koukoules 1948–57, 5:47–62; Rautman 2006, 103. Meats were cooked with generous amounts of leeks, onions, and garlic: *ODB* 2:1326.

[288]　I can find no such word; very likely an error in the text. The closest and most reasonable word is κατάφρακτα, or a coat of mail (for which see *LAnt* 316; *ODB* 1:183, 2:1114; Rautman 2006, 208–9), but this is only a guess. Drexl (who comments [1926, 304 ad loc.] "Kann ich nicht belegen") and Brackertz 1993 (who translates the line as "... besitzen bringt Glück") also are at a loss.

[289]　An example of antinomy in interpreting a symbol (cf. 269 above).

[290]　But this is not a good dream in Artemidorus 4.41.

[291]　Cf. *Somniale Danielis* ("Beiträge, IV") LXV: *ceram vel cereos viderit, gaudium significat*; cf. *Somniale Danielis* ("Beiträge, V") 32: *cereos facere aut candelabra illuminare, gaudium et iocunditatem significat*; cf. Achmet 129. The Byzantines preferred candles to olive oil lamps (for which see Morrisson and Sodini 2002, 203–4), starting in the seventh century: *ODB* 1:371; Rautman 2006, 105–6.

[292]　So too Achmet 234; cf. *Somniale Danielis* ("Beiträge, IV") LVII: *camelos videre & ab eis se viderit infestare, litem significat*.

[293]　So too Artemidorus 3.45; Achmet (106) interprets this as a profitable dream.

[294]　*Somniale Danielis* ("Beiträge, IV") CCL: *capillum se videre, incrementum significat*; see also Achmet 18 and 21; Artemidorus 1.18.
At first, the eastern Greeks wore their hair short (following the command of Paul in 1 Corinthians 11:14), but later they adopted a longer hair style. Hair demonstrated social status, and so the loss of hair, like the loss of beards, was a type of punishment. See the overall discussion in *ODB* 2:899; Treadgold 1997, 465, 473, 476, 486, 593.

[295]　So Artemidorus 1.22 (though this dream is good "for priests of the Egyptian gods, for buffoons, and for those whose custom it is to shave the head" [since the act is in accordance with custom or habit, not contrary to it, the interpretation is good]); also Achmet 21 and 31.

282. Having gray hair signifies gain.[296]
283. Sitting in a traveling coach[297] signifies illness.[298]
284. Safely coming down[299] from a slope is good.
285. Seeing or touching a bug indicates oppressive days.[300]
286. To fall off a cliff signifies misfortune.[301]
287. Eating raw meat signifies grief.[302]
288. Roasted meat, when dreamt of, signifies something good.[303]
289. Washing your head clean means freedom from every trouble.[304]
290. Dreaming of beautifying one's head signifies something good.[305]
291. Hearing dogs barking signifies an ambush laid by enemies.[306]
292. Dreaming of playing with dogs means friendship with your enemies.[307]

---

[296] *Somniale Danielis* ("Beiträge, IV") XLVII: *caput album habere, lucrum significat*; cf. Achmet 18: "If someone dreams that although young he was partly gray-haired, he will come into honor. If he dreams that he was already gray-haired and then got more gray hairs, he will increase even more in honor." The interpretation is based on the analogy of age (gray hair) ~ honor/respect.

[297] So I translate καρροῦχα; Brackertz (1993) translates as "Führwagen."

[298] For the interpretation cf. *Somniale Danielis* ("Beiträge, IV") CCXXXII: *sedere in somnis, infirmitatem significat.*

[299] I read κατέρχεσθαι for κρατεῖσθαι; cf. Anonymous 136.

[300] Cf. Artemidorus 3.8: "Bugs are symbols of cares and anxieties. For bugs, like anxieties, also keep people awake at night. Furthermore, they signify that discontent and dissatisfaction will arise among certain members of the household, especially among the women." Achmet (295) also gives a negative interpretation of bugs.

[301] Cf. *Somniale Danielis* ("Beiträge, IV") CCLXXII: *si videris, quod de altissimo cadas desubtus, ad pauperem bonum & ad divitem malum significat.*

[302] Artemidorus 1.70: "To eat raw flesh, however, is not at all auspicious. For it signifies the loss of part of our possessions, since our nature is unable to digest raw flesh"; cf. Achmet 240: "If someone dreams that he ate raw goat meat, he will fall ill and receive punishment from the authorities; if he ate raw mutton, he will slander and defame men, and so let the dreamer fear God and stand away from his evil deeds."

[303] In Achmet's dreambook, eating cooked meat is good in nearly every instance, no matter the meat's source, e.g., humans (87, 89), horse (230), cow (237), deer (240), lion (267), rabbit (276), cat (278), pig (279), snake (281), scorpion (283), eagle (284), peacock (287), and crane (288). See also Artemidorus 1.70.

[304] *Somniale Danielis* ("Beiträge, IV") LIV: *caput lavare, ab omni metu & omni periculo liberabitur.*

[305] Cf. 275 above.

[306] So too Artemidorus 2.11; Achmet 277; *Somniale Danielis* ("Beiträge, V") 45: *kanes latrantes videre vel ab eis infestare, ab inimicis tuis superabis*; *Somniale Danielis* ("Beiträge, IV") LII: *canes latrantes viderit, vel eis infestare, inimici tui te superare querunt significat.* In Byzantine iconography, dogs symbolised evil and the devil: *ODB* 1:644.

[307] Artemidorus 2.11; Achmet 277; *Somniale Danielis* ("Beiträge, V") 46: *kanes tecum ludere, gratias cum adversariis significat.* Cf. *Somniale Danielis* ("Beiträge, IV") LIII: *canes*

293.   If the soles of your shoes fall off, this means hindrance.[308]

294.   Crying in one's dream signifies joy.

295.   To be in flames signifies separation from one's wife.[309]

296.   Seeing lit wax tapers or handling them means good news.[310]

297.   [Dreaming of] extinguished wax tapers signifies something evil.[311]

298.   Dreaming of being deaf means freedom from worry.[312]

299.   Being hailed and not replying is good.[313]

300.   If one dreams that his head has been completely severed, this means loss.[314]

301.   A dream of very many dogs: you will incur many evils.[315]

302.   If you dream of grates[316] or if you seem to be shut up inside them, this signifies evildoing.[317]

303.   Dreaming of being burned alive means constant occupation with business matters.[318]

304.   Wanting to call out but not being able to do so signifies strife.

---

ludere viderit, gratiam significat. Hunting dogs were especially prized by the Byzantines; see the discussion in *ODB* 1:644; Rautman 2006, 56 (with bibliography in n. 20 on 59–60), 80, 184.

[308]   Cf. Artemidorus 2.5; Achmet 226. Three types of shoes were in usage among the Byzantines: high boots, open sandals fastened with leather straps, and shoes covering the feet. Boots were by far the most favored. The emperor wore red shoes; courtiers, black shoes; and laborers, white shoes. See Koukoules 1948–57, 4:395–418; *ODB* 2:795–6.

[309]   Also a negative interpretation in Achmet 158; cf. Artemidorus 2.9.

[310]   So Achmet 159.

[311]   So ibid., 159.

[312]   But cf. Achmet 48: "If someone dreams that he became deaf, [his wife or sister] will fall into spiritual illness through her obstinate sinning; but if he dreams that he was only partially deaf, her illness will likewise be partial."
The dream's interpretation may be based on the analogy that a deaf person is not troubled or concerned by events that occur around him or her.

[313]   The difference here, as opposed to 273, is the absence of μὴ δύνασθαι (not being able [to reply]). The interpretation may be based on the analogy that the person being hailed is of such status and power that he does not feel the need to acknowledge the greeting.

[314]   See Artemidorus 1.35.

[315]   Cf. *Somniale Danielis* ("Beiträge, IV") CCLXXXI: *si videris multos canes, de inimicis tuis te cavere significat.*

[316]   This is how I translate κάγκελλα; the word in modern Greek denotes railings, bars, or a balustrade (such as the balustrade separating the altar area of a basilica from the nave, for which see Sophocles 1975, s.h.v.; *ODB* 3:3023, s.v. "*templon*").

[317]   Cf. *Somniale Danielis* ("Beiträge, IV") LIX: *cancellos viderit aut in eis se reclusum videat, in aliqua calumpnia vel custodia detinetur.*

[318]   Cf. Artemidorus 2.52; Achmet 159.

305. Dreaming of becoming a *comes*[319] is bad for those who are a defendant in legal proceedings.[320]

306. Dreaming of a well-made bed signifies a good [life] with a woman.[321]

307. If you dream of a gold bedstead,[322] this signifies vexation.[323]

308. If you dream of becoming a dog, this means a very long time away from home.

309. Hot coals, when dreamt of, signify the scaring up of an enemy.[324]

310. Carrying jewelry [κόσμια] indicates honor along with envy.[325]

---

[319] I take κόμητα as the accusative of the word κόμης, which is the Byzantine word for the Latin *comes* (count). This was an honorary title used to denote various state offices such as the administration of the central treasury and the administration of the imperial domains; it could also describe military officers. See the discussion in Jones 1964, 1:104–6; *ODB* 1:484–5; Rosser 2001, s.v. "count"; Treadgold 1997, 316.

Brackertz (1993) takes the word much differently, as meaning "being hirsute" ("Zu träumen, man sei von unten bis oben behaart ..."); that is, he takes κόμητα as derived from κομήτης.

[320] A negative interpretation because of antinomy (normally one would want to achieve such a position of authority) or by analogy to the fear or anxiety that one would have when coming face to face with such a powerful person.

[321] The phrase μετὰ γυναικός can go with either the dream or its interpretation; thus, we could also translate as "to see that your bed is nicely spread out with a woman on it." I add "life" on the basis of Anonymous 190 (Κράββατον ἐστρωμένον καλῶς ἰδεῖν ζωὴν καλὴν μετὰ γυναικὸς δηλοῖ).

For the dream, cf. *Somniale Danielis* ("Beiträge, V") 87: *lectum suum formosum videre, uxorem fidelem accipiat*. Artemidorus 1.74: "A cushion, a couch, and all things pertaining to the bed indicate the dreamer's wife and his whole life. ... The outer rails of the bedstead, especially, signify the wife." Achmet (222) offers this series of analogies and associations of bed/mattress and woman: "If someone dreams that he got another mattress, he will get another wife. If he dreams that he fell asleep on a mattress in someone else's house, if he knows the homeowner, he will seduce that man's wife; if he does not know him, he will enter into fornication. If he dreams that he went off somewhere after tying up his mattress, he will leave his wife by going on a trip and on his return will discover her to have been chaste; and if he dreams that his mattress thickened and puffed out, he will find on his return that she has become pregnant through him. If he dreams that he owned an unfamiliar mattress, he will find among foreigners a woman analogous to the mattress's beauty and size and to the bedspread on it." The bed, on the other hand, symbolizes men for the following reason (222): "If [someone] dreams that a familiar or unfamiliar mattress was laying on [his bed] and that he was lying on it, he will find great power and joy: for the bed under him is made of wood and wood symbolises very powerful men; and however long he was on the bed is how long he will be exalted."

[322] So I translate κρεβάτι (κρεββάτι in modern Greek). Brackertz (1993) simply translates as "Bett."

[323] But cf. Artemidorus 1.74; *Somniale Danielis* ("Beiträge, IV") CLXVIII.

[324] Cf. the dream of eating coals in *Somniale Danielis* ("Beiträge, V") 48: *kardones comedere, inimici tui de te male loquentur*. But coals are a positive dream symbol in Achmet 158.

[325] Artemidorus (2.5) interprets this dream as auspicious for women, but inauspicious for men; cf. Achmet 256. For jewelry during Byzantine times, see Rautman 2006, 48–9, 263–4.

311. Flying downwards: take care lest you suffer loss.[326]

312. Snapping a branch off a tree [means] the renouncing of a friendship.[327]

313. Eating lion meat signifies [a lawsuit] with a legal adversary.[328]

314. Swimming signifies release from many evils.[329]

315. Handling meats means oppressive days and quarrels.

316. Receiving a young girl indicates increase in honor.[330]

317. Seeing dogs or being chased by them signifies hatred.[331]

318. Seeing or petting a ram is advantageous for those who work in finances, but evil for anyone else.[332]

319. Seeing or handling or eating human flesh indicates [getting] someone else's property.[333]

320. Seeing or handling or eating pork signifies motion in one's business.[334]

Beginning of the Letter Λ

321. Fresh chickpeas signify being penetrated phallically.[335]

322. Dreaming that a lion is approaching you in a hostile way points to an enemy.[336]

---

[326] See Artemidorus 2.68; Achmet 161.

[327] The interpretation is based on the analogies of snapping ~ severing, and tree ~ man.

[328] But in Achmet 267 the dream means that the dreamer will get wealth and power from a king, and will trample down his enemy.

[329] So too Achmet 174. But cf. *Somniale Danielis* ("Beiträge, IV") CCLXIII: *natare se videre, dampnum significat*; Artemidorus 1.64 and 2.27.

[330] Achmet 127 and 128; cf. *Somniale Danielis* ("Beiträge, IV") CXCVIII: *puellas accipere more, bonum tempus significat.*

[331] Achmet 277.

[332] But this is a positive dream in Achmet 240, where rams are interpreted as power and wealth; cf. Artemidorus 2.12, where rams are associated with kings or magistrates (cf. 1.70).

[333] So too Achmet 87 and 89; cf. Artemidorus 1.70.

[334] Pigs are not interpreted favorably in the Byzantine dreambooks; cf. *Somniale Danielis* ("Beiträge, V") 121: *porcos videre aut plumbum tractare, infirmitatem magnam significat*; and *Somniale Danielis* ("Beiträge, IV") CCX: *porcos viderit, infirmitatem significat.* But Artemidorus (1.70) considers eating pork the most auspicious of all dreams involving the eating of meats; cf. Mavroudi 2002, 344.

[335] I take the word μαλακία in the sense of someone who is a passive partner in homosexual relations (μαλακός), which is how ancient oneirocritic writers, especially Artemidorus, used the word; cf. 357 below. Achmet (204) interprets chickpeas as indicative of sorrows and anxieties. For λαθύριον (chickpea), see Stephanus 1954, s.h.v. Chickpeas were often eaten with olive oil and ground cumin (Dalby 2003, 210), or as a dessert if roasted (Dalby 1996, 90).

[336] Achmet 267; cf. Artemidorus 2.12; *Somniale Danielis* ("Beiträge, IV") CLXII: *leonem infestare, inimici seditionem significat.* In Byzantine art, the lion symbolised Jesus or the emperor, since both conquer their adversaries; but since the lion was considered a wild beast that roared, it

323. Dreaming that a wolf is approaching you in a hostile way means that an enemy will attack you.[337]

324. Dreaming of being stoned to death signifies being occupied in many business matters.[338]

325. A dream of brigands or evil men signifies profit.[339]

326. A lit lamp, when dreamt of, signifies profit.[340]

327. Dreaming of the plague:[341] be on your guard against official orders.[342]

328. Collecting bacon signifies effeminancy in your actions.[343]

329. Handling bacon signifies death for one of your relatives.[344]

---

could also symbolise evil men. Once the southern provinces of the Empire were lost, Byzantines rarely saw lions. See the discussion in *ODB* 2:1231–2.

[337] So too Achmet 274; cf. Artemidorus 2.12: "A wolf also signifies a violent enemy, rapacious and wicked, who attacks one in the open."

[338] But Artemidorus (3.48) interprets this dream as being slandered or undertaking a trip abroad.

[339] Cf. ibid., 3.2. Brigandage had political overtones in the Byzantine Empire, as many brigands were soldiers (former or active) or peasants in revolt: Bartusis 1981; *LAnt* 330 (late Roman period); *ODB* 1:325.

[340] Artemidorus 2.9: "A lamp burning brightly in a house is good. For it signifies an increase of fortune and wealth for everyone, marriage for those who are unmarried, and health for the sick"; cf. *Somniale Danielis* ("Beiträge, IV") CLXV: *luminaria se viderit, securitatem significat.*

[341] The first attack of the plague in Constantinople occurred in 541–44; see Allen 1979; Croke 2005, 71; Geyer 2002, 40–41; Laiou 2002b, 49–50; Morrisson and Sodini 2002, 193–5; Treadgold 1997, 196–207, 211–13, 214–23, 229–41, 246–58, 276–9, 298–9, 402–5. The fullest treatment is Horden 2005, where the plague is identified as EMP (early medieval pandemic) or bubonic plague (*Yersinia pestis*). The Black Death hit Constantinople in the mid-fourteenth century: *ODB* 3:1681; Treadgold 1997, 773, 806, 841–4 (where it is commented that perhaps a third of all the people in the Byzantine Empire died from the plague).

[342] Κέλευσις = the Latin *iussum.*

[343] But *Somniale Danielis* ("Beiträge, IV") CLVII: *lardum trectare, aliquis de parentibus eius morietur.*

[344] Brackertz (1993, 230–31 ad his Nicephorus 26) comments on *lardum* and other Latin loan words in the Byzantine dreambooks: "Das lateinische Element hat in der Gebrauchssprache der Byzantiner, sowohl in der gesprochenen wie auch in der geschriebenen, eine Rolle gespielt, so an unserer Stelle *armata* = *arma*; ebenso *kandela* = *candela* (Nikephoros 147), *lardos* = *lardum* (Daniel 328. 329), *sandalion* = *sandalium* (Germanos 217), *kodikelloi* = *codicilli* (Daniel 259), *karrucha* = *carrus* (Daniel 283), *karbuna* = *carbones* (Daniel 309) und öfter. Latein, das bis weit ins 6. Jahrhundert Amtssprache der obersten Reichsbehörden und des Hofes war, wurde unter Kaiser Herakleios I. (610–641) durch das Griechische abgelöst." (I remind the reader again that Brackertz followed Drexl's edition of Nicephorus for his translation and commentary, and so his references to Nicephorus are always at variance with my own references, which are taken from Guidorizzi's authoritative text.) For the use of Latin by the Byzantines, see also Croke 2005, 73–6 (a discussion of the extensive use of Latin during the time of Justinian); Dagron 1969; Fögen 1998, 12–16, 19–22; Triantaphyllides 1909 (old, but quite useful).

330. Dreaming of a running lion means a profitable business matter.[345]

331. Collecting stones[346] signifies illness.[347]

332. Dreaming of oneself as being dressed in white garments signifies joy.[348]

333. Picking fresh vegetables signifies effeminacy in your actions.[349]

334. Dreaming of being stoned to death means an accusation from one's enemies.[350]

335. Throwing a stone signifies loss.[351]

336. Seeing a pit[352] and then avoiding it signifies being freed from great trouble.[353]

Beginning of the Letter M

337. If you dream of bees in your house, this signifies enemies.[354]

338. Dreaming of bees coming out of your house: keep a lookout for enemies.

---

[345]   *Somniale Danielis* ("Beiträge, IV") CLX: *leonem currentem viderit, expeditionem negotii significat.*

[346]   It is hard to say whether λίθοι here means "precious gems" or simply "stones."

[347]   The interpretation, perhaps, is based on the fact that λίθος could also describe a stone in the kidney or in the bladder. For the dream cf. *Somniale Danielis* ("Beiträge, IV") CLXVI: *lapides mittere, egritudinem significat.*

[348]   See Mavroudi 2002, 366–7 for similar interpretations in Syriac Christian and Arabic dream literature.

[349]   But this is a favorable dream image in Achmet 204; cf. Artemidorus 1.67.

[350]   But cf. 324 above for a different interpretation of the same dream.

[351]   Cf. Artemidorus 3.48: "If the dreamer throws stones at someone, it signifies that he will speak badly about the man. But if someone throws stones at the dreamer, it indicates that the dreamer himself will be slandered. For stones resemble indecorous and contentious words." The analogy of throwing stones ~ throwing hurtful words is straightforward.

[352]   The word λάκκος can mean either a pit or a cistern. Brackertz (1993) translates the word in both ways: "Befindet sich jemand in einer Grube oder Zisterne ...." For the dream, cf. *Somniale Danielis* ("Beiträge, V") 115: *puteum fodere vel in eum cadere, calumniam gravem significat.*

[353]   See Artemidorus 2.24; Achmet 142.

[354]   Cf. *Somniale Danielis* ("Beiträge, IV") CCLXXXV: *si videris apes volare in domo tua, desertionem significat.* Cf. Achmet 282 on wasps: "If someone dreams that he saw yellow wasps entering a field or land, an enemy will come there on a predatory raid. And if he dreams that the wasps stung the inhabitants, the enemy will harm the inhabitants by analogy to the stinging; but if they stung no one, the enemy will do no harm whatsoever. If he dreams that the inhabitants drove the wasps away with smoke, the enemy will be driven off disgracefully and the inhabitants will be victorious."

Bee-keeping was a major source of sugar for the Byzantines; sugar taken from sugarcane was imported from Arabic lands, but was little used. See Kazhdan 1997, 56; Koukoules 1951 (cf. Koukoules 1948–57, 5:296–309); Laiou 1977, 30–31; Rautman 2006, 186 (with n. 22 on 197). Beekeeping also supplied wax for candles.

339. [Dreaming that] bees are brought to you signifies a rising-up of enemies.[355]

340. Eating honey signifies grief.[356]

341. Speaking with an eparch[357] signifies confusion.[358]

342. Flying with wings signifies a sea voyage.[359]

343. Going to bed with one's own wife is good for someone away on a trip.[360]

344. Going to bed with your daughter or sister indicates separation.[361]

---

[355] Artemidorus 2.22; but this is a good dream in Achmet 282. Cf. *Somniale Danielis* ("Beiträge, IV") CLXXXII: *mel accipere se viderit, caveat ne ab alio seducatur significat.*

[356] But this is a very auspicious dream in Artemidorus 1.72 and 5.83; also Achmet 241; see too the Arabic texts cited in Mavroudi 2002, 230. For honey in the Byzantine diet, see Laiou 2002b, 53; *ODB* 1:5 (for its use in abortions); Rautman 2006, 104–5, 186 (cf. 52 for its use as contraceptive).

[357] The word ἔπαρχος referred to a governor, in particular the governor of the city of Constantinople. (Among the Romans, the office was the position of urban prefect.) The eparch was the leading judge of the Byzantine emperor's tribunal. His duties included overseeing the criminal justice system of the city, supervising commercial and industrial activity, and taking care of all spectacles; he also looked after the guilds. See the extended discussion in Guilland 1980; also *ODB* 1:704; Ostrogorsky 1969, 249–50, who cites references that call the eparch "the father of the city"; Rautman 2006, 68–9, 75, 76, 90, 98–100; Rosser 2001, s.vv. "Eparch of the City" and "Book of the Eparch."

[358] A somewhat similar dream is in Achmet 126 (if we substitute "king" for "governor"), but there we have a very favorable interpretation: "If someone dreams that he spoke with a king he recognised, if he should remember the words, let him with full confidence hold on to them: for a king is symbolic of Christ and therefore never utters lies." Cf. also *Somniale Danielis* ("Beiträge, IV") CLXIII.

[359] So too Achmet 160. Brackertz (1993, 258 ad loc.) notes the nautical pun: "Wortspiel. Griech. *pteron* bedeutet sowohl Flügel als auch Segel, Ruder."

[360] But cf. *Somniale Danielis* ("Beiträge, IV") LXX: *cum coniuge sua concumbere, anxietatem significat.* Artemidorus (1.78) considers this a good dream, provided that the woman is submissive and willingly yields. The analogy is straightforward: the dream foretells that the dreamer will once again be in his own bed.

As I have commented earlier, despite pages of dreams in Achmet involving men having sex with other women, men, even animals and birds, a woman does not dream of having sex nor does she take any initiative. The closest to the latter is Chap. 128: "If someone dreams that a beautiful and well-dressed woman, either his own wife or someone else's, was in his house amorously playing with him and that he reciprocated, if he is a king or noble, he will have a year that will turn out in every respect according to his wishes." See also Mavroudi 2007, 57–60.

[361] Cf. Achmet 128: "If someone dreams that he had sex with his mother or sister, he will do good to a worthless man in a moment of self-censure and repentance"; *Somniale Danielis* ("Beiträge, IV") LXVII: *cum sorore concumbere, dampnum significat.*

For incest in Byzantium, see *ODB* 2:991–2; Vinson 2002, 418–19; Zhishman 1964, 215–53. Artemidorus calls incest and oral–genital sex "sexual actions in opposition to convention." Regarding incest with a family member (either male or female), the dream results generally are unfavorable, although this may not be the case, for example, if the male penetrator in the dream derives pleasure or profit from the intercourse. Dreams involving oral sex, however, never foretell goodness, not even for the person being fellated, since such dreams denote

345.   Being beaten with iron signifies sorrow.[362]

346.   Having sex with a dead person means a successful outcome[363] to your actions.[364]

347.   Speaking with a dead person signifies profit.[365]

---

impending harm and punishment. This negative interpretation by Artemidorus derives from the ancient Greek and Roman hostility toward fellatio. In Rome, for example, men who performed oral sex were considered so base and depraved that some were forced to pass themselves off as passive partners in anal sex (a status in itself the object of great opprobrium) simply to avoid the label of fellator, while oral rape was the worst possible degradation of a person, especially an adult male. See Richlin 1992, 145–51 (with notes on 248–9) for oral rape of men, 26–31 for reasons for the revulsion to oral sex (cf. 69, 99–100), and 132ff. for Martial's 60 poems dealing with oral sex. Cf. Skinner 2005, 18–19; Williams 1999, 197–203; Winkler 1990, 38. The medieval Arabs, like the Greeks and Romans, described fellatio as an unspeakable act, and when Artemidorus's dreambook was translated into Arabic, this section of the text was removed. Bellamy (1979, 34) notes that not a single reference to oral sex can be found in medieval Islamic popular literature; cf. Rowson 1991, 75 n. 8.

[362]   Iron is a good and a bad dream symbol in Artemidorus's dreambook; for example, 4.65: "Someone dreamt that he had sexual intercourse with a piece of iron just as one would have it with a woman. It came to pass that the man was condemned to slavery and was enchained in iron and had, as it were, intercourse with it. The illustrious Antipater remembered this example and told another man who had dreamt that he had intercourse with a piece of iron that he would be condemned to fight in a gladiatorial contest. But the dream did not come true in this way. Instead, the dreamer's penis was cut off"; 5.15: "Someone dreamt that he had an iron penis. He fathered a son who killed him. For iron is consumed by the rust that it produces from itself."

[363]   A subtle wordplay here, since ἔκβασις often described death.

[364]   Artemidorus 1.80: "To possess a corpse, whether male or female, with the exception of one's mother, sister, wife, or mistress, or to be possessed by a corpse is thoroughly inauspicious. For the dead are changed into earth. To possess them, therefore, signifies being thrust into the ground, and to be possessed by them means receiving earth into one's body." Achmet 131: "If someone dreams that he had sex with a dead man that he knew, he will do good to that man's heirs; but if the man was a stranger, he will trample down a very powerful enemy ruler. If someone dreams that a dead man was having sex with his [*sc.* the dreamer's] wife or daughter, he will receive profit and kindness from that man's heirs."

Sexual relations, as portrayed in all the Byzantine dreambooks, are cast in the framework of penetration and reception, domination and submission, profit and loss, taking pleasure and giving pleasure. Generally, the receptor of the penis can expect to receive some profit from the penetrator. To put it crudely, the person receiving semen will receive profit, and the one giving the semen will yield profit. Not all is loss for the penetrator, however, for he can expect joy and happiness, success in his business and way of life, and peace and stability in his domestic situation. It is by no happenstance that Achmet repeatedly uses the word *kosmos* (orderly rule) as a pun in conjunction with the *kosmos* (beauty) of the person who is penetrated. For example, "A woman [symbolises] a man's power and strength. And just as he dreams of her being beautiful/obedient [*kosmia*] or ugly/disorderly [*akosmos*], so it will turn out for him in everyday life—that is, in the former case, he will have happiness, but in the latter, sorrow" (124). Orderly sex makes for orderly success.

[365]   *Somniale Danielis* ("Beiträge, V") 33: *cum mortuo loquere, bonum persequitur*; *Somniale Danielis* ("Beiträge, IV") LXXVI: *cum mortuo loqui, grande lucrum significat.*

348.   Having sex with a prostitute means not a little profit.[366]

349.   Having sex with a virgin signifies spiritual distress.[367]

350.   Having sex with another man's wife signifies good profit.[368]

351.   Having sex with one's concubine signifies something good.[369]

352.   Having sex with one's own slave girl signifies strife.[370]

353.   Having sex with a man means that someone will completely subdue you.[371]

354.   Speaking with the emperor points to bad luck in one's activities.[372]

355.   Dreaming that you are having sex with an old woman signifies completion in your activities.[373]

356.   Dreaming that you are a cook means enjoying other people's property.[374]

357.   If you dream of being phallically penetrable [μαλακός], consider this the loss of your wife.[375]

---

[366]   Also a positive dream in Artemidorus 1.78 and Achmet 128. For prostitution in Byzantine brothels, inns, baths, and theaters and stadiums, see Leontsini 1989; *ODB* 3:1741–2; Rautman 2006, 27, 51; also Mavroudi 2002, 465. Some prostitutes became wealthy or worked in the imperial court, even becoming empress (Theodora) or mother of an emperor (Helena): *ODB* 3:1741. Justinian and Theodora founded the Convent of Repentance for women who wished to escape prostitution: Brubaker 2005, 432. Procopius in his *Secret History* spends much time describing Theodora's prostitution, immorality, and usurpation of manly roles; see Brubaker 2005, 433–6.

[367]   The interpretation is based on the association of virginity with spirituality. Achmet (128) describes a dream of sex with a virgin girl in very favorable terms: "If someone dreams that he had sexual intercourse with a virgin, if he is a king, he will discover the fulfillment of his chief joy and desire; if a commoner, he will get wealth from the authorities." But cf. *Somniale Danielis* ("Beiträge, IV") LXIX: *cum virgine concumbere, anxietatem significat*; *Somniale Danielis* ("Beiträge, V") 34: *cum virgine nubere, angustiam anime significat*.

[368]   So too Achmet 127 and 128; but cf. Artemidorus 1.78: "But it is not good to possess the legal wife of another man because of the law. For the dream signifies to the dreamer the same punishments to which men caught in adultery are subjected. Being possessed by someone with whom one is familiar, whatever his character, means profit for a woman."

[369]   Also a good dream in Artemidorus 1.78. Concubinage was viewed negatively by the Byzantine Church and government if the man also had a legal wife; it was tolerated if the man was unmarried. See Beaucamp 1990; Laiou 1984; *LAnt* 388–9 (heavy on Christian sources); Mavroudi 2007, 63–4; *ODB* 1:492.

[370]   This is an auspicious dream, however, in Artemidorus 1.78 and Achmet 128; but see Mavroudi 2002, 465.

[371]   But this is a good dream in Achmet 14 and 128; Artemidorus (1.78) considers it auspicious if the man is rich, but bad if the man is poor.

[372]   But cf. *Somniale Danielis* ("Beiträge, V") 38: *cum imperatore vel rege loquere, dignitatem magnam significat*; Artemidorus 4.31.

[373]   Cf. Achmet 127 and 128.

[374]   For the interpretation of cooks, see Artemidorus 3.56. For cooks (who at first combined their culinary talents with the sacrifice of animals), see Dalby 1996, 8–10, 162–67.

[375]   Cf. Artemidorus 5.65: "A man dreamt that his penis was covered with hair and that a thick shaggy fur suddenly started to grow on it all the way up to the farthest point of the tip. The man was a notorious catamite and indulged in every form of licentious pleasure, except that he

358. Entering your own house in a chariot: sure reliability in actions will be attributed to you.

359. Dreaming of being drunk signifies illness.[376]

360. Looking at the Dog Star signifies an accusation and bad luck.[377]

361. To dream of being involved in a battle signifies profit.[378]

362. A mill, when dreamt of, indicates lack of worry over one's activities.[379]

363. To dream that someone is the owner of a mill that is actively grinding means that the mill-owner [in the dream] will be in danger in a short while.

---

did not use his penis, as men customarily do. Accordingly, this part of his body was so inactive that even hairs grew on it. For it was not rubbed against any other body." See the exhaustive discussion in C. Williams 1999, 172–224 on passive partners; cf. Hubbard 2003, 7 with notes.

As we have seen above, the Byzantine dreambook writers, like Artemidorus, demonstrate that in their day sex consisted of male penetration of a submissive male or female in a discourse of dominance and power. Dreams involving heterosexual penetration—whether of prostitutes, wives (including other men's wives), and concubines—foretell profit, goodness, and happiness. The penetrator, if he receives pleasure from the act, will do good to that person or to someone related to the penetrated; or he will trample down and beat into submission his enemy (this is an example of power and domination in the sexual act in the dream reflecting power and domination in the waking realm). Overall, any dream involving sex is a good sign, but only insofar as the male penetrator experiences pleasure and in direct proportion to the submissive person's beauty, youth, and, most importantly, his or her willingness to be dominated and to obey the penetrator. Regarding male homoeroticism, if a man dreams of being the insertive partner, great goodness and profit will come his way, but if he is the one penetrated, he will be overpowered and subjected to great humiliation. In the dream above, we have an alternative interpretation for a dream of being penetrated: since the passive male partner is assimilated by association into the construct of woman, the dreamer's wife will die.

[376] So too *Somniale Danielis* ("Beiträge, V") 59: *ebrium se videre, infirmitatem significat*; Artemidorus 3.42. This is a good dream in Achmet 113, 114, 195, 196. The Church condemned drunkenness, with many theologians railing against it; see Basil the Great, "Against Drunkards," PG 31:444–64 (I owe this reference to *ODB* 1: 664); cf. Rautman 2006, 105.

[377] See the discussion of this dream symbol in Brackertz 1993, 258 ad loc.; see also Artemidorus 2.11 and 2.12.

[378] Cf. Achmet 155; but Artemidorus (2.31) considers this a bad dream, unless the dreamer is a soldier or someone who makes his money from matters related to war, such as arms manufacture.

[379] Cf. Achmet 193. Oxen, horses, and donkeys were used to grind grain or press olives in Byzantine mills: *ODB* 2:1374; Rautman 2006, 181–3. Water-mills became pervasive in Byzantium, starting in the fifth century; see Bouras 2002, 519; Bryer 2002, 110–11; Kazhdan 1997, 49; Laiou 1977, 68; Lefort 2002, 235–6; Morrisson and Sodini 2002, 197–9; Rautman 2006, 182–3 (with n. 17 on 196). A water-mill has been excavated in the agora of Athens. There were two types of water-mills: the so-called winter mill, which operated when a stream was flooded with water, and the yearlong mill. Windmills first appeared in the thirteenth century; see Bouras 2002, 519; Brett 1939; Bryer 2002, 111–12; Rautman 2006, 183 (with n. 18 on 196).

364. To dream of having sex with one's own mother, even if she is dead [in real life], signifies gain.[380]

365. Handling pearls points to evildoing in one's actions and grief.[381]

366. A short person who dreams of becoming taller[382] will have profit;[383] but a tall person who dreams of becoming shorter should expect loss.[384]

367. Working in marble signifies illness.[385]

368. Getting or eating an apple signifies displeasure and illness.[386]

369. If you dream that your mother has become a prostitute, some kind of danger will happen.

370. If someone beats you with a cane,[387] this is good.

371. Sitting with an old man or having sex with an old woman indicates completeness in your actions.[388]

372. Having sex with a prostitute indicates distress.[389]

Beginning of the Letter N

373. If you dream that a dead person has risen from the grave, this signifies profit.[390]

---

[380] Cf. *Somniale Danielis* ("Beiträge, IV") LXVIII: *cum matre [concumbere], securitatem significat*; cf. also ibid., CLXXII: *matrem suam mortuam aut vivam viderit, gaudium significat.*

[381] Pearls are a good dream symbol in Achmet 245, 246, 256 (interpretations based on Arabic sources; see Mavroudi 2002, 371–2).

[382] So I translate μικρὸν ὄντα μείζονα ὁρᾶν.

[383] Cf. *Somniale Danielis* ("Beiträge, V") 96: *minor maior se factum videre, potestates ei accrescunt.*

[384] Ibid., 91: *maior minor se factum videre, potestates ei minuuntur.* Cf. Artemidorus 1.50: "Regarding the quantitative transformation dreams—that is to say, if a man dreams that he changes from small to large, or from large to larger—it is auspicious, unless the person dreams that his great size exceeds the natural limitations of a man."

[385] Achmet (146) states that marble signifies powerful wealth and a long life.

[386] Apples are symbolic of a woman in Artemidorus 1.73 and Achmet 151 and 198 (as well as in the imagery of the Song of Songs in the Hebrew Bible); see Manuel 12 below. But Artemidorus (1.73) also interprets eating sour apples as indicating discord and quarrels (an analogy to the sour taste).

[387] Κάλαμος, which usually described a reed or a cane, also denoted the measuring device used to measure the distance between two vines in a vineyard: the closer the vines, the greater their quality. See *ODB* 2:1091.

[388] The interpretation is based on the analogy of old age ~ completeness. See also 346 and 353 above. Old people were generally considered wise, and were respected for their experience; see *ODB* 1:36; Rautman 2006, 9.

[389] This is contrary to the dream interpretation in 348 above. There is also a difference in the word to describe sexual relations: κοιμᾶσθαι here versus συνδοιάσαι.

[390] See Achmet 132; but this is a bad dream in Artemidorus 2.62.

374. A dream of nests of young birds indicates additional income in one's business.[391]

375. Dreaming of a fast moving cloud signifies struggle in one's actions.[392]

376. Throwing a bride out of your house: consider this throwing out a dead body.[393]

377. [To dream of] a church with God [inside it] signifies honor for any dreamer;[394] but dreaming that the church is on fire means quarrels.

Beginning of the Letter Ξ

378. If you dream that you are struck by a sword,[395] this signifies honor in your actions.[396]

379. To dream that you are a guest[397] [in someone's house] means a life of many changes; but if you have guests in your house, this signifies envy.[398]

380. A dream of vomiting means loss.[399]

381. Wood that has been cut from trees means gain.[400]

382. Dreaming of oneself as having blond hair signifies profit.

383. Scratching your hand indicates that you will get your hands on gold.[401]

---

[391] Cf. *Somniale Danielis* ("Beiträge, V") 99: *nidos avium qui invenerit, nuntius ei bonus accrescit.* See too Achmet 184 and 291.

[392] But Achmet (162) considers this a good dream. Artemidorus (2.36) interprets the symbol as either good or bad, depending on whether the cloud is white or black in appearance.

[393] Yet another dream that associates marriage with death.

[394] A dream of a Christian church has very negative connotations in the Arabic dream texts: Mavroudi 2002, 323–4. The bibliography on Byzantine churches is immense; see some of the literature cited in Rautman 2006, 279 n. 15 (note to his discussion on 274–6).

[395] The Byzantine sword, which was long and two-bladed, was used by both infantry and calvary; the Roman short stabbing sword (*gladius*) was abandoned after the sixth century. See *ODB* 3:2196; Rautman 2006, 205–6.

[396] See Achmet 121; but cf. *Somniale Danielis* ("Beiträge, V") 60: *ferro percussum se videre, desolationem significat.*

[397] I take ξένος here as "guest," although it can also mean "stranger" or "foreigner" (for which, see *ODB* 2:796–7). Brackertz (1993) translates as "Fremdling," which can denote both a foreigner and a stranger.

[398] *Somniale Danielis* ("Beiträge, IV") CXXIX: *hospites habere, invidiam significat*; cf. *Somniale Danielis* ("Beiträge, V") 78: *hospites supervenientes habere, insidias maximias significat.* A straightforward analogy (the guests will be jealous of your possessions).

[399] See the comment to 172 above.

[400] But this is considered a bad symbol in Achmet 143.

[401] I accept here Brackertz's translation: "Juckt dir die Hand, wirst du Geld bekommen." He comments (1993, 259 ad loc.): "Heute glaubt man in einigen Gegenden Griechenlands, daß das Jucken der rechten Hand Gelderwerb bedeutet, das der linken, daß man Geld ausgeben wird; in anderen Regionem zeigt das Jucken der Hand allgemein Gewinn oder Geldempfang an."

384.   Dreaming of bronze or marble statues is not good.[402]

385.   Carrying wood indicates grievous sins and hatred.

Beginning of the Letter O

386.   Wearing armor means security in your activities.[403]

387.   Handling weapons: you will be freed from every evil.[404]

388.   Sitting on a donkey foretells death for rich people and bad luck for poor people.[405]

389.   Dreaming of donkeys signifies great distress;[406] and if you see them raised up on their rear hooves[407] [or] running, this means strife.[408]

390.   Sitting on or seeing a white donkey means great honor.[409]

391.   Dreaming of donkeys pulling a plough signifies success after initial loss.[410]

392.   Dreaming that the sky is made of gold signifies evil for wealthy people, but [joy] for poor.[411]

393.   If someone dreams that the sky has fallen to the ground, this is most grievous for any dreamer.[412]

394.   Dreaming of touching the sky[413] is troublesome for anyone.

---

[402]   The ξόανον (often made of wood) was an image or statue of a god, as opposed to the statue (ἀνδρίας) that portrayed a person (see above 1, with comment). The negative interpretation in this dream may be because the statues could have depicted pagan gods.

[403]   Achmet 155; *Somniale Danielis* ("Beiträge, IV") V: *arma in somnis portare, tutamentum significat.*

[404]   See Achmet 155.

[405]   In the Hebrew Scriptures, kings rode donkeys rather than horses. For example, Solomon, when named king, entered Jerusalem while seated on a donkey (1 Kings 1:38–40). As one sign of his wrongdoing, Solomon accumulated horses and chariots (1 Kings 4:26–8, 10:26–9)—Mosaic law forbade the king from acquiring large numbers of horses: Deuteronomy 17:16.

[406]   Cf. *Somniale Danielis* ("Beiträge, IV") IV: *asinos vel edos viderit, crimen negotii significat.*

[407]   So I take ὠγκωμένος.

[408]   Cf. Achmet 233; *Somniale Danielis* ("Beiträge, IV") VII: *asinos clamantes aut solutos currere, aliquam litem adversarie significat.*

[409]   Achmet 233: "[A] white donkey [means that a dreamer's] good fate and grandeur will be through his wife and children."

[410]   Cf. Artemidorus 2.12; for ploughing in general, *Somniale Danielis* ("Beiträge, V") 20: *arare se videre, laborem significat* (a straighforward analogy).

[411]   Cf. Artemidorus 2.8.

[412]   Cf. ibid., 2.8.

[413]   The phrase οὐρανὸν ἅπτεσθαι can also mean "if the sky is on fire. ..." Brackertz (1993) translates as I do: "Im Traum den Himmel zu berühren ist für jedermann heikel."

395. Bringing a snake into your house [means that] a woman will enter your house.[414]

396. Dreaming of your teeth falling out [signifies that] a member of your family will die.[415]

397. Cleaning one's teeth points to one's own toils.[416]

398. Losing your teeth without feeling any pain indicates freedom from care.[417]

399. Dreaming that your teeth are black signifies illness.[418]

400. Seeing [or] handling earthenware pots: be on your guard lest something evil befall you.[419]

401. Birds sitting on their eggs signify good actions.[420]

402. A clock, when dreamt of, means change and confusion.[421]

403. Handling bones [means] profit;[422] but if you trip over them, this signifies separation of friends.

404. Having many eyes signifies gain.[423]

405. Having only one eye signifies bad luck in having children.[424]

---

[414]   For woman signified by snake, cf. *Somniale Danielis* ("Beiträge, IV") CCLXXXVI: *si videris columbram contra te venire, contra malas feminas te defendere ammonet*. Cf. Artemidorus 2.13: "Asps and vipers signify money because of their powerful poison and, for the same reason, they also mean rich wives. ..." But the snake can also symbolize the penis and sex (2.13): "But if the dreamer's wife has a reptile in her possession which she conceals in her bosom and in which she takes pleasure, she will commit adultery and, generally, with an enemy of the dreamer."

[415]   Artemidorus 1.31; Achmet 60 and 61 (with Mavroudi 2002, 453–4); *Somniale Danielis* ("Beiträge, V") 49: *dentes sibi cadere viderit, de parentibus suis aliquis morietur*.

[416]   But Achmet (65) interprets this dream as signifying that the dreamer will "beautify the children of his family with clothing and through good deeds."

[417]   Cf. Artemidorus 1.31. The opposite dream—losing your teeth with pain and blood—can be found in *Somniale Danielis* ("Beiträge, V") 50: *dentes inferiores aut molares cum sanguine et dolore <cadere>, plus proximum parentem perdere*.

[418]   Achmet (60) interprets black teeth as foretelling illness for family members, not for the dreamer.

[419]   Artemidorus (1.66) interprets earthenware as a good sign. The wealthier Byzantines, who considered this type of ware as very inferior in quality, preferred gold and silver plate; see Rautman 2006, 139, 169, 190–91, 261–3.

[420]   Cf. *Somniale Danielis* ("Beiträge, IV") CXXII: *gallinam ova parere, lucrum cum sollicitudine significat*. Achmet (292) interprets this dream unfavorably.

For chickens as a popular part of the Byzantine diet, see Kazhdan 1997, 55; Koukoules 1948–57, 5:68–75; Morrisson and Sodini 2002, 200; Rautman 2006, 186.

[421]   Cf. Artemidorus 3.66. The clock during the Byzantine era was either a sundial or a water clock (the more dependable method); see Koukoules 1948–57, 5:89–90; *ODB* 2:947. See also Rautman 2006, 4–5.

[422]   But cf. *Somniale Danielis* ("Beiträge, IV") CXCII: *ossa aliqua trectare, odium significat*.

[423]   Artemidorus 1.26; but cf. Achmet 52.

[424]   But cf. ibid., 52.

406. Eating fruit is a thoroughly truthful [dream].[425]

407. Growing your fingernails long signifies lack of care.[426]

408. A dream of fog [hovering] above the ground means change and confusion.[427]

409. Eating seafood dishes: profit will come to you.[428]

410. Drinking vinegar signifies strife.[429]

411. A snake, when dreamt of, indicates vexation.[430]

412. To dream of crowds of people: something good will happen for you.

Beginning of the Letter Π

413. Trapping a bird signifies profit.[431]

414. A dream of birds fighting among themselves signifies confusion.[432]

415. If you see a clear stream of water or drink from one, this signifies profit.[433]

---

[425] Ibid., 8 on eating fruits in Paradise: "If someone dreams that he ate [in Paradise] some of the fruit of its trees, he will find in his faith wisdom and knowledge: for the fruits of Paradise happen to [symbolise] divine and holy words. If he dreams that he gave some of the fruits to others, he will be a teacher to the extent that he shared and gave. If he dreams that he only took the fruit and did not eat or share them with others, he has received God's gifts and does not know it, and so he will not bring his fruit to perfection; if he did not eat the fruit but gave them to someone, he will be judged as vainglorious, while the recipient of the fruit will be saved."

[426] But cf. ibid., 74 and 75, where the dream relates to gain and to the slave who supervises the dreamer's treasures. See Artemidorus 1.22 on cutting fingernails.

Perhaps the interpretation here is based on the analogy that a person who grows his fingernails long enjoys a life of leisure and does not engage in manual labor.

[427] Achmet 163; cf. *Somniale Danielis* ("Beiträge, IV") CLXXXVII: *nebula super terram, nullum bonum significat.*

[428] For this meaning of the word ὀψάρια, see Dalby 2003, 218. For the dream, see Artemidorus 1.70. Perhaps fish are auspiciously interpreted above because of their symbolism in Christianity: see note 254 above.

[429] So too Artemidorus 1.66; cf. *Somniale Danielis* ("Beiträge, V") 17: *acetum vel absinthium bibere, molestiam gravem significat*; *Somniale Danielis* ("Beiträge, IV") XIX: *acetum bibere in somnis, infirmitatem significat.*

[430] See the extended discussion in Achmet 281.

[431] *Somniale Danielis* ("Beiträge, IV") II: *aves in somnis capere, lucrum significat.* Artemidorus (2.11) considers this dream inauspicious.

[432] *Somniale Danielis* ("Beiträge, V") 1: *aves in somnis qui contra se pugnare viderit, iracundiam significat.*

[433] Artemidorus 2.27; Achmet 174. Water was the basic beverage of the Byzantines, followed by wine (which was diluted, although "neat" wine was not uncommon: Dalby 1996, 193–4): *ODB* 1:287. Visitors to Constantinople commented on the salty taste of its water: Dalby 2003, 85–6. See also Koukoules 1948–57, 5:121–35, who states that milk was not popular; Dalby (2003, 72–3) argues, on the other hand, that Byzantines drank milk to a remarkable extent.

416.   If you see a flock of birds or struggle with them, this means something good for free people, but harm for slaves.[434]

417.   Receiving a [kiss] from an emperor means a good deed.[435]

418.   Dreaming that one is wealthy means poverty.[436]

419.   Flying in unknown lands signifies a journey from home.[437]

420.   Dreaming that one is wandering around lost[438] signifies great distress.

421.   If you see running water[439] or bathe or sail in it, this indicates disease.[440]

422.   Being victorious in a wrestling match signifies something good.[441]

423.   If you dream that running water is flowing out of your house, this signifies profit and happiness.[442]

424.   Dreaming of a pack of four-legged animals signifies an untimely quarrel.

425.   Seeing prostitutes and spending time with them signifies unexpected toil.[443]

426.   To dream of a boat running on an open sea signifies very great joy.[444]

427.   Sailing in one's dream indicates goodness and joy.[445]

---

[434]   Cf. *Somniale Danielis* ("Beiträge, IV") I: *aves in somnis qui viderit & cum ipsis pugnaverit, lites aliquas significat.*

[435]   The word φίλημα has been added by Drexl (1926). Cf. the general dream of kissing in *Somniale Danielis* ("Beiträge, IV") CXCVI: *osculum dare, dampnum significat.*

[436]   See Artemidorus 4.17.

[437]   Achmet 160.

[438]   So I translate πλανώμενον on the basis of *Somniale Danielis* ("Beiträge, V") 58: *errantem se videre, molestiam magnam significat.* Brackertz (1993) translates: "er komme vom Weg ab."

[439]   Normally the word πηγή denoted a fountain or spring (the most famous of which in Constantinople was the Sanctuary of the Virgin Mary outside the Theodosian Walls), but I take the word in a broader sense here because of πλεῦσαι.

[440]   Cf. Artemidorus 2.27.

[441]   See ibid., 1.60.

[442]   Cf. ibid., 2.27: "A river flowing out of a house signifies benefits for a man who is rich and very powerful. For he will rule the city and, in his quest for honor, he will spend much on behalf of the state. Many who are poor and needy will come into his home. For all men need a river. But for a poor man, it means that his wife or son or someone else in his household will be slanderously accused of having committed adultery and of having behaved indecently." Cf. *Somniale Danielis* ("Beiträge, IV") CVIII: *fontem in domo sua viderit aperiri, incrementum vel letitiam significant.*

[443]   Cf. Achmet 127. The interpretation differs from the one given in 348 above, and reflects the author's synthesis of sources.

[444]   See Artemidorus 2.23; Achmet 179.

[445]   Artemidorus 2.23; Achmet 178. In Byzantium, sailing was restricted to the months of April through October. Pilots stayed as close to land as possible, relying on landmarks, ports, and beacons. If the pilot lost sight of land, he consulted the stars and sun. See Avramea 2002, 77–88; *ODB* 2:1444; Rautman 2006, 148–9. Transport of goods by sea was more cost effective than by land: Haldon 2005, 34; *LAnt* 730–31; Treadgold 1997, 407.

428. Dreaming that a ship is on fire indicates confusion.[446]

429. Shearing sheep signifies loss.[447]

430. Having one's feet secured with shackles is good for slaves and the poor, but evil for the wealthy.[448]

431. Receiving or eating sweetmeats[449] signifies gain.[450]

432. Dreaming that a child has become old means loss of capital.[451]

433. Getting runaway child [slaves][452] signifies a plot by one's enemies.

434. Dreaming of any sort of calamitous collapse signifies failure in one's activities.[453]

435. If you dream that mice or cats are in your house, you will be involved in business with foreigners and make a profit.[454]

436. White sheep, when dreamt of, signify something good.[455]

---

[446] Cf. Achmet 179. Perhaps this dream can be related to "Greek fire," which was a napalm-like substance used by Byzantine ships. A mixture of oil, resin, and sulphur was heated and then pumped through a bronze tube. See Gregory 2005, 173; *ODB* 2:873; Rautman 2006, 210, 221–3 (with n. 27 on 231); Rosser 2001, s.v. "Greek Fire"; Treadgold 1997, 326–7, 435.

[447] *Somniale Danielis* ("Beiträge, V") 110: *oves tondere, damnum significat*; *Somniale Danielis* ("Beiträge, IV") CXCV: *oves viderit tonsas, dampnum significat.*

[448] Perhaps a good sign because the image of slaves in chains would be consistent with everyday reality (as we have seen, dreambook writers interpret symbols that reflect normal conditions as good), but for a freeperson such a condition would imply a drastic reversal of fortune. For the dream, cf. Artemidorus 3.35.

[449] For the meaning of παστίδη, see DuCange 1688, s.h.v.

[450] But cf. Achmet 241.

[451] Cf. Artemidorus 1.50.

[452] I have relied on Brackertz's (1993) translation for the phrase παιδία δέξασθαι εἰς φυγὴν: "Flüchtige junge Sklaven oder Sklavinnen aufzunehmen zeigt Anschläge von Feinden an."

[453] See Achmet 145 and 146.

[454] Cf. ibid., 275. But cf. *Somniale Danielis* ("Beiträge, IV") CLXXV: *mus & leo in somnis, securitatem significat.* Artemidorus (3.28) interprets a mouse as a household slave since "it lives in the same house as the dreamer, is nourished by the same food, and is timid."

[455] Artemidorus (2.12) considers white sheep a better sign than black sheep. According to Achmet 240, sheep symbolise joy, wealth, slaves, and, if they are white in color, goodness.

Sheep were the primary domesticated animal in Byzantium, supplying meat and cheese besides wool. Kazhdan (1997, 52) discusses the huge numbers of livestock that rich landowners possessed. For example, the fourteenth-century John Kantakouzenos of Thrace had 1,500 horses, 1,000 pairs of oxen, 5,000 cows, 50,000 pigs, 70,000 sheep (goats perhaps included), and hundreds of camels, donkeys, and mules; see also Laiou 1977, 173–4. A peasant, on the other hand, might own up to 300 sheep and goats. Cf. *ODB* 2:1242–3; see too Haldon 2005, 32; Laiou 1977, 67 (for holdings of oxen, pigs, and other livestock), and 2002b, 327–9, 340; Lefort 2002, 252; Rautman 2006, 185. See Morrisson and Cheynet 2002, 839–41 for the price of livestock in Byzantium.

The interpretation of the dream here is doubtlessly based on the Jesus' words that sheep will be on His right hand at the final judgement and will be called righteous: Matthew 25:31–3.

Beginning of the Letter P

437.   Eating or handling radishes: watch out for poison.[456]

438.   If you dream of roses being in your house, this signifies something good.[457]

439.   Seeing or receiving a staff indicates honor.[458]

Beginning of the Letter Σ

440.   Eating figs signifies illness.[459]

441.   Having a pale-colored body signifies hindrance in your actions.

442.   A dream of packsaddles [σάγματα][460] signifies loss and oppression.

443.   Hearing trumpets signifies tumult.[461]

444.   Seeing clear moonlight signifies the accomplishment of good deeds.[462]

445.   Seeing a moon in one of its lesser phases signifies loss.[463]

446.   A chair [σέλλα],[464] when dreamt of, is a harsh [sign].

---

[456]   But cf. Achmet 207: "If someone dreams that he was eating radishes, he will get a very minute amount of useless money; moreover, he will become a liar, a man of evil repute among the people, and an object of hate because of the foul smell of the belching [that results from eating radishes]. If someone dreams that a person brought him radishes, if he is king, he will soon receive news that is evil in proportion to the amount; if a commoner, he will have strife. If someone dreams that radishes were placed on his eating-table, if he is king, he will stir up his councilors because of an evil mandate; if a commoner, he will have domestic quarrels." Cf. Artemidorus 1.67.

[457]   Artemidorus (1.77) also considers this a good dream, except in the case of those who are at the point of death or who wish to hide (the reasoning is that the sweet smell of roses attracts people's attention); cf. *Somniale Danielis* ("Beiträge, IV") CCXVIII: *rosam viderit, valitudines significat*. Achmet (202) comments: "If someone dreams that his house was sprinkled with roses, if he is a king, he will receive joyous news because of the rose's sweet smell and redness; if a commoner, he will find happiness and wealth."

[458]   So too Achmet 211.

[459]   Cf. Artemidorus 1.73; Achmet 241; *Somniale Danielis* ("Beiträge, IV") CXIII: *ficum viderit, lites cum inportunis significat.*

[460]   I take this as "packsaddle"; see LSJ, s.h.v.; cf. Achmet 237 and modern Greek σάγμα.

[461]   Cf. Artemidorus 1.56.

[462]   See Achmet 217 (cf. Mavroudi 2002, 220–22); *Somniale Danielis* ("Beiträge, IV") CLV: *lunam albam viderit, lucrum significat*. But cf. *Somniale Danielis* ("Beiträge, IV") CLI: *lunam claram viderit, invidiam significant*. The different interpretations demonstrate that even the Latin Daniel dreambook of the tenth century was a conflation of different sources.

[463]   So too Artemidorus 2.36; Achmet 167.

[464]   It is difficult to know the exact meaning of σέλλα. If the word equals the Latin *sella* (for which, see Lewis–Short 1879, s.h.v.), there are various ways of translating it: a chair or stool; a chair carried (with poles) by slaves; a magistrate's chair; or a seat used for defecating. LSJ (s.h.v.) also cites instances of σέλλα meaning "saddle."

447. Seeing arrows or making them or handling them signifies fluctuation in one's actions.[465]

Beginning of the Letter T

448. Constructing one's own house signifies something good.[466]

449. Getting soft cheese signifies profit.[467]

450. Seeing a narrow, contracted opening or door and then wanting to enter or exit it but not being able to do so, points to distress.

451. An approaching bull [symbolises] an enemy.[468]

Beginning of the Letter Y

452. Getting cold water from a spring signifies long life.[469]

---

[465] Cf. Achmet 247; cf. *Somniale Danielis* ("Beiträge, V") 13: *arcum tendere vel sagittas emittere, angustiam magnam significat*; *Somniale Danielis* ("Beiträge, IV") XIII: *[a]rcum tendere vel sagittas mittere, laborem vel anxietatem significat.*

Arrows were discharged by infantrymen or calvary on horseback. The range of the infantryman's bow was nearly 1,000 feet, while the arrow shot from a calvaryman's bow, which was smaller and strung less tautly, traveled less than 400 feet: *ODB* 3:2192; Rautman 2006, 207.

[466] *Somniale Danielis* ("Beiträge, IV") CCCII: *si videris fabricare domum tuam, pecuniam tuam crescere significat*; *Somniale Danielis* ("Beiträge, V") 51: *domum suam edificare, consolationem significat*; Achmet 142. For Byzantine houses and their construction, see Gregory 2005, 241–2 (with bibliography); Rautman 2006, 90–94 (the capital), 123–33 (smaller cities), 162–3 (villages), 166–9 (country). Cf. Holum 2005, 101–2; *LAnt* (258–72), which discusses houses from the fifth through eighth centuries; *ODB* 2:953–4.

[467] But cf. Artemidorus 1.72. Cheese, most of which came from goats, comprised a significant part of the Byzantine diet: Koukoules 1948–57, 5:34–5 (and 326–30 for cheesemaking). Laiou (2002b, 53, with bibliography) notes the balanced diet of Byzantines: pulses, wine, fruits, vegetables, dairy products, meat and fish, etc. See also Koukoules 1948–57, 5:96–110; *ODB* 1:416–17; Rautman 2006, 46–7, 75, 94–6 (with nn. 18 and 20 on 117), 168–9.

[468] Cf. Artemidorus 2.12: "A bull signifies extraordinary danger, especially if it is threatening or pursuing, and also threats on the part of superiors, if the dreamer is a poor man or a slave." Achmet (236) interprets the bull as a threatening government official: "If someone dreams that his bull became wild [ἠγριώθη], the local magistrate will become furious [ἀγριωθήσεται] with him; and if he mastered the bull, he will overthrow the magistrate; but if the bull overpowered him, the magistrate will control him completely."

[469] Cf. Artemidorus 1.66; *Somniale Danielis* ("Beiträge, V") 66: *fontes videre aut in eis bibere, consolationem et letitiam significat*; *Somniale Danielis* ("Beiträge, V") 81: *in fontem lavare aut in claro flumine, letitiam cum lucro significat.* The key in interpreting water is its clarity, as is shown by a comparison with *Somniale Danielis* ("Beiträge, V") 82: *in fontem sordidum aut in flumen turbolentum, accusationem cum dampno significat.* As for bathing in cold water, cf. *Somniale Danielis* ("Beiträge, IV") CCLXXXIX: *si videris te in aqua frigida lavare, sanitatem*

453. If you see a wide body of water and then sail across it, you will be oppressed by the *dunatoi*.[470]

454. If you are given pigs, expect unforeseen profit.[471]

455. Seeing a body of agitated water or crossing over it or drinking from it means hindrance.[472]

456. A dream of water running into your house is evil for anyone.[473]

457. Drinking clear water signifies gain.[474]

458. Drinking water from a well indicates temporary toil.[475]

459. Wearing brand-new shoes [symbolises] unexpected profit.[476]

460. Drawing water from a well [means] useful gain.[477]

---

corporis significat. Hot water is interpreted unfavorably in *Somniale Danielis* ("Beiträge, IV") CCLXXXVIII: *si videris te in calida aqua lavare, dampnum corporis significat.*

In Byzantium, water from springs was deemed best, as it was cold, pure, and sweet-tasting. Water was imported into Constantinople through aqueducts, while cisterns were to be found throughout the city and up in the hills. See Croke 2005, 68–9 (with n. 41 on 82); *LAnt* 746, which reports that more than 80 open and roofed cisterns were built in Constantinople between the late fourth century and the early seventh; *ODB* 3:2191; Rautman 2006, 72–5 (with n. 5 on 115).

[470] Artemidorus (2.23) interprets this dream as a bad sign only if the waves' turmoil is due to a tempest. The interpretation above, like many others in this dreambook which bemoan the heavy-handed behavior of aristocrats, surely reflects the normal Byzantine person's fear and resentment of their social betters.

[471] A negative dream in Achmet 279, perhaps because of Arabic attitudes toward pork, although see Mavroudi 2002, 341–5; also *Somniale Danielis* ("Beiträge, IV") CCX: *porcos viderit, infirmitatem significat.* The dream above may have a positive interpretation, however, because the dreamer receives the pigs as a gift and therefore has increased his holdings. As mentioned above in notes 187 and 455, Byzantine farmers owned many more sheep and goats than pigs, although the largest landowners could own tens of thousands of them: *ODB* 3:1979–80; Rautman 2006, 185.

[472] Achmet 177; but this dream is positive in *Somniale Danielis* ("Beiträge, V") 65.

[473] Cf. ibid., 68: *flumen in domum suam intrare, periculum ipsa patietur.* Above in 423, water flowing out of one's house was interpreted favorably, but there the water was rushing out of the house. An incoming flood would be a bad dream in that the water could destroy or ruin property.

[474] Cf. Achmet 186.

[475] But this is an auspicious dream in Artemidorus 2.27 and Achmet 181.

[476] *Somniale Danielis* ("Beiträge, IV") XLIX: *calciamento novo calciari, lucrum ex insperato significat*; *Somniale Danielis* ("Beiträge, V") 43: *kalciamenta nova habere, gaudium et letitiam significat.* But Achmet (242) considers this dream a sign of sorrow and imprisonment.

[477] So ibid., 181.

Beginning of the Letter Φ

461. Seeing a prison or entering one means distress.[478]

462. Wishing to run away but not being able to do so points to hindrance.[479]

463. Carrying a load indicates freedom in your activities.[480]

464. A dream of many bald men signifies trouble.

465. If you dream of becoming bald, this means the loss of both profit and friendship.[481]

466. Receiving a light shows unexpected gain.[482]

467. If you dream of a nest of young birds, this signifies a profitable journey.[483]

468. A dream of picking lice off one's body signifies a time of inactivity.[484]

Beginning of the Letter X

469. Washing your hands with spices points to a lack of worry over your actions.[485]

470. If you dream of falling snow, this means that you will see harmonious agreements.[486]

471. Snow and frost, when dreamt of, signify faith.[487]

472. Handling or eating money points to sorrow.[488]

---

[478] Cf. *Somniale Danielis* ("Beiträge, IV") CCLVIII: *in carcere se videre, dampnum significat.*

[479] Cf. *Somniale Danielis* ("Beiträge, V") 31: *currere se non posse videre, infirmitatem significat.*

[480] Cf. Artemidorus 2.56. For loads in Byzantium, see *ODB* 1:274.

[481] So too Artemidorus 1.21; Achmet 31.

[482] Ibid., 158.

[483] But cf. *Somniale Danielis* ("Beiträge, IV") CLXXXV: *nidus* [*sc. nidos*] *avium viderit, agoniam negotii significat.*

[484] But this is a positive dream in Artemidorus 3.7.

[485] Cf. *Somniale Danielis* ("Beiträge, V") 95: *manus se lavare, a peccatis liberabis et a criminibus excusabis.*

[486] Cf. ibid., 100: *nivem videre, letitiam magnam significat; Somniale Danielis* ("Beiträge, IV") CLXXXVI: [*n*]*ives viderit, letitiam significat.* But see Nicephorus 132.

[487] Achmet 190: "Snow, hail, and ice signify sorrows, worries, and torments. If someone dreams that an area or district, where snow usually does not fall, was partly covered with snow, the inhabitants will experience non-productivity; and if the snow fell in large quantity, a great multitude of enemies proportionate to the size of the region will torment the populace. If, however, it is customary for snow to occur there, the misfortune will be even greater and more severe; and if this dream occurs during the winter, the misfortune will be milder: if during the summer, more oppressive and bitter." Artemidorus (2.8) interprets snow in a favorable light.

[488] Cf. *Somniale Danielis* ("Beiträge, IV") CCI: *pecuniam accipere, litem significat.* See Achmet 155 for dreams of money as signs of evil. Artemidorus (2.58) is ambivalent: "Some men maintain that money and all kinds of coins indicate bad luck. But I have observed that small

473. Finding or handling money signifies a struggle that will be difficult to deal with.

474. Dreaming of having a sepulchral mound raised over you signifies profit.[489]

475. Making a crucible points to the same thing.[490]

476. Using a crucible signifies honor.

477. Losing a crucible means the loss of one's ships.[491]

Beginning of the Letter Ψ

478. Getting half a loaf of bread[492] means the slipping-away of a friendship.

479. Getting or eating or merely seeing a loaf of white bread signifies harshness and strife for any dreamer.[493]

480. Getting a loaf of barley bread signifies joy in your life.[494]

---

coins and copper coins mean discontent and painful exchanges of words. However, silver coins symbolise discussions that involve contracts about important matters; gold coins, about matters that are even more important. It is always better to have just a few coins and not much money rather than a great deal, since a large amount of money signifies anxieties and griefs because it is difficult to manage."

For Byzantine coinage and money, see Gregory 2005, 218–19 (with bibliography on 219); Morrisson 2002; Morrisson and Sodini 2002, 212–19; Rautman 2006, 30–35 (with nn. 19–21 on 36–7); Treadgold 1997, 896 (brief bibliography).

[489] Achmet (131) interprets this dream as a sign of death and sorrow.

[490] Χώνη here symbolises wealth, probably because it was used to smelt metals and also signified in Byzantine Greek the treasury of the Church.

[491] Perhaps an association between trade and mercantile fleets, on which see Rautman 2006, 150–53.

[492] I translate ψωμὶ μέσον as in the modern Greek usage. Brackertz (1993, 261 ad loc.) comments: "Das alte Wort für Brot, *artos*, ist in der neugriechischen Volkssprache durch *psomi*, das altgriechische *psomion* = *psomos* (Achmet 119,20; 164,4) = Bissen, Brocken ersetzt worden."

[493] But cf. Artemidorus 1.69; Achmet 241; *Somniale Danielis* ("Beiträge, IV") CCIV: *panem candidum accipere, accusatorem significat.*

[494] So too Artemidorus 1.69; cf. *Somniale Danielis* ("Beiträge, IV") CCVI: *panem ordeacium accipere, letitiam significat.*

Among the Byzantines, white bread was considered the very best in quality, barley bread the lowest; see Dagron 2002, 446; Haldon 2005, 30–31; Koukoules 1948–57, 5:12–31; see also Chapter 5, note 11, below. Bread was baked in home ovens or at bakeries (for which see *ODB* 1:246, where it is commented that bakers were exempted from public service, as were their animals; cf. Dalby 2003, 64); see Dagron 2002, 453–6, with recent bibliography; Koukoules 1928; *ODB* 1:321; Rautman 2006, 102–3. According to studies cited in Kazhdan 1997, 46, in early Byzantium a person ate 3 to 6 pounds of bread per day, but after the loss of North Africa and other grain-producing areas like Siciliy and the steppes around the Black Sea (see Gregory 2005, 151–2; Kazhdan and Epstein 1985, 5; *ODB* 2:865; Treadgold 1997, 110, 239), the amount dropped to just over a pound. Laiou (2002b, 53) notes that the loss of grain in the Byzantine diet was compensated by the development of other crops and by more emphasis on items like

481. Handling [or] eating crumbs means life.

482. Skillfully[495] singing signifies great unity along with joy.[496]

483. Seeing or getting or eating various kinds of fish[497] signifies illness.[498]

484. Fleas, when dreamt of, point to harm inflicted by enemies.[499]

Beginning of the Letter Ω

485. To dream of raw eggs points to oppression and distress; hard-boiled eggs, on the other hand, signify wealth.[500]

486. Carrying a child on your shoulders is a grievous [sign].[501]

---

dairy products and meat (mutton and goat, followed by beef and pork); cf. Morrisson and Sodini 2002, 201. As for barley, this crop was grown in the Balkans (versus grain, which came mainly from Turkey); see Laiou 1977, 28–9; Lefort 2002, 251; Rautman 2006, 172–3. For a general discussion of the different types of grains and cereals, see Dalby 1996, 90–92. See Morrisson and Cheynet 2002, 822–8 for the price of wheat, and 828–9 for the price of barley and other cereals, throughout the history of the Byzantine Empire.

[495] So I translate ἐν συνέσει (Brackertz 1993 offers "In einem Verein zu singen"). See Sophocles 1975, s.v. "σύνεσις," for this word describing the Psalms in the Septuagint.

[496] Also Artemidorus 1.76; but Achmet (252) considers this dream symbolic of weeping and sorrow (an instance of antimony).

[497] Drexl (1926, 314 ad loc.) comments: "ψαπίκλεα ist vielleicht ὄψα ποικίλα." I translate accordingly.

[498] So too Artemidorus 1.70; cf. *Somniale Danielis* ("Beiträge, IV") CLXX: *maris pisces viderit, anxietatem gravem significat.*

[499] Artemidorus does not refer to fleas in his dreambook, but he regards gnats ("and anything of this kind") as enemies who will cause the dreamer harm. Mavroudi (2002, 438) quotes the Arabic dreambook writer Ibn Sîrîn: "The dream of fleas <signifies> weak enemies."

[500] Achmet 250: "If someone dreams that he was eating boiled eggs, he will get wealth from slaves' labors proportionately to how many he ate: for a bird signifies a female slave; and if he sucked raw eggs, he will receive distress and vexation at the hands of a female slave." See also Artemidorus 2.43. Eggs were eaten hard-boiled or were fried; they also were used in soufflés: Dalby 2003, 71; cf. Koukoules 1948–57, 5:66–8.

[501] But this dream is viewed favorably in Artemidorus 2.56. For children and childhood in Byzantium, see Rautman 2006, 54–6 (with n. 17 on 59).

Chapter 5

The *Oneirocriticon* of Nicephorus
The Dreambook of Nicephorus, Patriarch of Constantinople[1]

A

1. An eagle signifies an angel of God.[2]

2. Anyone who speaks with a king remains out of work.[3]

3. Being embraced by a man you love: count it as a profitable sign.[4]

---

[1] For the *titulus*, see Guidorizzi 1980, 51 ad loc.

[2] Artemidorus 2.20; Achmet 284. Brackertz (1993, 228–9 ad his 3) references the use of the eagle in the Bible and in iconography: "Im AT und NT [der Adler] ist er Symbol Gottes, zumal seiner Fürsorge. Er trägt seine Jungen auf Flügeln zu ihrem wahren Ziel empor (Ex 19,4). Als Bild und Erscheinungsform Gottes wird er zum Attribut der Evangelisten Johannes und Markus." See *ODB* 2:762 and 3:2227 for the fourfold symbolic imagery: man/Matthew, lion/Mark, ox/Luke, and eagle/John. There may be further associations here: the eagle symbolised the emperor of Byzantium, and there was an Angelos dynasty from 1185 to 1204; see Ostrogorsky 1969, 401–17. The imagery of the fourteenth-century poem, the *Poulologos*, in which the eagle is the emperor (*ODB* 3:1708) may be cited as a parallel.

The sixth-century Pseudo-Dionysius the Areopagite was responsible for much of Byzantine thought on angels through his treatise *Celestial Hierarchy*: see *ODB* 1:97, to which I owe this reference. The author divided angels into hierarchical realms—nine orders and three triads. (Interestingly, patriarch Nicephorus I, our supposed author here, was also responsible for developing angelology.) The Church condemned cultic worship of angels, but they were very popular in Byzantine popular culture. See also *LAnt* 298–9.

[3] But this is a most auspicious dream in Achmet 126 and in Arabic texts (Mavroudi 2002, 200–201).

[4] See Achmet 128. Guidorizzi (1980, 99 ad loc.) takes this dream in sexual terms: "Si allude qui, verosimilmente, ad un amore omosessuale." If this dream is indeed homoerotic, then we may adduce as a parallel Achmet's frequent references to male homoeroticism. In every instance of homoerotic sex, the dream is a good sign for the dreamer, provided that the penetrator is of a higher social status than the penetrated. That is, the submissive partner in the dream must be a male of a lower social class, eunuch, or slave. No dream of sex between males of equal social rank exists in Achmet. One possible exception occurs in the discussion on necrophilia; here, the penetrator and the penetrated may (apparently) be of the same status—at least, Achmet does not specify class or status: "If someone dreams that he performed sex on a dead man who was an acquaintance, he will do good to that man's heirs; but if the man was a stranger, he will trample down a very powerful enemy ruler" (131). In another dream, one that reinforces the concept of sex as a private act being translated into the public realm of profit and business, Achmet writes: "If someone dreams that a dead man was performing sex on his [*sc.* the dreamer's] wife or daughter,

4.   Walking on coals signifies harm at the hands of your enemies.

5.   If one is holding[5] pears, he will fail to achieve his hopes.[6]

6.   Moving sluggishly causes unlucky trips.[7]

7.   If you are deprived of your reason,[8] know that you will live in a foreign land.[9]

8.   Eating brown [δυσειδεῖς][10] loaves of bread signifies illness.

9.   Eating loaves of hot bread signifies illness.

10.   Eating loaves of white bread is an auspicious dream.[11]

---

he will receive profit and kindness from that man's heirs" (131). Overall, a person's submission to penetration by a male social superior—e.g., a religious leader, priest, king, or nobleman—is a very auspicious sign, since the submission foretells that the penetrated will receive some benefit or profit from the penetrator. This agrees with Artemidorus's dreambook on three basic points. First, sex is a reflection of social hierarchies: penetrators are of a social rank higher than the penetrated. Second, gender is not a concern in the act of penetration; whether the passive partner is male or female, young or old, slave or freeborn, is not important, provided that the social hierarchy is preserved. And third, sex is cast in terms of profit and loss, domination and submission, power and loss of power. See Chapter 4, notes 360–61, 364, 375.

⁵   As Guidorizzi (1980, 100 ad loc.) points out, κρατεῖν in Nicephorus is usually equivalent to κατέχειν.

⁶   But cf. Achmet 241: "If [someone dreams of] eating ripe pears, he will get moderate wealth from a cruel but very powerful man." Cf. Artemidorus 1.73: "Cultivated pear trees are a good sign. For even when their fruit is stored up, it does not rot, and if the pears are eaten immediately, in addition to their nutritional value, they provide a wine-like juice. I know that certain people make a kind of wine from them. But wild pears and common pears indicate benefits only for farmers. For others, they mean unpleasantness."

⁷   Guidorizzi 1980, 100 ad loc.: "L'interpretazione … è fondata su un nesso di causa ed effetto (movimenti difficili = viaggi faticosi)." He further comments on the use of the verb ποιεῖν to denote the dream as a causative force: "[L]'uso di ποιέω è mutuato dall'antica terminologia oniromantica (il sogno non preannuncia ma produce l'evento: la stessa situazione è altrove identificata dal nesso [τὸ ὄναρ] φέρει εἰς—ad es. ai vv. 33, 40, 41)."

⁸   It is hard to know how to translate ἀρθεὶς νόον; I have translated it in a more literal way. Guidorizzi translates: "Se voli con la mente …." He interprets (ibid., 100 ad loc.) the phrase as meaning that the dreamer has a mental perception of flying or being swollen with pride: "Il nesso ἀρθεὶς νόον è di interpretazione problematica. Il senso potrebbe essere, con valore traslato, «insuperbisi», oppure «volare»: pare più probabile la seconda soluzione, poiché la tradizione onirocritica è concorde nell'associare i viaggi in terra straniera ai sogni di volo …." Brackertz translates (1993, his 23): "Dünkt es dich, du seist in die Höhe getragen worden, wirst du in die Fremde ziehen." The word νόος denoted the intellect; see *ODB* 2:1001 for its theological and philosophical meanings in Byzantine literature.

⁹   Cf. Artemidorus 3.42.

¹⁰   Brackertz translates (1993, his 27) this word as "Graubrot"; Guidorizzi as "brutto." Guidorizzi (1980, 100 ad loc.) comments on this bread as the food of the poor: "Ἄρτος δυσειδής è il pane nero, dei poveri, in opposizione a ἄρτος καθαρός."

¹¹   Cf. Artemidorus 1.69: "It is good for a man to dream that he is eating the kind of bread to which he is accustomed. For to a poor man, black bread is appropriate, and to a rich man, white bread. The reverse not only indicates nothing good, but, above and beyond that, something bad. For white bread signifies sickness to the poor, and black bread signifies want to the wealthy. On

11.   Seeing stars is a very good sign for people.[12]

B

12.   If you walk on roof-tiles, you will avoid the harm of your enemies.[13]

13.   Receiving a book: know that you will receive honor.[14]

14.   Eating grapes indicates rainfall.[15]

15.   If you are obese,[16] you will be very dishonored.[17]

16.   Claps of thunder in one's dream are the words of messengers.[18]

17.   To be shut up in a deep shaft[19] is a terrible dream in every respect.

Γ

18.   Milk causes you to have a gentle demeanor.[20]

19.   Milk scatters the plans of your enemies.

20a.   If you laugh in your dream, you will be upset when you wake up.

20b.   If you laugh in your dream, you will have grievous ways.[21]

---

the other hand, barley bread means good luck for everyone. There is a legend that barley bread was the first food that men received from the gods. Wheat-meal and barley-meal mean the same as bread, but to a lesser degree."

[12]   See also Artemidorus 2.36.

[13]   The meaning is based perhaps on an association with the verb κερμιδόω (to make a roof from shields—that is, the *testudo*). For Byzantine roof-tiles, see Rautman 2006, 107–8, 114–15.

[14]   Cf. Artemidorus 2.45. Guidorizzi (1980, 100 ad loc.) comments how the differences in interpretation in Artemidorus and Nicephorus may be attributed to the different value that books assumed in each culture; cf. my remarks above in Chapter 4, note 89.

[15]   But cf. Artemidorus 1.73; *Somniale Danielis* ("Beiträge, IV") CCLXIX: *uvas acerbas videre, litem significat.*

[16]   So I take the phrase βρίθων τὸ σῶμα. Brackertz translates (1993, his 51): "Drückt dich schwere Last"; Guidorizzi (1980): "Se hai il corpo appesantito."

[17]   But cf. Achmet 87: "The flesh as a whole signifies every kind of wealth and money. If someone dreams that his flesh became fatter, he will acquire wealth and money in proportion to his weight."

[18]   In the case of ἄγγελος, it is often hard to determine whether "angel" or "messenger" is intended. I usually translate the word as "messenger" unless there is a specific marker (e.g., θεοῦ, as in 1 above). For thunder, see Artemidorus 2.8.

[19]   So I translate βυθῷ κρατεῖσθαι. Guidorizzi (1980) translates: "Essere rinchiusi in un pozzo"; Brackertz (1993, his 54): "In der Tiefe des Meeres zu versinken."

[20]   Pun between γάλα (milk) and γαληνός (gentle). This dream has a positive interpretation also in Artemidorus 4.62 and Achmet 237.

[21]   Guidorizzi (1980, 101 ad loc.) discusses the corrupt manuscript tradition here. There are two different versions in the Latin Daniel: *Somniale Danielis* ("Beiträge, IV") CCXVII: *ridere*

21. If you dream of becoming old, you will have privilege.[22]
22a. Eating sweets foretells bitterness for you.[23]
22b. If you eat sweets, you will have bitter ways.
23. Marrying a woman: consider this a change in your way of life.[24]

Δ

24. Plums, when eaten [in a dream], foretell illness.
25. The bites of dogs point to harm at the hands of your enemies.[25]
26. Names indicate the character of people appearing in your dream.[26]
27. Falling from a house: reckon this as harm.[27]
28a. Consider a sweet fragrance a foul odor.
28b. Consider a foul odor displeasure.[28]
29. If you receive gifts, you will not be far from making profit.[29]

---

aut stridentes viderit, tristitiam significat; and *Somniale Danielis* ("Beiträge, V") 126: *ridere aut ridentem videre, lucrum significat*. See my comment to Daniel 110.

[22] A pun between γέρων (old age) and γέρας (honor or privilege). Cf. Artemidorus 1.50. As Prof. Mavroudi observes, this is another example that Nicephorus operates at the level of "learned," not "folk," literature (see Chapter 1 above): the word γέρας is not vernacular, and so for someone to catch the pun, one would have to have some education in ancient literature.

[23] Achmet (249) views this dream, interpreted here negatively by antinomy, as foretelling goodness.

[24] A decidedly negative interpretation can be found in *Somniale Danielis* ("Beiträge, IV") CCXLIX: *uxorem ducere, dampnum significat*; an even more negative interpretation is given in Artemidorus 2.65.

[25] So too ibid., 2.12 and Achmet 277.

[26] So I translate δηλοῦσι κλήσεις τῶν ὁρωμένων τρόπους. So too Guidorizzi: "Le parole rivelano il carattere di coloro che appaiono in sogno"; he further observes (1980, 101 ad loc.) that "Il verso è assai oscuro." Brackertz translates (1993, his 160): "Namen offenbaren den Charakter derer, die man schaut"; he offers (236 ad loc.) a brief note of the importance of names in antiquity. See Laiou 1977, 108–41 for a fuller discussion of names in Byzantine society and how they were chosen: some names were derived from crafts and professions, some were toponymics, and still others came from family ties and nicknames. Also Rautman 2006, 19–20.

[27] The manuscript tradition here is divided. Most manuscripts have the reading δόμου πεσών (which I translate), but a few (as well as Germanus, which is an independent witness to the Nicephorean tradition) have δόμου πεσόντος (if one's house has fallen down). See Guidorizzi 1980, 101 ad loc.

[28] Cf. Achmet 105. The two traditions are interpreted differently: one according to antinomy, the other by analogy.

[29] A straightforward analogy.

E

30a.   If someone is burning incense, this is a bitter dream.

30b.   If someone fumigates you with incense, this is a bitter dream.[30]

31.   Mud is indicative of the soul's sordidness.[31]

32.   If someone is standing in a church, he will deal with accusations.[32]

33a.   Seeing a eunuch is altogether auspicious.[33]

33b.   Seeing a eunuch brings about a good result.[34]

34.   Eating with your enemies brings about reconciliation.[35]

35.   If a viper appears, it expresses harm caused by your enemies.[36]

Z

36.   A belt that has been cut in two quickly ends a trip.[37]

---

[30]   Cf. Achmet 28: "If someone dreams that he was fumigating people with a censer, he will give them words both piercing and sweet: piercing because of the fire, and sweet because of the sweet smell; he will also disclose one of his secrets to them."

Censers were used in churches, especially to fumigate the altar, the Gospel, and the Eucharist: *ODB* 1:397. Incense was also used at funerals, exorcisms, and when honoring a great person: *ODB* 2:991.

[31]   Cf. Artemidorus 3.29; Achmet 172.

[32]   A pun between ἐκκλησία (church) and ἔγκλησις (accusation).

[33]   Eunuchs enjoyed a very high status in Byzantium; see the discussion in Rosser 2001, s.v. "Eunuchs," and Brackertz 1993, 234 ad his 97, who comments that even patriarchs were eunuchs. Although there were laws against castrating children, some parents still castrated their sons to place them in the Byzantine administration (Kazhdan and McCormick 1997, 178; Treadgold 1997, 551); the *koubouklion*, for example, was the corps of palace eunuchs. Attitudes changed in the eleventh century, however, when manliness among the nobility was greatly emphasised. See Guilland 1967, 1:165–97; Kazhdan and McCormick 1997, 178–80; McCormick 1997, 236–7; *ODB* 2:746–7; Rautman 2006, 27–8 (with n. 15 on 36), 55–6, 87–8; Treadgold 1997, 117, 384, 423. Castration was also inflicted on certain people in order to prevent them from assuming the throne: Treadgold 1997, 431, 433, 455, 487.

For eunuchs as a positive dream symbol, see Achmet 97 and 99 (with Mavroudi 2002, 269); but cf. Artemidorus 2.69: "Sophists, poor men, priests of Cybele, castrated men, and eunuchs are also untrustworthy." The difference between the positive associations in Achmet and the Byzantine dreambooks and the negative ones in Artemidorus can be explained by variances in cultural attitudes.

[34]   But cf. *Somniale Danielis* ("Beiträge, IV") XCIV: *eunuchos viderit, dampnum significo.*

[35]   Cf. Artemidorus 2.2: "Dreams in which a person addresses and embraces his enemies indicate the end of their hostility."

[36]   Achmet 281; but Artemidorus (4.56) considers the viper a rich man or woman.

[37]   Cf. Achmet 242.

H

37a.   Holding nails: consider this the barbs of enemies.

37b.   Holding nails: look out for the barbs of enemies.[38]

Θ

38.   Seeing a tranquil sea is a favorable sign.[39]

39.   If you dream of dying, you will be without worries.[40]

40.   A cow, when seen [in a dream], brings about a good deed.[41]

41.   A shattered staff does not produce a good result.[42]

42.   Eating lettuce: this indicates bodily disease.[43]

43.   Doors that have collapsed mean harm for their owners.[44]

I

44a.   If you are up to your neck in mud, consider this to be harm to your soul.[45]

44b.   If you are floating[46] in mud, consider this to be harm to your soul.

45.   If you fall from a horse in your dream, you will end up in disaster.[47]

46.   Dreaming of black horses is not at all good.[48]

---

[38]   Cf. *Somniale Danielis* ("Beiträge, IV") LI.

[39]   But cf. Artemidorus 2.23; *Somniale Danielis* ("Beiträge, V") 88: *mare limpidum videre, expeditionem significat.*

[40]   A straightforward analogy. Cf. Achmet 132 (though in his 131, this same dream has an unfavorable interpretation); see also the dreams in Artemidorus 2.49.

[41]   So too Achmet 236 and 237.

[42]   Cf. ibid., 211.

[43]   So too Artemidorus 1.67. Guidorizzi (1980, 102 ad loc.) comments how the interpretation probably derives from the traditional cultural association of lettuce with death and sterility ("L'esito negativo attribuito alla lattuga riflette forse l'eco di antichi tabú agricoli, nei quali questa pianta [appartenente alla sfera rituale del marcio e del purtido] è connessa con la morte e la sterilità").

[44]   Cf. Achmet 146: "If someone dreams that the wall or balcony or arch of his house collapsed or that the wood was broken or that the door was unfastened or burned down, all these things signify the fall of the homeowner or of his relatives." See also Artemidorus 2.10.

[45]   Cf. ibid., 3.29; Achmet 172.

[46]   So πεπλευκώς; the usual meaning of "sailing in" does not make sense.

[47]   A wordplay between πίπτειν (falling) and πτῶσις (calamity). Falling off one's horse could be fatal. Saboris, the *strategos* of the Armeniac theme who had revolted and declared himself emperor in 668, fell off his horse during military exercises and subsequently died: Treadgold 1997, 320.

[48]   Cf. *Somniale Danielis* ("Beiträge, IV") LXXXVIII: *equo nigro sedere, anxietatem significo.*

47. Being captured by Ishmaelites:[49] consider this something good.[50]

48a. Eating fish is not unpleasant for you.

48b. Eating fish: you will cleave to unpleasantness.[51]

K

49. A smashed oil lamp dissolves scandal.[52]

50. Seeing the fruit of olive trees: this is auspicious.[53]

51a. If anyone is around a fox, he will soon see profit.[54]

51b. Meeting a fox: expect profit.[55]

52. If you cry in your dream, you will be absolutely happy.

53a. Holding keys indicates soundness of character.[56]

53b. Holding keys causes soundness of character.[57]

54. Holding a branch: expect to be accused.[58]

---

[49] So Ἰσμαηλίταις συσχεθέις. Guidorizzi (1980) and Brackertz (1993, his 140) both translate similarly: "Se sei oppresso dagli Ismaeliti," and "Dünkt es dich, du seist den Ismaeliten in die Hände gefallen." The verb συνέχω can also mean, in the passive voice, "to engage in close combat" (LSJ, s.h.v., 2.d.), and so the interpretation could be translated as "being involved in battle with Ishmaelites."

[50] The terms "Arabs," "Ishmaelites," and "Saracens" were interchangeable; cf. Gigli 1978, 77 n. 47. The Ishmaelites were the offspring of Ishmael, and therefore Arabs (northern Arabic tribes specifically). For a brief history of the Ishmaelites, see Brackertz 1993, 235 ad his 140. Guidorizzi (1980, 103 ad loc.) uses this verse to argue that the dating of this dreambook cannot predate the seventh century because of the mention of Ishmaelites ("[I]l verso è notevole perché offre l'unica indicazione cronologica sulla data di composizione del prontuario di ps.-Niceforo, che non può quindi risalire a prima della seconda metà del VII secolo"). For early Byzantine interactions with Arabs, see Greatrex 2005, 498–503 (with full bibliography); Gregory 2005, 164–70; *LAnt* 308; Treadgold 1997, 301–7 (bibliography on 905–7).

[51] Cf. Artemidorus 1.70 for both good and bad interpretations of eating fish: "It is also good to eat fish, especially when it is roasted, but no less so when it has been prepared in some other way—with the exception of small fish. For they have more bones than meat. They do not signify profit in any way, but rather hatred toward our nearest relatives, and vain hopes."

[52] A pun between κανδῆλα (oil lamp) and σκάνδαλα (scandal). But Guidorizzi (1980, 103 ad loc.) reads much more into this image: "Si tratta di una trasparente simbologia sessuale."

[53] Also a good dream in Artemidorus 2.25; cf. *Somniale Danielis* ("Beiträge, V") 109: *olivas colligere, lucrum significat.* Laiou (2002c, 321) calculates that ten or twelve olive trees were needed to meet a Byzantine household's needs.

[54] See too Artemidorus 2.12.

[55] A pun between κερδώ (fox) and κέρδος (profit).

[56] Guidorizzi (1980, 103 ad loc.) is unclear how to translate here τρόπων, which I translate in this instance as "character."

[57] See Artemidorus 3.54. For keys in Byzantium, see Vikan and Nesbitt 1980, 2–5.

[58] A pun between κλῆμα (branch) and ἐγκαλεῖσθαι (to be accused).

55.   If someone wears a collar,[59] he is not far from danger.

56.   Trees that have been cut down foretell the downfall of men.[60]

57a.   If you sit in feces, expect harm.

57b.   If you sit in feces, you will experience all manner of harm.[61]

58.   If you see crows, consider them demons.[62]

59.   Eating meat is not a good sign for anyone.[63]

60a.   If someone falls from a cliff, he will soon be unfortunate.

60b.   If someone falls from a cliff, this indicates an unlucky fate.

61.   Seeing barley brings one to a court of judgement.[64]

62.   Rams, when dreamt of, prepare easy trips.[65]

63.   The barking of dogs signifies harm from enemies.[66]

Λ

64.   A dream of lions indicates a multitude of enemies.[67]

65.   White hairs signify useful activities.[68]

---

[59]   Guidorizzi (1980, 103 ad loc.) states that the word can mean not only a collar (especially a dog collar), but also a pillory ("Κλοιός è il collare [specialmente dei cani] oppure anche la gogna"). LSJ, (s.h.v.), cites ancient texts that describe the κλοιός as a wooden collar used on prisoners, a meaning that could well explain the dream's interpretation.

[60]   To the references cited in my comment to Daniel 123, add Artemidorus 2.10: "If the trees that grow in front of the house are burning, it portends the death of the masters. As for the trees that grow inside the house, large trees burning likewise signify the death of the owners of the house: those whose names are masculine in gender signify the death of men; those whose names are feminine signify the death of women."

[61]   Cf. ibid., 2.26.

[62]   But cf. ibid., 2.20: "The crow indicates a long period of time, a delay in business affairs, and an old woman because of its longevity. It also indicates a storm, since the crow is the harbinger of storms."

[63]   But this is consistently a good symbol in Achmet—e.g., 87, 89, 127, 132, 158, 233, 234, 235, 237, 240, 267, 272, 273, 276, 278, 279, 280, 281, 283, 284, 287, 288.

[64]   A pun between κριθαί (barley) and κριτήριον (tribunal). Cf. Artemidorus 1.68; but in Achmet 208, barley foretells wealth and strength of body.

[65]   Also a positive sign in Artemidorus 2.12; but see Achmet 240.

[66]   See the various interpretations of this dream in Artemidorus 2.11; cf. Achmet 277.

[67]   But the lion symbolises a king, according to Artemidorus 2.12 and Achmet 267. As Prof. Mavroudi points out, the dream, with its association of lion with king, underscores how unpleasant it was for the average person to encounter imperial authority (in the form of tax collectors, soldiers, etc.).

[68]   But Achmet (18) offers a negative interpretation: "If someone dreams that the hairs on his head were completely white, let him know that whoever has power over him will be greatly oppressed; if he dreams that his beard was completely white, he himself will come into dishonor."

66. Dreaming that one has white skin: this is exceedingly auspicious.[69]
67. A wolf with its jaws agape signifies foolish habits.

M

68. Pearls indicate the flowing of tears.
69. Holding a dagger portrays a quarrel.[70]
70. Having a black face brings about lengthy sorrows.[71]
71. If a black person appears [in your dream], he is a harbinger of disease.[72]
72. If you are holding apples, expect to be united in love [ἔρως].[73]
73. Embracing your mother:[74] reckon this as a very good dream.[75]
74. Dreaming of pure people:[76] consider this propitious.[77]
75. Eating mushrooms points to a dose of poisons.[78]
76. The appearance of a mouse reveals a [previously hidden] character trait.[79]

---

[69] Ibid., 88: "If someone dreams that his skin turned from white to black like an Ethiopian's, he will be an untrustworthy and ludicrous liar; if a woman has this dream, she will become known as a prostitute and be divorced by her husband." The word "Ethiopian" was applied in Byzantine literature to any person of black color who lived in Africa, from the Atlantic to the Indian Ocean: *ODB* 2:733.

[70] A pun between μάχαιρα (dagger) and μάχη (quarrel). But this dream has a very good interpretation in Artemidorus 2.31 and Achmet 247.

[71] See my comment to 66 above. The color black is consistently considered a bad sign in Artemidorus—e.g., 2.11, 2.12, 2.36, 4.33.

[72] Racism and anti-Semitism occurred in the ancient world as well as in Byzantium. See, e.g., Avi-Yonah 1984; *ODB* 1:122–3; Williams 1935. See Maas 2005a, 16 (with nn. 58–9) and Matschke 2002b, 474–6 for Jews in Constantinople; De Lange (2005) gives an extensive discussion for the sixth century. The emperor Leo III, thinking his losses to the Arabs were due to God's wrath, tried to force all Jews to be baptised: Treadgold 1997, 350.

[73] So Achmet 198. See my comment to Daniel 368 for apples as a metaphor for women and sex.

[74] Guidorizzi (1980) takes this verse as denoting sexual relations. In dream 3 above, where we have the same phrasing (ἀνδρὶ πλακεῖς) as here (μητρὶ πλακεῖς), he translates as "se abbracci un uomo," but here he translates, "giacere in sogno con la madre." Although a sexual nature cannot be ruled out (cf. Daniel 364), I translate along the lines of Brackertz (1993, his 192): "Wenn du die Mutter umarmst. …"

[75] But see Artemidorus 1.79; Achmet 128.

[76] So μορφὰς ἀγνὰς. As Prof. Mavroudi comments, pure people would include children, saints, and individuals admired for their honesty and moral conduct.

[77] So too Achmet 150, but not so for the Arabic texts on which he usually relies; see Mavroudi 2002, 273.

[78] For the supposed poisoning of Caesar Augustus through mushrooms, see Tacitus, *Annals* 12.67. Dalby (2003, 76) records a warning by Cecaumenus to avoid mushrooms because of their deadly effects. But cf. Achmet 203 for more positive interpretations of mushrooms.

[79] See Artemidorus 3.28. The mouse is portrayed in Byzantine sources as a despicable and hated creature, since it destroys foodstuffs, books, and works of art: *ODB* 2:1360. The bracketed

N

77.   If you see dead people, you will experience the death of your affairs.[80]

Ξ

78.   Withered oak trees that appear [in a dream]: this is not a good sign.

79a.   Withered trees that are dreamt of: you will toil to no avail.

79b.   Withered trees that are dreamt of: [your] efforts [will be] useless.

80.   If you are holding a sword, expect [to find a weapon].[81]

81.   Having a plank of wood: consider this a good sign.[82]

O

82.   It is not good to dream that your teeth have fallen out.[83]

83.   To dream that a house is burning is good.[84]

84.   Turbid wine clearly signifies many sorrows.[85]

85a.   Wine that has been poured out stops sorrows [caused by] messengers.[86]

85b.   Wine that has been poured out stops angry quarrels.

86a.   Getting a cup of wine: expect a state of confusion.[87]

86b.   Getting a cup of wine: expect terrible quarrels.[88]

87.   Washing off mud points to release from worries.[89]

---

words in the translation are suggested by Prof. Mavroudi on the basis of the analogy to mice coming out and destroying things in a household while people are sleeping: nobody sees the mice's destruction, only the result of their presence.

[80]   A pun between νεκροί (dead people) and νέκρωσις (mortification).

[81]   Guidorizzi (1980, 37 and 105 ad loc.) discusses the various ways that later copyists tried, unsuccessfully, to fix the hopelessly mangled manuscript tradition. For his version of the text (translated here), Guidorizzi borrowed the verse as it appears in the Suda. The sword as a dream symbol is typically a sign of power; see Achmet 247, and my comment to Anonymous 393.

[82]   Perhaps so interpreted because ξύλον was often used to refer to the cross of Jesus?

[83]   Cf. Achmet 60 and 61.

[84]   Cf. *Somniale Danielis* ("Beiträge, IV") CCLCII: *si videris domum tuam ardentem, invenire te pecuniam significat*; but cf. *Somniale Danielis* ("Beiträge, V") 80: *incendia in quacunque domo videris, ipsa domus aliquod periculum obtinebit*; Artemidorus 2.10; Achmet 159.

[85]   So too ibid., 195.

[86]   Cf. ibid., 186.

[87]   Ibid., 186.

[88]   The most common interpretation according to the Byzantine dreambooks. The same interpretation appears in Mavroudi's Arabic texts (2002, 349–50).

[89]   Cf. Achmet 177.

88a. Relating a dream within a dream is a true dream.[90]

88b. Telling a dream in a dream is a true dream.

89.   Sitting on a donkey signifies unlucky ways.[91]

90a. Walking on a mountain: this signifies violence in one's affairs.

90b. Crawling on a mountain: this points to violence to one's affairs.

91.   Dreaming of olive oil: you will escape all harm.[92]

92.   Walking on snakes: you will destroy the barbs of your enemies.[93]

93a. If you are disturbed or troubled [ὀχλούμενος], know that you will live well.

93b. Being with disturbed or troubled people: this is an unfortunate sign.[94]

Π

94a. Being bound with shackles is extremely inauspicious.

94b. Carrying shackles in your hands: expect to come into danger.

95a. If someone dreams of a dove, this foretells joy.[95]

95b. If someone dreams of a dove, this brings about harm.

96.   If you are sitting on a rock, cherish good hopes.

97.   Washing one's feet points to an easy trip.[96]

98.   [Having] flat[97] feet points to a mass of sorrows.

---

[90]   So I translate Ὄναρ ὀνείρους νητρεκὲς πέλει λέγειν. That is, whatever dream narrative one may offer in a dream will come true (so Prof. Mavroudi paraphrases). Brackertz translates likewise (1993, his 229): "Spricht einer im Traum, so ist das ein wahrer Traum." Guidorizzi (1980) translates: "Sogno del sogno predice il vero."

[91]   But a positive dream image in Achmet 233, since the donkey, as Prof. Mavroudi points out, was the mode of transportation of a triumphant Semitic prophet and Achmet's source is Arabic. The negative interpretation above in a Christian text may be the result of an association with the horrible death that Christ suffered after His triumphal entrance on a donkey on Palm Sunday.

[92]   Achmet 241.

[93]   For the snake symbolising an enemy, cf. *Somniale Danielis* ("Beiträge, V") 135: *serpentem infestare, inimici tui superationem significat.* See too Artemidorus 1.64 and Achmet 281. There may be a reference to the spurious ending of Mark's gospel (16:9–20, specifically verse 18), where disciples are told that if they pick up snakes they will not be harmed.

[94]   Guidorizzi (1980, 93 ad loc.) comments on the two different methods of interpretation (antinomy, and cause and effect or simple analogy) in 93a and 93b: "Le due redazioni presentano qui (come al verso seguente) un testo assai differente, né è possibile definire quale abbia innovato; *a* propone un'interpretazione fondata su un rapporto di rovesciamento (turbamento = tranquillità: per questo schema, cfr. anche il. v. 52), *b* su un nesso di causa ad effetto."

[95]   Cf. Achmet 291; but Artemidorus (2.20) takes the dove as a sexually promiscuous woman.

[96]   But cf. *Somniale Danielis* ("Beiträge, IV") CCXI: *pedes lavare, anxietatem significat.*

[97]   So I translate πλατεῖς. Guidorizzi (1980) offers "grossi"; Brackertz (1993, his 263), "Plattfüße."

99.   If your feet are cut off, start no trip at all.[98]

100.   A tower[99] that has collapsed points to the death of magistrates.[100]

101a.   If you see a running foal, consider this an imperial official.

101b.   If you see a running foal, this is something mysterious.[101]

Ρ

102.   A needle in one's house points to a dose of poisons.[102]

103.   Flowing rivers personify enemies.[103]

Σ

104.   Eating cuttlefish results in a long illness.[104]

105.   Worms represent harm caused by enemies.[105]

---

[98]   Cf. Achmet 116 and 117.

[99]   The πυργός typically was a fortification tower (as I take it here), but it could also be a fortified residence, part of the fortifications of a monastery (a very notable example is the monastery of Saint Catherine in the Sinai, which was fortified by Justinian), or a watchtower in the country: see Bouras 2002, 505; Rautman 2006, 223.

[100]   A pair of analogies framed in a–b–a–b sequence: πυργὸς πεσὼν δείκνυσι ἀρχόντων μόρον.

[101]   Guidorizzi (1980) takes μυστικόν as referring to a friend or even secretary. Guilland (1968) discusses this word as the title of an illustrious imperial office. During the last half of Byzantium, the word denoted a high-ranking functionary close to the emperor: *ODB* 2:1431–2. In the first interpretation, I take the word as having this meaning (the Greek can be accusative masculine singular). In the second interpretation, the word is definitely neuter and so denotes "something mysterious"; Brackertz (1993, his 271) likewise translates: "Ein Fohlen laufen zu sehen bedeutet etwas Geheimnisvolles." Prof. Mavroudi suggests that some scribe changed the text before him since the administrative meaning of μυστικός was not obvious to him.

[102]   Or, "A needle points to a dose of poisons in one's household." Guidorizzi emends the manuscript reading of ῥαφίς or ῥαφανίς to ῥάφη, hence his translation of "rafano." See his extended discussion (1980, 106 ad loc.). He emends on the basis of Daniel 237 (for which see above). But sewing with a needle can symbolise magical spells: see Achmet 228. I have decided to retain the original reading, although Guidorizzi's emendation is perfectly fine.

[103]   Cf. Achmet 174. Given the harm and dangers that can occur through sudden river flow, the interpretation is clear.

[104]   Dalby (2003, 146, 155, 156) quotes several Byzantine texts that discuss how cuttlefish, which were eaten as appetisers or side dishes, or even as the main course (Dalby 1996, 72–3), cause raw or thick humors in the body. If the bad effects of this fish on the body was common knowledge, then this would explain the interpretation above.

[105]   Achmet 85: "If someone dreams that his stomach was filled with worms that were feeding off it, a group of strangers will come to his house and live off him until they cause him distress; if the dreamer is a king, he will draft a new army and enrich it; if a woman, she will become pregnant through fornication [an obvious analogy between worms (~ penis) in the stomach and sexual intercourse]. If someone dreams that his entire body was filled with flesh-

106. Wearing a black robe: this is not a good dream.[106]
107. [Wearing] a purple robe results in a long illness.[107]
108a. [Wearing] a white robe brings about a good result.[108]
108b. It is very good to be wearing a white robe in a dream.[109]
109. Wearing the emperor's robe: this is the dissolution of one's hope.[110]
110. If you grab hold of sparrows that then fly away, expect harm.[111]
111. Anyone who embraces a pillar should expect to receive divine grace.[112]
112. Eating figs points to the slanders of foolish people.
113. Smashing a dagger: this points to the crushing of enemies.[113]
114. If wasps appear [in a dream], they are the injuries inflicted by enemies.[114]

T

115a. Sitting on a wall: you will soon thrive.
115b. Sitting on a wall: know that you will be ready for action.
116a. Having one's hair cropped short: this is most grievous.[115]
116b. Having your hair cropped short points to harm to your business and property.
117. If your hair falls out, consider this to be great danger.
118a. Being led around like a blind man:[116] consider this very inauspicious.

---

eating worms, he will involuntarily become a feeder of people; if a poor man has this dream, he will be rich in proportion to the number of worms."

[106] Ibid.,156.

[107] But a very favorable dream in ibid., 157.

[108] Ibid., 156.

[109] Ibid., 215: "Although white garments signify goodness, this is true [only when a dreamer wears them] habitually."

[110] But cf. ibid., 157. Guidorizzi (1980) takes ἐλπίδος λύσις differently: "una speranza realizzata"; cf. Brackertz (1993, his 298): "Hoffnungen zunichte." I prefer to take λύσις in a negative way, as in 129 below, on the grounds that wearing imperial garments would not be appropriate for non-royalty (cf. Manuel 37).

[111] The interpretation of sparrows as symbolic of harm occurs also in Manuel 10; see below.

[112] In Byzantine culture, the column symbolised Jesus and the apostles (in the sense of "moral pillar" and "support"): *ODB* 1:483. There is also the biblical image of God as a pillar of smoke during the Israelites' departure from Egypt (Exodus 13:21).

[113] A wordplay here between συνθλᾶν (smashing) and θλίψις (crushing), with the metaphor of dagger as enemy.

[114] So Achmet 282, cited above in my comment to Daniel 337.

[115] See my comments to Daniel 89 and 280.

[116] So I take τυφλὸν φέρεσθαι; cf. Brackertz's translation (1993, his 312): "Scheint dir, du gingest als Blinder einher"; see his comments (1993, 241–2) ad loc.

118b. Being led around like a blind man: this is exceedingly auspicious.

Y

119. Water bursting up from below ground foretells enemies.[117]
120. Drinking clear sparkling water: expect happiness.[118]

Φ

121a. If a rabbit is seen [in a dream], it signifies a misfortunate way of life.[119]
121b. If a rabbit is seen [in a dream], it makes trips unlucky.
122. Having lice indicates deceit for those you live with.[120]
123a. Kissing arouses long battles with demons.[121]
123b. Kissing arouses long fights with enemies.[122]
124. Eating with a friend leads to a good deed.
125. The continuous lapping noise of the sea indicates the gradual disintegration of one's affairs.[123]
126. If the sea recedes, this is not auspicious for anyone.
127. Hearing a voice: this is a reliable dream.
128. Seeing the lights of heaven points to light shed on one's affairs.

---

[117] Cf. Achmet 182.

[118] Artemidorus 1.66.

[119] But cf. Achmet 276.

[120] Brackertz (1993, 242 ad his 324) comments: "Läuse waren im Mittelalter anscheinend ständige Gäste des gemeinen Mannes." Arabic dreambooks interpreted lice as money: Mavroudi 2002, 438.

[121] But cf. Achmet 135: "If someone dreams that he kissed someone for the sake of friendship and union, he will do good to that person out of love; but if because of sexual desire, he will be treated well by that man. If he dreams that he kissed a person on the neck, he will show kindness to that man; if on the shoulder, to the man's wives; if on the arms, to the man's brother or trusted slave; and so likewise regarding the other limbs as previously stated." Who gives and who receives a kiss matters according to the Latin Daniel dreambook: *Somniale Danielis* ("Beiträge, V") 111: *osculum accipere, lucrum significat*, versus *Somniale Danielis* ("Beiträge, V") 112: *osculum dare, dampnum significat*.

[122] Cf. Achmet 136: "If someone dreams that he kissed a known enemy for the purpose of reconciliation, he will hate him even more; but if the man is not an enemy, he will make that man privy to his secret."

[123] The gradual erosion of one's affairs is analogous to the gradual erosion of the shoreline by the water.

X

129. Washing your hands indicates the dissolution of worries.[124]

130. A black tunic points to a shameful way of life.[125]

131. A torn tunic[126] tears away the oppressive weight of worries.[127]

132. If snow appears [in a dream], it brings feuds with enemies.

Ω

133. Having and then cooking eggs signifies sorrows.

Appendix I[128]

Prologue I[129]

1. Above all else, be master of your passions and stomach,

2. And let tears fall from your eyes

3. As you make your prayers from the depths of your heart

4. And as you lift up your hands to your God and Lord.

5. For in this way you will be able to see clearly and concisely

6. The nebulous images that come from dreams.

7. A full stomach, a lot of drinking and the stupor [brought about]

8. By unmixed wine, the darkness of anxieties,

9. And mental despair cause false dreams.

---

[124] But cf. *Somniale Danielis* ("Beiträge, IV") CLXXX: *manus lavare, molestias graves significat.*

[125] The Byzantine tunic could be long or short, short-sleeved or long-sleeved: Rautman 2006, 48–9. At the imperial court, one's rank was denoted by the type of *khitōn* worn: *ODB* 3:2127–8.

[126] Brackertz (1993, 226 ad his Astrampsychus 97, which is the equivalent of this verse) says: "Griech. *chiton*, lat. *tunica*, ein kurzärmeliges Hemd aus Leintuch, das von Mannern wie Frauen getragen wurde."

[127] A wordplay between ῥαγεῖς (torn) and ἔρρηξε (tears away).

[128] See Guidorizzi's (1980) apparatus criticus, for which medieval and renaissance manuscripts contain each of the various verses in Appendix I.

[129] For the thoughts expressed in these prologues, see Artemidorus 1.1–2. In effect, the prologues recommend three ways for securing true dreams: sexual abstinence, good dietary regimen, and prayer. Guidorizzi (1980, 109 ad loc.) relates these principles to Christian incubation, citing Deubner 1900, 14–18. See Chapter 3 above for incubation practices in the Byzantine period.

Prologue II

10.   It befits to be sober in order to see [reliable] dreams,

11.   And not to be defiled by shameful passions,

12.   So that after being purified in soul and mind you can more easily

13.   Discern the [correct] interpretations of your dreams.

Prologue III

14.   You can perceive the completely true images of your dreams

15.   If you are sober, very pure, and without sordidness.

16.   Stay sober, my friend, and toss aside the indecent trickery of sexual matters.

A

17.   The dream of a rooster is a truthful one.

B

18.   Walking on thorns points to the ways of your enemies.[130]

19.   Walking in one's dream shows harm inflicted by enemies.

20.   Being kissed by the emperor signifies honor.

Γ

21.   If you are struck in the jaw: consider yourself free.[131]

22.   A dream while lying awake[132] is a true dream.

23.   If you are sitting naked, you will be stripped of your property.[133]

Δ

24.   Receiving letters that have been written in red ink:

25   Expect to receive very soon either an official rank of authority or death.[134]

---

[130]   Cf. Artemidorus 3.33; Achmet 211.

[131]   Brackertz (1993, 232 ad his 63) describes the historical background for this interpretation ("Die Freilassung eines Sklaven wurde durch einen Schlag auf dessen Wange bekräftigt").

[132]   That is, a vision. See ibid. (232 ad his 68) for discussion.

[133]   Cf. Achmet 118.

[134]   Brackertz (1993, 232 ad his 66) discusses how red ink was used in imperial documents ("Kaiserliche Befehle wurden in Byzanz auf scharlachrotem Papier geschrieben, die kaiserliche

26.   Dreaming of church feasts: know that these are gifts of God.[135]

27.   Eating pomegranates: expect to struggle with illness.[136]

28.   Having big ears results in gain.[137]

Z

29.   A dream of being girded: consider [this] to be profit-making for you.[138]

Θ

30.   A dream of wild animals talking: understand this as oppression.

31.   A dream of wild animals running: understand this as tumult.

32.   If you comb the hairs of your head, call it honor.[139]

I

33.   If someone dreams of horses, this signifies the appearance of messengers.

K

34.   It is good to eat fruits that are in season,[140]

35.   Yet [eating them] out of season causes you loss.[141]

Unterschrift erfolgte stets mit roter Tinte. Die purpurroten Schuhe waren das wichtigste Kennzeichen der Kaiserwürde"). See too *ODB* 1:17 and 2:995. The interpretation of the dream above is clear: the imperial document contains either a death warrant or a promotion in rank.

[135]   See Guidorizzi 1980, 110 ad loc. For church feasts, see Arranz 1979; Dihle 1992; *ODB* 2:781–2; Rautman 2006, 108–9, 114–15. The liturgical calendar was filled with feast days: 66 full feasts (not including Sundays) and 27 half-feasts.

[136]   Cf. Artemidorus 1.73: "Pomegranates mean wounds because of their color, tortures because of their prickles, slavery and submission because of the Eleusinian legend [that is, the story of Demeter and Persephone]." Cf. Achmet 151 and 198.

[137]   Cf. ibid., 48 and 49.

[138]   I translate Guidorizzi's text, which adds κερδοσύνην σοι (profit-making for you). Guidorizzi (1980, 110 ad loc.) discusses the corrupt nature of the text and his own emendation of Drexl's emendation ("Il testo è corrotto nei manoscritti; Drexl emenda in κέρδος σοι εἶναι; un altra soluzione potrebbe essere κερδοσύνην σοι; il senso complessivo del verso è communque chiaro").

[139]   See Artemidorus 2.6.

[140]   So too Achmet 200.

[141]   Cf. the dream given in ibid., 199: "A certain man came and consulted Sereim in the presence of several people: 'I dreamt that I climbed up an apricot tree and was eating some of the fruit.' Sereim said to him: 'You will receive goodness and charity from a wealthy man.'

36.   It is good to be flying: this [is] a good deed.[142]

37.   If olive oil is poured on your head, reckon this as good.[143]

38.   Holding lit wax candles: this is very good.

39.   Holding extinguished wax candles: this is inauspicious.

40.   If you are holding a hawk, you will certainly get what you want.[144]

41.   Crying in the dark foretells idle sorrow.

42.   Holding a sword is good for any dreamer.

Λ

43.   A dream of sitting at a pit: this is not auspicious.

M

44.   To be sleeping [among] grinding stones in a mill or to be among[145] them is an unlucky sign.

N

45.   Dead oxen indicate the years of a famine.[146]

46.   If someone is holding spun garments, you should expect sorrows.

Ξ

47.   Dreaming that the sea has dried up is the removal of evils.

After a considerable number of days, another man came to Sereim, who was with the very same people, and related the exact same dream as the previous man. Sereim told him: 'You will have grief and torments.' Now those sitting there were at a complete loss as to why Sereim, given the same dream, had rendered two different interpretations. Sereim responded: 'When the first man consulted me, it was the fruit-bearing season; but when the other man came, it was autumn. Therefore, the interpretation had to be changed.' And upon investigation they discovered that the events happened just as the dream interpreter had predicted."

[142] Ibid., 161.

[143] Ibid., 23.

[144] Cf. ibid., 285. For hawking in Byzantium, see Koukoules 1948–57, 5:395–8.

[145] So I take συνῶν; Brackertz translates (1993, his 196) as "bewohnen"; Guidorizzi (1980), as "esservi legato."

[146] See Achmet 237 (with Mavroudi 2002, 359–61). The parallel in the Hebrew Bible is Genesis 41. For famine and food shortages in Byzantium, see Laiou 2002b, 53–4; Treadgold 1997, passim, e.g., 480 (locusts in the late 920s), 495 (locusts in 961), 703 (locusts and bad weather in 1032–37).

O

48.   If a tooth is lost and another one again grows in its place,

49.   This represents gain and joy beyond expectation.[147]

50.   Having your teeth fall out: this is not a good sign.[148]

51.   A dream image of mist brings turmoil.[149]

52.   Being fed rice: expect to find profit.[150]

53.   Purple, when dreamt of, signifies disease.[151]

54.   Killing snakes: understand this as [killing] enemies.[152]

55.   Eyes that are not very large lead to life.[153]

56.   A snake, which is seen on one's bed, [means] prosperity.[154]

Π

57.   Every form of sexual intercourse[155] is indicative of lengthy desires.

58.   If you hold a partridge, know that you are possessing a woman.[156]

---

[147]   Artemidorus 1.31.

[148]   Cf. ibid., 1.31; Achmet 60, 61, 64, 65.

[149]   Guidorizzi (1980) translates ὀμιχλοειδὴς ὄψις as "un sogno confuso." Brackertz translates (1993, his 228) along my lines: "Der Anblick von Nebel oder Dunst ...." The word ζαλή (translated here as turmoil) has a variety of meanings, some literal (inclement weather) and others figurative (trouble or distress).

[150]   Cf. Achmet 208: "If someone dreams that he had a field of rice, he will get wealth along with much strife, lawsuits, and torment because of the labor involved in getting rice to grow; and if he dreams that he was eating rice, his wealth will come with greater evils."

Rice, as well as other foodstuffs like sugarcane, watermelons, spinach, and bananas, came from contact with the Islamic world: *LAnt* 281, 454.

[151]   But this is a favorable symbol in Artemidorus 1.54 and 2.3.

[152]   Ibid., 2.13 and 4.56.

[153]   Cf. Achmet 53.

[154]   But cf. Daniel 395 with the comment there.

[155]   For this meaning of μίξις, see LSJ, s.h.v. (and cf. modern Greek μῖξις). Guidorizzi (1980) translates euphemistically as "connubio"; Brackertz (1993, his 193) uses "Liebesfreuden."

[156]   Achmet 294: "The partridge represents a beautiful woman. If someone dreams that he found a domesticated partridge or had one in his house, he will get a beautiful and indulgent wife who will give him pleasure. If he dreams that he possessed or received from somebody a wild partridge, he will get a woman who, though beautiful, is quarrelsome and difficult of access. If he dreams that he had a partridge but then lost it, he will be separated from his wife. If he dreams that he was eating a partridge, he will receive from a woman wealth through apparel. If a pregnant woman dreams that she had a partridge, she will bear a daughter; if she is not pregnant, she will conceive and bear one. If a king dreams that he went hunting for partridges, he will find happiness in both his queen and women. If a king dreams that he was eating partridges, he will have sex with a desirable woman: for partridges on the whole signify women or daughters."

59.   Flying in one's dream announces a rank of honor.[157]

60.   A clear running spring dissolves the sorrows of the soul.[158]

61.   If the sky is falling, this does not foretell good things.

62.   Having your feet bound with shackles brings trouble.

63.   Leeks and onions both signify sorrows.[159]

64.   Smokeless fire has a good interpretation.

P

65.   Leaning on a staff announces rest.[160]

66.   Being beaten with a staff: view this as the acquisition of money.[161]

67.   The surf of a calm sea is altogether good.[162]

68.   The surf of a tumultuous sea points to sorrows.

Σ

69.   If your skin becomes black, this is not good for anyone.

70.   Wet skin indeed foretells sorrows.[163]

71.   If you dream of being rich, you will be poor.

72.   Sleeping in the dark is bad luck for anyone.

---

[157]   See ibid., 161 for discussion.

[158]   Cf. Artemidorus 2.27: "[Springs] overflowing with pure water mean good luck for all men, but especially for the sick and needy. For, to the sick, they are a sign of recovery; to the poor, they are a sign of wealth. For there is nothing so nourishing as water."

[159]   Achmet 204: "If someone dreams that he ate garlic or onions or leeks, he will have grief and weeping by analogy to these vegetables' bitterness. If he dreams that he did not eat any of these vegetables but was only holding them, the suffering will be less. If he dreams that he gave them to somebody he knew, that person will receive from him evil days in proportion to the number he gave. If he dreams that he was eating some of these vegetables cooked, he will experience moderate sorrow at the hands of the authorities because of the fire." Cf. Artemidorus 1.67.

[160]   Cf. Achmet 211. Artemidorus (5.51) relates the following dream: "A man dreamt that he heard someone saying that his staff was broken. He got sick and was paralysed. For the support of his body—that is, the strength and good health of his body—was signified by the staff. The same man, who was upset and annoyed that his paralysis lingered on, dreamt that his staff was broken. He regained his strength immediately. For he would no longer have any need for a support."

[161]   As we have seen repeatedly, someone who dreams of having something done to him or her, whether in the form of beating or sex, will receive benefits.

[162]   For the opposite interpretation, see Daniel 222 with comment ad loc.

[163]   So Achmet 171.

73. [Wearing] a red robe results in a good deed.[164]

T

74. Running in your dream causes strong fortunes.

Y

75. If you drink water, expect to come into profit.
76. If you hear hymns, understand this as struggles with neighbors.[165]

X

77. If a hawk flies from one's hand, this means harm [if the dreamer is a] magistrate.[166]
78. If someone is holding green grass, this brings about something good.[167]
79. If you are holding gold, you will end up not getting what you want.[168]

Ψ

80. If you dream of fleas, consider [this] to be seeing enemies.[169]
81. Drinking unmixed wine causes false dreams.[170]

Ω

82. Eating baked eggs leads to wealth.[171]

---

[164] Cf. ibid., 225.

[165] For Byzantine hymns, see Conomos 1984; Gregory 2005, 143; Treadgold 1997, 398.

[166] For the hawk and its interpretation, see Artemidorus 2.20.

[167] So Achmet 211.

[168] Gold is a sign of grief and distress in ibid., 255 and 256, but of goodness in Artemidorus 2.5 and 3.30; cf. *Somniale Danielis* ("Beiträge, IV") XVII: *aurum in somnis trectare, expeditionem negotii significat.* Cf. Daniel 2 with comment ad loc.

[169] See Achmet 295 for flies and mosquitoes as symbolic of enemies.

[170] This verse is related to the prologues above. The ancients, of course, diluted their wine; barbarians and uncivilised people drank unmixed wine, or so it was thought. Ammianus Marcellinus (15.12) describes the horrible effects of such wine on the minds and bodies of its drinkers. See the general discussion in *ODB* 1:664–5, on which this note is based.

[171] See my comment to Daniel 485. Dalby (2003, 216) refers to ὀφθὰ ὠιά (this is the phrase above) as *ouefs en cocette.*

Appendix II[172]

A

1. If you see an angel,[173] the city will have victories.[174]

2. A saint, when dreamt of, is a favorable image.[175]

3. Consider the Athinganoi[176] demons.

4. If a goat appears to you, you should understand[177] it as a savage enemy.[178]

5. If you see a rooster, expect a great slave.

6. Instead of seeing a saint, another person will appear in your dream.

7. If you own a grapevine, expect to be accused.

8. Being hung: expect to be seen lifted up in honor.[179]

---

[172] As noted in Chapter 1, each dream in Appendix II appears in only one or two of the 16 manuscripts that Guidorizzi collated. See Guidorizzi's (1980) apparatus criticus for the manuscript tradition of each particular dream.

[173] I take this ἄγγελος as "angel" and not as "messenger"; cf. Brackertz (1993, his 1): "Schaust du einen Engel, wird die Stadt den Sieg erringen." But Guidorizzi (1980) translates otherwise: "Se sogni un messaggero la città conquisterà vittorie."

[174] So too the Arabic text cited in Mavroudi 2002, 265–6.

[175] Cf. Achmet 150. For saints in Byzantine culture, see Gregory 2005, 113–18; Hackel 1981; Mango 1997; Treadgold 1997, 263–4.

[176] Brackertz (1993, 229 ad his 4) comments on this heresy and the actual Nicephorus: "Athinganer oder Melchisedekianer, eine Sekte, deren Anhänger Melchisedek, den Priesterkönig von Salem, für den Logos oder für den Hl. Geist oder für eine über Christus stehende göttliche Kraft hielten. Zentren dieser Sekte waren im 5. Jahrhundert Ägypten und Byzanz. Ihr Name drückt aus, daß sie mit Andersgläubigen keine Berührung haben wollten. … Von Nikephoros I … ist bekannt, daß er ein erbitterter Gegner der Athinganer und Paulikianer (= Manichäer) war." See also Gigli 1978, 77 n. 47. For good treatments of this heresy (constantly accused, falsely, of such practices as magic and astrology), see *ODB* 1:222; Rochow 1983; Starr 1936; Treadgold 1997, 429–30. Gypsies in the eleventh and twelfth centuries were called "Athinganoi," even though they had no connection with this sect: *ODB* 2:889.

[177] Guidorizzi (1980) has δόκα (you should expect); but Prof. Mavroudi emends to δόκει, a reading that I accept.

[178] Cf. *Somniale Danielis* ("Beiträge, IV") CXXVIII: *hircos vel capras viderit, expeditionem significat.* But the goat is a positive symbol in Achmet 240 and 262.

[179] Ibid., 89: "If someone dreams that by the order of his ruler he was forcibly and violently hung by the neck, he will be honored in glory in proportion to how high he was hung; and if the dreamer is sick or distressed, he will, after some violence, lose his condition and finally become happy. Likewise, if a king or magistrate dreams that he handed someone over to be hung, at first he will be angry and irritated at that man but later will honor him: however, the man will sin against God. If someone dreams that he ate the flesh of a hanged man, he will sinfully gain wealth from a man in high places in proportion to how much he ate." There is the obvious analogy between "being lifted up in honor" and "being hung"; the wordplay was common in

9. The resurrection of the dead results in justice.[180]

10. In addition to what is seen in a dream, words are also significant.

11. Massaging one's joints[181] signifies harm at the hands of enemies.

12. A bear that appears [in a dream]: think of it as a powerful enemy.

13. A stalk of wheat is interpreted as wealth [that will last] for years.

14. If you dream of being unruly [ἄτακτον], understand this as the appearance of a demon.

15. Consider flutes the laments and cries of grief.[182]

16. If you become insane, you soon will have wealth.[183]

17. If you dream of being mute, this is most heinous.[184]

18. If you see chaff, this swiftly leads to joy.

B

19. A spirited gait signifies progress in your life.

20. Falling into a deep hole signifies danger for you.

21. Acorns are a good sign, even if you dream of them only.

22. Arrows in a dream signify grief caused by poisons.

---

ancient literature and in the Christian Bible, e.g., Pseudo-Callisthenes 2.21.26; Artemidorus 1.2 and 2.53; John 3:14, 12:32–3. For a negative interpretation of a dream of being hung, see Artemidorus 2.50.

[180] Cf. Achmet 5: "If someone dreams of the resurrection of the dead, justice will be carried out in whatever place he saw the resurrection occurring. For if unjust people are living there, they will be punished; but if people are being wronged, they will quickly have right done to them: for God alone is the righteous judge in the resurrection of the dead, and because of this the interpretation is as reliable as one can possibly be."

[181] Guidorizzi (1980) translates as follows: "Logorare le articolazioni indica danno di nemeci." Brackertz (1993, his 24): "Stößt man sich an den Gelenken, droht Unheil von Feinden."

One could, perhaps, take ἄρθρα τρίβειν as implying masturbation. For ἄρθρα = genitals, see LSJ, s.h.v. If such a translation is correct, this is the only mention of masturbation in the Byzantine dreambooks. Artemidorus (1.78) comments on masturbation: "If a man dreams that he is masturbating privately, he will possess either a male or female slave, because the hands that are embracing his penis are like attendants. But if he has no servants, he will suffer a loss, because of the useless elimination of seed. I know of a slave who dreamt that he stroked his master's penis, and he became the companion and attendant of his children, for in his hands he held his master's penis, which is the symbol of his children. Then, again, I know of a slave who dreamt that his penis was stroked and aroused by his master's hands. He was bound to a pillar and received many strokes and was, in this way, extended by his master."

[182] But for a positive interpretation, see ibid., 1.56.

[183] It was popularly thought in Byzantium that demons caused insanity; for Byzantine medical explanations of insanity, see Dols 1984; cf. *ODB* 2:998.

[184] But cf. Daniel 22 and Achmet 63.

23.   Seeing or holding an herb: deem this as goodness.

24.   The barks of dogs: deem them as the words of enemies.

Γ

25.   The weasel, if dreamt of, is a female thief.

26.   If you pluck out the hairs of your beard, you will fall from your clan.[185]

27.   Marrying an old woman is an exceedingly useful dream.[186]

28.   Writing in your dream results in goodness.[187]

Δ

29.   Fingers and toes: these are [interpreted as] slaves.[188]

30.   Seeing the empress[189] is to be understood as [seeing] the Mother of God.[190]

31.   If you dream of a great serpent, this is a terrible emperor.

E

32.   Being lifted up after lying on the ground is a good sign.

33.   An eel, even if seen by itself, is a bad sign.

34.   Icons are to be interpreted as people.

35.   If you build a church, you will contract a marriage.[191]

---

[185]   Brackertz (1993, 232 ad his 59) notes that shaving a beard was considered a mortal insult, since it was punishment for those guilty of apostasy: "Der Bart war ein wesentliches Merkmal des östlichen Christentums; ihn abzuscheren galt als Todsünde, wenn nicht gar als Zeichen der Abtrünnigkeit." See the comment to Daniel 89 for a discussion of beards and social class.

[186]   Perhaps so interpreted because a man could inherit the old woman's property faster. We can also translate γαμηθείς as simply "going to bed with."

[187]   See Artemidorus 1.53.

[188]   So too ibid., 1.48 and Achmet 73 (though cf. 116).

[189]   Brackertz (1993, 233 ad his 75) comments on the history of the word δέσποινα as an address for the empress of Byzantium, although the word can refer to a woman of any rank; cf. note 41 to Manuel 10 below in Chapter 9. For a brief introduction to Byzantine empresses, see McCormick 1997, 243–7.

[190]   See *LAnt* 723–4 (with bibliography) for an excellent introduction to *Theotokos* as a word for the Virgin Mary; cf. *ODB* 3:2070, and the comment to Manuel 27 (note 115) below.

[191]   Cf. Achmet 12: "If a king dreams that he built a church, he will beautify a youthful girl and exalt her in proportion to the size of the church; if a commoner has this dream, he will acquire wealth through a woman's patronage; if an unmarried woman, she will get a husband; if a married woman, she will become a widow and then get another husband."

36. The fruit of an olive tree: you will come face to face with Hades.[192]

37. If you eat guts, you will profit off someone else's livelihood.[193]

38. Lying asleep on a rather large bed is exceedingly good.[194]

Z

39. A storm squall in a dream: you will soon have wealth.[195]

40. Burning-hot coals: you will have an icy road [παγετὸν δρόμον].[196]

41. Every type of boiling [denotes] oppression in your life.[197]

42. Drinking julep is a good sign in every respect.[198]

43. Eating dough is a thoroughly evil dream.[199]

44. If a woman receives a belt, this is an altogether useful dream.[200]

45. If you lose an animal, you will fall from honor.

H

46. If someone is carrying a distaff, this means an obstacle.

47. Daylight [that appears in a dream] is a good sign, while night and darkness are bad signs.[201]

48. Holding reins in your hands is a good image.[202]

49. Hearing echoes: consider this a very pleasant sign for you.

---

[192] In Byzantine literature and culture, the word Hades described not only the underworld (that is, hell), but also Death personified: *ODB* 2:891.

[193] Cf. Artemidorus 1.70.

[194] Up until the tenth century, the bed also served as a dining table; thereafter, the bed became a separate household item: *ODB* 1:276.

[195] But cf. *Somniale Danielis* ("Beiträge, V") 70: *grandinem vel tempestatem videre, dampnum significat*; Artemidorus 2.8.

[196] I cannot explain the interpretation except as an example of antinomy (hot coals symbolise ice).

[197] But a positive interpretation of this dream is given in Achmet 158.

[198] Like many of the dreams in Appendix II, this is borrowed verbatim or nearly so (in summative form) from Achmet (here, Chap. 95). Brackertz (1993, 234 ad his 103) comments on this Arabic loan word.

[199] In the Christian New Testament, yeast was proverbial for evil, sin, and hypocrisy; see, e.g., Matthew 16:6, 11; Luke 12:1; 1 Corinthians 5:6–8. On the day before the evening of the Passover meal, the head of the Jewish household conducts a ceremonious search of the house to remove all leaven. The Byzantines, as opposed to the Latin and Armenian churches, used leavened bread in communion: *ODB* 1:241.

[200] See Chapter 4, note 216.

[201] Cf. *Somniale Danielis* ("Beiträge, V") 137: *tenebras videre, infirmitatem significat*.

[202] Cf. Achmet 153.

Θ

50.   To dream of the summer harvest is [to see] the sickle of death.²⁰³

51.   If you see the summer harvest, expect to see people with the plague [θανατικοί].²⁰⁴

52.   A woman's vagina:²⁰⁵ you will see a naked tomb.

53.   A cloudy sky:²⁰⁶ this is not a good dream.

I

54.   A hawk that has flown from your hands [means] harm.

55.   Holding a hawk: you will soon get what you want.

56.   Falling into mud: this is a bad dream.

57.   A man plying a loom signifies strife.

K

58.   If you are wearing a cap,²⁰⁷ this is a good dream.

---

²⁰³   Brackertz (1993, 234 ad his 118) cites Joel 4:12–14 as a parallel. Cf. Achmet 208: "If a king or magistrate dreams that he saw in an unfamiliar place a field ready for harvest, his people will be assembled and prepared for war, and because the field was ready for harvesting they will be slaughtered immediately; but if there was a delay in the harvesting, there will be a proportionate delay in the slaughter. If a commoner has this dream, he will have wealth but also toil. If a king dreams that a field was being harvested or had already been harvested and that he realised that he owned this field, he will soon hear of the slaughter of his people; but if another person owned the field, he will hear of the slaughter of other people." For sickles in Byzantine agriculture, see Bryer 2002, 108–9; *ODB* 1:38–9.

²⁰⁴   So I translate θανατικοί, for which see Horden 2005, 143; cf. Guidorizzi (1980): "Sognare le messi: sono gli appestati." Brackertz, however, translates (1993, his 119): "Träumst du von Sommer und Ernte, wirst du um Menschen trauern." The analogy in the dream above is that just as the grain is cut down, so too people will be cut down through plague. For plague in Byzantium, see my comment to Daniel 327 (note 341).

²⁰⁵   So I translate Θῆλυ γυναικὸς γυμνὸν κατίδῃς τάφον. Guidorizzi's (1980) translation approximates mine: "Il grembo di una donna è una tomba aperta"; Brackertz (1993, his 120) takes Θῆλυ with γυμνὸν and so translates: "Schaust du ein nacktes Weib, wirst du das Grab eines Frauenzimmers sehen."

²⁰⁶   So I take θολὸς οὐρανός. Guidorizzi (1980) translates as "il cielo di fango" (the sky made of dirt or mud). I take θολός in its modern Greek sense of "foggy" or "cloudy."

²⁰⁷   This is the καμηλαυχίον, or the felt hat used by infantrymen in the tenth century; the word also denoted in late Byzantium the emperor's crown (the top of the hat contained gold); see Kolias 1982. See also Achmet 132 and 216, and the numerous references in Sophocles 1975, s.v. "καμελαύκιον"; also Piltz 1977 (I owe this reference to Prof. Mavroudi). Brackertz (1993, 235 ad his 146) comments on the word's Persian origin: "Das Wort ist persischen Ursprungs; es erscheint in den byzantinischen Quellen in verschiedener Bedeutung. Bei Achmet 168,15ff.

59. Being beheaded brings in gold.[208]
60. A cat is a female thief.[209]
61. Holding a raven is interpreted as a greedy guest.[210]
62. Barley, when it appears [in a dream]: you will have a trial.[211]
63. Onions and garlic indicate sorrows.[212]
64. If you dream of a comb, this says that you will kill.[213]

Λ

65. Leprosy, swamps, and wells all signify the arrogant behavior of prostitutes.[214]
66. Scabies: expect to come into very great profit.[215]

M

67. Lettuce indicates bodily disease.
68. Being drunk is very auspicious when you have this dream, for it [means] wealth.[216]
69. Eating honey: this is exceedingly unfavorable.[217]

---

bezeichnet es eine Kappe oder einen Hut. Ebenso heißt auch die kaiserliche Herrschaftsmütze, eine spitze weiße Haube, die mit Juwelen verschwenderisch besetzt war." Guidorizzi (1980) translates as "turbante."

[208] See the various interpretations in Achmet 120.

[209] Ibid. (278) also associates the cat with a male or female thief; Artemidorus (3.11) equates cats with adulterers, since cats "steal" birds and birds are likened to women.

[210] Or "stranger" (ξένος); it is hard to tell which is meant. Artemidorus (2.20) equates the raven with a thief or adulterer, while Achmet (240) interprets it as "a poor elderly man who is greedy and foreign-born."

[211] Perhaps a wordplay between κριθάριν and κρίσιν. The text is corrupt and unclear, as the line ends with θαρ, with a short/unaccented syllable missing (θαρ <˘>). Prof. Mavroudi suggests taking this word as θάρρος, and κρίσις as meaning "interpretation"; thus, "If you see barley, have confidence [ἔχειν θάρρος] in the interpretation."

[212] Cf. *Somniale Danielis* ("Beiträge, IV") XX: [a]*grimoniam edere, nuntium fedum significat.*

[213] A wordplay between κτένιον (comb) and κτύννυμι (to kill). The text is corrupt: Κτένιον ἰδὼν κτιννύει τοὖναρ λέγει; I read κτιννύειν. Prof. Mavroudi suggests reading λέγε instead of λέγει; thus, "If you dream of a comb, say that the dream kills"—that is, the dreamer will get killed.

[214] But cf. Artemidorus 2.27 and 3.47; Achmet 108 and 109.

[215] So too Artemidorus 3.47.

[216] So too the Arabic dreambooks cited in Mavroudi 2002, 345–8.

[217] An example of antinomy (the honey's sweetness symbolises unpleasantness).

70.   A nose, when dreamt of, speaks of thoughtful wisdom.[218]

N

71.   If you dream of a stinking corpse, you will see an enemy.

72.   If you have become dead, you will find release from worries.

73.   A dead person speaking: everything [that he says] is true.[219]

74.   A young man whom you dream of: this is an enemy.[220]

75.   If you appear as a young man [in a dream], this speaks of an insult[221] against you.[222]

76.   Swimming in the sea: it will be very good for you.

77.   Lying in bed afflicted with diseases causes the inroads of enemies.

Ξ

78.   To scratch oneself:[223] this is an evil dream for anyone.[224]

79.   If you are dwelling in a foreign land, you will be a guest in someone's house.[225]

80.   A dream of foreigners [or guests]: the interpretation also pertains to foreigners [or guests].

---

[218]   A pun between μύτις (nose) and μῆτις (wisdom); the two words were pronounced the same in Byzantine Greece. By the ninth century, ι, ει, η, ηι, οι, υ were all expressed by the same sound: *ODB* 2:1021.

The Greek is corrupt, and I have chosen to translate it as currently given in the text: Μύτιν ἰδὼν βούλευσις ἡ μῆτις λέγει. Prof. Mavroudi offers a very good emendation: Μύτιν ἰδὼν βούλευσιν ἢ μῆτιν λέγε (If you dream of a nose, say [that this indicates] thought or contemplation).

[219]   So too Artemidorus 2.69; cf. Achmet 132.

[220]   Cf. ibid., 127: "An unfamiliar youth always signifies an enemy; but if the youth is familiar, he represents either the youth himself or someone like him or someone with the same name."

[221]   In Byzantine Greek, the word ὕβρις meant an insult or injury inflicted on someone through words or action. The affront was even more horrible if done publicly. See the discussion in *ODB* 2:959.

[222]   Also a negative dream image in Artemidorus 1.50.

[223]   Drexl 1922 emends ξαίεσθαι in the manuscript to ξαίνεσθαι. Guidorizzi (1980) reads ξέεσθαι. Prof. Mavroudi suggests ξύνεσθαι (cf. modern Greek, ξύνω), which I translate here.

[224]   *Somniale Danielis* ("Beiträge, V", 142) has the opposite interpretation, and one more consistent with classical oneirocriticism, in that a person violently beaten will get benefits and profit. See my comment to Daniel 256.

[225]   Perhaps a wordplay between ξένην [γῆν] and ξένος. One could also translate as "If you are dwelling in a foreign land, you will become a foreigner."

81.   Dreaming of wooden statues: the interpretation is made in reference to people.

O

82.   Being obstructed in your journey opens up evil.

83.   Walking straight is good or leads to good things.

84.   A hen that is dreamt of: consider this a good female slave.

85.   If someone falls from the sky, he will not have a sure footing.[226]

86.   If you urinate in your dream, you will not worry about loss.[227]

Π

87.   To be struck on the cheek: this is exceedingly bad.[228]

88.   To be sitting on the ground is a most unfortunate sign.

89.   Holding washed [clothes]: expect sorrows.[229]

90.   If the sea freezes up, everything will turn out well.[230]

91.   Eating or holding a pita: deem this as gain.

92.   Seeing a chaste person:[231] this is a beneficial sign.

P

93.   Holding a staff: this means strength and [power].[232]

94.   Eating berries: expect a rain shower.

---

[226]   A straightforward analogy.

[227]   But cf. Achmet 47, where the opposite is true.

[228]   Lacerated cheeks are a very bad sign in Artemidorus 1.28.

[229]   This is the opposite of the usual (positive) interpretation of this symbol.

[230]   But cf. Achmet 190: "Ice signifies a great deal of sorrow. If someone dreams that the waters of a place were iced over, let him judge this as sorrow, grief, weeping, and sterility for the inhabitants by analogy to the freezing of the water; and if the dream occurs during the winter season, the suffering will be lighter; but if during the summer months, more oppressive and severe." Artemidorus (2.8) interprets ice as auspicious only if the dream occurs during the winter. (For Artemidorus, the dream is good since it is in accordance with one of the elements of interpretation—namely, time.)

[231]   Brackertz (1993, his 267) takes this word as referring to a saintly person: "Einen Heiligen zu schauen bringt Segen."

[232]   So ibid., 240 ad his 272: "In Ägypten und im Alten Orient war der Stab Symbol von Macht und Gewalt. Es ist bekannt, in wie starkem Maße die Gesalt des Moses in den byzantinischen Kaiserkult hineingewachsen war. Sein Stab war höchstes Herrschersymbol." Drexl added the bracketed word (κράτος) in his edition (1922).

95.   To be sewing in a dream: you will effect habits [that result in] power.

Σ

96.   Putrification is good: interpret this as release from debt.

97.   Being seized by Saracens[233] is an evil dream.

98.   Sweeping your own house is very bad.[234]

99.   If you eat flesh, expect something shameful.

100.   If you see a satyr, examine yourself as to what condition you are in.[235]

101.   An earthquake is a message of upheaval for everyone.[236]

102.   Collecting or eating beets means profit.

103.   If you are given grain, expect disease to befall you.

104.   Holding animal fat: expect that this means gain.

105.   If you dream of sparrows, expect quarrels and lawsuits.

106.   Washing your body: you will be released from anxieties.

107.   To see the Savior is good in every respect.[237]

---

[233]   That is, by the Arabs. See Brackertz 1993, 241 ad his 280: "In diesem Vers gebraucht Nikephoros den Ausdruck Sarazenen für Araber und deutet den Traum als unheilvoll. Die etymologische Herkunft des Wortes im umstritten. Während des ganzen Mittelalters wurden im christlichen Abendland alle Araber und Muslims, später auch die Türken, ja überhaupt die »Ungläubigen« schlechthin als Sarazenen bezeichnet." The use of the term "Saracens" for denoting Arabs is as early as the third century CE; see Bowersock 1987; *ODB* 1:149; also above, n. 50 (comment ad Nicephorus 47). See also Vasiliev 1935–68 for a history of the relations between Arabs and Byzantium. Muslim Arabs first appeared in the seventh century, with attacks on Byzantium occurring from the mid-seventh through the eleventh century, at which time the Turks became Byzantium's chief enemy in the East.

[234]   But cf. Achmet 187.

[235]   Cf. Artemidorus 2.37.

[236]   Cf. Achmet 145: "If someone dreams that there was an earthquake [σεισμός] in the region where he lived, this means a new edict from the king that will terrify and disturb [σείων] the inhabitants; and if the earthquake occurred everywhere, the edict will likewise be universal: if partial, so too the edict." (See Mavroudi 2002, 367–8 on this dream.) There may be subtle word-play here in Achmet, as *sēmeiōma* was the written report of a judicial verdict or an official's decision: *ODB* 3:1868. See also Artemidorus 2.41; cf. *Somniale Danielis* ("Beiträge, V") 139: *terre motum videre, aliqua malignitas supervenit.*

The Byzantines considered earthquakes portents of impending disaster or punishments sent by God in response to sin; see Vercleyen 1988; *ODB* 1:669–70. Earthquakes were commemorated in the Byzantine liturgical calendar; Croke (1981 and 2005, 71) discusses two such instances. In Constantinople, there was an annual procession to commemorate the great earthquake of 554 (Krueger 2005, 301). See also Croke 2005, 70–71, 76 (with nn. 64–72 on 82–3); Geyer 2002, 38; Treadgold 1997, 403, 405. The sixth-century scientist Anthemius of Tralles produced an artificial earthquake using steam power: *ODB* 1:109.

[237]   Achmet 11: "If someone dreams of our Lord God Jesus Christ and is aware that He is indeed Christ, he will have spiritual salvation, secular wealth, and very great victory; and if he

T

108.   A dream that occurs during the day is very clear [in its significance].[238]

Y

109.   Water pouring out from above announces enemies.
110.   If you drink the water of rivers, this brings toil.
111.   Drinking clear water: this is a very good sign.
112.   Weaving a textile: the interpretation calls for a journey.[239]

Φ

113.   To dream that another person is bald: expect a disturbance.
114.   The person who has lice will have a time of idleness.
115.   Gathering lice: you will have profit, but not much of it.
116.   If you are carrying a burden [φόρτον], you will likely not be saddled with a burden [φόρτον].
117.   A bright light seen in a dream: expect to be filled with joy.

X

118.   Holding reins in one's hand: a good dream.

---

also talked with Him, let him cling without hesitation to everything that Christ said to him, and he will be blessed. If he saw Christ in some unknown house and that he went inside and did not come out, let him know that he will soon die but that he will nevertheless be saved, and his heirs will be loaded with honors and wealth." For the Arabic parallels, see Mavroudi 2002, 271–6.

[238]   Prof. Mavroudi takes this verse as meaning that the most truthful dream is seen during a midday nap, since at that time one is closer to a state of wakefulness. I would add that it was a commonplace in ancient cultures that dreams closest to dawn are the most significant. The reason is obvious: one remembers with greater clarity and vividness whatever one dreams when closest to waking consciousness.

[239]   Achmet 261: "If someone dreams that he was weaving in his house, if he usually does this, he will find profit in his work in proportion to the amount of work stretched out on the loom; but if he normally does not weave, he will go away on a trip and profit from it in proportion to the quality of the loom. ... If someone dreams that he was assembling a loom, he will go on a short trip because of the brief time it takes to put a loom together. If he put thread in his loom, he will prepare for a trip; but if the loom belonged to someone else, he will get another person ready." See Dagron 2002, 444–5 for the weaving of linen; he discusses how in urban centers the manufacture of linen cloth and clothing was done in homes and specialised workshops. The twelfth-century Jewish traveler Benjamin of Tudela noted that weaving was a trade for many Jews: Treadgold 1997, 703; also *ODB* 3:2032, where Benjamin is quoted as referring to the 2,000 Jews working in silk in Boeotian Thebes (see Chapter 4, note 255, above).

119. To be pushed around by the hands [of other people] indicates neglect.

120. Geese seen in a dream: consider them good female slaves.[240]

Ω

121. To be pale-looking: this dream brings evil.

---

[240] Achmet 293: "Geese signify profitable and mild-tempered slaves. ... On the whole, male and female geese are judged as male and female slaves; and whatever these geese experience in a dream will so turn out for these slaves."

Chapter 6

The *Oneirocriticon* of Astrampsychus

1. Speaking in a dream: this is a true dream.
2. Moving sluggishly causes unlucky trips.
3. Flying well: this is [a sign] of a good deed.
4. Laughing in your dream: you will have grievous ways.[1]
5. Crying in your dream: you will be absolutely happy.
6. Eating with enemies brings about reconciliation.
7. If you dream of dying, you will have grievous ways.[2]
8. A foul smell: consider this as displeasure.
9. If someone fumigates you with incense, this is a bitter dream.
10. If you dream of being old, you will have privilege.
11. Running in a dream causes strong fortunes.
12. Washing your hands indicates the dissolution of worries.[3]
13. Washing one's feet means freedom from worries.[4]
14. Washing your torso[5] means freedom from worries.
15. Having your hair cropped short points to harm to your business and property.
16. If your hair has fallen out, this results in great danger.
17. A dream of having white skin: this is exceedingly auspicious.
18. If your skin has become black, this is not good for anyone.
19. Being embraced by your mother: this is a good dream.

---

[1] The vast majority of dreams in this dreambook are interpreted in a simplistic manner: antinomy, puns, and straightforward analogies. We do not see the more sophisticated methods (etymology, literary allusions, metonymy) so evident in the Byzantine dream key manuals. This fact, coupled with the use of accentual rhythms (rather than metrical units), could point to a general readership.

[2] So too Achmet 131; cf. *Somniale Danielis* ("Beiträge, V") 36: *cum mori se viderit, calumnie graves ei advenient.* This interpretation is the opposite of Nicephorus 39. See Chapter 1 for a discussion of the relationship between the verses in this dreambook and Nicephorus's dreambook.

[3] A wordplay between λούω (to wash) and λύω (to free someone).

[4] But cf. Nicephorus 97 for a different interpretation.

[5] So I take ὅλμος.

20. Being embraced by a man you love very much is profitable.[6]

21. Every form of sexual intercourse is indicative of lengthy toils.[7]

22. Kissing arouses long battles with enemies.

23. Having flat feet signifies sorrows.

24. If your feet have been cut off, start no trip at all.[8]

25. If you are obese,[9] you will be very dishonored.

26. If you are deprived of your reason, know that you will live in a foreign land.

27. Being[10] blind is altogether good in every respect.

28. A dream of wearing a white robe is very auspicious.

29. Wearing a black robe: this is not a good dream.[11]

30. Wearing a purple robe results in a lengthy illness.

31. [Wearing] a red robe results in a good deed.

32. Wearing the emperor's robe: this is the loss of hopes.

33. A torn tunic tears away the oppressive weight of worries.

34. A belt that has been cut in two quickly undoes a trip.

35. Looking at the stars is a very good sign for people.

36. Claps of thunder in a dream are the words of messengers.

37. Seeing the lights of heaven points to light shed on one's affairs.

38. Snow, when dreamt of, brings fights with enemies.

39. If you dream of dead people, you will experience the death of your affairs.

40. Withered trees that are dreamt of: [your] efforts [will be] useless.

41. Pearls indicate the flowing of tears.

42. Milk scatters the plans of your enemies.

43. Milk is representative of[12] a gentle demeanor.

44. Mud is indicative of the soul's sordidness.

45. A clear running stream of water dissolves the sorrows of the mind.[13]

---

[6] See the comment to Nicephorus 3. Here, by way of variation, we have a superlative adjective. As noted above in Chapter 1, the verses in Astrampsychus are related to family *b* of the Nicephorean manuscript tradition; they often show variations, however, even with that branch.

[7] In Nicephorus, Appendix I, 57, we have "desires" rather than "lengthy toils"; once again, our text is an independent witness of Nicephorus's dreambook.

[8] But cf. Achmet 116.

[9] I change πρήθων τὸ σῶμα to βρίθων τὸ σῶμα; cf. Nicephorus 15 and Germanus 20.

[10] Here we have φαίνεσθαι, but in Nicephorus 118a and 118b φέρεσθαι.

[11] For the colors in this and the subsequent verses, see Achmet 156.

[12] The texts read πράξενον; I emend to πρακτικόν or to πρόξενον (which I translate here).

[13] In Nicephorus, Appendix I, 60, the reading is λύπας ψυχῆς (sorrows of the soul).

46. Wine that has been poured out of vessels stops sorrows.[14]
47. Turbid wine clearly signifies many sorrows.
48. Receiving a cup of wine: expect terrible quarrels.
49. Water bursting forth from below ground foretells enemies.
50. Drinking clear sparkling water: this is a useful sign.[15]
51. The flow of a river destroys the joy of your enemies.[16]
52. Standing in a church results in an accusation.
53. If you are sitting naked, you will be stripped of your property.
54. Sitting in feces: you will experience all manner of harm.
55. Sitting on a rock: cherish good hopes.
56. Sitting on a wall: expect to be fortunate.
57. Sitting at a pit: this is not auspicious.
58. Walking on coals signifies harm at the hands of enemies.
59. Walking on roof-tiles: you will cause harm to your enemies.[17]
60. Crawling on a mountain: this points to violence to one's affairs.
61. Walking on snakes: this destroys the barbs of enemies.
62. Floating in mud: consider this as harm to your mind.[18]
63. Falling off a cliff points to an unlucky fate.
64. Eating sweets: you will have bitter ways.
65. Eating grapes indicates rainfall.
66. Eating figs points to slanderous words.[19]
67. Eating lettuce: this signifies bodily disease.
68. If you drink dirty water, you will be amid sorrows.
69. Laying hands on children: expect danger to come.[20]
70. The one holding a pear will fail in his hopes.
71. Holding nails: look out for the barbs of enemies.
72. A shattered staff does not produce a good result.

---

[14] The dream, with the addition of the word "vessels," differs from both the *a* and *b* families of the Nicephorus dreambook.

[15] This is at variance with Nicephorus 120.

[16] Nicephorus 103 reads: ʽΡύσις ποταμῶν δυσμενῶν δηλοῖ κάραν.

[17] Here we have φέροις, as opposed to the φύγῃς in Nicephorus 12.

[18] We have νοῦς here, as opposed to ψυχή in both the *a* and *b* families of Nicephorus (see Nicephorus 44a and 44b).

[19] At variance with Nicephorus 112, which reads: σῦκα βιβρώσκειν φληνάφων δηλοῖ ψόγους (Eating figs points to the slanders of foolish people). Astrampsychus has βρῶσις σύκων δείκνυσι φληνάφοις λόγοις.

[20] I do not know if we should take this dream as having a sexual connotation. If it does involve sex, we may compare Artemidorus 1.78, which states that a dream of having sex with a child will have an evil outcome if the child (male or female) is less than ten years of age; having sex with a child 11 years and older is an auspicious symbol, even if the child is the dreamer's.

73. Grabbing hold of the tails of animals: you will get everything you want.

74. Holding keys indicates soundness of character.

75. Holding a branch: expect to be accused.

76. Holding a dagger portrays a quarrel.

77. Holding spun [garments]: expect sorrows.

78. Grabbing hold of a sparrow that then flies away: expect harm.

79. Embracing a column: expect divine grace.

80. The smashing of a dagger points to the crushing of enemies.

81. A hawk that flies out of one's hands means harm for magistrates.

82. If you are holding gold, you will end up not getting what you want.

83. Having and then eating eggs signifies sorrows.

84. Cattle, when dreamt of, bring about a good deed.

85. A dream of black horses is not at all good.

86. A dream of white horses signifies the appearance of messengers.[21]

87. Dreaming of lions points to fights with enemies.[22]

88. Doves, when dreamt of, are indicative of losses.

89. If you see a running foal, this is something mysterious.

90. The bites of dogs point to harm at the hands of enemies.

91. A wolf with its jaws agape signifies meaningless words.[23]

92. The appearance of a mouse: you will be servile in character.[24]

93. Dead cattle indicate years of famine.

94. If wasps appear [in a dream], they are injuries inflicted by enemies.

95. A rabbit, when dreamt of, causes unlucky trips.

96. A dream of olive oil: you will escape all harm.

97. Seeing a tranquil sea is a favorable sign.

98. The continuous lapping noise of the sea indicates agitation in your affairs.[25]

99. Swimming in a stormy sea signifies sorrows.

100. Swimming in a calm[26] sea: this is a good dream.

101. Being around a fox: expect profit.

---

[21] Nicephorus, Appendix I, 33 does not have the λευκῶν that appears here.

[22] Nicephorus 64 has στίφη, while here we have μάχας. We may attribute this to the more formal vocabulary that Nicephorus uses, as opposed to the vernacular that we see in Astrampsychus. See Chapter 1 in more detail for the differences in meter and language between Nicephorus's dreambook and the verses in this dreambook.

[23] Nicephorus 67 reads τρόπους, as opposed to λόγους here.

[24] A wholly different interpretation in Nicephorus, where the mouse is interpreted as revealing "a [previously hidden] character trait."

[25] A different interpretation in Nicephorus 125.

[26] In Nicephorus, Appendix II, 76, the word ἡμέρας is omitted.

Chapter 7

The *Oneirocriticon* of Germanus

The Dreambook of Germanus, Patriarch of Constantinople

Beginning of A

1.   Being embraced by a man you love: this is useful.[1]

2.   If you are deprived of your reason, know that you will live in a foreign land.

3.   Seeing the stars is a very good sign for people.

4.   If one is holding a pear, he will fail in his hopes.

5.   Moving sluggishly causes unlucky trips.

6.   A rooster, when dreamt of, is a truthful dream.

7.   An eagle, when seen in a dream: consider this an angel of God.

8.   Anyone who speaks with the emperor remains out of work.

9.   Eating loaves of white bread is an auspicious sign.

10.*   A staff, my friend,[2] indicates a very great man.[3]

11.   Eating loaves of hot bread signifies illness.[4]

12.*   Holding silver: this is a good dream.

13.   Walking on coals signifies harm at the hands of your enemies.

14.*   To ascend a high place signifies something good.

15.*   To be going up from height to height is good for some people, but evil for others.

16.*   A bear approaching you in a hostile way signifies grief.

17.*   Dreaming that your brother or a relative has died: this points to life.[5]

---

[1]   A slight change from Nicephorus 3.

[2]   The author uses words or phrases like this to convey an informal style; cf. 150, and 238 below. Some ancient epithets like φίλος (friend) were used throughout the Byzantine period: *ODB* 1:18.

[3]   I use an asterisk to show that the entry in question does not appear in Nicephorus's dreambook. The vast majority of these non-Nicephorean dreams and interpretations may be found in Daniel and Achmet.

Drexl (1923, 433) considers this dream as coming from Nicephorus, but it does not appear there; perhaps he thought it a gloss on Nicephorus, Appendix II, 93.

[4]   So too Manuel 9; but cf. Achmet 241.

[5]   A modified version of Daniel 15.

18.*   Blood trickling out of your mouth points to loss.[6]

Beginning of B

19.   Walking on roof-tiles points to the snares of enemies.[7]

20.   If you are obese, you will be very dishonored.

21.   Receiving a book: know that you will receive honor.

22.   To be shut up in a deep shaft is terrible in every respect.

23.   Eating grapes foretells rainfall.[8]

24.   Claps of thunder in one's dream are the words of messengers.

25.*   A dream of cattle fighting means struggles in your actions.

26.*   Eating beef signifies sorrows.

27.*   Dreaming that one is taking a stroll means something bad.

Beginning of Γ

28.   Milk scatters the plans of enemies.

29.   If you dream of becoming old, you will have privilege.

30.   If you are sitting naked, you will be stripped of your property.

31.*   A crane gives advance notice of a destitute man.[9]

32.   If you laugh in your dream, you will have grievous ways.[10]

33.   Marrying a woman: consider this a change[11] in your way of life.

34.   Being struck in the jaw: consider yourself free.

35.*   Having a long tongue is a very good sign.[12]

---

[6]   A commonplace in Achmet, as we have seen. See my comment to Daniel 35; cf. Artemidorus 1.33 and 1.61.

[7]   A different interpretation is given in Nicephorus 12.

[8]   The manuscript is incomplete here; the text reads Βότρεις ἐσθίειν ὀμβρικὴν δηλοῖ φυ. To complete the sentence, I have borrowed κλίσιν from Nicephorus 14.

[9]   So Achmet 288: "On the whole, the crane signifies a poor man. ... If someone dreams that he found one or more cranes, he will meet a proportionate number of poor men from whom he will derive no profit. If someone dreams that he was raising cranes in his house, he will feed poor people and this will be to his glory; but if he dreams that he slaughtered them, he will do these poor people harm. If he dreams that the cranes left his house and flew away, he will be released from a company of beggars."

[10]   As commented in Chapter 1, verses in both Germanus and Astrampsychus are related to family *b* of the Nicephorean family of manuscripts, though not always closely.

[11]   The manuscript reads τρόπον; but Nicephorus 23 has τροπήν, which I adopt here.

[12]   Cf. Achmet 62.

36.   Eating sweets is a bitter sign for you.[13]

37.*   If one of your relatives dreams of his own birthday, he will soon die.[14]

38.*   Drinking milk signifies happiness in your life.

Δ

39.   Consider a foul odor displeasure.

40.*   Having two heads foretells the joining of a friendship.

41.*   If you dream of two suns, you will have longevity of days.

42.   Names indicate the character of people appearing in your dream.

43.   The bites of dogs point to harm from your enemies.

44.   If you receive gifts, you will not be far from making profit.

45.   A house that has collapsed: reckon this as harm.[15]

46.   Plums, when eaten [in a dream], speak of illness.

47.*   Dreaming that you are running means that you will soon see profit.

48.*   Being unable to run signifies hindrance.

49.*   Dolphins, when dreamt of, symbolise good news.[16]

E

50.*   Getting beautiful garments signifies gain.

51.*   Looking down from a height: expect freedom from care.[17]

52.   If someone fumigates you with incense, this is a bitter dream to see.

53.*   Being anointed with olive oil: expect a good opportunity.

54.   Mud is indicative of the soul's sordidness.

55.   Seeing a eunuch brings about a good result.

56.   Eating with your enemies brings about reconciliation.

57.   If a viper appears [in a dream], it expresses harm caused by enemies.

58.   Standing in a church causes accusations.

---

[13]   Here Germanus's interpretation clearly is independent of family *b* in the Nicephorean manuscript tradition.

[14]   See Anonymous 43 for a different interpretation.

[15]   See the discussion above to Nicephorus 27. For the dream, cf. *Somniale Danielis* ("Beiträge, V") 52: *domum suam destruere vel cadere, dampnum significat*; *Somniale Danielis* ("Beiträge, V") 53: *domum suam ardentem videre, scandalum vel periculum significat.*

[16]   Based on Daniel 130.

[17]   Partially based on Daniel 189.

59*.   Holding an elephant's tusk means illness.[18]

60.*   Ivory statues, when dreamt of, signify fear.[19]

61.*   Reading a letter points to happiness.

62.*   Touching the sky is a very good sign.

63.*   Eating venison is auspicious.

64.*   Handling eels means fear.[20]

65.*   Being kicked by any sort of animal is a bad sign.

66.*   Bathing in a well: expect gain.

67.*   Offering prayers: you will see personal goodness.

Z

68.*   Leavened dough, when dreamt of, is a good thing.[21]

69.*   If you are wearing a belt, expect profit whenever you dream this.

70.*   Playing chess signifies a contest for you.[22]

71.   A belt that has been cut in two quickly ends a trip.

H

72.*   [To dream that] the sun has fallen from the sky: this is auspicious.

---

[18]   But cf. Achmet 268; cf. *Somniale Danielis* ("Beiträge, IV") XCVI: *eborum, inpeditionem significo*; cf. *Somniale Danielis* ("Beiträge, IV") XCVII: *eborum emere aut vendere, tristitias maximas significat.*

[19]   But this is a favorable symbol in Artemidorus 2.39. For Byzantine ivory workmanship, see Cutler 2002, 578–81; *LAnt* 521–2 (use of ivory in diptychs and large pieces of furniture).

[20]   Loosely based on Daniel 148.

[21]   But yeast is a bad sign in itself; see Nicephorus, Appendix II, 43, with comment ad loc.

[22]   Achmet 239: "If someone dreams that he was playing chess with a friend, the two will come to mutual blows over capital gain, and the victor [of the chess game] will get it and also accomplish what he is eager for; but if he dreams of playing a stranger, he will bloodlessly fight with an enemy, and to the victor of the game will come the fulfillment of his desires. If a king or great magnate or polemarch dreams that he was playing chess as if he were playing war, he will fight hostile enemies; and if he won the game, he will fulfill his every wish in the war: if not, he will be beaten by the enemy. If he dreams that while playing chess he captured more pieces than did his opponent, he will enslave more of the enemy; if not, the opposite: however, the rout in the battle will not be universal [for some pieces still remained]. If a king or great magnate or polemarch dreams that his chessboard was lost or stolen or broken, he will lose his army and come into very great sorrow." See Brackertz (1993, 244 ad loc.) on chess as a borrowing from the Persians; *LAnt* (460), however, considers the game's origin to be northern India, and dates it to the sixth century. The game was very popular among the educated elite in Byzantium: Koukoules 1948–57, 1:219–21; Rautman 2006, 57. The pieces originally were foot soldiers, horses, chariots, and elephants.

73.   Holding nails: you are looking at the barbs of your enemies.

74.*   A mule means a life overseas for you.[23]

75.*   If you dream of giving birth to the sun, consider this to be my king.[24]

76.*   [A dream of] the sun standing still: expect honor.

77.*   To dream of a brightly shining sun: this signifies danger.

78.*   To dream of clear sunshine signifies gain.

79.*   [If you dream that] the sun and moon are taking the same trajectory or shining at the same time, this signifies strife throughout the world.[25]

80.*   [To dream that] the sun and moon are moving all over the sky signifies separation of husband and wife.[26]

Θ

81.   If you dream of dying, you will be without worries.

82.   A cow, when seen [in a dream], results in an evil state of affairs.[27]

83.   Doors that have collapsed mean harm for their owners.

84.*   Worshipping God or calling upon Him means that you will be released from every sort of evil.

85.*   Kissing God: you will be held accountable for a situation you do [not][28] foresee.

86.   Eating lettuce means bodily disease.

87.   A shattered staff does not produce a good result.

88.   Seeing a tranquil[29] sea is a favorable sign.

89.*   A dream of hot waters bubbling up: this is bad.

90.*   Placing your trust[30] in God is an exceedingly good dream.

91.*   A dream that the sea is being swept with heavy waves: expect harm.

---

[23]   So Achmet 232.

[24]   Cf. ibid., 166: "If any woman whatever dreams of giving birth to a sun, she will give birth to a king." The sun was a focal point of Byzantine imperial propaganda: *ODB* 2:910. For childbirth in Byzantium, see *ODB* 1:290-91; Rautman 2006, 52–4. The phrase "my king" (βασιλεύς μοι) is close to the formulaic address "your majesty" (βασιλεύς σου; for which, see *ODB* 1:18).

[25]   A loose compilation of Daniel 205 and 215.

[26]   A variation on Daniel 209.

[27]   Nicephorus 40 reads πράξιν (deed), as opposed to τάξιν (state of affairs). Nicephorus also has a favorable interpretation (a good deed), showing the independence of the Germanus tradition from the original Nicephorean text.

[28]   Drexl 1923 adds οὐ on the basis of Daniel 228.

[29]   Drexl emends γενῶσαν to γελῶσαν.

[30]   Drexl (1923, 438 n. 8) suggests reading θεωροῦντα (beholding) instead of θαρροῦντα in the manuscript.

92.* Dreaming that the sea has dried up is a bad sign.

I

93. If you dream that your garment has been torn, you will be rid of the oppressive burden of worry.[31]
94. A dream of black horses is not good.
95. Falling from a horse: consider this to be great disaster.
96. If you are floating in mud, this points to harm to your soul.
97. Dreaming of [white] horses indicates the appearance of messengers.
98.* Eating fish: you will not continue to experience goodness.
99. Being captured by Ishmaelites: this is auspicious.
100.* Sitting on a white horse is a good sign.

K

101. Being around a fox: expect profit.
102. If you cry in your dream, you will be absolutely happy.
103. If you are holding a hawk, you will certainly get what you want.
104. If you are sitting in feces, you will experience all manner of harm.
105. The barking of dogs signifies harm from enemies.
106.* Holding a burning oil lamp signifies grief.[32]
107. Holding extinguished wax candles is unfortunate.[33]
108. Holding lit wax candles: this is useful.
109. Flying well: this is [a sign] of a good deed.
110. Eating raw meat: this is not a good sign.
111. Trees that have been cut down foretell the fall of men.
112. Falling off a cliff means an untimely fate.
113. Barley, when seen [in a dream], results in a court of judgement.
114. Ravens, when dreamt of, are to be considered demons.
115. If someone wears a collar, he is not far from danger.
116.* Rams, when dreamt of, prepare easy trips.
117. A smashed oil lamp destroys scandal.
118. Holding a branch: expect to be accused.
119. Holding keys signifies soundness of character.

---

[31] But cf. Achmet 157.
[32] But cf. ibid., 159.
[33] See ibid., 159.

120. Seeing the fruit of olive trees: this is auspicious.

121.* Beautifying your head is a good sign.

122.* A pillar that has fallen down points to the death of a magistrate.

Λ

123.* Dreaming of taking a bath is good.

124. Dreaming that one has white skin: this is useful.

125. Lions, when dreamt of, end strife with enemies.[34]

126. [Wearing] a white robe in a dream results in very great goodness.

127. Sitting at a pit: this is not good for oneself.

128. A wolf with its jaws agape signifies the ways of foolish people.[35]

129.* Handling bacon: a relative of yours will die.

130. White hairs signify useful activities.

M

131.* Speaking with a dead person: expect profit.

132.* A dream of bees coming out [of your house] reveals enemies.

133.* Being struck with a sword signifies sorrow.

134. Embracing your mother is a very good dream.

135. A mouse, when dreamt of, is an indicator of evils.

136. Holding a dagger portrays a quarrel.

137. Dreaming of pure people: this is a sign of good will.

138. Pearls indicate the flowing of tears.

139. Holding apples: consider this being united in love.

140. [Having] a black face brings about lengthy sorrows.

141. Eating mushrooms points to a dose of poisons.

142. To be sleeping amid grinding stones or to be among them is an unlucky sign.

N

143. Holding spun [garments]: expect sorrows.

144. Swimming in a calm sea: this is a good dream.

---

[34] Different interpretation in Nicephorus 64.

[35] This interpretation is different from what appears in Astrampsychus 91 and Nicephorus 67.

145.   Dead oxen indicate years of famine.

146.   Being sober is appropriate for the appearance of dreams.

Ξ

147.   Holding a sword: expect to be in arms.

148.   Withered trees, when dreamt of, are useless labors.

149.* Carrying wood causes spiritual oppression.

150.* Vomiting[36] in one's dream causes loss, my friend.

151.   Dreaming that the sea has dried up is the removal of evils.

152.* Eating dry cheese signifies disease.[37]

153.* Precious wood signifies kingship.[38]

O

154.* Growing teeth: understand this as gain.

155.   Dreaming of olive oil: you will escape every kind of harm.

156.   Washing off mud points to release from worries.

157.   Being with disturbed or troubled people: this is an unfavorable sign.

158.   Sitting on a donkey signifies unlucky ways.

159.   Getting a cup of wine: expect terrible quarrels.

160.   Crawling on a mountain points to violence to one's affairs.

161.   Turbid wine clearly signifies many sorrows.

162.   Relating a dream within a dream is a true dream.

163.* Wine that has been emptied out of vessels stops sorrows.

164.   Wine that has been poured out stops angry quarrels.

165.* A dream on Saturday results in temporal power.[39]

166.* A dream of mist: expect disease soon afterwards.[40]

167.* Eating hard-shelled seafood signifies illness.[41]

---

[36]   Drexl (1923, 442 ad loc.) notes: "ξεράν = ἐξεράν (ausspeien), s. Stephanus s.v."

[37]   Cf. Achmet 251.

[38]   Cf. ibid., 126 on wood and kings: "If someone dreams that he found and procured so many pieces of the wood of the cross of Christ that he had the entire cross, he will become king and be very religious."

[39]   For the days of the week in Byzantium, see Rautman 2006, 4–5.

[40]   So Achmet 163: "If someone dreams that he ... encountered mist, he will suffer illness by analogy to ... the mist's darkness." Galen (6.632 Kühn) interprets a dream of mist as indicative of disease caused by black bile.

[41]   The opposite interpretation is found in Achmet 300: "If someone dreams that he ate a crab or some other hard-shelled creature, he will get ... moderate health: for many medical

168.* If someone [dreams of] entering a strange house, he will die soon afterwards.[42]

169.* Unripe fruits signify illness.

170. To dream that your teeth have been wrenched out signifies something bad.

171. To see a house burning is auspicious.

172.* A domestic bird signifies a slave.

173.* Dreaming of birds that are capable of swimming: expect joy.[43]

174.* Killing a snake: you will conquer an enemy.

175.* Wine of the best vintage: expect joy.

II

176.* Pigeons, when dreamt of, give evidence of harm.[44]

177. Washing your feet points to an easy trip.

178. Having flat feet signifies sorrows.

179. Carrying shackles in your hands: expect dangers to come.

180. Every form of sexual intercourse gives evidence of lengthy desires.

181. If your feet are cut off, start no trip at all.

182. Holding an ugly child results in illness.

183. Having your feet bound with shackles: understand this as something troublesome.

184. If you see a running foal, this is something mysterious.

185. A tower that has collapsed points to the death of a magistrate.

186. Sitting on a rock: let [the dreamer] have happy hopes.

187.* Warming yourself at a fire: you will find wealth.[45]

188.* Someone who treads grapes in a wine vat will serve someone of high authority.[46]

189.* Mud foretells for you anxiety and anguish.

---

treatments are often made from these creatures."

[42]   The interpretation is based perhaps on the analogy of death as a change of residence or abode.

[43]   Cf. Artemidorus 2.20–21.

[44]   Ibid. (2.20) considers the pigeon very auspicious for sexual affairs.

[45]   Achmet 158: "If someone dreams that he tried to light a fire in order to warm himself, if he did light it and so became warm, he will stand in need of a magistrate and become rich by analogy to the heat: for coolness generally signifies poverty."

[46]   Ibid., 195: "If someone dreams that he was making wine by treading on grapes in a vat, he will serve a person of very great authority and be entrusted with very important administrative matters."

190.* Pepper, when dreamt of, gives evidence of quarrels.[47]

191.* An ape signifies a very crafty enemy.[48]

192.* A stork foretells an illustrious man.[49]

193. A clear running stream dissolves the sorrows of the soul.

194.* A pack of dogs signifies a pack of evil men.

P

195. Receiving a staff brings great honor.

196. The flow of a river points to an enemy.

197.* Wearing rags: this brings great danger.

198. A needle in a dream signifies the way to poisons.

199.* Roses in your house signify something good.

Σ

200. [Wearing] a white robe results in something very good.

201. Grabbing hold of sparrows that then fly away: expect harm.

202. [Wearing] a red robe results in a good deed.

203. Wearing a black robe: this is a thoroughly evil dream.

204. [Wearing] a purple robe results in a lengthy illness.

205. Smashing a dagger points to the crushing of enemies.

206. Sleeping in the dark is a sign of bad luck for anyone.

207. Having black skin: this is not good for anyone.

208. Worms point to harm caused by enemies.

209. Eating cuttlefish results in a long illness.

210. Smashing a knife points to the slaughter of enemies.

---

[47] Ibid. 205: "On the whole, pepper represents for any dreamer lawsuits, quarrels, and sorrows. … If someone dreams that he found or procured pepper, he will have lawsuits and sorrows both within and outside of his house. If he dreams that he ate pepper, he will suffer punishment at the hands of the authorities in proportion to the amount and the bitterness. If he dreams that he bought pepper with a scale, he will receive sorrows and duress from a tribunal because of the scale's balance. If he dreams that he distributed pepper to some people, he will goad men into quarrels in proportion to the amount of pepper." Cf. *Somniale Danielis* ("Beiträge, V") 118: *piper tractare, ab inimicis tractari.*

[48] Achmet 136: "If someone dreams that he kissed an animal, he will find profit and goodness in life; but if he kissed an ape, he will come to know a fickle but weak enemy who will deceitfully befriend him." Cf. Artemidorus 2.12.

[49] Achmet 288: "If someone dreams that he found stork feathers, he will get proportionate wealth from an illustrious man."

211.   Eating figs signifies the slanders of foolish people.

212.   Wearing the emperor's robe brings hope.

213.   Embracing a pillar: expect divine grace.

214.   If wasps appear [in a dream], they are injuries inflicted by enemies.

215.* If someone dreams of erecting a cross, he will find joy.[50]

216.* A wreath in a dream signifies a king.[51]

217.* Wearing sandals foretells taking a trip.[52]

218.* Wearing a multicolored robe signifies oppression.[53]

219.* An earthquake clearly signifies tumults in some region.

220.* Mustard, when seen in a dream, gives evidence of illness.[54]

221.* Dreaming that your wife is dead is good.[55]

T

222.   Having your hair cropped short: this indicates harm to your affairs.

223.   If your hair falls out, this causes great danger.[56]

---

[50]   See ibid., 150. A form of Christian sympathetic magic was using a cross to mark tilled fields in order to protect them from natural disasters like hail, floods, and locusts: *ODB* 3:1699.

[51]   See Achmet 245; cf. *Somniale Danielis* ("Beiträge, IV") XL: *coronam cuiusque rei accipere, letitiam significat*; *Somnium Danielis* ("Beiträge, V") 27: *coronam accipere, honorem significat*. Brackertz (1993, 247 ad loc.) distinguishes between the crown and the wreath: "Die Byzantiner unterschieden zwischen der Krone (*stemma*) und dem Kranz (*stephanos*). Das Stemma war die kaiserliche Krone, Stephanos im Sinne von Krone bezeichnet auch die Hochzeitskrone, die die Kaiser anläßlich ihrer Hochzeit aus der Hand des Patriarchen empfingen, ferner die Krone der Märtyrer."

[52]   So Achmet 226.

[53]   So Artemidorus 2.3.

[54]   Achmet 205: "Mustard signifies the same things as onions—namely illness, sorrow, and weeping. ... If someone dreams that he found or picked up mustard seeds, he will experience illness and sorrow in proportion to the amount. If he dreams that he was eating food with mustard, he will have sorrow and weeping by analogy to the bitterness. If he dreams that he prepared mustard seeds for eating, he will accuse many men and injure them; and if he ate the mustard, he will partake of their sorrow."

[55]   Drexl (1923, 445 ad loc.) offers the amusing comment that he cannot understand the meaning of this entry ("Diesen Satz kann ich nicht belegen").

[56]   Cf. this dream with the dream recorded in Achmet 20: "A certain noble of the caliph Mamun dreamt that he anointed his entire body and that all his bodily hairs fell off, except for his pubic hairs that then grew even longer. The noble sent one of his men to pretend that he, the slave, had dreamt this and to consult the interpreter. But the interpreter said to him: 'A noble saw this dream; you did not. And he will come into danger and nothing of his wealth, except for his wives, will be left for him.' After a few days, the dream turned out just as predicted." Achmet so interprets this dream because of an analogy of pubic hairs to women (male genitals and things associated with them such as underwear and pubic hairs are signifiers of woman). Byzantine dreambook writers do not refer to armpit hairs or pubic hairs and are relatively silent, at least

224. Being led around like a blind man: this is exceedingly auspicious.

225.* [A dream on] the first day of the week is a true dream.[57]

226. Running in your dream causes strong fortunes.

227. Sitting on a wall: expect to be prosperous.

228.* If someone dreams of eating fresh cheese, this is auspicious.[58]

229.* If someone dreams of eating dry cheese, this is inauspicious.[59]

230.* A peacock, when dreamt of, signifies for you wealth and glory.[60]

231.* Listening to someone sing: expect to be oppressed.[61]

232.* The turtle dove and ring dove, when dreamt of, are good signs.[62]

---

compared to Artemidorus and Achmet, on sexual organs and sexuality. Achmet's supposed Arabic identity permitted him much greater freedom to discuss vividly topics such as bestiality and male–male and male–female sex. Female–female relations, however, are not mentioned by any postclassical oneirocritic writer, including Achmet. Brown (1989, 69ff.) shows that men in medieval and early modern Europe were willing to *disbelieve* that female homoeroticism occurred: it garners the scantest of mention until the mid-seventeenth century. Brown offers reasons for this silence: for example, lesbianism was not seen as a serious threat; women were merely trying to emulate men (hence, lesbianism actually served to reaffirm, not subvert, social hierarchy); and people possessed an imperfect knowledge of male and female biology. Boswell (1989, 32) points out that censure of gay women was extended to the woman who assumed the "man's" role in the relationship, not to the "passive" partner: "At the outset sexual deviance is perceived only in women who violate the sex role expected of them by playing an active part in a female–female romantic relationship. The 'passive' female, who does not violate expectations of her sex role by receiving, as females are thought naturally to do, the attentions of her 'husband,' is not considered abnormal."

[57] It is not clear if Germanus means "a dream occurring on the first day of the week" or "a dream involving the first day of the week."

[58] So Achmet 251; cf. *Somniale Danielis* ("Beiträge, IV") LV: *caseum recentem accipere, lucrum significat.*

[59] So Achmet 251.

[60] Ibid., 287: "If someone dreams that he found a peacock, he will have much wealth, a rank of authority, and a most beautiful woman. If he dreams that he had a tame peacock at home, he will get a wealthy woman and beget an illustrious son because of the shiny luster of the peacock's feathers. If someone dreams that he was eating a peacock's flesh, he will get wealth from a king or a very great man: for the peacock often signifies a king because of the beauty and majesty of its feathers and because of the crest on its head. If he dreams that he was eating the flesh of a female peacock, he will get wealth from a very great woman. If he dreams that his peacock died or became lost, he will find sorrow, poverty, and a successor to his rank; and if the peacock was female, the misfortune will likewise happen to his wife." Cf. Artemidorus 4.56.

Wealthy Byzantines populated their gardens with peacocks as a form of adornment, with the peacocks sometimes eaten as food: Koukoules 1948–57, 5:408–9. Peacocks appear in Byzantine painting as symbols of paradise and salvation: *ODB* 3:1611–12.

[61] Cf. *Somniale Danielis* ("Beiträge, V") 101: *nuptias facere vel cantatrices videre, planctum et laborem significat.* For singing in Byzantium, see Wellesz 1961.

[62] So too Achmet 291; see also Artemidorus 2.20.

Y

233. Drinking clear sparkling water: this is useful.

234. Drinking turbid water: you will experience sorrows.

235.* If you get a piece of wild boar [meat], expect sudden gain.[63]

236. Water bursting forth from below signifies enemies.

237.* Sprinkling water [in your house]: consider this to be domestic oppression.

238.* Dreaming of truffles:[64] understand this, in my opinion, as your woman.[65]

239.* Wearing brand-new shoes means something exceedingly good.

240.* Wearing old shoes: you will incur loss.

Φ

241. Kissing rouses up long fights with enemies.

242.* Destroying[66] lice signifies deceits[67] for those who live with you.

243. Hearing a voice: consider this a reliable dream.

244. Eating with friends results in an evil deed.[68]

245. The continuous lapping noise of the sea indicates agitation in your affairs.

246. A rabbit, when dreamt of, causes unlucky trips.

247. Seeing the lights of heaven points to light shed on one's affairs.

248.* Eating dates signifies something good.[69]

249.* If someone [dreams of] setting lice on fire, this burns up his wealth.

---

[63]   Cf. Achmet 279; but the boar is an unfavorable sign in Artemidorus 2.20.

[64]   Drexl (1923, 446 ad loc.) comments on this word: "Zu ὕτνα (statt des gewöhnlichen ὕδνα) vgl. ἴτνον bei Du Cange, Gloss. Append. und das heutige ὕτανα oder ὕτινα." The word is equivalent to the Latin *tuber*, which was a delicacy favored by the Romans (Pliny, *Natural History* 19.2.11, 19.3.13; Juvenal 5.116, 119); it could be eaten raw, put in salads, boiled and smothered with garum (fish sauce), or grilled on skewers.

[65]   Γύναιον, not found elsewhere in the Byzantine folk dreambooks and Achmet, was a term of endearment and of insult. LSJ (s.h.v.) offers examples of its use in a "contemptuous sense." (Perhaps this explains Brackertz's [1993] translation, "üble Wieber.")

[66]   Here we have φθεῖρας φθείρειν (which is a nice pun), as opposed to φθεῖρας φέρειν (having lice) in Nicephorus 122.

[67]   I emend δούλους to δόλους; cf. Nicephorus 122.

[68]   An opposite interpretation of Nicephorus 124.

[69]   Achmet 241: "If someone dreams that he … found dates that had been gathered at the roots [of a palm tree] and that he ate some and then took the rest, he will get a proportionate amount of wealth from a woman through fornication; and if he gave some of the dates to others, the woman will benefit others too."

X

250.   If snow appears [in a dream], this brings about enmity with enemies.

251.   Washing your hands indicates the dissolution of worries.

252.   If a hawk flies from one's hands, this means harm for those who are magistrates.

253.   If someone is holding green grass, this brings about something good.

254.   A torn tunic tears away the oppressive weight of worries.

255.*   Holding gold: you will end up not getting what you want.

Ψ

256.   Fullness of the stomach points to false dreams.[70]

257.   Unmixed wine causes false dreams.

[Ω]

258.*   Carrying your child on your shoulders: this is an unfortunate sign.

259.   Holding eggs most certainly signifies sorrows.

---

[70]   This and the next verse, like verse 146 above, are related to the prologues in Appendix I of the Nicephorus dreambook.

Chapter 8

The Anonymous *Oneirocriticon*
An Additional [Dreambook] Drawn from the Experience of the Wise

[Beginning of A]

1. If someone dreams that he was made of gold or silver, he will suffer hindrance to great actions.[1]

2. Handling any type of silver vessel means profit in your activities.

3. Drinking wormwood signifies difficult quarrels.[2]

4. Making statues of men means the acquisition of sincere[3] and trustworthy friends.

5. If someone dreams of lambs and young goats, this means profit for himself through his activities.[4]

6. Ascending a high place on horseback signifies freedom for slaves and something good for anyone else.

7. To dream that one has been beheaded indicates getting rid of great trouble;[5] others say that he will lose his master.[6]

---

[1] Artemidorus 1.50: "If a slave, male or female, dreams that he is made of silver or gold, he will be sold, so that he is converted into silver or gold. If a poor man has the dream, he will grow rich, so that a substance of that sort will surround him; if the man is rich, he will be the victim of plots, since everything made of silver and gold invites many designing people. For every sick man, this dream clearly portends death. ..."

[2] Brackertz (1993, 262 ad loc.) comments on the medicinal use of wormwood: "Der Wermut (griech. *Apsinthion*) galt als ein guts Mittel gegen Schmerzen und Leiden aller Art. Man trank ihn im Sommer vor der Mahlzeit, weil man glaubte, er sei der Gesundheit zuträglich; s. Dioskurides 3,23. Der General Kekaumenos rät seinem Sohn: »Trinke auch keine Medizin oder sonst einen Absud. Wenn du aber etwas trinken willst, was deinem Magen hilft, dann trinke Absinth«."

[3] So I take γνήσιος; cf. Brackertz (1993), who translates as "echte."

[4] Cf. *Somniale Danielis* ("Beiträge, V") 3: *agnos vel hedos habere, consolationem significat.*

[5] Achmet 120: "If someone dreams that he was decapitated and his head became separated from him, if he is a slave, he will be set free; if he is ill, he will be cured; if he has sorrow or debt, he will lose it; if he is a king, his anxiety, fears, and worry will change into joy."

[6] I take "others say" as implying that the author has consulted other dreambooks (see comment to 411 below); as we will see, Manuel also says that he used several sources in writing his dreambook. Here, however, our author is exaggerating, as he may have used only Achmet's

8.   Leaping from a ship onto dry land signifies a change of residence.

9.   To be gazing about from a lofty place indicates the formation of a powerful friendship.

10. Lightning, when dreamt of, means unexpected gain.

11. To dream that one is barefoot or is walking barefoot foretells loss.

12. Handling flour means gain.[7]

13. If someone dreams that his brother or sister or relative died, this signifies an additional period of life for him.

14. If someone dreams that he saw someone separating fighting roosters, the person in the dream should be on guard so as to avoid evil.

15. To dream that one is sick signifies heavy distress.

16. To dream that one is deaf and dumb means great joy.

17. If you are swept away by a river, be careful not to suffer anything bad.[8]

18. Looking at the stars means profit.

19. Wearing armor signifies honor.[9]

20. Blood coming out of your mouth means danger.

21. Seeing or holding newly grown thistles means a rising-up of your enemies.

22. A bear approaching with someone's property[10] signifies quarrels.

23. To dream of a grapevine [growing] or planted in any place whatever means a useful and good period of time.

Beginning of B

24. If someone is being carried by another person, this signifies a shameful situation for him [*sc.* the dreamer].

25. If someone is sitting on oxen that are plowing, this means an honorable appointment for him.

26. A dream of cattle running signifies joy.

27. A dream of cattle grazing signifies joy and profit.[11]

---

dreambook: both interpretations come from Achmet (the first interpretation from Chap. 120, the second from Chap. 121).

   [7]   Achmet 208: "If someone dreams that he had some flour, he will have more glorious wealth. ..." Wheat meal could be eaten with milk or made into a type of porridge: Dalby 2003, 187.

   [8]   Cf. Achmet 173.

   [9]   So also ibid., 155.

   [10] So I take ἐν χρήμασί τινος ἐρχομένη; cf. Brackertz's (1993) "Ein Bär, der über jemandes Habe herfällt. ..." Note that I do not agree with his translation of ἐρχομένη as "falling upon" or "assailing," but simply translate it as "coming."

   [11] The opposite interpretation is found in Daniel 57 (see also the comment to the dream).

28.   Thin[12] cattle point to a bad year.[13]

29.   To dream that cattle are fighting signifies joy and profit.

30.   Eating beef means grief and displeasure.

31.   Eating butter foretells good news from afar.

32.   Bathing in a bathtub[14] means sudden commotion.

33.   Gathering or eating acorns signifies freedom of action as well as profit.

34.   Getting and holding a palm leaf signifies honor.

35.   Hearing thunder in the sky means good news.

36.   To be holding dice and then to see them fall out of your hands signifies the loss of life.

37.   Walking on roof-tiles means escaping the trap of your enemies.

Beginning of Γ

38.   Having a dirty beard is good for those involved with lawcourts, but evil for anyone else, especially the poor.

39.   Having sex with an old woman means an abundance of things.

40.   A beard that falls out or is shaved off is a terrible sign for any dreamer.

41.   A white beard signifies worries; other [dream interpreters] say it is honor.

42.   Whoever eats a sweet dessert will be beset by many evils.

43.   Whoever dreams of a birthday party will soon die.

44.   Drinking milk means happiness.

45.   Seeing gold or silver letters of the alphabet in any place whatever is an altogether good sign for a craftsman, but a bad sign for anyone else.

46.   To dream that you are having sex with a woman you know signifies something good.[15]

47.   To dream of letters tattooed on your body signifies blows.

48.   Laughing in one's dream means sorrow.

49.   Making wedding preparations means dangerous loss.

50.   Walking around barefoot indicates loss.

51.   Being hit in the jaw signifies freedom.

---

[12]   The manuscript has τρεῖς, but Drexl emends to τρυσσοί. He observes (1925b, 352 ad loc.): "Wenn man das τρεῖς der Hs lässt, so finde ich für den Satz keinen Beleg. Bei Achmet S. 215 Z. 3 und 14 deuten *magere* Rinder auf schlechte Jahre. So schreibe ich τρυσσοί (nach Hesychios = schwächlichen) was. ..."

[13]   See Mavroudi 2002, 360–61.

[14]   Or, "bath-house."

[15]   For whom? The man? The woman? Or if the woman is married, her husband? Achmet would say that the good fortune would come to the husband, since, although the penetrator gives benefits to the penetrated, all benefits fall to the woman's "head"—that is, her husband.

Beginning of Δ

52. Having additional fingers means additional wealth.

53. Wearing a silver ring means freedom from every evil, while wearing an iron ring means additional capital.

54. To dream of having a diadem signifies prosperity and something good.[16]

55. Fruit-bearing trees, when dreamt of, means income, but withered trees signify failure.

56. To dream of trees being cut down indicates loss for free people, but gain for slaves.

57. To dream of trees being rooted out signifies war and the fall of people.

58. To dream that you are unable to run means hindrance to your actions.

59. Running means sudden gain.

60. To dream of a very large serpent and then being chased by it signifies at first fear, but then afterwards honor.[17]

61. Having two heads means a union of friends.

62. To dream of a dolphin signifies good news.

63. To dream of demons indicates distress.

64. If you dream of sending gifts to someone else, take care not to suffer loss.

65. Making a will means failure in one's affairs.

66. The person who sees a very large serpent entering his house will have something good.

67. Handling nets means doing poorly and failing in one's affairs.

68. Dreaming of two suns signifies a longer life for the dreamer.

69. Smelling a foul odor signifies depression.

70. Receiving gifts means profit.

Beginning of E

71. To dream that one is in armor signifies unexpected honor without danger.

72. Seeing or chasing deer signifies envy without danger.

73. Eating venison means something good.

74. Sitting on an elephant foretells great honor.

75. Seeing an elephant or being chased by one means that enemies will prevail.

---

16. See Achmet 256.

17. I translate, following the reading in Daniel; cf. Drexl 1925b, 354 ad loc.: "Vgl. Ps-Daniel 80, wo statt unseres φόνον das wohl richtigere φόβον steht." The manuscript reads: Δράκοντα ἰδεῖν καὶ διώκεσθαι παρ' αὐτοῦ μὲν φόνον, ἔπειτα δὲ τιμὴν δηλοῖ (Seeing a large serpent and then being chased by it signifies at first murder, but then afterwards honor).

76. Being stripped of one's clothes is good for the ill, but a sign of difficulty for all others.

77. Reading an epistle means a source of new joy.[18]

78. Seeing a conflagration in any place whatever signifies danger.

79. Praying means a prosperous period of time.

80. Receiving one's freedom in a dream foretells goodness and profit for free people, but evil for slaves.

81. To pour or rub olive oil on oneself signifies a prosperous period of time.

82. Drinking olive oil means illness.

83. Eating olives signifies something good.

84. Seeing reptiles approaching you in a hostile way means the rising-up of your enemies.

85. Taking off your clothes means bitter loss.

86. Wearing a wreath made from an olive or oak or laurel tree signifies a trip with toil.

Beginning of Z

87. Wearing a belt in a dream means expenses[19] as a result of a trip.

88. Losing your belt is a bad sign, as is a belt that is cut in two.

89. To lose an animal means falling from great honor.

Beginning of H

90. Collecting or driving-in nails signifies loss.

91. Seeing bright sunlight means gain.

92. To dream that the sun is blood-red in color signifies loss.

93. Seeing two suns means a second source of authority.

94. Not seeing clearly the shining or risen sun means danger throughout the world.

95. If the sun and moon are traversing the sky together, this means unpleasantness and quarrels.

96. To dream of the sun rising in the east is a very good sign.

97. To see the sun moving under the clouds means profit and a good deed.

---

[18]   "New" by analogy to the news that is contained in the letter.

[19]   I take πορεία here as "traveling expenses" (for this meaning of πορεία, see LSJ, s.h.v.). The line could also be translated as, "Wearing a belt in a dream signifies the march of a journey."

98.   To dream of the sun and moon moving about here and there signifies the separation of husband and wife.

99.   To dream that the sun has fallen from the sky signifies something good for the dreamer, but something bad for the king.[20]

Beginning of Θ

100.   To dream of a wild animal talking like a human signifies distress; being with wild animals, the same.

101.   To dream of wild animals fighting each other means fear without danger.

102.   To dream of subduing and humbling a wild animal means that you will make friends with your enemies.

103.   To dream that wild animals are running signifies some tumults.

104.   To dream of the summer harvest[21] out of season means the death of people.

105.   Seeing God or worshipping Him or asking Him for something means freedom in all things.

106.   Whoever dreams that God is leaving his house will leave home.

107.   Whoever kisses God will be held accountable for a situation that he did not foresee.

108.   Seeing God in a wide-open area means freedom from worry.

109.   If the door of your house is damaged or missing, this means the loss of your wife.

110.   A shattered staff foretells something evil.

111.   If someone dreams of dying, he will be without worry.

Beginning of I

112.   Dreaming of wearing bright clothes signifies pleasure.

113.   To dream of becoming stronger means profit in one's activities.

114.   Catching sight of a cavalryman signifies quarrels and displeasure.

---

[20]   In oneirocritic literature, the sun symbolises a king (cf. Mavroudi 2002, 209–14), and so only he will be affected by the danger symbolised by the sun falling from the sky.

[21]   Perhaps θέρος here means "summer." Thus, "if you dream that it is summer contrary to the time of year. ..." But "harvest" is best, since we then have an analogy between the cutting of the grain and the cutting-down of people. Cf. 263 below.

115. Sitting on a white horse means additional capital; if on a grey steed, news along with loss; if on a chestnut-brown horse,[22] a profitable trip;[23] if on a horse of great stature, an additional span of life; if on a black horse, [loss].[24]

116. Falling off a horse means falling from life.

117. To be captured by Ishmaelites means something good.

118. Fish, when dreamt of, mean the disturbance of an enemy.

119. Eating fish signifies unpleasantness.

120. Frying fish[25] means tuberculosis.[26]

121. Wearing clothes made entirely of silk signifies envy.

122. Washing your clothes means release from displeasure and shame.

123. Wearing clothes that are stained or dirty does [not] signify something good.[27]

124. Flying without wings is good for those in foreign lands, but for the rest it is inauspicious.

125. Flying about here and there signifies tumultuous times.

126. If a man is weaving a textile, it means strife.[28]

127. Wearing multicolored clothes means fear and punishment.

128. Losing your clothes denotes grief.[29]

129. Wearing white clothes signifies joy; yellow clothes, illness; green clothes, faith.[30]

130. To dream that a textile is being woven without [the agency of] a man or woman signifies something good.

---

[22] Drexl 1925b, 357 ad loc.: "βάδιος = kastanienbraun; s. Stephanus s.v."

[23] But cf. *Somniale Danielis* ("Beiträge, IV") XCI: *equo castaneo sedere, negotium fedum significo.*

[24] The phrase ζημίαν σημαίνει has been added by Drexl, who (1925b, 357 ad loc.) comments: "<ζημίαν σημαίνει> (in der Hs ist eine kleine Lücke) ergänze ich nach Ps.-Daniel 157"; cf. *Somniale Danielis* ("Beiträge, IV") LXXXVIII: *equo nigro sedere, anxietatem significo*; see my comment to Daniel 246.

[25] Τηγανίζω = ταγηνίζω. Artemidorus (2.42) considers the frying-pan a greedy woman.

[26] A pun on τῖξις, which also means "a melting-away" (or "thawing," as in modern Greek), as food would do in a hot pan. The emperor Constantine III died of tuberculosis: Treadgold 1997, 307.

[27] Cf. Achmet 156. I accept Drexl's (1925b) addition of οὐ to the text.

[28] Both men and women wove materials like flax, wool, cotton, and silk. Although weaving was a domestic job, there were professional weavers in Constantinople (especially in the silk industry). See Koukoules 1948–57, 2.1:215–17; *ODB* 3:2193.

[29] Achmet (156) also considers this dream a sign of sorrow, but he predicts that the dreamer's wife will be the one to grieve.

[30] So Achmet 156, who consistently in his dreambook associates the color green with faith, and the color yellow with disease. Sirriyeh (2006, 213) discusses green as a symbol of righteousness and piety in Islam, and how the virtuous will have green robes in the afterlife (so the Koran); cf. Mavroudi 2002, 337–40.

Beginning of K

131.   Eating parsley means a shameful piece of news.

132.   Eating a gourd points to illness.

133.   Seeing or handling a wax candle signifies good news.

134.   To read imperial documents[31] or to see them being read foretells a happy period of time.

135.   To dream that cymbals are being played or being held or to dream that people are dancing signifies strife and lamentation.

136.   Walking downhill signifies something good.

137.   To dream of a short-sleeved tunic[32] signifies profit through a woman.[33]

138.   Seeing or touching bed bugs signifies days full of worry.

139.   Cackling crows or ravens signify a profitable business.

140.   Seeing dogs or being chased by them means great animosity.

141.   Playing a cithara denotes an unlucky day.

142.   Eating or handling red cherries signifies illness.[34]

143.   To dream of candles being kindled signifies [good][35] opportunities; to hold extinguished candles, the opposite; to hold candles again in the same condition, a protracted period of time. Thick candles [are interpreted] as years, while slender ones as months and days depending on their quality and quantity.[36]

---

[31]   One could take κονδάκια in its other meaning as a short hymn containing the substance of a church feast. But I follow Brackertz (1993), who translates as an imperial document: "Liest oder vernimmt einer den Worlaut eines kaiserlichen Schreibens ...." As Prof. Mavroudi points out to me, the original meaning of κονδάκιον was "scroll," referring to a small rod (made of wood, ivory, or other material) around which a document was rolled. Imperial documents remained rolls long after the codex came into wide usage, and so imperial documents could still be called κονδάκια.

[32]   The κολόβιον is a transliteration of the Latin *colobium*; see the numerous references in Sophocles 1975, s.h.v.

[33]   In Achmet's dreambook, all undergarments, especially underwear, signify a man's wife; see, for example, 156.

[34]   Perhaps a pun between κεράσια (cherries) and κέρασμα (a word used by ancient physicians to denote an affliction of two or more illnesses). Prof. Mavroudi offers the following observation: "[The reason for the interpretation] is perhaps something more pedestrian: even today in villages (where cherry trees are), it is well known that climbing a cherry tree and eating until your heart's content can make you sick in the stomach, cause diarrhea, etc."

[35]   I have added καλούς.

[36]   See Achmet 301 for a discussion of how a dream symbol is variously interpreted in terms of days, weeks, months, and years. For example: "Now if someone consults you about a dream, ask him in return at what hour he saw the dream. For from the first to the third hour of the night, [we calculate that] the dream will turn out at some point up to 20 years; from the third to the sixth hour, up to 15 or ten or eight years; from the sixth to the ninth hour, up to five or four or three years; from the ninth hour to dawn, up to one year or six or three months or one month

144. Falling off a cliff means something evil.

145. Eating or handling human flesh means that you will get someone else's property.

146. Being chased by a camel signifies violence at the hands of a powerful man.

147. Sitting on a camel means gain.

148. If you dream of becoming a *comes*,[37] this is not a good sign for state functionaries and legal defendants.

149. Chasing after a camel signifies goodness.

150. Holding a vine signifies an accusation.

151. To dream of oneself as a hunter or as running to hunt means gain.[38]

152. Seeing thunderbolts is good for slaves, but for all others, especially the poor, [this dream] is bad, for it is a sign of misfortune.

153. Eating any kind of heart means a quarrel in the house of the dreamer.[39]

154. Calling out to someone and not being answered back is a terrible sign; but if the person answers back, this means something good.

155. A dream of having a hernia: the dreamer will fall into many misfortunes.[40]

156. To dream of having long flowing hair signifies gain.

157. To dream of having gray hair: this too is a sign of gain.

158. Defecating on your bed means illness.

159. Climbing up a mast signifies only a little good.[41]

160. To dream that you are deaf means freedom from care.

161. To dream that your head is shaven means loss.

162. Beautifying or washing your head means goodness.

163. Receiving the heads of dead people means profit from those who hold power.[42]

164. Washing dirt off your head signifies escape from every trouble.

---

or even within ten days; the dream at daybreak will turn out that very day or [after] two or three days." Cf. Artemidorus 1.2 for a similar discussion of how times and days affect interpretation.

[37]   In Daniel 305 (early Byzantium), the word means "prefect" (see comment ad loc.); but at the time of this manuscript (fourteenth century), the word denoted a lower official or a subaltern officer of the naval and army units: *ODB* 1:485.

[38]   *Somniale Danielis* ("Beiträge, IV") CCXLIII: *venationem facere, lucrum significat.*

[39]   For the Byzantines' eating of animal hearts, see Dalby 2003, 144, 157, 160. Hearts were considered nourishing if they were well cooked.

[40]   So too Achmet 98.

[41]   But Artemidorus (2.23) considers the mast to have symbolic importance only for the ship's master.

[42]   Cf. Achmet 132: "If a king dreams that the heads of men who had died in battle were brought to him, he will be master of the heads of hostile nations." Κεφαλή consistently is interpreted in the Byzantine dreambooks as someone who wields power over other people—e.g., a wife, slaves, subjects, etc.

165. Sitting in a four-wheeled coach means illness.

166. To dream that a dog is playing with you means friendship with an enemy.

167. To dream that you have become a dog means that you should expect a very long absence from home.[43]

168. Hearing dogs howl means the snares of enemies.

169. Eating roasted meat signifies something good.

170. Eating the flesh of a woman means unexpected profit.

171. Dreaming of very many dogs signifies averting one's enemies.

172. Swimming means release from many evils.

173. Carrying jewelry means honor with envy.

174. Getting a young girl[44] denotes an increase in honor.

175. Eating raw meat means fornication.

176. Crying foretells something good.

177. Sitting in a wagon means animosity and grief.

178. Breaking a branch off a tree signifies separation from a friend.

179. Pulling an oar indicates a period of time filled with unrest.

180. If you dream of falling down, this means abuse.

181. If the soles of your shoes fall off, this signifies hindrance.

182. Flying downwards signifies that you will suffer loss.

183. Eating lion meat means victory over one's adversary.

184. Walnuts piled up in any place whatever indicate great profit.[45]

185. Finding the wood of a walnut tree means that you will find an advantageous situation.[46]

186. Finding or handling or eating a yellow-colored fruit signifies illness.[47]

187. To dream of a cypress tree [growing] in some place indicates seeing an aristocratic woman.[48]

---

[43]   But see Artemidorus 1.50.

[44]   Brackertz (1993, 265 ad loc.) comments on this word: "Das griech. Wort *kore* = Mädchen wird euphemistisch auch für Freudenmädchen, Dirne gebraucht. Im Neugriechischen ist noch heute der Ausdruck *koritsia* üblich."

[45]   Cf., however, *Somniale Danielis* ("Beiträge, IV") CLXXXIV: *nuces colligere, lites significat*; Achmet 198.

[46]   Ibid., 151: "If someone dreams that he was sitting under the shade of a walnut tree, he will meet a wealthy man, who, however, will be miserly because of the stony nature of walnuts; however, the two men will be on happy terms with each other."

[47]   See also ibid., 151.

[48]   Ibid., 151: "If someone dreams that a cypress tree ... grew inside his house (and this dream can be seen only by a noble, not by someone unworthy and poor), let him know that the cypress tree signifies the queen's status because of the tree's beauty and sweet smell and because by nature it never fades or sheds its leaves. ... If a king dreams that a cypress tree was in his

188.   Drinking dog milk means fear and lengthy disease.[49]

189.   If someone dreams that a dog is biting and shaking his clothes, this signifies dishonor inflicted by his enemies.[50]

190.   Dreaming of a well-made bed indicates a good life with a woman.

191.   A slave boy[51] signifies joy.

192.   Eating dog meat means profit from an enemy's wealth.[52]

193.   Eating cat meat indicates profit through a thief.[53]

194.   Finding a cat's skin signifies profit from the property of every thief.[54]

195.   Being scratched by a cat's claws means a very grave illness.[55]

196.   Fighting with a cat and then tying it up foretells the fettering of a thief.[56]

197.   Meeting a crow signifies that you will meet a certain liar.[57]

198.   Gnats or mosquitoes mean oppression and anxiety; and if you see a throng of them, this refers to a throng of enemies.[58]

199.   Eating a crab denotes profit from a crooked man.[59]

200.   To dream of your own clavicles signifies a powerful victory over your enemies.[60]

201.   To dream that your penis is erect means that you will acquire honor and children.[61]

---

palace, if he does not have a queen, he will get one; if he has one, he will delight in her, beget children in proportion to the tree's branches and height, and have a long life."

[49]   This verse is copied verbatim from ibid., 277.

[50]   Cf. ibid., 277.

[51]   Brackertz (1993, 266 ad loc.) comments on this word: "Griech. *kopelios*, neugriech. *kopelli* = Bursche, Diener." He also references Artemidorus 4.10 for the interpretation.

[52]   Cf. Achmet 277.

[53]   Ibid., 278.

[54]   Ibid., 278: "If someone [dreams that he] found or picked up a cat's tail, he will seize all of a thief's property."

[55]   Ibid., 278: "If someone dreams that while fighting with a cat he was wounded by its claws, he will suffer very severe illness and be filled with sorrow."

[56]   Cf. ibid., 278: "If someone dreams that he fought with or killed a cat, he will put a thief into bonds and slay him; and if he recognises the cat, he will know the thief: if not, the thief will be a stranger."

[57]   Cf. ibid., 290.

[58]   Cf. ibid., 295.

[59]   Ibid., 300: "The crab signifies a crooked man who cannot be corrected because of the crab's twisted manner of walking."

[60]   So too ibid., 69; although in the previous chapter (68), he interpreted them as concubines: "The clavicles signify concubines, who are more desirable than lawful wives. If someone dreams that his clavicles became larger, he will show love to those wives he desires and he will take pleasure in his concubines; if a married woman has this dream, she will make love to another man; if she is unmarried; she will become a common prostitute."

[61]   So ibid., 95; see Mavroudi 2002, 390.

202. If your penis is cut off, this signifies the death of a child as well as punishment.[62]

203. Finding human dung means that you will find unjust profit; and if you eat this dung, this means profit procured through sin.[63]

Beginning of Λ

204. Wearing a white garment means effeminacy.[64]

205. If you dream of being stoned, this means that your enemies will accuse you.

206. Handling bacon indicates the death of relatives.

207. Gathering chickpeas means illness.

208. To see a wolf approaching in a hostile way means the appearance of enemies.

209. To see a lion approaching you in a similar [hostile] way means a great enemy.

210. To dream of a running lion means a profitable matter.

211. Hurling a stone signifies loss.

212. Gathering stones indicates illness.

213. To dream of brigands signifies gain.

214. To dream of a burning lamp means concealment[65] of affairs.[66]

215. To dream that a wolf has eaten means redemption from great distress.

216. Sitting at a pit is an evil sign.

217. If you dream of a peregrine hawk, you will see a soldier arrive.[67]

218. If you kill a peregrine hawk, you will strike down a ruthless man.

---

[62] See Achmet 95.

[63] Ibid., 105: "If someone dreams that he picked up human dung, he will derive enjoyment of some money that, however, will be badly spoken of because of the foul smell of dung. ... If he dreams that he ate human dung, he will gain his enemy's gold amid sin and strife; but if he ate animal dung, his profit will be greater and his sin less." Besieged people could be reduced to eating excrement for sustenance: see my comment to Daniel 182 (note 196).

[64] Or simply "weakness." Cf. Brackertz (1993), who translates both ideas: "Ein weißes Kleid zu tragen weist auf Schwäche und Krankheit" ("Schwächer" can also refer to male impotence).

[65] So ἀποκρυφή; for which, see Sophocles 1975, s.h.v. The interpretation is an example of antinomy, since normally a brightly burning torch would reveal where one's goods have been hidden or would cast light on one's activities.

[66] This dream means the revealing of secrets according to Achmet 159; cf. Artemidorus 2.9.

[67] See Achmet 289. For the λούπη (= "Taubenfalke" according to Drexl [1925b], although Brackertz [1993] translates as "Weih"), see DuCange 1688, s.h.v.

219. Whoever eats roasted rabbit meat will receive illness and wealth from a woman.[68]

220. Whoever chases a rabbit will desire a woman who is a prostitute.[69]

Beginning of M

221. To be gathering something with someone older signifies profit.

222. Sitting with an older man signifies the same.

223. To dream that one is drunk means illness.

224. Seeing magicians[70] means shame and an accusation.

225. If you dream of a mill, this signifies freedom from worry in your activities.

226. If you dream that your mother is alive, even if she is [in reality] dead, this signifies gain.

227. Seeing or handling small pearls signifies misfortune;[71] [other dream-interpreters] interpret them as tears.[72]

228. To dream that someone who is young has become older[73] signifies gain; the opposite, however, means loss.

229. Seeing or touching marble signifies illness.

230. Eating or holding apples means strong love with a woman.

231. Seeing your mother involved in prostitution means danger.

---

[68]   The interpretation is based on two analogies: roasting ~ illness (fever), and meat ~ wealth; see Achmet 276, on which the interpretation is based. See Dalby 2003, 209 for Byzantine recipes of cooked hare.

[69]   So too Achmet 276: "If someone dreams that he was chasing a rabbit, he will fall in love with, and pursue, a prostitute. If he dreams that while chasing the rabbit he hurled a rod or some other object at it, if he hit it, he will satisfy his desire: if not, she will frustrate him and embitter him as well."

[70]   I take *magoi* not as eastern Magians, but in its popular Greek connotation of magician (cf. Brackertz's "Magier"), for which see *ODB* 2:1266. See Abrahamse 1982 for a discussion of the word *magos*. Cf. Achmet 12: "If someone dreams that he was a *magos*, he will be a lover of riches and wealth: for magicians are worldly-minded and think nothing of the retribution in the hereafter" (this is borrowed from several Arabic texts: Mavroudi 2002, 327–8; cf. Sirriyeh 2006, 218 who takes the word as meaning "Zoroastrian"). The Byzantines were ambivalent about magicians. Although magicians were utterly condemned by the Church and by legal statutes, they were approached for love-spells, poisons for destroying rivals, spells for destroying neighbors' crops, etc. See Krueger 2005, 305–6 for examples of spells, curses, and amulets.

[71]   So Daniel 365; but this is a favorable dream in Achmet 245: "If someone dreams that he found or received from somebody pearls or precious gems, he will discover the splendor of holy dogmas in proportion to the stones' size and shininess"; cf. ibid., 246 and 256.

[72]   The latter interpretation is to be found in Nicephorus 68; cf. Astrampsychus 41 and Germanus 138.

[73]   The word ἡλικία can refer to age or stature. I take it in the former sense on the basis of Daniel 11.

232. If you dream of bees coming out, think of enemies coming against you.

233. Eating bees signifies grief.

234. If you find honey on the honeycomb, you will find wealth through violence.

235. Eating honey boiled with spices means grief.

236. If you see millstones in some place, it signifies a message from your enemies.

237. To dream of ants moving about in a house indicates forthcoming death.[74]

238. To dream of ants coming into your house signifies disease and a large family.[75]

239. To dream of grain-bearing ants coming out of your house means release from both disease and an evil family.[76]

240. If you see a monkey, you will see a wealthy but not very powerful enemy.

241. Wearing a necklace made with precious gems and pearls signifies a position of authority.[77]

Beginning of N

242. Nests of birds mean a surplus in your means of livelihood.

243. To dream that a corpse has risen from the dead denotes gain.

244. To dream of the dead indicates that your business will be dead.

245. To dream of oneself as dead signifies loss.[78]

246. To dream of clouds moving quickly means struggle in your activities.

247. A bride leaving a house indicates death.

248. To dream of a church with God inside signifies honor.

---

[74] Cf. *Somniale Danielis* ("Beiträge, IV") CIX: *formicas quascumque viderit, lites maximas significat*. Cf. Artemidorus 1.24: "To dream that ants are entering one's ears is auspicious for sophists. For the ants are like young men who attend courses. But for other men, the dream prophesies death. For ants are children of the earth and they go down into the earth."

[75] Achmet 296: "Ants for the most part signify death. If someone dreams that a mass of ants appeared from a hole in his house, this means his imminent death. If someone dreams that ants were walking down a road and then entered his house, he will, quite simply, become ill and his family of slaves will increase."

[76] Ibid., 296: "If someone dreams that ants were coming out of his house while carrying grain, he will be released from illness, an evil household, and the fear that has been afflicting him. If someone dreams that ants were on his threshing-floor or in his granary, he will have sorrow and be poor."

[77] Ibid., 256: "If someone dreams that he was wearing a necklace made with gems and pearls, he will receive a rank that carries the authority to govern people, and he will govern them well. If he dreams that the necklace became lost or stolen, he will lose his position. If he dreams that the pearls and gems were removed, he will act evilly toward his subjects."

[78] But in other dreambooks, this dream indicates a lack of worries; see, e.g., Nicephorus 39 and Nicephorus, Appendix II, 72.

249.   A bride who has put on jewelry will soon die.

250.   Nodding to someone means the disclosure of a secret.[79]

251.   Nodding to a woman means that you will discover joy.[80]

252.   [A dream of] falling sick and being given up [for dead] means a lesser amount of wealth.[81]

Beginning of Ξ

253.   If you dream of being a stranger,[82] this is indicative of a life subject to changes.

254.   Dreaming of oneself in a foreign place means unexpected gain.

255.   To dream that guests are in your house means envy.

256.   Shaving means loss.

257.   Worshipping a wooden idol means that you will petition someone, but you will not be heard.[83]

258.   If someone who is away in a foreign land dreams of the resurrection of the dead, he will quickly see his homeland.[84]

259.   A dream of yellow wasps signifies a marauding expedition by enemies.

---

[79]   Achmet 125: "If someone dreams that he nodded to a friend, he will divulge his secret to him and entrust him with wealth, provided that the man perceived the nod. If he nodded to an unfamiliar old man who noticed the nod, the dreamer's fate will be for the better; if he knows the old man, the dream's result will happen to that man." The word νεῦμα (nod) also meant a musical sign that stood for musical notes attached to sacred words: *ODB* 2:1461, 1495.

[80]   Ibid., 124: "If someone dreams that he nodded to a woman, if she indicated yes in return, he will find in that year joy analogous to the woman's beauty; but if she indicated no, he will have sorrow analogous to her ugliness, and things will be for him the opposite of what he wants." Cf. 125: "If someone dreams that he nodded to an elegant woman who reciprocated, he will derive profit from seasonable agricultural activities; if he has no [fields], he will derive joy and profit from his business."

[81]   So ibid., 132.

[82]   Or, "if you dream of being a guest in someone's house." Given the interpretation, the above translation seems more appropriate. See also Daniel 379 with my comments ad loc.

[83]   Achmet 12: "If someone dreams of worshipping a wooden idol, he will stand in need of some evil nobleman, but he will not be heard regarding what he requests. If someone dreams of worshipping an idol constructed on a wooden platform, he will be the leader of a false heresy against the Word." See Mavroudi 2002, 328–31 for Arabic dreambook parallels.

Both the Hebrew Bible and the Christian New Testament insist that prayers offered to pagan gods are useless, since no god but Yahweh exists. See, e.g., 1 Kings 18:26–9; 2 Kings 19:17–19; Psalms 115:5–8 and 135:15–18; Isaiah 44:9–20. Also *ODB* 2:982.

[84]   Achmet 7: "If someone dreams of the resurrection of the dead, this signifies freedom from bonds and an end to wars, and the relatives of the inhabitants [of the region where the dream occurred] who are overseas will soon see them, and they will receive from the king honors and gifts of wealth."

260. Receiving a donkey from someone as a hospitality gift means unexpected joy.

261. If someone dreams of lying on somebody else's mattress that has been set upon a bed, this means joy and power.

262. Gathering dry fodder means wealth.

263. Seeing some unfamiliar tract of land being harvested signifies the slaughter of strangers.

264. Finding a dry brick denotes wealth.

265. Sitting on an unfamiliar horse means happiness with another man's wife.[85]

266. Eating dry cheese signifies a shameful matter.

Beginning of O

267. Wearing armor means security in what one does.

268. Handling armor signifies freedom from every danger.

269. Drinking vinegar means quarrels.

270. Sitting on a black donkey means death.

271. A dream of donkeys indicates great troubles.

272. Seeing white donkeys or riding on them means glorious honor.

273. Hearing the braying of donkeys or seeing them either let loose or running means envy.

274. A dream of plowing donkeys means inactivity along with loss.

275. To see the sky a flaming color means calamity throughout the world.[86]

276. Touching the sky means difficulty for all dreamers.

277. If the sky has fallen to the ground, this means hindrance to one's activities.

278. To dream of a snake on your bed means that you will marry an unmarried woman; but if she already has a husband, this dream means that she will become a widow.

279. To lose one's teeth means the death of relatives; but if the teeth grow back, this signifies gain.

280. Cleaning your teeth means that you will devour other people's labors.

281. Taking out your teeth without pain means freedom from worry.

282. Having black or exceedingly white teeth means illness.

---

[85]   Cf. ibid., 14: "If someone dreams of sitting on the Pharaoh's steed or saddle-horse, if he did so with the Pharaoh's consent, the Pharaoh will give him a woman of the royal family; if without his consent, the dreamer will mount the Pharaoh's daughter from behind and this will become known."

[86]   Cf. *Somniale Danielis* ("Beiträge, V") 28: *caelum flammeum videre, aliquod iniquitatis toto orbe accrescit.*

283. If you see your own reflection, you will have a long life.[87]

284. If you dream of having a clear reflection, this is a good sign; but if the reflection is poor, you will experience many evils.[88]

285. Birds sitting on their eggs signify something good.

286. To hear musical instruments being played means a quarrel with your neighbors.[89]

287. Touching bones indicates gain.

288. Drinking dark wine means weakness of body.

289. Simply drinking wine [...][90]

290. Wine that has been poured out indicates the stopping of strife.

291. To dream of small eyes means loss.

292. Losing your eyes signifies death.

293. Eating yellow-colored or acidic-tasting fruit means illness.[91]

294. To dream of fruits in season is a good sign.

295. Gathering bones of any sort means that you will lose trustworthy friends.

296. Having long fingernails indicates a lack of worry over one's business.

297. Eating your fingernails signifies that you will consume other people's labors.

298. To dream of fog right above the ground signifies the turbulence of affairs throughout the world.

299. A dream of dancers means happiness.[92]

300. Drinking white wine means joy; but if it is diluted with water, oppressive sorrow.

301. If you kill a snake, you will conquer your enemy.

302. Seeing or touching sea birds signifies that you will find something desirable.[93]

---

[87] *Somniale Danielis* ("Beiträge, IV") CI: *faciem suam in quacunque re viderit, vita longa ei datur.* See also Achmet 248, although he interprets the dream as referring to a brother or, if the dreamer has no brother, to a very close friend.

[88] Artemidorus (2.7) interprets along the same lines.

[89] For Byzantine music, see Koukoules 1948–57, 2:39–44 (instruments); Rautman 2006, 276–8 (with n. 19 on 279), 293.

[90] A lacuna exists in the text.

[91] Cf. Achmet 151.

[92] Cf. Artemidorus 1.76.

[93] See Achmet 134 for the benefits derived from dreams of bestiality with such birds. Achmet had earlier stated (133) that if someone is penetrated by an animal, then he or she can expect to receive some profit from a man who is an enemy; but if he penetrates the animal and receives pleasure from the act, he will overpower an enemy to whom he will later show good: "If someone dreams that he performed sex on a domesticated animal, he will trample down an enemy to whom he will later show kindness: however, that man will not show gratitude in return. If he dreams that a wild animal performed sex on him, he will receive great goodness from an enemy

Beginning of Π

303. To dream that a tower has collapsed: this means the death of a great magistrate.

304. Sitting on rocks indicates good hopes.

305. Having your feet cut off means idleness and inactivity.[94]

306. Holding birds points to unexpected profit.

307. Seeing a stream of water means release from great oppression; and if you drink from it, [bad] news; if you are sailing or swimming in it, illness.[95]

308. A dream that a spring is bubbling up in your house: this means gain.

309. Walking uphill sideways means toil; going downhill sideways, a good period of time.

310. Seeing storage jars or looking inside them signifies fresh news.[96]

311. Whoever dreams that he is rich will become poor.

312. Whoever dreams that he is wandering around will be greatly distressed.

313. Running on foot means a sum of cash.[97]

314. Fighting on foot means honor.

315. Speaking with sheep signifies illness.

316. Shearing sheep denotes loss.

317. Tending sheep means gain.[98]

318. If you are sitting upon black sheep, watch out lest you lose even the clothes on your back; but if upon white sheep, it signifies something good.[99]

319. To acquire a very large number of milk-producing sheep means joy and wealth.[100]

---

in proportion to that animal's size and strength. In sum, whoever dreams of performing sex on any man or woman or animal will do good to that person or thing."

[94]   Ibid., 117: "If someone dreams that … his feet were cut off, if he is wealthy or very powerful, he will be deprived of his slaves and end up being punished; if he is poor, he will soon die: for a poor man gets his sustenance by walking with his feet, while a rich man can have no feet and still live—albeit painfully—by being attended to by slaves."

[95]   Cf. *Somniale Danielis* ("Beiträge, IV") CXXXV: *in flumen natare, anxietatem significat.*

[96]   But cf. Artemidorus 1.74.

[97]   So I translate διάφορον; for this meaning, see LSJ, s.h.v., 4b. Brackertz (1993) translates as "klingenden Lohn."

[98]   Most Byzantine shepherds practiced transhumance, often travelling significant distances from home; see *LAnt* 281; *ODB* 3:2105.

[99]   See Artemidorus 2.12.

[100]   Achmet 240: "If someone dreams that he found or bought a very large number of milk-giving sheep, he will get wealth, happiness, and slaves in proportion to the number of sheep. If the dreamer is a king, he will reduce a nation to slavery and make it tributary to him, and he will be happy in proportion to the number of sheep."

320. [To dream of] shepherding sheep and then losing them means great poverty.[101]

321. Drinking sheep milk signifies joy.[102]

322. Eating raw mutton signifies a bad personal reputation.[103]

323. If one dreams of a skinned sheep in his house [οἴκῳ], it signifies his own [οἰκεῖον] death.[104]

324. Eating sheep heads means unexpected gain and longevity.[105]

325. Eating a sheep's liver signifies a very large quantity of gold.[106]

326. Handling pepper or mustard means illness, sorrow, and weeping.

327. Buying pepper signifies strife in your house; and if you eat it, it signifies punishment.

328. Dreaming that a young child has died means good hope and gain.

329. Dreaming that a young child has grown old indicates sorrow and loss.

330. Playing with a young child means rather quick profit.[107]

331. If you receive any kind of bird whatsoever, this signifies glory and a good deed.

332. Playing in private with a young child means joy.

333. To dream of a herd of quadrupeds indicates untimely toils.

334. Seeing prostitutes and having sex with them foretells sudden tumult.

335. To dream of a ship running on the open sea means great joy.[108]

---

[101] Ibid., 240: "If someone dreams that he was shepherding sheep, he will receive rank and power over people in proportion to the number of sheep." For shepherding in Byzantium, see Bryer 2002, 103–4; Koukoules 1948–57, 5:310–25.

[102] Cf. ibid., 240 on goat milk: "If someone dreams that he was drinking goat milk, this means joy and wealth. If a king dreams that he was drinking it in a vessel, he will experience joy and exultation and have sex with a woman, all in proportion to the vessel's beauty and the milk's sweetness."

[103] See ibid., 240 for eating cooked mutton (as well as parts of a sheep like the feet, liver, and tail), and for the horrible consequences of eating raw goat meat.

[104] See ibid., 240.

[105] Ibid., 39: "If someone dreams of eating the boiled head of a sheep, he will get wealth as well as profit from a man of high rank, although he will do so with difficulty [because of the symbolic significance of boiling]. If he dreams that the sheep's head was roasted, he will fight his enemy to strip him of his wealth and he will win; however, his enjoyment of the wealth will be accompanied by punishment because of the roasting from the fire. If someone dreams that he ate an uncooked head, he will become exceedingly rich amid very great sins"; cf. ibid., 40. See Dalby 2003, 143 for a treatise on foods that recommends eating heads, though with pepper or mustard to avoid emesis.

[106] So Achmet 240. Dalby (2003, 71) records a Byzantine text that recommends the liver of an animal as being especially nourishing.

[107] Cf. *Somniale Danielis* ("Beiträge, IV") CXLII: *infantes viderit & cum ipsis luderit, felicitatem temporis significat.*

[108] Cf. *Somniale Danielis* ("Beiträge, V") 97: *navigium videre, nuntium bonum significat.*

336.   Sailing in your dream signifies something good.

337.   Seeing a ship that has been set on fire means upheaval.

338.   Dreaming that a ship is standing on dry ground signifies grief in your house; if it is sailing on dry land, loss.[109]

339.   To see from far away a ship loaded with goods means good news.[110]

340.   Sailing when it is foggy or dark indicates idleness.[111]

341.   Seeing one's father either alive or dead means happiness.

342.   To dream of any type of purple garment means illness.

343.   Receiving or eating a pastelli[112] denotes profit.

344.   Eating plentiful snacks or dishes of food[113] signifies partnership along with gain.

345.   Seeing the suburbs on fire means failure.[114]

346.   To dream of someone telling you your fortune: this indicates strife.[115]

347.   If someone dreams of mice or cats living in his house, this indicates individuals outside of one's family along with profit.[116]

348.   Birds fighting with each other signify strife.

Beginning of P

349.   If you handle or eat radishes, watch out for poison.

350.   To dream of radishes set out on a table signifies the carrying-out of an evil plan.[117]

---

[109]   Cf. Achmet 178; but see Artemidorus 2.23.

[110]   *Somniale Danielis* ("Beiträge, IV") CLXXXIII: *naves viderit, bonum nuntium significat.*

[111]   Perhaps an allusion to the fact that ships had to be pulled into harbors when faced with poor weather or when pilots could not see the sun or stars for navigation purposes.

[112]   Drexl (1925b, 369 ad loc.) describes the παστέλις as a sesame-and-honey concoction ("ein Gemisch von Sesam und Honig [in Neugr.]; s. Du Cange s.v."). Cf. Brackertz's (1993, 270) note ad loc.: "eine Süßigkeit, die aus Sesam und Honig bereitet ist." Cf. Koukoules 1948–57, 5:113.

[113]   Dalby (2003, 72, 98) takes προσφάγια as meaning various cheeses; Koukoules (1948–57, 5:32–3) extends the meaning to include dishes of fish, meat, and fruits. The meaning "snacks" comes closer to the meaning intended here.

[114]   Cf. *Somniale Danielis* ("Beiträge, IV") CXXXIV: *incendia in quocumque loco viderit, aliquod periculum significat.*

[115]   Artemidorus (2.69) offers an extremely unfavorable opinion of fortune-tellers.

[116]   The interpretation comes from the analogy that such creatures, like the foreigners they symbolise, would live in one's house and eat the food there.

[117]   Achmet 207: "If someone dreams that radishes were placed on his eating-table, if he is king, he will stir up his councilors because of one of his evil mandates; if a commoner, he will have domestic quarrels." Prof. Mavroudi observes that dishes of radishes are set out on the table of the Last Supper in many late Byzantine frescoes (e.g., Saint Nicolas Orphanos in Thessaly

351. Sowing or transplanting radishes means evildoing and slander.[118]

352. To dream of pine resin or pitch or sulfur indicates some act of violence.[119]

353. Gulping something down in a dream signifies a drug used for treating illness.

354. Gathering roses means joy received through a wicked person.[120]

355. To dream of roses strewn around one's house signifies great joy and good news.[121]

356. Holding a staff in a dream signifies a good friend.

357. A staff that falls out of your hands signifies the loss of a good friend.

358. Beating someone with a staff means beneficence for the person beaten.[122]

359. Handling a pomegranate, if it is sweet, foretells wealth from a rich man; but if it is acidic, it signifies sorrow.[123]

Beginning of Σ

360. To dream of oneself crucified means honor from a great person.[124]

[early fourteenth century]); the reason, perhaps, is that the radishes symbolise the evil plan that Judas hatched.

[118] So Achmet 207.

[119] *Somniale Danielis* ("Beiträge, IV") CCXIX: *resinas vel sulphur viderit, grandes molestias significat.*

[120] Achmet 202: "If someone dreams that he was gathering roses, he will receive happiness from a man who will be wicked because of the rose's thorns."

[121] Ibid., 202: "If someone dreams that roses were strewn in his house, if he is king, he will receive news of joy because of the rose's sweet smell and red color; if a commoner, he will find happiness and wealth."

[122] The interpretations here and in 356 and 357 are drawn from ibid., 123 and 211.

[123] This is a paraphrase of ibid., 151: "If someone dreams that he owned a pomegranate tree, if the fruit was sweet, he will meet a wealthy man with whom he will be on sweet terms; but if the fruit was sour, he will meet a cruel man by whom he will be oppressed in proportion to the amount of fruit."

[124] Cf. ibid., 90: "If someone dreams that he was crucified, if he is poor, he will become rich; if he is already rich, he will obtain even more money, but this will come with violence and punishment. If someone dreams that he was scourged with straps of rawhide before he was crucified, he will be exalted before the people and have power over them in direct measure to the [amount of] flogging. If he dreams that after he was crucified he came down from the cross, he will fall from the height of his honor and his wealth will disappear. If he dreams that he was crucified and then set on fire, he will be exalted and be a ruler of people; however, he will later suffer a violent death on the battlefield because of the violence that fire symbolises."

Constantine the Great abolished crucifixion and replaced it with hanging on the *phourka* (a fork-shaped gallows) and execution by sword: *ODB* 2:768, 3:1622; Rautman 2006, 30–31. Islamic countries still practiced crucifixion at this time. See also Artemidorus 2.53 for the numerous methods of interpreting a dream of crucifixion, and Mavroudi 2002, 174–88. Cf. also Nicephorus Appendix II, 8 (with comment ad loc.) for the association of being lifted up while hung (or crucified) with the gaining of honors.

361. Receiving any type of wreath indicates happiness.

362. Wearing a wreath on one's head means great honor.

363. Receiving a wreath together with a palm leaf signifies mastery over one's enemies.

364. Wearing a wreath made of roses means something good, provided that roses are in season [at the time of the dream]; if they are out of season, it indicates torment.[125]

365. Having a laurel wreath tree signifies something good for everyone.

366. Having a cypress wreath signifies illness.

367. Having a gold or silver crown also means illness.[126]

368. Wearing a crown made with precious stones or pearls foretells great honor.[127]

369. Finding sugar means finding great profit.[128]

370. Having a pale-looking body means hindrance to one's actions.

371. Dreaming of your spouse signifies that you will find good friends or a good deed.

372. To dream that your wife is set up in prostitution signifies danger for you personally.[129]

373. To dream that one's wife is dead is a good sign for any dreamer.

374. Torturing[130] your wife means loss of capital.

375. Wearing shackles made for the feet[131] means lengthy grief.

376. To dream of a bloody moon signifies loss.[132]

---

[125] So too Artemidorus 1.77.

[126] See ibid., 1.77. Perhaps there is a subtle association here: στέφανοι were also marriage crowns, and given the persistent oneirocritic association of marriage with death, this may explain the interpretation here.

[127] Achmet 245.

[128] Ibid., 249 on sugar: "If someone dreams that he was eating sugar, he will have joy and sweet wealth. If he dreams that he was eating sugared flat-cakes, he will have good days equivalent to the number of cakes: for if he ate only one cake, he will have one good day or month or year; if two or more, likewise in proportion. If he dreams that he was eating sugar that had been broken into bits, he will find wealth that will last for very many days; and if he gave some of this sugar to people, he will do good to others. If he dreams that the sugar was dissolved in water, he will grieve over his wealth and find opposition. If he dreams that he carried a large quantity of sugar into his house, he will get much wealth without toil and worry. If he dreams that he distributed sugar to poor people, he will admonish people by word and deed." See Dalby 2003, 227 for cane sugar.

[129] Achmet (128) states that the danger predicted by such a dream will happen to the woman, not to the dreamer.

[130] So βασανίζειν; cf. Brackertz's (1993) "mißhandelt."

[131] For συμποδισμός, see Stephanus 1954, s.h.v.

[132] *Somniale Danielis* ("Beiträge, IV") CLIII: *lunam sanguinem viderit, damnum significat.*

377. To dream of the waning moon signifies profit.

378. To dream of a bright moon indicates good actions regarding one's affairs.

379. To dream of the moon in any of its lesser phases signifies loss.

380. To dream of the moon at its fullest phase is a good sign for those under duress; otherwise, it is bad.

381. Hearing trumpets means a disturbance.

382. [To dream of] striking oneself on iron signifies worries.

383. Dreaming of any kind of rusty iron means some sort of illness.

384. Whoever dreams of serving in the army as a bodyguard:[133] watch out lest he sin or be impeded in some way.

385. Climbing a staircase[134] signifies hindrance.[135]

386. Eating the flesh of corpses means freedom from care.

387. Seeing or shooting arrows signifies opposition to your actions.

388. An earthquake taking place in a dream signifies confusion in the world.

389. Dreaming of darkness means illness.

390. Eating black grapes means confusion and oppressive strife.

391. Eating cuttlefish denotes disease.

392. Wearing women's clothing means shame and dire straits.[136]

393. Holding a sword signifies profit: and if the sword is bare and without a sheath, this foretells the death of one's own wife; if the sword is broken, it indicates the death of a child.[137]

394. If one puts on sandals and then goes for a walk, this signifies a journey; but if one wears them without taking a stroll, the dreamer will marry a woman.[138]

---

[133] This is a loan word, from the Latin *speculator*. *Speculator* often meant a scout or spy, but in imperial Rome it denoted a soldier, just below to a centurion in rank, who acted as a bodyguard; this is how Brackertz (1993) takes it ("Leibwächter"). Sophocles (1975, s.h.v.) also translates as "executioner."

[134] The word σκάλα ("stairs" according to Sophocles 1975, s.h.v.) also denoted mooring-stations for fishing-boats to unload their catches.

[135] But this is a negative symbol in Artemidorus 2.42.

[136] Achmet 266: "If someone dreams that he was wearing feminine garments contrary to habit, he will find suffering, constraint regarding his wealth, fear of the authorities, and analogous dishonor. If he dreams that he was wearing an outer cloak like a woman, a secret calamity will lead him to the brink of destruction. If he dreams that he was wearing his wife's clothes, he will experience humiliation and dishonor regarding his wife; if he dreams of wearing another woman's clothes, he will be humiliated publicly." The Council of Trullo (692) outlawed cross-dressing: Brubaker 2005, 444. For transvestite nuns in Byzantium, see Gregory 2005, 141–2.

[137] See Achmet 155, on which this interpretation is based. Isaac Comnenus minted coins depicting himself holding an unsheathed sword; this symbolised his right to rule through conquest: *ODB* 2:1011; Treadgold 1997, 598.

[138] See Achmet 266 for details.

395.   If your mattress is stolen, this signifies the loss of your wife.[139]

396.   Eating or having parsnips [means] the expectation of wealth.

397.   If you own sparrows, expect injustice at the hands of a friend.[140]

398.   If you possess many small sparrows, expect lawsuits and quarrels with friends.

399.   To dream that sparrows came in and chirped in one's house signifies an expenditure on the house [either because of it][141] or on account of some blood relative.

Beginning of T

400.   Anointing your hair with oil means increase in wealth.[142]

401.   To see the hairs on your head beautiful and long signifies honor and glory for a magistrate, and for a poor man wealth.[143]

402.   If the hairs on your head are cut off, for the emperor this signifies a diminution of his treasuries; for other men, poverty; for a woman, sorrow over her husband.[144]

403.   To dream that the hairs of one's beard are plentiful and thick—that is, more than necessary: this signifies destitution and sorrow.[145]

404.   Having grey hair means for a ruler diminution of honor; for other people [it signifies] poverty;[146] again, to have completely white hair signifies sorrow for all dreamers.

405.   If the hairs of one's moustache have increased, this signifies [for a powerful magistrate][147] an increase in his household and glory; for anyone else, profit and wealth.

---

[139]   The bed always signifies a woman in oneirology (cf. *Somniale Danielis* ["Beiträge, V"] 87 and Daniel 306). Cf. Achmet 149: "If someone dreams that a priest entered his [*sc.* the dreamer's] house and fell asleep on his bed, he will become friends with that priest who, however, will deal treacherously with him by mounting his wife"; 247: "If someone dreams that he found or received sheets or woollen covers for his bed, he will get a wife analogous to their beauty."

[140]   But cf. ibid., 298.

[141]   Drexl adds this phrase; see his comments (1925b, 373) ad loc.

[142]   Cf. Achmet 23.

[143]   Based on ibid., 18.

[144]   Based on ibid., 21.

[145]   Ibid., 22: "If someone dreams that his beard reached a beautiful length, he will acquire even greater wealth; but if it grew longer than what is fitting, he will come into sorrow and illness[: however, his afflictions will be] moderate, since he [can always trim the beard and thus] make it beautiful again."

[146]   Ibid., 18.

[147]   Drexl (1925b) adds this phrase on the basis of Achmet 42, from which this dream and interpretations are drawn.

406. If the hairs of one's moustache fall out, this indicates poverty and ill repute.[148]

407. If your armpit hairs increase, this indicates that your daughters and the other lawfully begotten women of your family will be wealthy.[149]

408. Finding a strung bow signifies a journey and a happy return from it.

409. Holding bows and arrows means victory over one's enemies.

410. A broken bow [signifies] fear of one's enemies and illness of one's wife.[150]

411. Finding a bow and arrows[151] signifies power.[152]

412. Being struck by an arrow means grievous illness.[153]

413. If the wall of your house falls down, it means the death of your wife and loss; but if you rebuild it, this signifies that you will get more wealth through her.[154]

414. Singing or eating is a good sign.

415. To dream of a dead man walking around signifies good news.

416. To dream of oneself as dead and carried out for burial signifies freedom from all of one's sorrows.[155]

417. Seeing or eating or owning bulls signifies very great honor.

418. Eating dry cheese means a shameful deed; fresh cheese, on the other hand, is a good dream.

Beginning of Y

419. Drinking boiling-hot water means illness; but if the water is ice-cold, a long span of life.[156]

---

[148]   Achmet 41.

[149]   Ibid., 41: "If someone dreams that his armpit hairs grew in number and length, he will see wealth in his daughters: if he has no daughters, he will see it in the younger of the women connected to him by kinship; but if he dreams that the hairs were burned off or fell out, the result will be to the contrary for his daughters or kinswomen."

[150]   But see ibid., 155.

[151]   Here we have σάγιτται versus βέλη in 409 above. The difference in vocabulary may be attributed to the use of several sources.

[152]   See Mavroudi 2002, 459 for discussion.

[153]   Cf. Achmet 247.

[154]   So ibid., 146.

[155]   See ibid., 132; cf. Artemidorus 2.49: "To dream that one is dead, that one is being carried out for burial, or that one has been buried foretells freedom for a slave who is not entrusted with the care of the house. For a dead man has no master and is free from toil and service. But for a slave who has been entrusted with the care of the house, it signifies that death will rob him of his trusteeship." For death and burials in Byzantium, see *ODB* 1:340–41; Rautman 2006, 10–12, 45–6; and Daniel 181 (with comment ad loc.).

[156]   See Artemidorus 1.66.

420. Getting cold water from a spring means longevity.

421. Drinking river water means that you will soon have toil.

422. Drinking muddy water or crossing such water signifies passion.

423. Drinking clear water means gain.

424. If you eat the meat of a hyena, be on your guard to avoid suffering a magic [spell] cast by an evil woman.[157]

425. Begetting a son means affliction.[158]

426. Dense forests mean defeat at someone's hands.[159]

427. Wearing shoes [...][160]

Beginning of Φ

428. Seeing or approaching a friend means gain.

429. Spending time in prison denotes distress.

430. Seeing a large group of bald people signifies oppressive trouble.

431. Seeing that one is bald means the loss of both friends and capital.

432. Wanting to flee but not being able to do so means hindrance.

433. To dream of having a boil on one's foot is a good sign for slaves and the poor, but a horrible sign for the wealthy.[161]

434. Bathing in a well means gain.

435. If one is thrown into prison and placed in chains, he will fall into many evils.

436. Carrying a load means freedom.

437. Receiving a light means gain.

---

[157] Achmet 273: "The hyena represents an evil woman who is a sorceress, a poisoner, and an enchantress. If someone dreams that he was sitting on a hyena, he will have sex with such a woman. If he dreams that he threw a stone or missile at it, he will offer words and answers that will come between them. If he dreams that while fighting a hyena he killed it with a spear, he will forcibly have sex with this type of woman. If he dreams that he was eating hyena meat, he will be enchanted by this woman for a period of time proportionate to how much he ate. If he dreams that he was drinking hyena milk, he will find that his money has been lost, and he will become poor." Artemidorus (2.12), interpreting a hyena as a hermaphrodite, refers to the writings of Aelian and Aristotle on the subject.

[158] See Artemidorus 1.14.

[159] Cf. ibid., 2.28. Lefort (2002, 261–2) discusses forests in the Byzantine Empire; cf. Rautman 2006, 170–71; *ODB* 1:40, 3:2168. Perhaps the interpretation is based on the many military disasters that resulted from ambushes in forests; a particularly notorious example was the defeat suffered by Varus and his three legions in 9 CE in the Saltus Teutoburgiensis.

[160] Another lacuna in the text.

[161] In this context, we may adduce the story of Job, a man who was "the greatest of all the people of the east."

438.   To dream of a bird's nest signifies profit.

439.   A light is a good sign.

440.   Eating with a friend or the emperor signifies something good.[162]

---

[162]   Drexl (1925b, 375 ad loc.), bracketing these last two dreams and interpretations, comments: "439 und 440 sind hinter dem Schlusskreuz von erster Hand in Klammern angefügt."

Dreams beginning with the letters χ, ψ, and ω are missing in the manuscript.

Chapter 9

The *Oneirocriticon* of Manuel II Palaeologus

A Dreambook by Manuel Palaeologus[1]

1. Fish

Fish are interpreted as fear and a lack of resolve,[2] since they tremble and are easily frightened [περιφόβους].[3] [This applies] only to live fish, for fish that have been prepared for eating signify profit.[4]

2. Hard-Shelled Fish

Lobsters, crabs, crawfish, and other hard-shelled fish point to injurious loss that will come at the hands of enemies who are immoderate in their actions.[5] [This is the type of dream] that Phakrases had.[6]

---

[1]   The title can also be translated as "A Dreambook for Manuel Palaeologus." That is, Manuel is not the author, but the recipient. My thanks to Prof. Mavroudi for this astute observation.

[2]   I take ἀβουλία in its modern Greek sense.

[3]   See Artemidorus 2.14.

[4]   See ibid., 1.70 and 2.18. The area around the Golden Horn in Constantinople was the scene of tremendous catches of tuna; the Black Sea offered fish such as tuna and mackerel, as well as caviar. See Dalby 2003, 15, 35–7, 65–8.

[5]   See Artemidorus 2.14; but cf. Achmet 300. On fasting days, hard-shelled fish were popular for religious reasons (they lacked blood): Dalby 2003, 93–4. See also Dalby 1996, 73–4 for further discussion of hard-shelled fishes eaten by the Greeks; also Koukoules 1948–57, 5:87–8.

[6]   The Phakrases family had many members serving in secular and religious positions during the Palaeologan period (*ODB* 3:1645–6). A likely candidate for the person above is Manuel Phakrases, who served as a dignitary of Manuel II and is attested to in 1409, when he participated in a synod in the capital.

Some of the names in this treatise cannot be located in standard reference texts such as *Prosopographisches Lexicon der Palaiologenzeit*; but they would have been known to the original readers.

3. Finger rings

The finger ring [δακτυλίδιον] is to be interpreted as an advance deposit of money [ἀρραβῶνας][7] over an unimportant matter. And if it breaks, then this foretells the undermining of the agreement that had been contracted [ὑπισχνουμένου].[8]

4. Mice

If mice appear in someone's house roaming up and down, all the secrets [μυστήρια] of the homeowner will be revealed. For the mouse [μῦς] derives its name from the [verb] μύω—that is, to shut one's eyes [καμμύω].[9]

5. Blind People

Likewise, if someone dreams that a blind man was walking in his [*sc.* the dreamer's] house, let him know that a hidden secret is being wrought in [that house]. And if [he dreams that] this man recovered the sight in one of his eyes, the concealed secret will be half revealed; but if the man regained his full sight, the secret will be brought completely to light.[10]

6. Dogs and Asses[11]

Dogs and evil animals point to enemies. And if someone dreams that while riding he was bitten by one of these animals and that he then dismounted and was left alone far from the rest of the army, he will suffer harm at the hands of his enemies and he will lose his rank of authority.[12]

7. Wells, Water Tanks, and Drinking Vessels

Wells, water tanks, and any vessel capable of holding liquids are interpreted as women.[13] If someone dreams that he drank water from any of these items, he will

---

[7] The *arrabōn* was a payment of money that functioned as the guarantee or advance deposit in anticipation of a fuller (and more legally binding) transaction. See *ODB* 1:185–6.

[8] Along the same lines, *Somniale Danielis* ("Beiträge, IV") CXXI: *gemmam de anulo perdidisse, aliquid admittit*; cf. Achmet 257.

[9] The same etymology appears in Stephanus 1954, s.v. "μῦς." But see Chantraine 1968–80, 3:725. For Manuel's method of etymology, see the discussion above in Chapter 2.

[10] Cf. Artemidorus 1.26. In Manuel's own life, an event analogous to the dream above occurred after he replaced Andronicus IV Palaeologus as heir to the throne; Andronicus was subsequently blinded, but ended up losing sight in only one eye.

[11] Μοχθήριον = the Latin *asinus*. See Stephanus 1954, s.v. "μοχθηρός."

[12] So too Achmet 277.

[13] Ibid., 47: "If someone dreams that he urinated into some vessel that he owned, he will have sex with his wife; but if the vessel belonged to someone else, he will have sex with another

satisfy his pleasure with a woman. But if he merely washed himself with the water and did not taste it, he will only exchange words and pleasantries [χαριεντισμόν] [with her].

If [someone] dreams that from far away or by going near a well or cistern[14] or fountain[15] or pool of water (which is to be interpreted as a wealthy and reputable woman),[16] he did not drink from the water at all, nor did he wash himself [in that water], he will fall into great anxiety[17] and dangerous concern and worry generated by a woman for a reason other than erotic passion, as was mentioned. If [he dreams that] he fell into such a well or cistern or pool, he will be in danger because of a woman.

8. Hats[18]

If someone dreams of wearing a broad-brimmed conical hat—especially if he normally does not wear one in everyday life—and that he was also holding a staff and merrily walking up and down in the royal palace [παλάτιον], you should know that he will succumb to a harsh and terrible illness and be at the point of death.[19] However, he will return to health because of the staff's appearance [in the dream].[20]

---

man's wife." 181: "If someone dreams that he was drawing water from a well he built, if the water was clear, he will by analogy get wealth from a virgin girl; if foul, illness and sorrow from her. If he dreams that he gave others some of this water to drink, through this girl he will enrich or oppress these same people in accordance with the water's clarity or murkiness." 186: "The drinking cup signifies a woman. If someone dreams that he received a glass drinking cup with water inside it, he will get a woman who will bear a child: for glass symbolises a midwife. If he dreams that although the cup was cracked the water stayed inside, the woman will die but the child will live; but if he dreams that the water flowed out but the cup was preserved, the opposite."

[14] Constantinople had numerous cisterns, both open and covered, with many located in the hills. The water supplied by these cisterns was critical, since the city had no river and few natural springs. See the discussion in *ODB* 1:518–19, on which my comments are based.

[15] So βρῦσις, as in modern Greek. The fountain symbolised salvation in Christianity, due to its association with the fountain of life in Genesis 2:10; see *ODB* 2:801.

[16] But cf. Artemidorus 2.27: "Streams, springs, and fountains overflowing with pure water mean good luck for all men, but especially for the sick and needy. For, to the sick, they are a sign of recovery; to the poor, they are a sign of wealth. For there is nothing so nourishing as water. But if they are dried up and without water, they signify the exact opposite for everybody."

[17] I take ἔννοια in its modern Greek sense.

[18] So I take σκιάδιον (cf. LSJ, s.h.v., and also in modern Greek). The word in classical antiquity meant "parasol." During the Palaeologan period, it was a type of hat worn by the emperor and his courtiers; it appears to have been a conical hat with a broad brim, with its design and fabric (embroidery, ornaments, etc.) denoting the rank of the wearer. See *ODB* 2:904. The *skiadion* could also be an ecclesiastical headdress worn by priests and deacons: *ODB* 3:1910.

[19] Cf. *Somniale Danielis* ("Beiträge, IV") CXXXIII: *in platea vel palatio deambulare, anxietatem significat*. For the palaces in Constantinople, see McCormick 1997, 233–6; Rautman 2006, 86–8. There were five imperial palaces by the year 425, with more to follow: *LAnt* 630.

[20] As we have seen, the staff is a symbol in Byzantine dreambooks of strength, honor, and power; thus, the staff in the dream above signifies that the dreamer will regain his strength.

9. Hot and Cold Pita Bread,²¹ White²² Bread, and Coarse Bread²³

If someone dreams of eating hot pita bread, he will be afflicted with consumption.²⁴ But if he dreams of eating one cold, he will get the profit that he had lost but that no one else had wanted. If someone dreams of eating white [καθαρός] bread, he will get profit sufficient for his life's sustenance;²⁵ but if the bread was hot, he will fall ill. If someone dreams that he was eating pieces of coarse bread [κυβαρούς] or that someone gave him some pieces that he then shared with others, he will experience danger, inaction, humiliation, abuse from his enemies, and capture in battle. This is precisely how we can interpret events related in the war story concerning Sountzērakis, the son of Mesōthaniatē, and Leontopardos, the *protospatharios*:²⁶ Tzērakis was taken prisoner and put into chains by the enemy for a rather long period of time, while Leontopardos died after being struck in the mouth with a spear.

---

²¹ Πῆτα probably equals the Byzantine πίττα (= πίτυρος [ἄρτος] = πιτυρίας), which was a bread made of bran. The Roman term was *panis sordidus* or *panis plebeius*. Bread made from bran was considered worthy only of peasants: *ODB* 1:321, cf. 2:865. The word also described a flat pie prepared with dough and filled with cheese or vegetables, for example.

²² For this meaning of καθαρός—that is, bread made from fine flour—, see the many references in Sophocles 1975, s.h.v., and Koukoules 1948–57, 5:12–15. The Roman equivalent was *panis candidus*, which contained top-quality flour.

²³ Κιβαρός (here written κυβαρός) = the Latin *cibarius*. As Rautman (2006, 95) comments, dark bread was eaten only in times of duress. Discussion in Koukoules 1948–57, 5:12, 20, 21; cf. Nicephorus 10 with comment ad loc.

²⁴ For this meaning of πύκνωσις, see Stephanus 1954, s.h.v. For the dream, cf. Achmet 241, where it is interpreted as a sign of wealth, although the wealth will come with pain and chastisement because of the fire used to heat the bread.

²⁵ The dream is so interpreted because bread was the basic staple in the Byzantine diet.

²⁶ The *spatharioi* (sword-bearers) at first formed part of the Byzantine emperor's bodyguard and were eunuchs (Ostrogorsky 1969, 249). By the eighth century, the title was honorific and was ultimately discarded by the eleventh century; cf. Rautman 2006, 204. The Leontopardos cited here is called the πρωτοσπαθάριος, which was a title given to civil officials who exercised duties at court (e.g., overseeing judicial proceedings); the term also denoted the commander of the military forces in the various themes comprising the Byzantine Empire. See Guilland 1967, 2:99–131; *ODB* 3:1935–6; Oikonomides 2002, 1009–10; Ostrogorsky 1969, 249, 367; Rosser 2001, s.v. "Protospatharios." For the themes of the provincial system, see, among others, Gregory 2005, 178–81, 203–4; *ODB* 3:2034–5; Treadgold 1997, 314–22, 373–5, 381–3, 442–3, 540–49, 595–606.

10. Eagles, Partridges, Doves, Swallows, Nightingales, and Sparrows[27]

Eagles signify tumults and disturbances involving the emperor,[28] while the other birds [mentioned above] signify struggles involving his magistrates [ἄρχοντες].

Partridges indicate much talked-about and tumultuous affairs of noble women, because these birds sing excessively.[29]

Doves denote straightforward and honest situations that are not characterised by deceit.[30]

Crows signify the words and disturbing actions of evil women who gossip.[31]

The swallow reveals news and messages regarding loved ones who are living far away.[32]

The nightingale signifies the announcement of a very desirable and happy affair,[33] for when spring comes it immediately goes around the groves and settles down there; it then composes intricate and wonderful [songs], clearly proclaiming and announcing the common rebirth [of nature], and continuously charms passers-by with a multitude of songs filled with grace and sweetness.[34]

---

[27]   For the interpretations of the various kinds of birds in this section, see the Index of Dream Symbols for comments in previous dreambooks. I shall adduce only a few examples in the subsequent notes, mostly to demonstrate Manuel's limited acquaintance with Artemidorus and Achmet.

[28]   The double-headed eagle was a symbol of the Palaeologan dynasty. The idea of the two heads was that the emperor looked simultaneously to the West and to the East: *ODB* 1:669.

[29]   Cf. the comment to Nicephorus, Appendix I, 58. Artemidorus (4.56) interprets the partridge as a man who loves honors.

[30]   But the dove signifies a woman in both Achmet 291 and Artemidorus 2.20 Also at variance with Manuel's interpretation is *Somniale Danielis* ("Beiträge, IV") XLV: *columbas viderit, aliquam tristitiam significat.*

[31]   But Achmet (290) considers the crow as symbolic of a liar and extorter; Artemidorus (2.20) interprets it as time-delays, an old woman, and a storm.

[32]   But Achmet (286) comments: "[S]wallows ... signify a land army. If someone dreams that flocks of these birds came to a region, if locusts were there, a king will dispatch a land army in proportion to the number of birds in order to avenge and succor that place; but if the birds did not come to eat the locusts but instead damaged the trees there, an enemy will come and maltreat the inhabitants in proportion to the birds' damage in the dream: but if the birds did no harm and it was not the time for crops, a number of soldiers will come but inflict no harm. On the whole, these birds signify for any dreamer a land army." See also Artemidorus 2.66.

[33]   In this instance, there is agreement with Achmet 286 ("The nightingale is judged as news which will be sweet by analogy to the sweetness of the bird's voice") and Artemidorus 2.66.

[34]   For this image, cf. ibid., 2.66 on the swallow: "[The swallow's] chirping is not a threnody, but a song that serves as a prelude and exhortation to work. That this is so can be seen from the fact that a swallow in winter does not fly or utter a sound. ... But when the spring arrives, the swallow is the first to come out in order to point out, so to speak, the work that each must do. And when she appears, she never sings in the evening but at dawn, when the sun is rising. And she reminds every man that she encounters of the work that lies ahead." The paragraph above has a very close parallel, in imagery and description, to a passage in one of Manuel's letters, 45.191–208 (Dennis's 1977 edition).

Sparrows signify confusion and distress regarding a vulgar and uncouth[35] crowd—that is to say, the peasantry.[36] If someone dreams that he was impeded[37] by sparrows, he should know that he is about to experience a very great attack and a [potentially] fatal demise at the hands of commoners. And if in this dream he escaped from the birds, he will be delivered from these dangers; but if the birds overpowered him, he will be overpowered by commoners and have a full measure of evil. Such [is the dream that] the great interpreter[38] of the Syrians had: he barely escaped the grave danger hanging over him, for about 12,000 people had surrounded him when it was rumored that the hill next to Galata[39] was being sold to the Franks[40]

---

[35]   According to Stephanus 1954, s.v. "συμφερτώδης," this word is equivalent to ἀγύρτης.

[36]   Χωριάτης, which is modern Greek for "peasant," can also denote a crude and boorish person. For the disdain of the Byzantine intellectual toward peasants, see Kazhdan 1997, 70.

[37]   Instead of ἐκυκλώθη, perhaps we can read ἐκωλύθη (was surrounded) as we read below: "12,000 people had surrounded him ...."

[38]   The word διερμηνευτής, when modified by μέγας as here, described the chief interpreter who participated in embassies, served as translator for other officials, and attended to documents written in other languages. See *ODB* 2:1004; Oikonomides 1985, 172–3.

[39]   Galata was a suburb of Constantinople where the Genoese had quarters (thanks to a treaty with the Byzantine emperor in 1267) and enjoyed huge customs revenues. The Venetians had been given warehouses and quays in the area directly across from Galata in return for helping Byzantium in the eleventh century in repelling the Normans. War later occurred between the Genoese and the Venetians in 1294, with the Genoese being attacked in Galata. The Byzantines sided with the Genoese, but were forced to come to terms with the Venetians due to a lack of ships. See Matschke 2002b, 476–7; also Treadgold 1997, 748, 773–5, 780–82. The *Annales Ianuenses* (the official record of the commune of Genoa) is a primary source for relations with Byzantium between 1099 and 1294: see *ODB* 1:104.

Galata had strategic importance because its fortress protected the great harbor chain that was raised to keep ships from entering the harbor of Constantinople. During the Fourth Crusade, Galata was captured and the chain broken, thereby allowing the Crusaders' fleet to storm into the harbor and take the city.

The particular episode referred to above is not known; however, mob violence was not uncommon in Constantinople. For example, the family and friends of the fourteenth-century *megas doux* Alexius Apocaucus were frequently singled out for mob attacks because of Alexius's reign of terror (*ODB* 1:134–5), while Andronicus I was dismembered by a mob in the Hippodrome in 1185, after he had been tortured and mutilated by Isaac Comnenus (Treadgold 1997, 654–6). Prof. Mavroudi adduces Nicephorus Gregoras, the historian and scholar, who after his death was dragged through the streets of Constantinople; see also *ODB* 2:874–5.

[40]   For the relations between the Franks and Byzantium, see Ostrogorsky 1969, passim. Manuel spent time in France (in 1400 and 1401–1402: see Barker 1969, 171–8, 202–3, 219–20, 536–9; Ostrogorsky 1969, 440; Treadgold 1997, 787–9), to solicit aid in turning back the Turkish army under the command of Bayazid. An expedition from Charles, King of France, had come earlier in 1399 to Manuel's aid to relieve Constantinople; despite some preliminary success in removing the Turks from areas around the city, more help was needed and so Manuel left to secure it: Treadgold 1997, 787.

by the empress[41] through his agency.

11. Horses, Donkeys, and Mules

If someone dreams of seeing a person riding a beautiful and healthy horse of short stature [σύντομον], he is about to hear a good but concise [σύντομον] report about his public standing, influence, and powerful actions.[42] But if the horse was sluggish and maimed and therefore had difficulty moving, he will hear words that are odious and fraught with great danger—words that he will definitely accept.[43] And if the dreamer is enjoying good fortune [εὐτυχής] and is held in high esteem [ἔνδοξος], he will soon become unfortunate [δυστυχήσει] and lose his honor [δόξαν].[44] This was the dream that the Grand Duke[45] had after his brother-in-law the Palaeologan was drowned: he had acquired such a horse[46] even though he had saturated it with blows and lashes.[47]

If someone dreams that he was riding a donkey, he is about to be promoted, resulting in his own gain [ὠφέλειαν] and success [προκοπήν].[48] For the word "donkey" [ὄνος] is derived from the [verb] ὀνεῖν, which means "to derive advantage" [ὠφελεῖν] and

---

The word Φράγκοι acquired a variety of meanings over the centuries. At first, the word described the Frankish tribe, then in the tenth century to the Germans, then in the eleventh to the Normans and to the French, and ultimately to Roman Catholics living anywhere in Europe.

[41]   The word δεσποίνη had a variety of meanings: the empress, one of her daughters, or even the queen mother. Given the unknown nature of the episode referred to, I am uncertain how the word should be translated here.

[42]   Cf. Artemidorus 1.56; Achmet 152. Mavroudi (2002, 205), in discussing the Achmet passage, quotes from the dreambook of Ibn Qutayba: "The dream interpreters said: The horse is might and power. Whoever dreams that he was on a tractable horse that was gently behaving according to his wishes and the implements of the horse were perfect for him, he will obtain might, power, honor and valor among the people commensurate with the obedience of the horse to him."

[43]   But cf. Achmet 152: "If someone dreams that he was riding a well-bred but lame horse, he will experience sorrow and hindrance in whatever he is working to achieve."

[44]   A beautifully written sentence, with the puns occurring in a sequence of a–b–a–b.

[45]   The *megas doux* was the admiral of the Byzantine fleet (a title first used in 1092); see Gregory 2005, 266; Guilland 1967, 1:542–51; Ostrogorsky 1969, 368, with discussions of people who held this post on 395, 447, 461, 493, 501; Rosser 2001, s.v. "doux." The family of the Konstostephanoi virtually controlled this position: *ODB* 2:1330. By the thirteenth century, the *megas doux* commanded land armies too. It was also a title conferred on foreigners: *ODB* 2:1330.

The simple title of *doux*, without the modifier *megas*, was applied either to a subordinate to the governor (*stratēgos*) of a theme or, after the late eleventh century, to the governor of a theme. See also *ODB* 1:659.

[46]   Here, ἄλογος means "horse"; see Sophocles 1975, s.h.v. (cf. modern Greek ἄλογο).

[47]   Mavroudi (2007, 53 n. 17) relates this dream directly to the life of Alexius Apocaucus, who was Grand Duke and died in 1345 (see *ODB* 1:134–5). She notes that the circumstances of his brother-in-law's death (without mention of the dream, of course) are given by the contemporary historian Kantakouzenus (*Histories* 3.71).

[48]   Cf. Achmet 233.

"to succeed" [προκόπτειν].[49] Besides, [a donkey is also called] ἀείδαρος[50] because it is always beaten by the one who drives him with a stick.[51] And if he dreams that he was thrown headlong off the donkey, he will die or fall into misfortune.[52]

The camel signifies difficulties and a situation that is hard to manage[53] because of its hump and curved shape.[54]

The mule likewise is a very evil dream symbol, since its breed is a mixture of the horse and donkey and it is willfully mischievous and mean.[55]

12. [Apples,] Peaches,[56] and Plums

Apples and peaches are interpreted as a love affair.[57] But for prudent [σώφρονας] people, these fruits refer to exultation and movement to words over something else that they desire; but even in the case of chaste people, they might signify a chance discussion of a love affair.

Plums indicate the evil words of a most evil and troublesome woman. They also signify illness, since they overpower a person's tent—that is to say, his body.[58]

---

[49]   Artemidorus (2.12) adduces the same derivation: "[Donkeys] also indicate good luck in other undertakings because of their name [ὄνοι]. For they signify that one will derive profit [ὄνασθαι] and pleasure from the business at hand."

[50]   That is, "continually struck"; see Stephanus 1954, s.h.v. Cf. modern Greek γάϊδαρος.

[51]   The donkey's beatings are interpreted as profit, since Byzantine oneirocritics associate beatings with benefits and goodness for the dreamer.

[52]   Cf. Achmet 233: "If someone dreams that he fell off a donkey, he will become exceedingly poor."

[53]   I can find no other occurrence of the word δυσκαταχέριστος.

[54]   See the discussions, though, in Achmet 234 and 235.

[55]   Cf. ibid., 232, where there is a pun on δύστοκος. Achmet first interprets the mule as a horrible symbol on the fact that it cannot have offspring (*dustokos*). He further deems it as loss of money and property since *tokos* also means "money interest" (for interest rates in Byzantium, see *ODB* 2:1001–3), and so a mule, which is *dustokos*, foretells difficulty (*dus-*) in gaining profit (*tokos*).

[56]   I take ῥοδάκινα as peaches, as in modern Greek; see also Sophocles 1975, s.h.v. LSJ translates as "nectarines."

[57]   For apples in this traditional sense, see Artemidorus 1.73, 2.25; Achmet 151; full discussion in Littlewood 1993 (with earlier bibliography).

[58]   So too Achmet 141. There is a wordplay here, as Manuel takes δαμάσκηνον (plum) as a combination of δαμάζω (overpower) and σκῆνος (tent/body). The interpretation may also be based on the analogy of dried plums (prunes) "overpowering" a body when eaten in quantity. See Dalby 2003, 194 for the popular derivation of the Greek word for plum from the Syrian city of Damascus. "Tent" as a term for the human body is biblical: see 2 Peter 1:14 and 2 Corinthians 5:1–10.

13. Pomegranates and Figs

Pomegranates that are eaten in a dream signify illness.[59] Figs, on the other hand, denote slander,[60] accusations, and words that will bring the dreamer dishonor, although these words will not be true, but false.[61]

14. Very Large and Small Trees[, Roses, and Pears]

Very large trees are interpreted as noble and well-born men,[62] and their falling-down signifies death [for such a man]. Likewise, concerning small [μικρά] trees: these refer to insignificant [μικρούς] people and a lesser fortune and fate.

Roses[63] denote erotic women who generate desire, but only through their words, not through their deeds.

Pears denote failure in whatever [the dreamer] hopes for.[64]

The walnut tree is interpreted as important but troublesome women.[65]

15. Grapevines

The grapevine signifies family.[66] If [someone dreams that] a vine had white grapes that some people then picked, this means grief caused by the death of a layperson; but if the grapes were black, a monk or a nun[67] will die.[68] The physician Synesius

---

59   Cf. Artemidorus 1.73.

60   Perhaps a wordplay between σῦκον (fig) and συκοφαντία (slander or defamation).

61   Artemidorus (1.73) and Achmet (241) agree, but only if the figs are not ripe.

62   As we have seen, trees are judged as men in the Byzantine dreambooks and in Artemidorus 2.19, although individual trees like the cypress and palm may refer to women.

63   I take τριακονταφυλλέαις as equivalent to the modern Greek τριαντάφυλλα.

64   But Artemidorus (1.73) and Achmet (241) interpret the pear in a positive manner.

65   But Achmet (198) interprets the walnut tree as a man, not as a woman. It seems that in many cases where Achmet interprets a symbol as referring to a man, Manuel interprets it as referring to a woman.

66   The interpretation derives from the vine stem being analogous to the central family unit, and the clusters of grapes being analogous to children with their own families.

67   So I translate [μιὰ] ἀπὸ τῶν μοναζουσῶν on the basis of Sophocles (1975), who says (s.v. "μονάζω"): "ἡ μονάζουσα = μοναχή." For monks, monastic life, and monasteries in Byzantium, see Kazhdan and Epstein 1985, 86–95; Rautman 2006, 233–55 (with notes and bibliography on 255–6). For nuns and nunneries, see *ODB* 3:1504–5; nunneries comprised 15 per cent of all monasteries in Byzantium.

68   According to Achmet 200, white grapes are a more favorable dream symbol than black grapes (black is always a bad omen). Manuel's interpretation here may be based on an association of the grapes' black color with the black robes of the monastic orders.

had this dream right before his father-in-law the *actuarius*[69] died; he himself later died.[70]

16. [Wine,] Onions, Garlic, Leeks, and Similar Vegetables

Wine is interpreted as bitter anger and wrath,[71] just as onions, garlic, leeks, and cardamom are so interpreted, for their pungency moves a person to passionate wrath.[72]

Legumes[73] that are eaten [in a dream] point to profit by chance.[74]

17. Frankish Clothes and Colors

Frankish clothes signify the greatest freedom and [indeed] reveal freedom,[75] just as the Franks, Tartars, Turks, Indians, Scythians, and every race of people indicate freedom.[76]

Clothes that are white in color are good to dream of; those that are red and blue signify honor and esteem; those that are yellow, green, or black point to bitterness and wrath;[77] those that are purple denote honor.[78]

---

[69]   In imperial Rome, *actuarius* denoted a writer who used shorthand. In early Byzantium, the person was a record-keeper and distributed military pay and provisions. By the twelfth century, the word also described a court physician, a meaning doubtlessly intended here. See *ODB* 1:50 (cf. 3:1673) for a history of this term.

[70]   Achmet (36) interprets a dream of black grapes as follows: "A certain noble of the caliph Mamun came and consulted Sereim the dream interpreter. He said: 'I have a vine at home that produces white grapes, but in one of my dreams this same vine grew black grapes.' Sereim replied: 'One of your wives is pregnant through your Ethiopian slave.' And so the dream turned out, for the woman bore a black child from the Ethiopian."

[71]   Byzantine oneirocritics typically associate wine with anger and quarrels; Achmet, however, interprets it as money and gain.

[72]   So too Artemidorus 1.67 and Achmet 204.

[73]   Or cabbage (so modern Greek). For the growing of legumes in Byzantium, see Lefort 2002, 251–2; Lefort points out that over 100 kinds of vegetables were grown in the Empire.

[74]   There is a wordplay here between λάχανον (legumes) and λάχος (chance). The latter may also be translated as "inheritance"; thus, "Legumes that are eaten [in a dream] point to profit gained from an inheritance." For inheritance in Byzantium, see Laiou 1977, 104–5, 157–8, 188–202.

[75]   At first sight, a surprising interpretation coming from a Byzantine emperor and given the usual pejorative meaning of the word (*ODB* 2:803); but see note 40 above.

[76]   As stated above, Manuel sought help from many quarters in his quest for help against the Turks, and so visited Russia, the Pope, the Doge of Venice, and the kings of France, England, and Aragon. This may explain the reason for the interpretation here.

[77]   Perhaps the black color is associated with black bile. (In ancient—and modern—Greek, χολή means both "bile" and "wrath.")

[78]   Achmet and Manuel do not agree on how to interpret colors. For example, Achmet interprets green as faith, and purple as royalty.

18. Belts and Shoes

The belt is interpreted as power and strength. Thus, its removal [παρασάλευσις] is to be compared to weakness and loss of power.[79]

Shoes [represent] bonds,[80] and so losing them [or] throwing them away [denotes] freedom from evils.

19. The Penis

If someone dreams that his penis was erect and strong,[81] he will see himself in control over all his activities.[82] But if he dreams that his penis was flaccid and in a contracted position, he will be weak, prove unsuccessful,[83] and be defeated by his enemies.[84]

20. Head Hair and Beards

The hairs of the head, if they are long and plentiful, [symbolise] many worries and anxieties.[85] Their falling-out indicates very great freedom.[86]

---

[79]   There is a pun on χαυνότης, which means "weakness" as well as "loosening [a belt]." The interpretation is based on the belt being a Byzantine mark of power; see Daniel 199 and comment ad loc.

[80]   Perhaps the interpretation is based on an analogy between tying the laces of shoes (or the straps of sandals) and binding feet with bonds.

[81]   I take ἔντονος as "erect" and in opposition to χαῦνος (flaccid) in the next line.

[82]   So Artemidorus 1.45; Achmet 95 and 97.

[83]   The word ἄπρακτος can also mean "impotent"; see LSJ, s.h.v.

[84]   Cf. Achmet 95: "The penis is judged as a man's reputation, power, and children. If someone dreams that his penis was large and erect, his reputation will be widespread and he will beget sons; and if the dreamer is a king, he will be long-lived and his son will succeed him. If a king dreams that his penis was sticking way out and that someone came along and grabbed hold of it, his dominion will increase and the person in the dream, having come to know his secrets, will become his coregent; if the dreamer is a commoner, he will have an increased livelihood. If a woman dreams that she had a penis, she will bear a son who will honor her family. If someone dreams that he had two penises, if he already has a son, he will have a second son; if he has no son, twin boys. If someone dreams that his penis was cut off, his son will die and he will die soon after him; but if he dreams that the penis was not completely cut off, his wife will bear a son who will die, and he will grieve, although his sorrow will turn [into happiness]. If someone dreams that his penis reached a fantastic length, he will be great and famous and see happiness in his son. But if he dreams that his penis was small and flaccid, he will fall from honor and be poor, while his children will experience disease and helplessness."

[85]   The opposite interpretation is given in *Somniale Danielis* ("Beiträge, V") 41: *kaput cum longis crinibus <habere>, fortitudinem significat.*

[86]   The exact opposite meaning appears in Achmet, passim (e.g., 18, 21, 22, 30, 31); cf. also Artemidorus 1.18–22 and Nicephorus 117.

The beard is interpreted as family and an assembly of friends,[87] and so beardlessness signifies the loss of both family and friends.

21. The Nose

The nose is interpreted as honor.[88] If someone dreams that blood was flowing from his nose, his plans will suffer harm.[89] And if the blood flowed from both nostrils, the harm will be total; but if from one nostril only, the harm will likewise be half.

22. The Eyes

The eyes are judged as friends and beloved relatives.[90] If someone dreams that he lost one of his eyes or even both of them, he will be deprived of much loved friends and blood relatives.[91]

23. Phlebotomies

If someone dreams of undergoing a phlebotomy, he will suffer the loss of both his family and a substantial amount of property.[92]

24. Sailing and Capsising

If someone dreams that he was sailing on a small boat or skiff on the sea and that he either was sailing alone or had rowers with him, sooner or later he will see a corpse carried out for burial or will hear news that someone has died. If he dreams that he

---

[87] But cf. *Somniale Danielis* ("Beiträge, IV") XXXI: *barbatum se viderit, ornamentum significat.* Cf. Achmet 34 and 35, where the beard is interpreted as grandeur and wealth.

[88] So Achmet 56 and 57; cf. Artemidorus 1.27.

[89] Cf. Achmet 57: "If the king dreams that his nostrils were so stuffed up that he could not smell, let him know that the man who is the first to report to him on secular administrative matters will fall in danger along with himself; for the intellect judges good and bad smells through the nose."

[90] But for Achmet the eyes represent faith, reputation, and spiritual illumination; see the many dreams in his Chaps 52–6.

[91] Artemidorus 1.26: "To dream that one is blind in both eyes signifies the death of the children, brothers, or parents of the dreamer: of his children, for the reason [that children are missed when absent and they guide and lead their parents when they grow old], of his parents, because a man's eyes, like his parents, are the causes of his seeing the light of day."

[92] So Achmet 32; cf. 33: "One must know that blood, like hairs, signifies a person's wealth and power, although more often than not the interpretation is wealth. And so however much blood someone dreams is taken from him, whether through cupping or phlebotomy, will be the amount of property he will lose."

boarded a large ship,[93] he will enter the presence of the emperor or a great magistrate who in power is second only to the emperor himself.[94] If he dreams that one of these vessels sunk because of a tempest, let him know that a person of great authority[95] will be sentenced to death or lose his rule.[96] If he dreams that the vessel was running swiftly thanks to a fair wind and was cutting across the sea in a straight direction [δι' εὐθύτητος], he will see the magistrate of his land and district—or even the prince himself—prosperous and blessed, keeping very straight [εὖ μάλα διευθύνοντα] the helms of his glory and dealing with matters of state.[97]

25. Swords and Daggers

The sword is judged as power, manliness, strength, and grandeur,[98] bestowed either by the emperor or a magistrate or by virtue of one's own innate ability. And if someone dreams that his sword was lost or was broken in pieces, he will see his power and glory undermined and his fate will be misfortune and disaster.[99]

The dagger is interpreted as war and the ability to fight one's enemies.[100] And if someone dreams that he was wearing a sharpened dagger, he will be manly and, with strength and alacrity, rout his enemies. But if he lost this dagger, he should know that he will be reconciled with his enemies and live peacefully with them. And if he dreams that this dagger was broken in two [ἐτήθη], he will be beaten [ἡττηθῆναι] by his enemies.[101]

---

[93]   The καράβις was a warship; this, then, would explain the interpretation above of coming before someone in very high authority. The Καραβισιάνοι were the sailors of the first fleet of Byzantium, but were replaced in the eighth century by the Κιβυρραιῶται. See *ODB* 2:1105–6. Makris (2002, 92–3) describes how the Byzantine long warships, which had 230 rowers and Greek fire, had a cruising speed of five knots and a battle speed of seven knots; by the twelfth century, however, the dromons and Greek fire had both been discontinued, due to the Byzantines' adoption of Western technology. See also Rautman 2006, 150–53 (with nn. 17–21 on 155), 201–12 (with nn. 14–16 on 230).

[94]   So Achmet 180.

[95]   The word αὐθέντης originally denoted a murderer; but in late Byzantine Greek (as in modern Greek), it meant a master or someone who wielded power; the word also appears in Section 35 below, where it definitely refers to a master.

[96]   Cf. Artemidorus 2.23; Achmet 179.

[97]   This is the well-known ship of state analogy in Greek literature; see, e.g., Page 1955, 179–96 for Alcaeus's political poems; cf. Plato, *Laws* 758A and Book 6 of his *Republic*; Horace, *Odes* 1.14. For the dream, cf. Achmet 178: "If someone dreams that after he embarked he was sailing under a fair wind, he will be prosperous and find analogous favor from a magistrate"; cf. Artemidorus 2.23.

[98]   Ibid., 2.31: "A dagger and a straight sword signify the courage of the dreamer, the strength of his hands, and the boldness of his spirit." So also Achmet 247.

[99]   Cf. *Somniale Danielis* ("Beiträge, V") 5: *arma in somnis perdere aut frangere, dampnum significat*. There may also be a wordplay here, since καταφορά denoted a sword blow as well as a calamity; see LSJ, s.h.v.

[100]   So too Achmet 247.

[101]   Perhaps a wordplay here.

26. Bread Rolls[102]

Large bread rolls are judged as a trek that will last one year and turn out to be profitable because of the fineness [of the flour]; coarse bread, as distress and a trip that will last one year; small bread rolls, as a journey lasting one month—that is to say, [...];[103] the small καλήτζα roll,[104] as a trip lasting seven days, [that is to say,] for a week. Likewise, sesame bread points to a yearlong period of banishment[105] that will turn out to be profitable, pleasant, and altogether quite nice.[106]

27. Churches and Icons

If someone dreams that he entered Hagia Sophia for some reason,[107] he should know that this is to be interpreted as a universal [καθολικήν] upheaval of the cosmos [κόσμου] that will be shared by all,[108] for this is the universal [καθολικήν][109] church for Christians.[110] But if he entered some other church, the upheaval and tumult will be only slight.[111] And if he dreams that while he was walking around the church[112]

---

[102] The κουλλίκιον (= κολλύριον, so Sophocles 1975, s.h.v.) was a bread roll; cf. the modern Greek κουλ(λ)ούρα, for which see Koukoules 1948–57, 5:24–5, 30.

[103] A lacuna in the text, according to Delatte 1927–39 (comment ad loc.). The missing word, doubtlessly, would have meant either a short trip or a month's period of time.

[104] I cannot locate this word in any of the standard dictionaries.

[105] The word περιορισμός was equivalent to the Latin *deportatio*. The modern Greek meaning is "confinement." In Byzantium, *periorismos* described a person's legal punishment; besides confiscation of his property by the state, a person was confined within prescribed boundaries, such as a monastery, island, or a predefined area of the Empire. See the discussion in *ODB* 2:770.

[106] Sesame has a very positive interpretation in Achmet 204, since it produces a rich oil; but cf. Artemidorus 1.72. For sesame bread, see Koukoules 1948–57, 5:30.

[107] For this church, see Gregory 2005, 128–30; *ODB* 2:892–5; Rautman 2006, 82–5 (with bibliography in n. 14 on 117). Hagia Sophia was also known as the "Great Church" (Μεγάλη Ἐκκλησία). It was burned twice in riots and also hit by earthquakes; see *ODB* 2:892–5; Van Nice 1965–86. See Majeska 1997 for a discussion of the emperor's activities in Hagia Sophia in coronations, liturgies, and the once-annual censing of the church's sacred vessels. No dreambook writer, not even Manuel, refers to the magnificent and awe-inspiring imperial processions—in particular, the one entering Hagia Sophia—which were a hallmark of Byzantium. For an introduction to the processions, see Cavallo 1997a, 4–5; McCormick 1997, 248–52.

[108] The word κόσμος denoted the universe, while οἰκουμένη specified the earth (the "inhabited land"). Thus, Manuel implies that the tumult will affect all of creation.

[109] Of course, this is the word from which we get "Catholic." In modern Greek, the word denotes the Roman Catholic Church, while ὀρθόδοξος (correct thinking) describes the Greek Orthodox Church. Cf. Gregory 2005, 1.

[110] Manuel used relics for security in loans or to secure favor from leaders in the West; see Barker 1969, 131 with n. 15, 176–7, 183, 265, 511–12. For Manuel's faith (devout Orthodoxy), see Barker 1969, 408.

[111] Achmet (222) states that a church symbolises a child or the heir of one's property.

[112] Manuel uses *naos* in a general sense. Technically, the *naos* was the functional and symbolic center of the church where worshipers assembled for services. See *ODB* 2:1436 for

he was carrying a sword or other weapons or was wearing a crown or carrying a tree bough, he should know that during that storm and tumult the people will see him conquering, receiving military triumphs, and being superior to everyone else. And if he also saw the icons of the holy martyrs[113] and ascetics[114] or heard the voices of the *Theotokos*[115] and the angels, he will face an even greater upheaval and tumult but he will be proved righteous in battle.[116] The appearance of icons is interpreted through no method other than the fact that they and churches are further decorated with [the use of] tesserae [ψηφίδων], and a judgement is called ψῆφος.[117] If he dreams that he was chanting or singing[118] or was playing a cithara or musical harp, he will grieve greatly;[119] but if [someone else] was playing these instruments[120] in his presence, he himself will hear bitter and intolerable orders[121] or be told them by his close friends.

If someone dreams that he became a priest,[122] he will depart on a short trip and conduct some profitable business,[123] for the word "priest" [ἱερεύς] is derived from

---

a discussion of the *naos*'s religious symbolism.

[113]   A good introduction to the growth of the cult of martyrs in late antiquity may be found in *LAnt* 567–8.

[114]   For a discussion of the word ἀσκητής, see Sophocles 1975, s.h.v.; *LAnt* 317–18.

[115]   See the excellent monograph by O'Carroll (1982) on the Theotokos in both the Roman Catholic and the Greek Orthodox tradition; also Wallen 1960. Manuel wrote a liturgical poem to Theotokos; see Barker 1969, 432, 436, 438. In his letters, however, Manual does not use Θεοτόκος, but rather θεομήτηρ (e.g., 39.32, 57.16, 61.12 Dennis 1977).

Nestorius, the founder of the Nestorian heresy, insisted that since Mary was mortal she could not be the mother of God; thus, he rejected the word Theotokos and used *Christotokos*—that is, "bearer of the Christ": see Gregory 2005, 103–4. Nestorius, however, later grudgingly accepted the use of Theotokos (*LAnt* 604), and the term no longer was a matter of controversy.

[116]   For martyrs in dreams, see Achmet 11; for icons, ibid., 150.

[117]   A pun here, since ψῆφος meant not only a mosaic pebble, but also the stone used in casting votes (hence, "judgement"). For the mosaics in Hagia Sophia, see Whittemore 1933–52; cf. Cutler 2002, 557–61 and L'Orange and Nordhagen 1966.

[118]   The word τραγωδεῖν often meant in Byzantine Greek "to sing"; cf. modern Greek τραγουδῶ. For the choirs in Hagia Sophia, see *ODB* 3:1903–4; for chant in early Christian and Jewish religious practices in general, *LAnt* 370–71.

[119]   So too Achmet 252.

[120]   I take ὄργανα here as "instrument" and not as "organ," since the organ was used not in churches but in imperial ceremonies: *ODB* 3:1532. The emperor had a small band that played at formal functions and ceremonies. For musical instruments in Byzantium, see Koukoules 1948–57, 5:239–44; *ODB* 2:1426–7.

[121]   The word μανδᾶτον = the Latin *mandatum*; in Byzantine Greek, μανδᾶτον often denoted an imperial command or edict. For the word used to designate someone with legal representation, see ibid., 2:1281.

[122]   The bishop was the head of every church community; the priest acted more as his assistant and took care of individual parishes: ibid., 1:291–2. The Eastern priests did not need to be celibate, as in the West: ibid., 2:1169; Treadgold 1997, 260, 454.

[123]   Cf. Achmet 149: "If someone who is a layperson dreams that he was appointed priest, if he is a royal official, he will receive a very great and important rank from the king; if he is poor or a commoner, he will follow a very great man and receive honor and favor from him."

the [verb] ἵημι (to send)—that is, πέμπω (to send).¹²⁴ If he dreams that a priest came to him from far away, he will see a person who has been sent by someone from far distant lands.¹²⁵ If he dreams that a bishop was conversing with him, he will see an honored friend of his [returning] from a trip.¹²⁶ If he dreams that he became a bishop, he will receive an illustrious public office from the emperor¹²⁷ or despot¹²⁸ or autocrator¹²⁹ and Augustus¹³⁰ or Caesar,¹³¹ and he will go away on a trip.

If someone dreams that he was fumigating someone with incense, he will cause someone to become embittered through a death, or he himself will die and his close friend will be the cause of this misfortune or be partly responsible for his bitter death through evildoing or cowardice.¹³²

If someone dreams that he got a blessing from a bishop or received the Holy Gospel [εὐαγγέλιον] from him, he will hear good news [ἀγγελίαν] and useful¹³³ words from a magistrate who will come from far away.¹³⁴

---

¹²⁴ For a different etymology, see Chantraine 1968–80, 2:458–9.

¹²⁵ Cf. Achmet 149.

¹²⁶ I am not sure if ταξείδιον here means "military expedition" or simply "trip." For bishops and the role they played in Byzantium, see Holum 2005, 107–9; *LAnt* 341–3, which discusses the growth of their political, theological, and economic power; *ODB* 1:291–2; Van Falkenhausen 1997.

¹²⁷ Βασιλεύς was used to denote the Byzantine emperor from 629 until the end of the Empire; before 629, the Latin titles *imperator*, *Caesar*, and *Augustus* were used. See Ostrogorsky 1969, 106–7. The oft-used title *Basileus Rhōmaiōn* (King of the Romans) caused all sorts of problems with the West, where the Holy Roman Emperor ruled. *Rhōmaios* was what a Byzantine called himself: Gregory 2005, 1; Treadgold 1997, 804, 813.

¹²⁸ Δεσπότης was a term originally created in the twelfth century to denote the heir-apparent to the Byzantine throne (see Ostrogorsky 1969, 338, 530; Rosser 2001, s.v. "Despot"). The Palaeologan emperors granted the title to their sons and to those people who ruled over imperial tracts of lands or territories such as Epirus, the Morea, and Thessalonica. For Manuel applying the title to himself, see Barker 1969, 9–10 n. 23 (see 6 n. 12 for bibliography on the title). The word is given to many people in Manuel's letters. To cite just a few examples (using Dennis's 1977 edition): Christ (8.19), the king of Cyprus (32.20), Manuel himself (49.11), Theodore I Palaeologus, governor of Morea (13.1).

¹²⁹ Αὐτοκράτωρ usually denoted the senior emperor if there were two or more co-emperors (Ostrogorsky 1969, 113 n. 3, 129). According to Rosser 2001, s.v. "Autokrator," the Palaeologan emperors used the word to denote the reigning emperor and also the "heir-presumptive among the co-emperors"; see further Ostrogorsky 1969, 480. The emperor Heracleius first introduced the term in 629.

¹³⁰ Σεβαστοκράτωρ = the Latin *Augustus*.

¹³¹ Rosser (2001, s.v. "Caesar") comments that this word referred to the emperor's sons up until the eleventh century, at which time it became an honorific title, often bestowed on foreign rulers. See also Guilland 1967, 2:25–43.

¹³² Cf. Achmet 28 and 29. The interpretation derives from antinomy: the sweet smell of incense versus the bitterness of death.

¹³³ Perhaps a pun between χρηστός (useful) and Χριστός (Christ); the two words were pronounced the same at this time.

¹³⁴ Cf. Achmet 10 and 11.

28. Fire

A fierce flame with or without smoke carried into someone's house foretells a disaster or even bad luck; fire used for lighting, however, signifies wealth and glory.[135] And if [he dreams that] this flame was extinguished, it reveals lack of profit in the homeowner's activities, as well as significant poverty and melancholy brought on by various preoccupations.[136]

29. Oil Lamps

The oil lamp is judged as a woman.[137] If [someone dreams that] a lamp became extinguished, a woman is going to die or lose her sense of modesty. If there is a virgin girl living in his [*sc.* the dreamer's] house and [he dreams that] the lamp was extinguished by the flight of a bird, she will be corrupted by a stranger;[138] for the lamp's light represents the kindled torch of the girl's soul.[139]

Burning coals signify harm at the hands of enemies.[140]

30. Houses

Magnificent houses are judged as great happiness and life for their owners. If [such houses] are destroyed in a dream, they reveal fortunes brought low through death and misfortune.[141]

31. Getting a Wife

If someone dreams of getting a wife who was wonderful and graceful in beauty, he will experience a new way of life filled with honor. But if the woman was ugly, the opposite will happen—that is, he will have a vulgar and shabby existence. If he got either one of these women through illicit means, he will remain fixed [in the

---

[135]   Cf. ibid., 158 and 159.

[136]   But this dream symbolises death, according to ibid., 159.

[137]   A parallel is Artemidorus 1.74, where the lamp stand is interpreted as a woman.

[138]   The Byzantine penalty for deflowering a virgin involved marriage (if the girl was of sufficient age) or a monetary fine. The word Manuel uses here, φθορά, was the actual legal term to describe the deflowering of a virgin, an act that was distinguished from rape: *ODB* 3:1772; cf. Vinson 2002, 421. Freud considered dreams of flying as symbolic of sexual activities, specifically the sensation of having an erection; see Freud 1980, Chap. 6e.

[139]   Cf. the dream in *Somniale Danielis* ("Beiträge, IV") CCLXXXVII: *si videris aquilam volantem, uxorem tuam rapere mortem significat.* Achmet 159: "Whatever lights illuminate a house signify for any dreamer goodness, glory, and power; likewise, the extinguishing of these lights means the contrary." For the Byzantine analogy of the candle as an image of eternal light, see *ODB* 1:372.

[140]   Cf. *Somniale Danielis* ("Beiträge, IV") LVIII: *carbones qui se viderit edere, inimici tui de te mala loquuntur.*

[141]   So too Achmet 146; cf. Artemidorus 2.10 and 4.30.

analogous lifestyle]; but if [he got her] in a friendly way, simply put he will soon be released from this [way of life].

32. Adornment[142] of Women

If a woman dreams that she was beautifully adorned, she will appear even more worthy of respect and will acquire as well a more illustrious [reputation] in the eyes of her husband and in the eyes of those she happens to meet.[143] And if she dreams of also carrying a mirror, she will be seen as most excellent, wonderful, and very becoming in her lifestyle. The same interpretation applies even if a man has this dream.[144]

33. Different Kinds of Meats and Dairy Products [γάλακτα]

Mutton eaten without its fat signifies a lawsuit and disputes.[145] And if the meat is juicy,[146] this means profit from the lawsuit's resolution.

Pork points to conspicuous profit.[147] Beef signifies a boisterous[148] lawsuit,[149] although its fat represents a kind of freedom.

Olive oil, sweet oils,[150] and linseed oil all signify distress.[151]

Milk points to the calmness[152] of mind that arises from realising one's hope.[153] Cheese [denotes] anxiety and worry, although not so in the case of dry cheese.[154]

---

[142] Κόσμησις can also refer to a woman's conduct, not just to her physical beauty. See the discussion above in Chapter 4, note 364.

[143] Cf. Achmet 128 on a woman's adornment/good conduct and the goodness that this yields. For the ideal of women's behavior in the time of Manuel, see *ODB* 1:277, 2:763–4. For cosmetics and their relationship to social status, see *ODB* 1:536.

[144] Cf. Achmet 248. As Mavroudi (2007, 55) points out, this is the only actual mention of a woman having a dream in Manuel's dreambook (the "someone" in Section 39 can be masculine or feminine). This lack of a woman's perspective reflects the "primarily male" readership of the text—an observation that I would extend as applicable to all ancient and medieval Greek dream texts.

[145] So Artemidorus 1.70.

[146] So I take λιπώδης (= the Latin *pinguis*); the modern Greek sense is "fatty" or "greasy."

[147] So too Artemidorus 1.70; Achmet 279.

[148] A wordplay here between μετὰ βοῆς and τὸ βόϊον.

[149] But see Achmet 237, where eating beef symbolises very great wealth.

[150] I take μύρον here to mean "sweet oil" (Achmet uses it in the same sense). The word meant any sort of oil extracted from sesame, nuts, fruits, flowers, and the like: *LAnt* 455; *ODB* 3:1627–8.

[151] Perhaps the meaning is based on analogy to the crushing that occurs when extracting liquid from olives or seeds.

[152] A common wordplay in all the Byzantine dreambooks: γάλα (milk) and γαλήνη (calmness, serenity).

[153] Cf. Achmet 241.

[154] This is the opposite of ibid., 251.

Buttermilk[155] [symbolises] calmness that comes from even greater happiness, for the sharpness of its taste is mild.

Cream,[156] βουρλόγαλον,[157] whey cheese,[158] and young cheese foretell an altogether sweet and delightful situation.[159]

34. Flying

If someone dreams of flying [right above] the ground, he will be exalted in the region where he lives.[160] If he ascended to a high altitude but could still be seen flying [to the people below], he will depart to a foreign land[161] where he will be viewed as honorable and as one who can make money.[162] But if he ascended way beyond the clouds and so completely disappeared, he is about to be deprived of life.[163] This was the dream that the son of Lebēnēs[164] had right before he died.

35. Hats[165]

If someone dreams that he lost his hat, if he is still a virgin [παρθένος], he will lose his sense of virtuous decency by falling into debauchery.[166] If he has a wife, he will lose her to death or because of some other reason. If he has a master, he is about to be far removed from that man's success and aid or he will be insulted in some way on the very same day [as when the dream occurs].

---

[155] So I take τὸ ὀξύγαλαν; cf. Koukoules 1948–57, 5:121–2. See also Dalby 2003, 220, although elsewhere (1995, 66, 200) he offers the translation of "yogurt."

[156] So I take τὰ ἄνθα τοῦ γάλακτος. Cf. modern Greek ἀνθόγαλα.

[157] I cannot locate this word. Perhaps we can read βουτυρόγαλα or something like βουκολόγαλα, but these are only guesses.

[158] The word ἀνθότυρος denoted (and still so today in Greece) an unpasteurised cheese made from sheep or goat's whey and mixed with milk. See Dalby 2003, 73–4, and Koukoules 1948–57, 5:32.

[159] Cf. *Somniale Danielis* ("Beiträge, IV") LV: *caseum recentem accipere, lucrum significat.*

[160] So Artemidorus 2.68: "If a man dreams that he is flying not very far above the earth and in an upright position, it means good luck for the dreamer. The greater the distance above the earth, the higher his position will be in regard to those who walk beneath him"; so too Achmet 160.

[161] Cf. Artemidorus 2.68: "[Dreaming of flying] is good if this does not happen to a man in his own country, since it signifies emigration because the person does not set his foot upon the ground. For the dream is saying to some extent that the dreamer's native land is inaccessible to him."

[162] So Achmet 160.

[163] So ibid., 160.

[164] Or Lebēnos, since the phrase ὁ τοῦ Λεβήνου is ambiguous.

[165] For the meaning of this word, see note 18 above.

[166] I take ἀκολασία as the opposite of σωφροσύνη (sense of decency).

36. Staffs and Clubs

If someone dreams that he received a royal staff, he will get from the emperor honor, fame, support, and a magistracy.

The club is judged as power and mighty strength, along with harshness.[167]

37. Thrones[168]

If someone dreams of sitting on the royal throne, quite simply he will find a magistracy, glory, and magnificence.[169] But if people were paying him homage while he was wearing a crown, diadem, and purple shoes,[170] he will experience dishonor, worthlessness, animosity, and an accusation at the hands of many people.[171]

38. Snakes, Dragons, Lizards, and Frogs

If someone dreams that a snake was slithering toward him, he is about to experience harm at the hands of enemies and a catastrophe that will result in a very evil reputation.[172] If he dreams that a dragon was raised up and poised for attack, he will see a haughty and arrogant tyrant[173] and master of a nation come to fight or to wage war and cause people to die.[174] But if this dragon was fatally wounded [κατετρώθη]

---

[167]   Perhaps "harshness" by analogy to the fact that clubs were used to administer beatings.

[168]   The word θρόνος denoted the official seat of the emperor, versus his ordinary seat, the σκάμνον; the *thronos* usually had a footstool with it. See *ODB* 3:2083 for discussion.

[169]   But cf. Achmet 259: "If a king dreams that another man was sitting on his throne, that man will plot against him because of the daring of his action in the dream; but if the man was dressed in royal garments, he will be the king's successor."

[170]   Shoes dyed with purple from murex shells—as well as purple trousers, cloak, and handkerchief—denoted the Byzantine emperor: *LAnt* 382. Purple shoes were the exclusive prerogative of the emperor, and so it was common for a rebel to put them on in order to signify his usurpation of the throne: *ODB* 2:2135, 2146.

[171]   Obviously, there were boundaries not to be crossed even in a dream; perhaps Manuel (if he indeed is the author) wrote this as a warning to possible conspirators against the throne. As Prof. Mavroudi comments, the interpretation also reflects the general principle in dreambooks, going back to Artemidorus and also reflected in Achmet, that certain kinds of clothes (e.g., black for monks) are good for those who use them in everyday life or are entitled to wear them in everyday life. If they did not use such clothes in waking life, then the interpretation is bad. This is a good observation, since one of the main guidelines of interpretation stressed by Artemidorus is whether the action in a dream is consistent with, or contrary to, custom and habit (see above Chapter 2, note 10).

[172]   So Artemidorus 2.13 and Achmet 281.

[173]   The word τύραννος often denoted a rebel usurper in Byzantine Greek.

[174]   Perhaps there is an association of the word "dragon" with *drakontion*, which was a special pole-mounted dragon mask with a banner or streamer attached to it. This pole served as a windsock for the archers of the Byzantine army. See Rautman 2006, 216.

or was consumed by a lightning bolt, the dreamer will see this ruler wiped out and put to death.[175]

If someone dreams that lizards attacked him, let him know that he will experience bitterness and an attack at the hands of people who, though weak, are evil, vile,[176] bitter, and cause very great distress.[177]

If someone dreams of croaking frogs, he will see contemptible and vulgar people who will inflict tumult and distress either on themselves or on others.[178]

39. Pregnancy

If someone dreams of tending to[179] trees [or] plants, he will establish ties of kinship through nuptials.[180]

If someone dreams of being pregnant, he will become sick in some way,[181] but after nine months have passed, he will be freed of his illness, for a baby is interpreted as bodily disease [πάθος] according to two [dreambook] accounts.[182] And if indeed he gave birth to a child, a secret affliction will be brought to light.[183]

---

[175]   Achmet 281: "If someone dreams that a dragon was chased away by thunder and lightning, let him know that this means war and the fall of an enemy king in that region."

[176]   A pun on the word χαμερπή (which I translate in its modern Greek meaning): the word is composed of χαμαί (on the ground) and ἕρπειν (crawl), and thus can describe not only lizards but people with analogous characters (or their occupation, since peasants worked close to the ground).

[177]   Cf. Artemidorus 4.56: "Those whose appearance is less dreadful than their power as, for example, venomous spiders, water salamanders, and lizards, indicate small, contemptible men who are, however, in a position to harm one badly."

[178]   Achmet (283) interprets frogs as evildoing enemies of little repute. Cf. *Somniale Danielis* ("Beiträge, IV") CCXXIV: *ranas viderit, anxionem* [*sic* for *anxietatem*] *significat*. Artemidorus (2.15) interprets frogs as cheats and beggars.

[179]   The text has φιλιάζω. Sophocles (1975) says that the verb is equivalent to φιλιόομαι (to be friends with), although it is closer to φιλέω in meaning. However, Prof. Mavroudi offers the brilliant emendation of φυλλιάζω—that is, to prune trees or to take care of trees; although such a word would be a *hapax legomenon*, it would make perfect sense and so I use it here. (I would note that φιλιάζω and φυλλιάζω were pronounced the same and so could have led to some confusion.) In any case, the sentence seems wholly out of place given the title of this section and the following sentence.

[180]   No matter how we take φιλιάζω, there is an analogy between the roots of trees and plants and the roots (family and friends) that one establishes through marriage.

[181]   So too Artemidorus 1.14.

[182]   But ibid. (1.14) says that death will be the result (children are a bad dream symbol since they take a lot of effort to raise). I take λόγοι here as "accounts" (thus, Manuel has found in two different sources his interpretation), as opposed to "reasons" (that is, "a baby is interpreted as bodily disease for two reasons").

[183]   For many other possible interpretations of this same dream, see ibid., 1.14 and Achmet 127 and 128.

40. Kissing [φίλημα] Children [and Death of Children]

If someone dreams that he kissed the child of a woman who is not his wife, he will fall passionately in love with that woman and be sexually aroused; she, on the other hand, although also aroused, will guard herself against his passion. And if [he dreams that] this child died or was baptised [ἐβαπτίσθη] by someone, [he himself] will be plunged into the sea, flounder, and then die. For baptism [βάπτισμα] is [to be judged as] divine pity and death, and when one comes up out of the [baptismal] water this signifies the common resurrection of the dead that will take place;[184] for it is clear that [people] die in Christ [when they are baptised].[185]

41. Hunting Rabbits

If someone dreams that he was hunting a rabbit, he will gain power and a magisterial position over people.[186] And if he caught it alive and completely domesticated it, he will restore to this people peace, a tame existence, and progress. But if he killed the rabbit, he will ruin and completely destroy [his people].

42. Wolves

If someone dreams that a wolf entered the city [Constantinople], you should know that there will be either a great plague that will strike the city and destroy the citizens, or a man so arrogant[187] that he will cause the ruin of everyone.[188]

43. Bees

If someone dreams of bees, this is to be interpreted as a raid[189] and attack by enemies or as a rebellion by the common people.[190]

---

[184] Prof. Mavourdi comments that in the Greek Orthodox Church, children are baptised as infants by being completely immersed three times in the waters of a baptismal font. This would explain the association of baptism and children here.

[185] Cf. Achmet 179: "If someone dreams that he was crossing a river or sea in a ship, the ship represents his salvation and his lack of fear before his enemies; but if the ship came into danger, he will lose his salvation and become ill: but if the boat crossed over, he will be fruitful in his way of life." Manuel's phrase "die in Christ" appears very frequently in the New Testament and theological treatises; see, e.g., 1 Thessalonians 4:16 and Romans 6:8.

[186] This is contrary to the proverbial notion that rabbits are cowardly; see LSJ, s.v. "λαγώς."

[187] So γαῦρος. The use of this rather infrequent word may have come from an unconscious association with the verb γαυγίζω (to bark or to yelp).

[188] See Artemidorus 2.12; but cf. Achmet 274.

[189] I read ἐπιβολή, instead of the textual reading ἀποβολή.

[190] So too Achmet 282; Artemidorus 2.22: "[Bees] generally indicate that the dreamer will be destroyed by a mob or soldiers. For bees are analogous to crowds and armies since they obey a leader." During the time of Manuel, a peasant might own up to 30 beehives (*ODB* 1:130) to

44. Sheep

If someone dreams that sheep entered his house, he is about to see his dearly loved friends coming to stay there. But if [he dreams of] goats, he will behold people from foreign countries, who may or may not be ambassadors,[191] coming to his house; this dream is thus interpreted because goats are on the left hand of Christ the Savior, the true God.[192]

Lambs are interpreted as tender affections [μικρὰ φίλτρα] for children.[193]

45. Eggs

If someone dreams of holding eggs in his hands, he is about to be thrown out of his house or country; and the number of eggs he was holding will be the number of days he will be gone from his friends, relatives, and other [dear ones]. But if he already is on a trip [when this dream occurs], his absence will be a matter of months, not days. If he dreams of cracking the eggs open or eating them, he will be prevented and hindered from traveling.[194]

46. Graves

If someone dreams that he was passing the time in a graveyard and saw bare bones there, he will greatly repent[195] over himself and over matters related to his way of

---

produce honey; honey was used for sugar and for making candles, medicines, and alcoholic beverages; cf. Daniel 337 with comment ad loc.

[191]   For ambassadors and the diplomatic service at this time, see *ODB* 1:75, 634–6.

[192]   The biblical reference is Matthew 25:31–3. The interpretation appears to be based on a series of associations: goats ~ sinners ~ barbarians/foreigners. The Byzantines thought that the Empire was the extent of the civilised world and that all other peoples were in effect barbaric: *ODB* 2:796–7.

[193]   I am not sure whether this genitive is objective or subjective, but have decided to take it as objective as this makes more sense of the passage (as opposed to reading "tender affections of small children"). For the dream, cf. Achmet 240: "If someone dreams that he found or picked up a lamb, he will have a desirable child. If he dreams that he was eating lamb, he will have the wealth he has been seeking and have good health. If he dreams that he came across a large herd of lambs, he will be happy and rejoice in proportion to the number of lambs."

[194]   But eggs symbolise wealth and young slaves according to ibid., 250; Artemidorus (2.43) interprets eggs as both auspicious and inauspicious.

[195]   I do not take κατάνυξις in its classical sense of "bewilderment," but in its common Byzantine meaning of "piety" or "devotion" and in its modern Greek meaning of "repentance." The idea, as I take it, is that the dreamer, after being confronted by this frightening specter of the finality of death, will repent of his lifestyle and become more pious.

life,[196] [and he will become fearful of an accusation on account of the changeability, corruption, and constant hope of human nature].[197]

---

[196] Cf. *Somniale Danielis* ("Beiträge, V") 73: *hossa mortuorum vel corpora videre, labores maximas significat*; Achmet 132: "If someone dreams that he took from a dead man's grave a bone or flesh, he will get from a person in authority money that comes with terror."

[197] All the words translated within the brackets are contained on fol. 318ᵛ, except for the phrase "fear of an accusation" (φόβου κατηγορίας), which is on fol. 318ʳ. Delatte (1927–39, 524 ad loc.) expresses doubt whether this portion of text even is part of the dreambook ("iure dubites num textus f. 318ᵛ ad idem opusculum pertineat. Reliqua pagina vacat").

Bibliography of Works Cited

A. Roman Imperial and Byzantine Dreambooks

Achmet Dreambook
Drexl, F. (ed.). 1925a. *Achmetis Oneirocriticon*. Leipzig.
—— *English translation*: Oberhelman, S. M. 1991. *The Oneirocriticon of Achmet: A Medieval Greek and Arabic Treatise on the Interpretation of Dreams*. Lubbock, TX.
—— *German translation*: Brackertz, K. 1986. *Das Traumbuch des Achmet ben Sirin*. München.

Anonymous Dreambook
Drexl, F. 1925b. "Das Anonyme Traumbuch des cod. Paris. gr. 2511," *Laographia*, 8: 347–75.
—— *German translation*: Brackertz 1993 (see Section B below).

Artemidorus Dreambook
Pack, R. (ed.). 1963. *Artemidori Daldiani Onirocriticon libri quinque*. Leipzig.
—— *English translation*: White, R. 1975. *The Interpretation of Dreams = Oneirocritica by Artemidorus*. Park Ridge, NJ.
—— *French translation*: Festugière, A. J. 1975. *Artemidore, La clef des sognes*. Paris.
—— *German translation*: Brackertz, K. 1979. *Artemidorus von Daldis, Das Traumbuch*. München.
—— *Greek translation*: Mavroudi, M. 2002. *Artemidorou Oneirokritika*. Athens.
—— *Italian translation*: Del Corno, D. 1975. *Artemidoro, Il libro dei sogni*. Milano.

Astrampsychus Dreambook
Opsopaeus, S. (ed.). 1599. *Astrampsychi Oneirocriticon*.Venetiae.
Rigaultius, N. (ed.). 1603. *Artemidori Daldiani et Achmetis Sereimei F. Oneirokritika: Astrampsychi et Nicephori versus etiam oneirokritiki: Nicolai Rigaultii ad Artemidorum notae*. Lutetiae.
Brodersen, K. 2006. *Astrampsychos: Das Pythagoras-Orakel und über magische Steine, über Traumdeutung, Liebesbindezauber*. Darmstadt.
—— *German translation*: Brackertz 1993 (see Section B below); Brodersen 2006 (above).

Daniel Dreambook
Drexl, F. 1926. "Das Traumbuch des Propheten Daniel nach dem cod. Vatic. Palat. gr. 319," *Byzantinische Zeitschrift*, 26: 290–314.

—— *German translation*: Brackertz 1993 (see Section B below).

Germanus Dreambook
Drexl, F. 1923. "Das Traumbuch des Patriarchen Germanos," *Laographia*, 7: 428–48.
—— *German translation*: Brackertz 1993 (see Section B below).

Manuel Dreambook
Delatte, A. 1927–39. *Anecdota Atheniensia*, 2 vols (2:511–24). Liège and Paris.

Nicephorus Dreambook
Drexl, F. 1922. "Das Traumbuch des Patriarchen Nikephoros," in A. M. Koeniger (ed.), *Festbage A. Ehrhard: Beiträge zur Geschichte des christlichen Altertums und der byzantinischen Literatur*, 94–118. Bonn.
Guidorizzi, G. 1980. *Pseudo-Nicephoro: Libro dei sogni*, Collana di Studi e Testi, 5. Naples.
—— *German translation*: Brackertz 1993 (see Section B below).
—— *Italian translation*: Guidorizzi 1980 (see above).

B. Lexica and Dictionaries

Adler, A. 1967–71. *Suidae Lexicon*. Stuttgart. (Referenced as Suda.)
Arndt, W., and F. Gingrich (eds and trans). 1958. *A Greek–English Lexicon of the New Testament and Other Early Christian Literature: A Translation and Adoption of the Fourth Revised and Augmented Edition of Walter Bauer's* Griechisch-Deutsches Wörterbuch zu den Schriften des Neuen Testaments und der übrigen urchristlichen Literatur. 2nd edn. Chicago.
Bowersock, G. W., Peter Brown, and Oleg Grabar (eds). 1999. *Late Antiquity: A Guide to the Postclassical World*. Cambridge, MA and London. (Referenced as *LAnt*.)
Chantraine, P. 1968–80. *Dictionnaire étymologique de la langue grecque: Histoire des mots*. 4 vols in 5. Paris.
DuCange, Ch. 1688. *Glossarium ad scriptores mediae et infimae graecitatis*. 2 vols. Lyons.
Hornblower, S., and A. Spawforth (eds). 2003. *Oxford Classical Dictionary*. 3rd rev. edn. Oxford. (Referenced as *OCD*[3].)
Kazhdan, A. P., and A.-M. Talbot (eds). 1991. *Oxford Dictionary of Byzantium*. 3 vols. Oxford. (Referenced as *ODB*.)
Lampe, G. W. H. 1976. *A Patristic Greek Lexicon*. Oxford.
Lewis, Ch., and Ch. Short. 1879. *A Latin Dictionary, Founded on Andrews' Edition of Freund's Latin Dictionary, Revised, Enlarged, and in Great Part Rewritten*. Oxford.
Liddell, H., and R. Scott. 1968. *A Greek–English Lexicon*. Revised and augmented by H. Jones. 9th edn. Oxford. (Referenced as LSJ.)
Migne, J. P. 1857–1904. *Patrologia cursus completa. Series graeca*. 161 vols. Paris. (Referenced as PG.)
Rosser, J. H. 2001. *An Historical Dictionary of Byzantium*. London.

Schmidt, M. 1965. *Hesychii Alexandrini Lexicon.* 5 vols. Amsterdam.

Sophocles, E. 1975. *A Greek Lexicon of the Roman and Byzantine Periods (from B.C. 146 to A.D. 1100).* Hildesheim.

Stephanus, H. 1954 [1572]. *Thesaurus graecae linguae.* 9 vols. Graz.

C. Modern Literature

Abrahamse, D. 1982. "Magic and Sorcery in Hagiography of the Middle Byzantine Period," *Byzantinische Forschungen,* 8: 3–17.

Alexander, P. J. 1958. *The Patriarch Nicephorus of Constantinople.* Oxford.

Allen, P. 1979. "The 'Justinianic' Plague," *Byzantion,* 49: 5–20.

Arranz, M. 1979. "Les 'fêtes théologiques' du calendrier byzantin," in A. M. Triacca and A. Pistoia (eds), *La liturgie, expression de la foi,* 29–55. Rome.

Avi-Yonah, M. 1984. *The Jews under Roman and Byzantine Rule.* Jerusalem and New York.

Avramea, A. 2002. "Land and Sea Communications, Fourth–Fifteenth Centuries," in Laiou 2002a, 57–90.

Bar, Shaul. 2001. *A Letter That Has Not Been Read: Dreams in the Hebrew Bible.* Detroit.

Barker, J. 1969. *Manuel II Palaeologus (1391–1425).* New Brunswick, NJ.

Bartusis, M. 1981. "Brigandage in the Late Byzantine Empire," *Byzantion,* 51: 386–409.

Bauer, W. 1964. *Rechtgläubigkeit und Ketzerei im ältesten Christentum.* 2nd edn. Tübingen.

Baus, Karl. 1940. *Der Kranz in Antike und Christentum.* Bonn.

Beaucamp, Joelle. 1992. *Le statut de la femme à Byzance (4ᵉ–7ᵉ siècle), I: Le droit impérial.* Paris.

Beck, H. G. 1971. *Geschichte der byzantinische Volksliteratur.* Munich.

Behr, Ch. 1968. *Aelius Aristides and the Sacred Tales.* Amsterdam.

Bellamy, J. A. 1979. "Sex and Society in Islamic Popular Literature," in A. L. al-Sayyid-Marsot (ed.), *Society and the Sexes in Medieval Islam,* 23–41. Malibu.

Belting, H. 1990. *Bild und Kult: Eine Geschichte des Bildes vor dem Zeitalter der Kunst.* Munich.

Berger, A. 1982. *Das Bad in der byzantinischen Zeit.* Munich.

Blum, Ch. 1936. *Studies in Artemidorus' Oneirocritical Book.* Upsala.

Boissonade, J. F. 1962 [1844]. *Anecdota Nova.* Hildesheim.

Boswell, J. 1989. "Revolutions, Universals, and Sexual Categories," in Duberman *et al.* 1989, 17–36.

Bouras, C. 2002. "Aspects of the Byzantine City, Eighth–Fifteenth Centuries," in Laiou 2002a, 497–528.

Bowersock, G. W. 1987. "Arabs and Saracens in the Historia Augusta," in *Bonner-Historia Augusta-Colloquium 1984–1985,* 71–80. Bonn.

Brackertz, K. 1993. *Die Volks-Traumbücher des byzantinischen Mittelalters.* Munich.

Braun, J. 1924. *Der christliche Altar in seiner geschichtlichen Entwicklung.* 2 vols. Munich.

Brett, G. 1939. "Byzantine Water-Mill," *Antiquity*, 13: 354–6.

Brooks, S. H. 1987. *Matthew's Community: The Evidence of His Spiritual Sayings Material.* Sheffield.

Brown, J. 1989. "Lesbian Sexuality in Medieval and Early Modern Europe," in Duberman *et al.* 1989, 67–75.

Brown, P. 1988. *The Body and Society.* New York.

Brubaker, L. (ed.). 1998a. *Byzantium in the Ninth Century: Dead or Alive? Papers from the Thirtieth Spring Symposium of Byzantine Studies, Birmingham, March 1996,* Society for the Promotion of Byzantine Studies, 5. Aldershot.

————. 1998b. "Byzantine Culture in the Ninth Century: An Introduction," in Brubaker 1998a, 63–71.

————. 2005. "The Age of Justinian," in M. Maas 2005a, 427–47.

Bruce, F. F. 1988. *The Canon of Scripture.* Leicester and Downers Grove, IL.

Bryer, A. 2002. "The Means of Agricultural Production: Muscle and Tools," in Laiou 2002a, 101–13.

————, and J. Herrin. 1977. *Iconoclasm.* Birmingham.

Büchsenschütz, B. 1964 [1868]. *Traum und Traumdeutung im Altertum.* Weisbaden.

Butler, S. A. 1988. *Mesopotamian Conceptions of Dreams and Dream Rituals.* Münster.

Calofonos, G. 1984–85. "Dream Interpretation: A Byzantine Superstition?," *Byzantine and Modern Greek Studies*, 9: 215–20.

————. 1990. "Manuel II Palaeologos: Interpreter of Dreams?," *Byzantinische Forschungen*, 16: 447–55.

Cambiano, G. 1980. "Une interprétation 'matérialiste' des rêves *Du régime IV*," in M. D. Grmek (ed.), *Hippocratica: Actes du colloque hippocratique de Paris (4–9 septembre 1978)*, 88–96. Paris.

Cameron, Alan. 1976. *Circus Factions: Blues and Greens in Rome and Constantinople.* Oxford.

Cavallo, G. 1981. "Il libro come oggetto d'uso nel mondo bizantino," *Jahrbuch der Österreichischen Byzantinistik*, 31: 395–423.

————(ed.). 1997a. *The Byzantines.* Translated by Th. Dunlap, T. L. Fagan, and Ch. Lambert. Chicago.

————. 1997b. "Introduction," in Cavallo 1997a, 1–13.

Conomos, D. E. 1984. *Byzantine Hymnography and Byzantine Chant.* Brookline, MA.

Conybeare, F. 1901. "Les sacrifices d'animaux dans les anciennes églises chrétiennes," *Revue de l'histoire des religions*, 44: 108–14.

Cooper, K. 1996. *The Virgin and the Bride: Idealized Womanhood in Late Antiquity.* Cambridge, MA.

Cormack R. 1998. "Away from the Centre: 'Provincial' Art in the Ninth Century," in Brubaker 1998a, 151–63.

Croke, B. 1981. "Two Early Byzantine Earthquakes and Their Liturgical Commemoration," *Byzantion*, 51: 122–47.

————. 2005. "Justinian's Constantinople," in M. Maas 2005a, 60–86.

Cutler, A. 2002. "The Industries of Art," in Laiou 2002a, 555–87.

Dagron, G. 1969. "Aux origines de la civilisation byzantine: Langue de culture et langue d'État," *Revue Historique*, 241: 23–56.

_____. 1974. *Naissance d'une capitale: Constantinople et ses institutions de 330 à 451*. Paris.

_____. 1978. *Vie et Miracles de S. Thiècle*. Brussels.

_____. 1985. "Rêver de dieu et parler de soi: Le rêve et son interprétation d'après les sources byzantines," in Gregory 1985, 37–55.

_____. 2002. "The Urban Economy, Seventh–Twelfth Centuries," in Laiou 2002a, 393–461.

Dalby, A. 1996. *Siren Feasts: A History of Food and Gastronomy in Greece*. London and New York.

_____. 2003. *Flavours of Byzantium*. Totnes.

De Lange, N. 2005. "Jews in the Age of Justinian," in M. Maas 2005a, 401–27.

De Stoop, E. 1909. "Onirocriticon du prophète Daniel dédié au roi Nabuchodonosor," *Revue de Philologie*, 33: 93–111.

Del Corno, D. 1962. "Richerche sull'onirocritica greca," *Rendiconti dell'Istituto Lombardo, Classe di Lettere, Scienza morali e storiche*, 96: 334–66.

_____. 1969. *Graecorum de re onirocritica scriptorum reliquiae*, Collana di testi e documenti per lo studio dell'antichità, 26. Milan.

_____. 1975. "I sogni e la loro interpretazione nell'età dell'impero," *Aufstieg und Niedergang der römischen Welt*, II: *Principat* 16, 2: 1505–18.

Delatte, A. 1935. "La méthode oniromantique de Blaise l'Athénien," in *Mélanges offerts à Octave Navarre par ses élèves et ses amis*, 115–22. Toulouse.

Delehaye, H. 1925. "Les recueils antiques de miracles des saints," *Analecta Bollandiana*, 43: 5–85, 305–25.

Dennis, G. T. 1977. *The Letters of Manuel II Palaeologus*, Corpus Fontium Historiae Byzantinae, 8. Washington, DC.

Detorakis, Th. 1996. "Τὰ Βυζαντινὰ ὀνειροκριτικά: δύο νέα χειρόγραφα," *Palimpsōston*, 16: 65–74.

Deubner, L. 1900. *De incubatione capita quattuor*. Leipzig.

_____. 1907. *Kosmas und Damian: Texte und Einleitung*. Leipzig.

Dihle, A. 1992. "La fête chrétienne," *Revue des Études Augustiniennes*, 38: 323–35.

Dinzelbacher, P. 1981. *Vision und Visionsliteratur im Mittelalter*. Stuttgart.

_____ (ed.). 1989. *Mittelalterische Visionsliteratur: Eine Anthologie*. Darmstadt.

DiTommaso, L. 2003–2004. "Greek, Latin, and Hebrew Manuscripts of the *Somniale Danielis* and *Lunationes Danielis* in the Vatican Library," *Manuscripta*, 47/48: 1–42.

_____. 2005. *The Book of Daniel and the Apocryphal Daniel Literature*, Studia in Veteris Testamenti Pseudepigrapha, 20. Leiden.

Dols, M. 1984. "Insanity in Byzantine and Islamic Medicine," *Dumbarton Oak Papers*, 38: 135–48.

Duberman, M. B., M. Vicinus, and G. Chauncey (eds). 1989. *Hidden from History: Reclaiming the Gay and Lesbian Past*. New York.

Duffy, J. 1984. "Some Observations on Sophronius' Miracles of Cyrus and John," *Journal of Theological Studies*, 35: 71–90.

Dulaey, M. 1973. *Le rêve dans la vie et la pensée de saint Augustin*. Paris.

Dunbar, D. G. 1986. "The Biblical Canon," in D. A. Carson and J. D. Woodbridge (eds), *Hermeneutics, Authority, and Canon*, 315–42. Grand Rapids, MI.

Edelstein, E. J., and L. Edelstein. 1945. *Asclepius*. 2 vols. Baltimore.

Ehrlich, E. L. 1953. *Der Traum im Alten Testament*, Beiheft zur Zeitschrift für die alttestamentliche Wissenschaft, 73. Berlin.

Eitrem, S. 1991. "Dreams and Divination in Magical Ritual," in C. Faraone and D. Obbink (eds), *Magika Hiera*, 175–87. Oxford.

Epe, A. 1995. *Wissensliteratur im angelsächsischen England: Das Fachschrifttum der vergessenen artes mechanicae und artes magicae. Mit besonderer Berücksichtigung des Somniale Danielis: Edition der (lateinisch-) altenglischen Fassungen*. Münster.

Fahd, T. 1966. *La Divination Arabe: Études religieuses, sociologiques et folkloriques sur le milieu natif de l'Islam*. Leiden.

Ferch, A. J. 1983. "The Book of Daniel and the 'Maccabean Thesis,'" *Andrews University Seminar Studies*, 21: 129–41.

Fischer, S. 1982. *The Complete Medieval Dreambook: A Multilingual, Alphabetical "Somnia Danielis" Collection*. Bern and Frankfurt-am-Main. 1982.

Fögen, M. Th. 1998. "Reanimation of Roman Law in the Ninth Century: Remarks on Reasons and Results," in Brubaker 1998a, 11–22.

Förster, M. 1910. "Beiträge zur mittelalterlichen Volkskunde, IV," *Archiv für das Studien der Neueren Sprachen*, 125: 39–70.

_____. 1911. "Beiträge zur mittelalterlichen Volkskunde, V," *Archiv für das Studien der Neueren Sprachen*, 127: 31–84.

_____. 1921. "Das älteste kymrische Traumbuch (Um 1350)," *Zeitschrift für celtische Philologie*, 13: 55–92.

Foerster, W. 1972–74. *Gnosis: A Selection of Gnostic Texts*. Translated by R. McL. Wilson. 2 vols. Oxford.

Frère, J. 1983. "L'aurore de la science des rêves: Aristote," *Ktema*, 8: 27–37.

Freud, S. 1953–74. *The Standard Edition of the Complete Psychological Works of Sigmund Freud. Translated from the German under the General Editorship of James Strachey, in Collaboration with Anna Freud, Assisted by Alix Strachey and Alan Tyson*. 24 vols. London.

_____. 1980. *The Interpretation of Dreams*. Translated by James Strachey. New York.

Gage, E. 2004. *North of Ithaka: A Granddaughter Returns to Greece*. New York.

Gager, John. 1992. *Curse Tablets and Binding Spells from the Ancient World*. Oxford.

Geyer, B. 2002. "Physical Factors in the Evolution of the Landscape and Land Use," in Laiou 2002a, 31–45.

Gigli, G. 1978. "Gli onirocritici del cod. Paris. Suppl. Gr. 690," *Prometheus*, 4: 65–86, 173–88.

Grabar, A. 1984. *L'iconoclasme byzantin: Le dossier archéologique*. 2nd edn. Paris.

Greatrex, G. 2005. "Byzantium and the East in the Sixth Century," in M. Maas 2005a, 477–509.

Greenfield, R. P. H. 1995. "A Contribution to the Study of Palaeologian Magic," in H. Maguire (ed.), *Byzantine Magic*, 117–53. Cambridge, MA.

Gregory, T. (ed.). 1985. *I sogni nel medioevo, seminario internazionale Roma, 2–4 ottobre 1983*. Lessico Intellettuale Europeo, 35. Rome.

_____. 1986. "The Survival of Paganism in Christian Greece," *American Journal of Philology*, 107: 229–42.

_____. 2005. *A History of Byzantium*. Malden, MA–Oxford–Carlton, Victoria.

Guidorizzi, G. 1973. "L'opuscolo di Galeno 'De dignotione ex insomniis,'" *Bollettino del Comitato per la Preparazione dell'Edizione Nazionale dei Classici Greci e Latini*, 21: 81–105.

_____. 1977. "I prontuari oniromantici bizantini," *Recondiconti Istituto Lombardo*, 111: 135–55.

Guilland, R. 1967. *Recherches sur les institutions byzantines*. 2 vols. Amsterdam.

_____. 1968. "Études sur l'histoire administrative de l'Empire Byzantin: Le mystique ho mystikos," *Revue des Études Byzantines*, 26: 279–96.

_____. 1980. "Études sur l'histoire administrative de l'Empire Byzantin— L'Éparque, I. L'éparque de la ville," *Byzantinoslavica*, 41: 17–32, 145–80.

Guillaume, A. 1950. *Prophétie et divination chez les Sémites*. Paris.

Hackel, S. (ed.). 1981. *The Byzantine Saint*. London.

Håland, E. J. 2004. "Greek Festivals, Modern and Ancient: A Comparison of Female and Male Values," PhD diss., University of Bergen.

Haldon, J. 1998. "The Byzantine State in the Ninth Century: An Introduction," in Brubaker 1998a, 3–10.

_____. 2005. "Economy and Administration: How Did the Empire Work?," in M. Maas 2005a, 28–59.

Hanson, J. S. 1980. "Dreams and Visions in the Graeco-Roman World and Early Christianity," in *Aufstieg und Niedergang der römischen Welt*, II: *Principat 23*, 2: 1395–427.

Harrauer, C. 1997. "Astrampsychos," *Der Neue Pauly*, 2: 121–2.

Harrington, D. 1991. *The Gospel of Matthew*. Collegeville.

Holowchak, M. A. 2001a. *Ancient Science and Dreams: Oneirology in Greco-Roman Antiquity*. Lanham, MD.

_____. 2001b. "Interpreting Dreams for Corrective Regimen: Diagnostic Dreams in Greco-Roman Medicine," *Journal of the History of Medicine*, 56: 382–99.

Holum, K. G. 2005. "The Classical City in the Sixth Century: Survival and Transformation," in M. Maas 2005a, 87–112.

Hopfner, Th. 1937. "Traumdeutung," *Paulys Real-Encyclopädie der classischen Altertumswissenschaft*, 6A: 2233–45.

Horden, P. "Mediterranean Plague in the Age of Justinian," in M. Maas 2005a, 134–60.

Hubbard, Th. K. 2003. *Homosexuality in Greece and Rome: A Sourcebook of Basic Documents*. Berkeley–Los Angeles–London.

Husser, J.-P. 1999. *Dreams and Dream Narratives in the Biblical World*. Biblical Seminar, 63. Sheffield.

Joly, R. 1960. *Recherches sur le traité pseudo-hippocratique Du régime*. Paris.

_____ (ed., trans., and comm.). 1984. *Hippocrate, Du Régime*, Corpus Medicorum Graecorum, 1.2.4. Berlin.

Jones, A. H. M. 1964. *The Later Roman Empire: 284–602*. 3 vols. Oxford.

Kany-Turpin, J., and P. Pellegrin. 1989. "Cicero and the Aristotelian Theory of Divination by Dreams," in W. W. Fortenbough and P. Steinmetz (eds), *Cicero's Knowledge of the Peripatos*, 220–45. New Brunswick, NJ.

Karlin-Hayter, P. 2002. "Icon Veneration: Significance of the Restoration of Orthodoxy," in Sode and Takács 2002, 171–83.

Kazhdan, A. P. 1997. "The Peasantry," in Cavallo 1997a, 43–73.

_____, and A. W. Epstein. 1985. *Change in Byzantine Culture in the Eleventh and Twelfth Centuries*. Berkeley–Los Angeles–London.

_____, and M. McCormick. 1997. "The Social World of the Byzantine Court," in Maguire 1997, 167–92.

Kenny, M. 1996. "Distinguishing between Dreams and Visions in Ninth-Century Hagiography," *Gouden Hoorn*. Online journal, with Kenny's article accessible at <http://www.isidore-of-selville.com/goudenhoorn/41margaret.html>.

Keskiaho, J. 2005. "The Handling and Interpretation of Dreams and Visions in Late Sixth- to Eighth-Century Gallic and Anglo-Latin Hagiography and Histories," *Early Medieval Europe*, 13.3: 227–48.

Köpstein, H. 1966. *Zur Sklaverei im ausgehenden Byzanz*. Berlin.

Kolias, T. 1982. "Kamelaukion," *Jahrbuch der Österreichischen Byzantinistik*, 32/33: 493–502.

Koukoules, Ph. 1928. "'Ονάματα καὶ εἴδη ἄρτων κατὰ τοὺς Βυζαντινοὺς χρόνους," *Epeteris Hetaireias Byzantinōn Spoudōn*, 5: 36–52.

_____. 1948–57. *Βυζαντινῶν βίος καὶ πολιτισμός*. 6 vols in 9. Athens.

_____. 1951. "'Η μελισσοκομία παρὰ Βυζαντινοῖς," *Byzantinische Zeitschrift*, 44: 347–57.

Krueger, D. 2005. "Christian Piety and Practice in the Sixth Century," in M. Maas 2005a, 291–315.

Kruger, S. F. *Dreaming in the Middle Ages*, Cambridge Studies in Medieval Literature, 14. Cambridge.

Krumbacher, K. 1897. *Geschichte der byzantinischen Litteratur von Justinian bis zum Ende des oströmischen Reiches, 527–1453*, Handbuch der klassische Altertumswissenschaft. Munich.

Kühn, C. G. 1964–65 [1821–33]. *Claudii Galeni Opera omnia*. 22 vols. Hildesheim.

Laiou, A. 1977. *Peasant Society in the Late Byzantine Empire*. Princeton, NJ.

_____. 1981. "The Role of Women in Byzantine Society," *Jahrbuch der Österreichischen Byzantinistik*, 31: 233–60.

_____. 1984. "Contribution à l'étude de l'institution familiale en Épire au XIIIᵉ siècle," *Fontes Minores*, 6: 284–300.

_____ (ed.). 2002a. *The Economic History of Byzantium from the Seventh through the Fifteenth Century*. 3 vols. Washington, DC.

_____. 2002b. "The Human Resources," in Laiou 2002a, 47–55.

_____. 2002c. "The Agrarian Economy, Thirteenth–Fifteenth Centuries," in Laiou 2002a, 311–75.

Lamoreaux, J. C. 2002. *The Early Muslim Tradition of Dream Interpretation*. Albany, NY.

Lamza, L. 1975. *Patriarch Germanos I. von Konstantinopel*. Würzburg.

Lascaratos, J. 2004. "Miraculous Ophthalmological Therapies in Byzantium," *Documenta Ophthalmologica*, 81: 145–52.

Le Goff, J. 1985. "Le christianisme et les rêves (IIe–VIIe siècles)," in Gregory 1985, 171–218.

_____. 1992. *The Medieval Imagination*. Translated by Arthur Goldhammer. Chicago.

Lee, A. D. 2005. "The Empire at War," in M. Maas 2005a, 113–33.

Lefort, J. 2002. "The Rural Economy, Seventh–Twelfth Centuries," in Laiou 2002a, 231–310.

Leontsini, S. 1989. *Die Prostitution im frühen Byzanz*. Vienna.

Littlewood, A. R. 1993. "The Erotic Symbolism of the Apple in Late Byzantine and Meta-Byzantine Demotic Literature," *Byzantine and Modern Greek Studies*, 17: 83–103.

_____. 1997. "Gardens of the Palaces," in Maguire 1997, 13–38.

L'Orange, H. P., and P. J. Nordhagen. 1966. *Mosaics from Antiquity to the Middle Ages*. London.

Lopez, R. S. 1945. "Silk Industry in the Byzantine Empire," *Speculum*, 20: 1–42.

Lorand, S. 1957. "Dream Interpretation in the Talmud—Babylonian and Graeco-Roman Period," *International Journal of Psycho-Analysis*, 38: 92–7.

MacAlister, S. 1992. "Gender as Sign and Symbolism in Artemidoros' *Oneirokritika*: Social Aspirations and Anxieties," *Helios*, 19: 140–60.

_____. 1996. *Dreams and Suicides: The Greek Novel from Antiquity to the Byzantine Empire*. London and New York.

McCormick, M. 1997. "Emperors," in Cavallo 1997a, 230–54.

Maas, M. (ed.). 2005a. *The Cambridge Companion to the Age of Justinian*. Cambridge.

_____. 2005b. "Roman Questions, Byzantine Answers: Contours of the Age of Justinian," in M. Maas 2005a, 3–27.

Maas, P. 1903. "Der byzantinische Zwölfsilber," *Byzantinische Zeitschrift*, 12: 278–323.

Mack, B. L. 1993. *The Lost Gospel: The Book of Q and Christian Origins*. San Francisco.

Magdalino, P. 1998. "The Road to Baghdad in the Thought-World of Ninth-Century Byzantium," in Brubaker 1998a, 195–213.

Maguire, H. 1996. *The Icons of Their Bodies*. Princeton, NJ.

_____ (ed.). 1997. *Byzantine Court Culture from 829 to 1204*. Washington, DC.

Majeska, G. P. 1997. "The Emperor in His Church: Imperial Ritual in the Church of St. Sophia," in Maguire 1997, 1–11.

Makris, G. 2002. "Ships," in Laiou 2002a, 91–100.

Mango, C. 1975. "The Durability of Books in the Byzantine Empire, A.D. 750–850," in *Byzantine Books and Bookmen: A Dumbarton Oaks Colloquium, 1971*, 29–45. Washington, DC.

_____. 1997. "Saints," in Cavallo 1997a, 255–80.

Markopoulos, A. 1998. "The Rehabilitation of the Emperor Theophilos," in Brubaker 1998a, 37–49.

Martin, L. T. 1979. "The Earliest Versions of the Latin *Somniale Danielis*," *Manuscripta*, 23: 131–41.

_____. 1981. *Somnia Danielis: An Edition of a Medieval Dream Interpretation Handbook*, Lateinische Sprache und Literatur des Mittelalters, 10. Frankfurt.

Matschke, K.-P. 2002a. "Mining," in Laiou 2002a, 115–20.

_____. 2002b. "The Late Byzantine Urban Economy, Thirteenth–Fifteenth Centuries," in Laiou 2002a, 464–95.

Mavroudi, M. 2002. *A Byzantine Book on Dream Interpretation: The Oneirocriticon of Achmet and Its Arabic Sources*, The Medieval Mediterranean: Peoples, Economics, and Cultures, 400–1453, 36. Leiden–Boston–Köln.

_____. 2007. "Taʿbīr al-Ruʾyā and Aḥkām al-Nujūm References to Women in Dream Interpretation and Astrology Transferred from Graeco-Roman Antiquity and Medieval Islam to Byzantium: Some Problems and Considerations," in Beatrice Gruendler and Michael Cooperson (eds), *Classical Arabic Humanities in Their Own Terms: Festschrift für Wolfhart Heinrichs on His 65. Birthday from His Students and Colleagues*, 47–67. Leiden.

Mély, F. de, and C. E. Ruelle. 1896–1902. *Les Lapidaires de l'antiquité et du moyen age*. 3 vols in 4. Paris.

Metzger, B. 1987. *The Canon of the New Testament: Its Origin, Development, and Significance*. Oxford.

Michenaud, G., and J. Dierkens. 1972. *Les rêves dans les Discours sacrés d'Aelius Aristide IIe siècle ap. J.C.: Essai d'analyse psychologique*. Mons.

Mihăescu, H. 1981. "Les termes byzantines *birryn, birros,* 'casque, tunique' et *gouna* se fourrune," *Revue des Études Sud-Est Européennes*, 19: 425–32.

Miller, P. Cox. 1986. "A Dubious Twilight: Reflections on Dreams in Patristic Literature," *Church History*, 55: 153–64.

_____. 1994. *Dreams in Late Antiquity: Studies in the Imagination of a Culture*. Princeton, NJ.

Moreira, I. 2003. "Dreams and Divination in Early Medieval Canonical and Narrative Sources: The Question of Clerical Control," *The Catholic Historical Review*, 89.4: 621–42.

Morrisson, C. 2002. "Byzantine Money: Its Production and Circulation," in Laiou 2002a, 909–66.

_____, and J.-P. Sodini. 2002. "The Sixth-Century Economy," in Laiou 2002a, 171–220.

_____, and J.-C. Cheynet. 2002. "Prices and Wages in the Byzantine World," in Laiou 2002a, 815–78.

Muthesius, A. 2002. "Essential Processes, Looms, and Technical Aspects of the Production of Silk Textiles," in Laiou 2002a, 147–68.

Nicol, D. M. 1976. "*Kaiseralbung*: The Unction of the Emperors in Late Byzantine Coronation Ritual," *Byzantine and Modern Greek Studies*, 2: 37–52.

O'Carroll. M. 1982. *Theotokos: A Theological Encyclopedia of the Blessed Virgin*. Wilmington, DE.

Oberhelman, S. M. 1980. "Prolegomena to the Byzantine *Oneirocritica*," *Byzantion*, 50: 487–504.

_____. 1981. "The Interpretation of Prescriptive Dreams in Ancient Greek Medicine," *Journal of the History of Medicine*, 36: 416–24.

_____. 1983. "Galen, *On Diagnosis from Dreams*," *Journal of the History of Medicine*, 38: 36–47.

_____. 1986. "The Interpretation of Dream-Symbols in Byzantine Oneirocritic Literature," *Byzantinoslavica*, 46: 8–24.

_____. 1987. "The Diagnostic Dream in Ancient Medical Theory and Practice," *Bulletin of the History of Medicine*, 61: 47–60.

_____. 1990. "The Hippocratic Corpus and Greek Religion," in B. Clarke and W. Aycock (eds), *The Body and the Text: Comparative Studies in Medicine and Literature*, Comparative Literature Series, 22, 141–60. Lubbock, TX.

_____. 1993. "Dreams in Graeco-Roman Medicine," *Aufstieg und Niedergang der römischen Welt*, II: *Principat* 37, 2: 121–56.

_____. 1994. "On the Chronology and Pneumatism of Aretaios of Cappadocia," *Aufstieg und Niedergang der römischen Welt*, II: *Principat* 37, 1: 941–66.

_____. 1997. "Hierarchies of Gender, Ideology, and Power in Ancient and Medieval Greece and Medieval Islam," in J. W. Wright and E. Rowson (eds), *Homoeroticism in Medieval Islam*, 55–93. New York.

Önnerfors, A. 1960. "Zur Überlieferungsgeschichte des sogennanten *Somniale Danielis*," *Eranos*, 58: 142–58.

Oepke, A. 1954. "*Onar*," in *Theologisches Wörterbuch zum Neuen Testament*, 5: 220–38.

Oikonomides, N. 1985. "La chancellerie impériale de Byzance du 13ᵉ au 15ᵉ siècle," *Revue des Études Byzantines*, 43: 167–95.

_____. 2002. "The Role of the Byzantine State in the Economy," in Laiou 2002a, 973–1058.

Oppenheim, A. L. 1956. *The Interpretation of Dreams in the Ancient Near East*, Transactions of the American Philosophical Society, 46. Philadelphia.

Oppenheim, P. 1931. *Das Monchskleid im christlichen Altertum*. Freiburg im Breisgau.

Ostrogorsky, G. 1969. *A History of the Byzantine State*. Translated by J. Hussey. 2nd edn. New Brunswick, NJ.

Ousterhout, R. 1998. "Reconstructing Ninth-Century Constantinople," in Brubaker 1998a, 115–30.

Paffenroth, K. 1997. *The Story of Jesus according to L*. Sheffield.

Page, D. 1955. *Sappho and Alcaeus: An Introduction to the Study of Ancient Lesbian Poetry*. Oxford.

Palm, A. 1933. *Studien zur hippokratischen Schrift Peri diaitēs*. Tübingen.

Parry, A. 2004. "Dreams and Visions: Dream Interpretation and Analysis—Talmudic Style," in A. Parry, *The Complete Idiot's Guide to the Talmud*, 146–54. New York.

Patlagean, E. 1997. "The Poor," in Cavallo 1997a, 15–42.

Pearcy, L. 1988. "Theme, Dream, and Narrative: Reading the *Sacred Tales* of Aelius Aristides," *Transactions and Proceedings of the American Philological Association*, 118: 377–91.

Pelikan, J. 1990. *Imago Dei: The Byzantine Apologia for Icons*. Princeton, NJ.

Piltz, E. 1977. *Kamelaukion et mitra: Insignes byzantins impériaux et ecclesiastique*. Stockholm.

_____. 1997. "Middle Byzantine Court Costume," in Maguire 1997, 39–51.

Preisendanz, K., *et al.* 1973–74. *Die griechischen Zauberpapyri*. 2dn edn. 2 vols. Stuttgart.

Price, S. R. F. 1990. "The Future of Dreams: From Freud to Artemidorus," in David Halperin, J. Winkler, and F. Zeitlin (eds), *Before Sexuality: The Construction of Erotic Experience in the Ancient Greek World*, 365–87. Princeton, NJ.

Rapp, C. 2005. "Literary Culture under Justinian," in M. Maas 2005a, 376–400.

Rautman, M. 2006. *Daily Life in the Byzantine Empire*. Westport, CT and London.

Reinhold, M. 1970. *The History of Purple as a Status Symbol in Antiquity*. Brussels.

Reiss, E. 1896. "Astrampsychos," *Paulys Real-Encyclopädie der classischen Altertumswissenschaft*, 1: 1796–7.

Richlin, A. 1992. *The Garden of Priapus: Sexaulity and Aggression in Roman Humor*. Rev. edn. New Haven.

Richter, W. 1963. "Traum und Traumdeutung im Alten Testament," *Biblische Zeitschrift*, 7: 202–20.

Rochow, I. 1983. "Die Häresie der Athinganer im 8. und 9. Jahrhundert und die Frage ihres Fortlebens," *Studien zum 8. und 9. Jahrhundert in Byzanz*, 163–78. Berlin.

Rosenthal, F. 1965. "From Arabic Books and Manuscripts, XII: The Arabic Translator of Artemidorus," *Journal of the American Oriental Society*, 85: 139–44.

Rotonardo, S. 1998. *Il sogno in Platone: Fisiologia di una metaphora*. Naples.

Rowson, E. 1991. "The Categorization of Gender and Sexual Irregularity in Medieval Arabic Vice Lists," in J. Epstein and K. Straub (eds), *Body Guards: The Cultural Politics of Gender Ambiguity*, 50–79. New York and London.

Schilbach, E. 1970. *Byzantinische Metrologie*. Munich.

Schneider, A. M. 1941. "Brände in Konstantinopel," *Byzantinische Zeitschrift*, 41: 382–9.

Semeraro, M. 2002. *Il 'Libro dei sogni di Daniele': Storia di un testo 'proibito' nel Medioevo*. Rome.

Ševčenko, N. P. 1998. "Canon and Calendar: The Role of a Ninth-Century Hymnographer in Shaping the Celebration of Saints," in Brubaker 1998a, 101–14.

Sirriyeh, E. 2006. "Muslims Dreaming of Christians, Christians Dreaming of Muslims: Images from Medieval Dream Interpretation," *Islam and Christian—Muslim Relations*, 17: 207–21.

Skinner, M. 2005. *Sexuality in Greek and Roman Culture*. Malden, MA.

Sode, Claudia, and S. Takács (eds). 2002. *Novum Millennium: Studies on Byzantine History and Culture, Dedicated to Paul Speck, 19 December 1999*. Aldershot.

Sodini, J. P. 2002. "Marble and Stoneworking in Byzantium, Seventh–Fifteenth Centuries," in Laiou 2002a, 125–42.

Sommer, M. 1984. *Die Gürtel und Gürtelbeschläge des 4. und 5. Jahrhunderts im römischen Reich*. Bonn.

Speck, P. 1998. "Byzantium: Cultural Suicide?," in Brubaker 1998a, 73–84.

Starr, J. 1936. "An Eastern Christian Sect: The Athinganoi," *Harvard Theological Review*, 29: 93–106.

Stein, D. 1980. *Der Beginn des byzantinischen Bilderstreites und seine Entwicklung.* Munich.

Stewart, Ch. 2002. "Erotic Dreams and Nightmares from Antiquity to the Present," *The Journal of the Royal Anthropological Institute*, 8: 279–309.

Stewart, R. 2001. *Sortes Astrampsychi, III.* Munich and Leipzig.

Talbot, A.-M. 1997. "Women," in Cavallo 1997a, 117–43.

_____. 2002. "Pilgrimage to Healing Shrines: The Evidence of Miracle Accounts," *Dumbarton Oaks Papers*, 56: 153–73.

Tannery, P. 1898. "Astrampsychos," *Revue des Études Grecques*, 11: 96–105.

Terzaghi, H. (ed.). 1944. *Synesii Cyrenensis Opuscula.* Rome.

Tihon, A. 1981. "L'astronomie byzantine (du Vᵉ au XVᵉ siècle)," *Byzantion*, 51: 603–24.

Trapp, E. *et al.* 1976–94. *Prosopographisches Lexicon der Palaiologenzeit.* 12 vols. Wien.

Travis, J. 1984. *In Defense of the Faith: The Theology of Patriarch Nikephoros of Constantinople.* Brookline, MA.

Treadgold, W. 1997. *A History of the Byzantine State and Society.* Stanford, CA.

Triantaphyllides, M. 1909. *Die Lehnwörter der mittelgriechischen Vulgärliteratur.* Strasbourg.

Tuckett, C. M. 1996. *Q and the History of Early Christianity: Studies on Q.* Edinburgh.

Turville-Petre, E. O. G. 1968. "An Icelandic Version of the *Somniale Danielis*," in Allan H. Orrick (ed.), *Nordica et Anglica: Studies in Honor of Stefán Einarsson*, 19–36. The Hague.

Van der Eijk, P. J. 2004. "Divination, Prognosis and Prophylaxis: The Hippocratic Work 'On Dreams' (*De Victu* 4) and Its Near Eastern Background," in H. F. J. Horstmanshoft and M. Stol (eds), *Magic and Rationality in Ancient Near Eastern and Graeco-Roman Medicine*, 187–218. Leiden and Boston.

Van Falkenhausen, V. 1997. "Bishops," in Cavallo 1997a, 172–96.

Van Lieshout, R. G. A. 1980. *Greeks on Dreams.* Utrecht.

Van Nice, R. L. 1965–86. *St. Sophia in Istanbul: An Architectural Survey.* 2 vols. Washington, DC.

Van Voorst, R. E. 2000. *Jesus outside the New Testament: An Introduction to the Ancient Evidence.* Grand Rapids, MI.

Vasiliev, A. A. 1935–68. *Byzance et les Arabes.* 3 vols. Brussels.

Vegleris, E. 1982. "Platon et le rêve de la nuit," *Ktema*, 7: 53–65.

Vercleyen, F. 1988. "Tremblements de terre à Constantinople: L'impact sur la population," *Byzantion*, 58: 155–73.

Vikan, G. 1984. "Art, Medicine, and Magic in Early Byzantium," *Dumbarton Oaks Papers*, 38: 65–86.

_____, and J. Nesbitt. 1980. *Security in Byzantium.* Washington, DC.

Vinson, M. P. 2002. "The Christianization of Sexual Slander," in Sode and Takács 2002, 415–24.

Von Staden, H. 1989. *Herophilus: The Art of Medicine in Early Alexandria.* Cambridge.

Walde, C. 1999. "Dreams in an Auspicious Age: The Greek Interpreter of Dreams, Artemidorus," in D. Shulman and G. Stroumsa (eds), *Dreams and Dreaming in the History of Religion*, 121–42. Oxford.

_____. 2001. *Antike Traumdeutung und moderne Traumforschung*. Düsseldorf.

Wallen, G. A. 1960. *Theotokos: Eine ikonographische Abhandlung über das Gottesmutterbild in frühchristlicher Zeit*. Utrecht.

Waszink, J. H. 1964. *Studien zum Timaioskommentar des Calcidius*. Leiden.

Weber, G. 1998. "Traum und Alltag in hellenistischer Zeit," *Zeitschrift für Religions- und Geistesgeschichte*, 50: 22–39.

_____. 2000. *Kaiser, Träume und Visionen in Prinzipat und Spätantike*, Historia Einzelschriften, 143. Stuttgart.

Wellesz, E. 1961. *A History of Byzantine Music*. 2nd edn. Oxford.

Whittemore, T. 1933–52. *The Mosaics of St. Sophia at Istanbul*. 4 vols. Oxford.

Wilkenhauser, A. 1939. "Die Traumgeschichte des Neuen Testaments in religiongeschichtlicher Sicht," in *Pisculi: Studien zur Religion und Kultur des Altertums F. G. Dölger dargeboten*, 320–33. Münster.

_____, 1948. "Doppelträume," *Biblica*, 29: 100–111.

Williams, A. L. 1935. *Adversus Judaeos*. Cambridge.

Williams, C. 1999. *Roman Homosexuality: Ideologies of Masculinity in Classical Antiquity*. New York and Oxford.

Wilson, N. 1975. "Books and Readers in Byzantium," *Byzantine Books and Bookmen: A Dumbarton Oaks Colloquium, 1971*, 1–15. Washington, DC.

Winkler, J. J. 1990. *The Constraints of Desire*. New York and London.

Wittmer-Butsch, M. E. 1990. *Zur Bedeutung von Schlaf und Traum im Mittelalter*. Krems.

Zeitlin, S. 1975. "Dreams and Their Interpretation from the Biblical Period to the Tannaitic Time: An Historical Study," *The Jewish Quarterly Review*, 66.1: 1–18.

Zhishman, J. 1964. *Das Eherecht der orientalischen Kirche*. Vienna.

Index of Dream Symbols

General Index